Millennium: Journal of International Studies
The London School of Economics
and Political Science
Houghton Street
London   WC2A 2AE
E-mail: millennium@lse.co.uk
Web site: http://www.e-millennium.ac

IMPLEMENTATION AND WORLD POLITICS

Implementation and World Politics

How International Norms Change Practice

Edited by
ALEXANDER BETTS AND
PHIL ORCHARD

OXFORD
UNIVERSITY PRESS

OXFORD

UNIVERSITY PRESS

Great Clarendon Street, Oxford, OX2 6DP,
United Kingdom

Oxford University Press is a department of the University of Oxford.
It furthers the University's objective of excellence in research, scholarship,
and education by publishing worldwide. Oxford is a registered trade mark of
Oxford University Press in the UK and in certain other countries

Published in the United States of America by Oxford University Press
198 Madison Avenue, New York, NY 10016, United States of America

British Library Cataloguing in Publication Data
Data available

Library of Congress Control Number: 2014936677

ISBN 978–0–19–871278–7

Printed and bound by
CPI Group (UK) Ltd, Croydon, CR0 4YY

Links to third party websites are provided by Oxford in good faith and
for information only. Oxford disclaims any responsibility for the materials
contained in any third party website referenced in this work.

Acknowledgements

Most academics and students study international relations because they want to make the world a better place. Of course, understanding and explanation require methodological and theoretical rigor but most of us, ultimately, hope that our research and ideas are somehow relevant. We study war and peace because we ultimately want less of the former and more of the latter. We study international norms, for example, because we believe that the laws and principles developed by international society can make a difference to human rights, humanitarian response, or development outcomes.

Yet sometimes—just occasionally—there is a disjuncture between the abstract level at which theories of world politics are developed, and the people to whom they ultimately relate. A significant proportion of scholarship on international institutions in particular is focused on the "global" level—looking at what exists in Geneva or New York or emerges through the work that takes place in multilateral forums, international treaty bodies, or at the headquarters of international organizations. What work on international institutions, in general, and on international norms, in particular, has largely failed to do is to explore whether and how those structures actually make a difference in practice.

This book represents an attempt to close that analytical gap. It tries to make sense of what happens to international norms after they have emerged at the international level and states have signed and ratified them; to dig a little further down into the micro-level politics of international norms. It explores how the same international norms sometimes translate in radically different ways at national and local levels, or within particular organizations, and how this process can have profound effects on people's lives. It tries to understand what happens to international norms at implementation. How do they change and adapt? What explains variation in practice? Which actors and structures matter for shaping whether implementation actually takes place, and on whose terms?

The idea for this edited volume emerged from an initial conversation at the annual convention of the International Studies Association (ISA) in New Orleans in 2010. Attending a panel on the institutionalization of norms, featuring Neta Crawford, Michael Barnett, Peter Walker, and Thomas Weiss, we asked the panelists a set of questions relating to how they would conceive the line between existing international relations accounts of normative institutionalization, and subsequent processes of implementation. There was recognition that international relations had no adequate or consistent answer to this question. This sparked a conversation between the editors about whether there is a missing analytical step—a "normative institutionalization–implementation gap"—that might be the basis of a research project.

Based on those conversations, and our own reflections on the two issue-areas that we know best, refugees and internally displaced persons, we decided to apply for an International Studies Association Venture Grant to support a workshop to be held at the subsequent ISA meeting in Montreal in 2011. This enabled us to draft the basis of our conceptual framework (now the Introduction to this volume) and pull together a group of scholars working on international norms in relation to a cross-section of different issue-areas with a broadly humanitarian or people-focused purpose. The scholars who attended that workshop helped us significantly to refine the framework and eventually became the contributors to this volume.

We owe a debt of gratitude to a number of people and institutions for helping us in the development of the book project. Above all, we wish to thank our contributors for their excellent work and for submitting and revising chapters in a timely way. We especially wish to acknowledge the role that conversations relating to a previous project, "Regimes as Practice," notably with Anna Schmidt, played in helping to develop some of our ideas relating to implementation. The ideas in the volume have also developed through a series of presentations and suggestions by colleagues, and we would like to thank among others Michael Barnett, Alex Bellamy, Stephen Bell, R. Charli Carpenter, Jeff Checkel, Tim Dunne, Jean-Francois Durieux, Martha Finnemore, Jim Hollifield, Andrew Hurrell, and Martin Weber.

Institutionally, we wish to first and foremost thank the International Studies Association for recognizing the value of this work and funding it with the venture grant. In so many ways this book carries a "made at ISA" label and illustrates the value of the Association. The MacArthur Foundation funded the research on which a significant part of Alex's input is based. We also wish to acknowledge the ongoing support of our host institutions, the University of Oxford and the University of Queensland. We are grateful to Dominic Byatt at Oxford University Press for supporting this project from its inception. Finally, Phil would like to thank Victoria, as always, for her support and inspiration (and proof-reading) and Charlotte and Kate for putting up with Daddy's work. Alex would like to thank Emily for reasons that go beyond excellent advice on the cover design.

Alex and Phil
September 2013

Contents

Contents

Part III Policy Norms

List of Figures and Tables

FIGURE

TABLES

List of Abbreviations

APB	Atrocities Prevention Board
BiH	Bosnia-Herzegovina
CAR	Central African Republic
CICC	Coalition of the International Criminal Court
DPKO	Department of Peacekeeping Operations
DRC	Democratic Republic of Congo
ICC	International Criminal Court
ICFY	International Court on the Former Yugoslavia
IDP	internally displaced person
IFRC	International Federation of the Red Cross
IGO	inter-governmental organization
INGO	international non-governmental organization
IO	international organization
MENA	Middle East and North Africa
MHA	Ministry of Home Affairs
NGO	non-governmental organization
OAS	Organization of African States
OCHA	Office for the Coordination of Humanitarian Affairs
OHCHR	Office of the High Commissioner for Human Rights
OSCE	Organization for Security and Cooperation
PMC	private military company
PMSC	private military and security company
R2P	responsibility to protect
RSD	refugee status determination
SOD	Summit Outcome Document
UN	United Nations
UNHCR	UN High Commissioner for Refugees

List of Contributors

Miriam J. Anderson is an assistant professor of political science at Memorial University, having completed her Ph.D. at the University of Cambridge in 2010. She researches peace processes, post-conflict reconstruction, and transnationalism in war and peace. She is currently completing a book manuscript, "Windows of Opportunity: How Women Seize Peace Negotiations for Political Change," and co-chairs an international working group on transnational actors and conflict outcomes. Dr Anderson has published in *Politics and Gender, Refugee Studies,* and *Intervention and Statebuilding*. She became interested in issues of refugee return and property repossession as a result of her work as a human rights officer for the Organization for Security and Cooperation in Europe in Croatia from 1999–2002.

Urvashi Aneja is an Associate Professor at the Jindal School of International Affairs (JSIA) at the OP Jindal Global University, India. She is also the Director of the Center for Global Governance and Policy at JSIA, where she is leading a year-long project on the changing architecture of the international humanitarian system, focusing especially on the role of emerging donors such as India, and the impact of new information and communication technologies on the humanitarian sector. Urvashi has a Ph.D. in International Relations from the University of Oxford. Her doctoral research examined the manner in which international humanitarian NGOs interpret and implement the legal regime for humanitarian assistance in political emergencies, examining specifically on the cases of Sri Lanka and Afghanistan. At Oxford, Urvashi also co-founded the Oxford Humanitarian Group, an interdisciplinary research group that seeks to bridge the divide between academics and practitioners working on humanitarian issues.

Alexander Betts is Director of the Refugee Studies Centre and Associate Professor in the Department of International Development at the University of Oxford. His research focuses on the international politics of refugees, migration, and humanitarianism, with a focus on Sub-Saharan Africa. His recent books include *Forced Migration and Global Politics* (Wiley-Blackwell, 2009), *Protection by Persuasion: International Cooperation in the Refugee Regime* (Cornell University Press, 2009), *Refugees in International Relations* (with Gil Loescher, Oxford University Press, 2010), *Global Migration Governance* (Oxford University Press, 2011), *UNHCR: The Politics and Practice of Refugee Protection* (with Gil Loescher and James Milner, Routledge, 2012), and *Survival Migration: Failed Governance and the Crisis of*

Displacement (Cornell University Press, 2013). He has worked as a consultant to UNHCR, OCHA, UNDP, IOM, UNICEF, and the Council of Europe, and received research grants from the MacArthur Foundation, the Leverhulme Trust, and the Economic and Social Research Council. He has also held teaching and research positions at Stanford University, the Université Libre de Bruxelles, and the University of Texas at Austin.

Brian L. Job is Professor of Political Science and currently Associate Director, Institute of Asian Research, University of British Columbia. His teaching and research interests have concerned the evolving security order of Asia and regional, multilateral security cooperation, especially unofficial, Track 2 diplomacy—this in conjunction with the Council on Security Cooperation of the Asia Pacific, of which he served as Regional Co-chair and Canadian Member Committee Chair. Job established and directed the Canadian Consortium on Human Security. His current research agenda focuses upon the development and implementation of norms regarding human security, R2P, and the protection of civilians, with particular attention to their relevance to emerging powers.

James Milner is Associate Professor in the Department of Political Science at Carleton University in Ottawa, Canada. In recent years, he has undertaken field research in Burundi, Guinea, Kenya, India, Tanzania, and Thailand, and has presented research findings to stakeholders in New York, Geneva, London, Ottawa, Bangkok, Nairobi, Dar es Salaam, and elsewhere. He has worked as a consultant for the UNHCR in India, Cameroon, Guinea, and its Geneva headquarters. He is author of *Refugees, the State and the Politics of Asylum in Africa* (Palgrave Macmillan, 2009), co-author of *UNHCR: The Politics and Practice of Refugee Protection* (Routledge, 2012), and co-editor of *Protracted Refugee Situations: Political, Human Rights and Security Implications* (UN University Press, 2008).

Phil Orchard is a Lecturer in International Relations and Peace and Conflict Studies at the University of Queensland, where he directs the Masters in International Studies program, and a Research Associate with the Asia-Pacific Centre for the Responsibility to Protect. He holds a Ph.D. from the University of British Columbia, and previously worked as the assistant to the representative of the UN Secretary-General for Internally Displaced Persons. His research focuses primarily on international efforts to provide institutional and legal forms of protection to civilians and forced migrants. He is the author of *A Right to Flee: Refugees, States, and the Construction of International Cooperation* (Cambridge University Press, 2014). His work has been published in *Global Governance, International Affairs,* and the *Review of International Studies,* among other journals.

Emily Paddon is the Rose Research Fellow in International Relations at Lady Margaret Hall, and Associate Faculty at the Blavatnik School of Government,

University of Oxford. She is co-founder of the Oxford Central Africa Forum (OCAF) and a fellow of the Rift Valley Institute. Emily's academic research focuses on the politics and practices of United Nations peacekeeping, humanitarianism, and civilian protection in Sub-Saharan Africa. She has carried out research projects in the region for NGOs and various donors.

Christian Peratsakis is a Project Manager at Socrata, and previously served as AidData's Technical Manager at Development Gateway. His research focuses on the evolving aid architecture, climate finance tracking, and South–South cooperation. Christian received an MA from the LBJ School of Public Affairs at the University of Texas-Austin, and a BA from the College of William and Mary.

Sarah Percy is Professor of International Relations at the University of Western Australia. She has published widely on mercenaries, private security companies and the private military industry; and piracy in Somalia. She is interested in topics at the intersection of international law and international relations.

Anna Schmidt currently works for the European Union as Governance and Security Advisor for Somalia. Previously she was a fellow at the Institute of Development Studies at the University of Sussex, where she also coordinated the MA in Governance and Development. Her research focuses on international relations and political governance issues with particular emphasis on "global public policy," humanitarian emergencies and forced migration, conflict analysis and post-conflict reconstruction, as well as human rights, democratization and security issues. She has extensive research experience in conflict and post-conflict settings across Sub-Saharan Africa. Anna Schmidt holds a Ph.D. in Political Science from the University of California at Berkeley. In 2006–7 she was Jean Monnet Fellow at the European University Institute in Florence.

Michael Bluman Schroeder is Professorial Lecturer and Interim Director of the Global Governance, Politics and Security Program, a graduate program at American University's School of International Service. His research interests include the UN system, global governance, and political leadership in international organizations, particularly the influence of the UN Secretary-General on the organization's adaptation to historical changes in world politics. His other research projects examine the political dynamics shaping the evolution of UN electoral assistance, inter-organizational cooperation in peace operations, and the evolving role of the UN Secretary-General in international crises. His most recent work appears in the journal *Global Governance*.

Anastasia Shesterinina is a Ph.D. candidate at the Department of Political Science and Liu Scholar at the Liu Institute for Global Issues at the

University of British Columbia. She specializes in international relations and comparative politics. Her fieldwork-based doctoral dissertation research explores the patterns of organized collective political violence in the "post-conflict" case of Abkhazia, a breakaway territory of Georgia. Anastasia has presented her work at major political science conferences in the United States, Canada, and Europe. Her research has been supported by the Social Sciences and Humanities Council of Canada, the Security and Defence Forum Program, the Liu Institute for Global Issues, and the Faculty of Graduate Studies at the University of British Columbia.

Alana Tiemessen is presently a Post-Doctoral Fellow in the Department of Political Science at the University of Chicago. Her broad research interests are on international and transitional justice, conflict resolution, and human rights. Alana's current research projects address the politicization of the International Criminal Court, the ICC's relationship with domestic politics, and the use of judicial intervention as lawfare. She received her Ph.D. in Political Science from the University of British Columbia.

Scott D. Watson is Associate Professor of International Relations in the Department of Political Science at the University of Victoria. He holds graduate degrees from University of Waterloo (MA Political Science) and University of British Columbia (Ph.D. Political Science). He is the author of *The Securitisation of Humanitarian Migration* (Routledge, 2009), and has published in *Millennium: Journal of International Studies, International Migration, Security Dialogue*, and *International Political Sociology*, among others. He is currently researching projects on "Sport (Inter)Nationalism" and on "The Politics of Aid Acceptance and Refusal: Sovereignty, Modernity and Order."

Catherine Weaver is Associate Professor at the LBJ School of Public Affairs at the University of Texas at Austin, USA, where she directs the MA program in Global Policy Studies and co-directs the research program on Innovations for Peace and Development. She conducts research on global economic governance, the political economy of global development aid, and the use of GIS (geographic information system) technology to track and map international development and climate adaptation aid worldwide. In addition to numerous journal articles and book chapters, she is the author of *Hypocrisy Trap: The World Bank and the Poverty of Reform* (Princeton, 2008) and co-editor (with Nicola Phillips) of *International Political Economy: Debating the Past, Present and Future* (Routledge, 2010), and co-editor (with Manuella Moschella) of *Handbook of Global Economic Governance: Players, Power and Paradigms* (Routledge, 2014).

Jennifer M. Welsh is Professor in International Relations at the University of Oxford, co-director of the Oxford Institute for Ethics, Law and Armed

Conflict, and a Fellow of Somerville College. In 2013, she was appointed by the UN Secretary-General to serve as his Special Advisor on the Responsibility to Protect. Professor Welsh is a former Jean Monnet Fellow of the European University Institute in Florence, and was a Cadieux Research Fellow in the Policy Planning Staff of the Canadian Department of Foreign Affairs. She has taught international relations at the University of Toronto, McGill University, and the Central European University (Prague). Professor Welsh is the author, co-author, and editor of several books and articles on international relations, the evolution of the notion of the "responsibility to protect" in international society, the UN Security Council, and Canadian foreign policy. She was the Distinguished Visiting Fellow at Massey College (University of Toronto) in 2005, and a 2006 recipient of a Leverhulme Trust Research Fellowship and a Trudeau Fellowship. Professor Welsh has also served as a consultant to the Government of Canada on international policy, and acts as a frequent commentator in Canadian media on foreign policy and international relations. She has a masters and doctorate from the University of Oxford (where she studied as a Rhodes Scholar).

1

Introduction

The Normative Institutionalization-Implementation Gap

Alexander Betts and Phil Orchard

International norms matter in world politics. Whether these are formal legal standards like treaties or informal customs and principles, norms are influential in shaping the behavior of states. Until now, however, international relations (IR) scholarship has tended to focus on the process by which norms, shared understandings of appropriate behavior for actors with a given identity (Finnemore and Sikkink 1998: 891), influence world politics through the process of "institutionalization." Institutionalization is generally understood to be an international process and refers to the way in which norms emerge at the international level and become reflected in international law and organizations, with treaty signature and ratification by individual states seen as an important signal of institutionalization (Finnemore and Sikkink 1998). Institutionalization can tend to presage a process of norm diffusion, whereby these institutionalized norms move downwards to the state level, or across states through a process of adoption or mimicry (Checkel 1999: 88; Simmons et al. 2007; Sharman 2008). Once states have signed and ratified treaties, the task of IR scholarship is implicitly understood to be complete.

However, the focus on institutionalization leaves open a significant puzzle for scholars of international norms: states that have the same or similar levels of institutionalization of the same international norms may nevertheless exhibit significant variation in how those norms play out in practice. Just because two states have signed or ratified the same international norms, or similarly incorporated them within domestic law, does not necessarily mean that they will be similarly implemented.

This analytical gap matters. Norms—especially people-centred norms such as human rights, development, or humanitarian norms—ultimately only have significance insofar as they translate into practice. Norms may well be reflected in formal mechanisms, such as international treaties, or informal understandings, such as principles, and in the policy of individual states and organizations.

However, unless we understand and explain the conditions under which such norms actually make a difference to people's lives "on the ground," then we are left with an incomplete picture of the role of international norms in world politics.

The importance of norms in world politics is well documented. They both constrain and constitute the behavior of states and other transnational actors. They do so through providing incentives and by socializing states and other actors through a range of mechanisms that include the transformation of domestic legal systems and bureaucracies.

Dominant accounts of international norms, however, have two main weaknesses. The first is that international institutionalization—even as potent a step as signature or ratification of a treaty—cannot be assumed to equal compliance or implementation. Second, existing accounts assume a static view of norm content. As Krook and True have argued, norms are processes, works in progress, which "tend to be vague, enabling their content to be filled in many ways and thereby to be appropriated for a variety of different purposes" (2012: 104). Consequently, if what we really care about is not just whether states sign onto or ratify particular international norms but rather how those states actually understand the norms, how they interpret and practice them, then there is an analytical step missing in existing IR scholarship. Yet, despite a growing array of scholarship looking at how norms are interpreted and transformed within regional, national, and local politics (Autesserre 2009; Acharya 2004; Checkel 1997; Cortell and Davis 2000), there remains no coherent or consistent conceptualization of the "normative institutionalization-implementation gap" within constructivist IR scholarship.

In order to address the analytical gap, this chapter develops the concept of "implementation," which it understands as *a parallel process to institutionalization which draws attention to the steps necessary to introduce the new international norm's precepts into formal legal and policy mechanisms within a state or organization in order to routinize compliance.*[1] Implementation is critical to the norm emergence process; yet with few exceptions, it tends to be neglected. In emphasizing the role of institutionalization, IR scholarship has had a tendency to focus on why states sign on to or accept a new international norm. In effect, successful international institutionalization is seen as a clear outcome, providing an end-state to the norm emergence process. In contrast, we argue that fully accounting for variation in what norms do in practice relies upon explaining implementation as a distinct phase of normative contestation.

This volume focuses on a clear empirical gap between internationally institutionalized norms and the practice of states and other organizations. We argue that this observed gap occurs because a parallel process to that of

---

[1] While the concept of implementation has been used in international relations, it remains conceptually underdeveloped (Acharya 2004; Autesserre 2010; Deere 2009; Sandholtz and Sweet 2004; Schmidt 2006).

institutionalization—implementation—is critical to understanding how states and other actors interpret new norms and hence shapes whether important international norms make any difference or not in terms of outcome. It is only once these parallel processes are successfully completed that a norm can be considered to be internalized or settled.[2]

To do this, we examine a range of people-centred issues. These are issues designed primarily to assist and protect individuals within the spheres of human rights, aid, humanitarianism, peacekeeping, intervention, and displacement. The choice of these issues is deliberate—as Keck and Sikkink have noted, norms against violations of such basic rights are nearly universal: "Not all cultures have beliefs about human rights (as individualistic, universal, and indivisible), but most value human dignity" (1998: 205; see also Sundstrom 2005: 429–30). Consequently, each of the norms the individual chapters examine are either clearly institutionalized or well on the way to institutionalization. And yet each of the chapters also documents clear variance in state practice which institutionalization at the international level cannot explain. Furthermore, these are the policy fields where the institutionalization-implementation gaps really matters.

We argue that implementation processes play important roles in ensuring that states and other organizations comply with new international normative understandings for four reasons. The first of these is that in only rare cases can new international norms be considered institutionalized without some form of implementation process—and these rare cases are usually situations where the new norm has already been accepted within the state at the domestic level or within the organization and as such represents the status quo. The second is that implementation can be critical in determining how a new norm actually functions by increasing its precision—new adopters may have accepted a normative understanding, but without implementation this understanding may be ill-defined or imprecise. The third is that the implementation process itself can open up a new arena for interpretation and contestation of the norm by relevant actors, with the result that the adopted norm is understood differently across states and other international actors. Alternatively, this new period of contestation may cause the implementation process to "stall out" or otherwise fail, with the result that the international norm is gradually undermined or ignored. The fourth reason is that the implementation process results in clear and observable standards, which may be some of the only clear evidence that the norm has in fact been accepted. Thus, it is frequently evidence of successful

---

[2] Though note that, even once settled, this does not mean that the norm is automatically treated as valid—as Frost has argued, a norm is settled "where it is generally recognized that any argument denying the norm (or which appears to override the norm) requires special justification." Violating a settled norm should therefore trigger either a process of justification or will be undertaken clandestinely (Frost 1996: 105–6).

implementation which is transmitted back to the international level in order to monitor compliance with the norm. In other words, implementation draws our attention to a new phase of normative political contestation at the domestic level within the state or within organizations. This may result in the reinterpretation or undermining of new international norms.

Implementation has been ignored because of a conflation with other terms within IR scholarship, a conflation that neglects its role as a critical process. In particular, "implementation" has frequently been elided with the concepts of "institutionalization" on the one hand and "compliance" on the other, in ways that are often unhelpful for acquiring clear analytical insights into the processes through which international norms are shaped and channelled within states and organizations.

This introductory chapter will begin by discussing why implementation is a necessary complement to these two other concepts. We then provide an alternative conception of the norm life-cycle model which includes these two distinct processes—institutionalization and implementation—and allows domestic actors and institutions to play key roles in the contestation process. With this foundation laid, we then focus on the mechanisms by which normative understandings are transmitted downwards into the state by elaborating a basic framework for identifying the processes of norm contestation within implementation. Finally, the chapter engages in a discussion of the types of methodology required for engaging in implementation research.

IMPLEMENTATION AND NORM EMERGENCE

Finnemore and Sikkink (1998)'s widely cited norm life-cycle model analytically distinguishes between two distinct processes: "institutionalization" as an international process and "implementation" as a domestic process, and their model self-consciously focuses on the former rather than the latter. For them, the focus is primarily on international processes rather than the effects of domestic factors such as implementation. Thus the life-cycle suggests new norms are actively built by norm entrepreneurs; early-adopting states then socialize other states to follow them through a variety of mechanisms, including legitimation effects, self-esteem effects, and pressure for conformity. Once a critical mass of states adopts a new norm, it passes a threshold or tipping point (Finnemore and Sikkink 1998: 896–906). Following this, norms are so widely accepted that they "are internalized by actors and achieve a 'taken-for-granted' quality that make conformance with the norm almost automatic" (Risse and Sikkink 1999: 15). At this third state, international or regional demonstration effects occur and "international and transnational norm influences become more important than domestic politics for effecting norm change" (Finnemore and Sikkink 1998: 902).

For them, institutionalization plays an important—even critical—role as it "contributes strongly to the possibility for a norm cascade both by clarifying what, exactly, the norm is and what constitutes violation (often a matter of some disagreement among actors) and by spelling out specific procedures by which norm leaders coordinate disapproval and sanctions for norm breaking" (Finnemore and Sikkink 1998: 900; Legro 1997). This focus on institutionalization as an international-level process (see also Keck and Sikkink 1998; Risse et al. 1999) sees the new norm gaining precision as states clarify their understandings (Percy 2007b: 389; Lutz and Sikkink 2000).

An alternative scholarship does focus on institutionalization as explained by domestic-level processes (see Acharya 2004; Checkel 1999, 2007; Cortell and Davis 2000; Wiener 2007, 2008). But these two waves of scholarship treat institutionalization in distinctly different ways, with an institutionalization "line" that exists on a spectrum, from signing and ratifying international treaties at one end, to the adoption of domestic legislation, policies, and even standard operating procedures, at the other end.

In contrast, we contend that it is useful to analytically distinguish between what should be identified as two distinct processes. In this mode, institutionalization primarily reflects an *international process*, which can be defined as how norms emerge at the international level and become reflected in international law and organizations, and are signed, ratified, and adopted by particular states (see Finnemore and Sikkink 1998: 900). Implementation is a parallel process to institutionalization. However, at what stage these processes occur is variable, as the implementation process is triggered by a *state or organizational commitment to the emerging norm*.

Depending on when these commitments occur, the implementation process may be triggered prior to, during, or following clear markers of institutionalization at the international level. In other words, the process of implementation *may* sequentially follow the initial institutionalization process; however, there is nothing axiomatic about this, and so we choose to conceptualize implementation as a parallel process that may even interact with institutionalization. The commitments that trigger implementation may speed the institutionalization process; but this also means the implementation process may occur before the norm has been institutionalized at the international level. Consequently, the implementation and institutionalization processes are dynamic, with one feeding in to the other and vice versa. The implementation process may lead to increased precision for the norm at the international level, or even to substantial changes, as the implementation process alters how the norm is understood within the state or organization and hence as these new understandings are communicated to the international realm.

This demarcation also helps to distinguish *compliance* from institutionalization or implementation. This is not always clear in the literature. Checkel (1997: 475–6), for example, argues that compliance "seeks to establish the domestic mechanisms through which states obey the injunctions embodied in regime norms." Thus, he equates compliance with changes at the domestic level designed to ensure obedience to norms. This, however, conflates two distinct properties: implementation as a *process* which furthers adoption of the new norm, and compliance as an *act* whereby the state follows an existing norm.

For rationalists, compliance by itself means relatively little. Simmons notes that "'high compliance rates' should not be mistaken for important treaty effects, since most treaties just reflect the easy commitments governments were willing to implement even in the treaty's absence" (Simmons 2009: 116). Regimes with high compliance rates, in other words, may simply be formalizing "the status quo" (O'Neill et al. 2004: 165). Alternatively, high compliance rates may reflect state self-interest due to reciprocity, reputational effects, and side-payments or linkages (Simmons 2009: 117; Keohane 1984; Hasenclever et al. 1997). The common thread here is that in both cases the state is making a deliberate decision whether or not to comply with a given norm or institution.

A similar view permeates the constructivist view of compliance, based on whether an actor's behavior conforms with a rule or norm (Raustiala and Slaughter 2002: 539). As Franck (1990: 24) notes, the legitimacy of a rule exerts "a pull towards compliance on those addressed normatively because those addressed believe that the rule or institution has come into being and operates in accordance with generally accepted principles of right process." Thus, here it is the property of the norm which, being perceived as legitimate by the state (or other party), guides it towards compliance.

Consequently, while motivations for compliance differ, both constructivists and rationalists accept that compliance refers to the act of rule-following, rather than the mechanisms which cause the state to do so, and thus marks an absolute property: either the state complies or it does not. While a state may follow a rule with little effort, without implementation compliance may be a fair-weather process since neither states nor other organizations have made strong commitments nor adopted measures to restrict their behavior (Chayes and Chayes 1993; Mitchell 2005: 65–6). Defection will be easier without such constraints, and therefore failures to comply (or norm violations in other words) should be more common where implementation processes have either not occurred or not been completed.

Hence, clarifying implementation as a process distinct from institutionalization and compliance provides three clear benefits. First, it enables us to explain variations in state behavior toward clearly institutionalized norms. Implementation disaggregates two distinct processes of political contestation— one around the emerging norm, the other around its implementation—and recognizes that even once a norm is formally institutionalized it will continue to be subject to political contestation as implementation processes continue to occur within states and organizations. Thus the norm emergence process is neither necessarily linear nor static (Sundstrom 2005). Renewed contestation means the norm may be subject to reinterpretation or redefinition. But this also means that the implementation process may have real power to affect how the norm is understood at the international level (Schmidt 2006: 73–5).

Second, it allows for a more expansive view of the role played by both domestic institutions and by non-state actors. Privileging the international level means ignoring norms that are deeply rooted in other types of social entities, including regional, national, and subnational groups (Legro 1997: 32), but also "sets up an implicit dichotomy between good global or universal norms and bad regional or local norms" (Acharya 2004: 242). Instead, as Risse (2007: 268) notes, irrespective of how the new norm has emerged, these "normative commitments need to be implemented in the domestic practices of states and societies." This is aided by a cultural match with existing norms and beliefs (Risse and Sikkink 1999: 271; see also Sundstrom 2005: 420–4; Checkel 1999). But it is also furthered through the activities of local agents. As Acharya notes, such agents build congruence (through discourse, framing, grafting, and cultural selection) between the new norm and local beliefs and practices. Without these actors driving such a localization process, norm diffusion strategies that seek to supplant, rather than adapt, local practices will likely fail (Acharya 2004: 247–9). Thus, local actors are highly significant for defining *how* it is that a norm manifests in practice. Indeed, non-state actors may play the role of norm entrepreneurs, norm vectors, or even norm spoilers in ways that fundamentally transform the process of norm contestation. We will theorize both the causal processes through which implementation occurs and the differing agents who may be critical within the process.

Finally, introducing implementation as a theoretical concept has an additional benefit: it allows us to disaggregate between different types of norms. As already noted, an institutionalization process focused on the international tends to privilege formal norms, enacted through legal treaties. But not all norms take on such properties or reflect such a process. Instead, we suggest norms follow a three-form typology: ideally, they can be divided into sets of treaty, principle, and policy norms. Needless to say, in many cases these lines may be blurred and over time norms may progress from an informal, principled, status to full legalization.

We make this move for two distinct analytic reasons. The first is that such a division helps to better understand the institutionalization process occurring—whether the norm is being reflected in an international treaty, within policy at the international level, or within less formal processes such as UN General Assembly Resolutions, Conference Declarations, or other non-binding forms. The second is that we suggest the form of the norm will also be affected by potentially mobilizing different sets of norm entrepreneurs and institutions.

Treaty Norms

International treaties or other agreements are frequently seen as critical to the normative evolutionary process. Legalization, it is widely suggested, frequently marks the point when a new norm reaches its threshold or tipping point (Goldstein et al. 2000: 399; Finnemore and Sikkink 1998: 900; Khagram et al. 2002: 15) and "signal a seriousness of intent that is difficult to replicate in other ways" (Simmons 2009: 5). There is no question that treaty norms are important, nor that they provide the clearest observable commitment on the part of the state (Simmons 2009: 8). Treaty norms, by their nature, are clearly articulated and the implementation process is easier to observe as it works through the highest levels of government. Due to this visibility, it is frequently easier to assess government implementation efforts and for other actors— including non-governmental organizations (NGOs) and international organizations (IOs)—to hold governments to account.

But there are three major issues with an assumption that international treaties mark a better normative standard or clearer outcome than other normative forms. The first is that the nature of treaty norms does not create different effects in and of itself. As Finnemore notes, legal norms tend to be powerful "because they have legitimacy. They are viewed as 'binding', as having qualities of 'oughtness'" (Finnemore 2000: 702–3; Deitelhoff 2009: 34). Given that, as Hurd argues, legitimacy refers to "the normative belief by an actor that a rule of institution ought to be obeyed" (1999: 381), any settled norm bears this property. Consequently, their binding nature is important, but other norms can reflect similar properties.

The second is that international treaties, rightly, are seen to be more precise than more informal norms. As Diehl et al. argue, "a well-designed treaty or international regime should ideally include mechanisms to ensure implementation and compliance" (2003: 45), hence such treaties should have fewer implementation issues than other emerging international norms. But even legal treaties may lack clarity prior to implementation—"it is often unclear," Victor et al. note, "exactly what changes in behaviour will be required to meet international commitments" (1998: p. xi; Halliday 2009: 273). Even within the formal context of the European Union, Van Kersbergen and Verbeek find that norms once adopted may continue to mean different things to different actors. They suggest norm adoption may simply usher in "a new phase of battle over the norm itself" as norm practice "reveals to the actors involved what affected parties actually intend the norm to mean" (Van Kersbergen and Verbeek 2007: 218–19, 222). Sandholtz similarly notes that norms cannot cover every contingency and hence "the inescapable tension between general norms and specific actions ceaselessly casts up disputes, which in turn generate arguments, which then reshape both rules and conduct" (2008: 101, see also Sandholtz and Sweet 2004). Further, some international treaties are deliberately imprecise (Percy 2007b: 390). As Percy argues in her chapter with respect to the norm against mercenaries, the legal convention required such a complex and cumulative definition that it has never been implemented on the battlefield, yet "states *knew* that the resulting law was likely to be unworkable but felt like they could not adjust it without losing the sense of what they found objectionable about mercenaries" (Percy, this volume, Chapter 4).

The third is that international treaties have a higher profile, and hence may be more likely to mobilize domestic interest groups against them: they "may seek to block national implementation of international normative changes when their political or economic interests may be harmed by such implementation" (Diehl et al. 2003: 61). Thus, formal legal agreements can be subject to variable forms of implementation, triggered by international economic and ideational pressure as well as variable levels of domestic socialization and capacity (Deere 2009). For example, in examining the efforts of the Coalition for the International Criminal Court (CICC) to aid the domestic implementation of the Rome Statute, in their chapter Schroeder and Tiemessen find that, even with a formal treaty that has large numbers of signatories, domestic implementation can lag. Here, the CICC's efforts to support domestic NGOs have been critical in creating unique approaches to the implementation issues in different countries. Aneja similarly finds that how a norm is implemented can trigger opposition from domestic actors but also from governments, while Betts finds that the core aspects of the international refugee regime such as non-refoulement can be stretched by individual governments based on parochial interests.

Principle Norms

Principle norms are distinguished from treaty norms in two ways. First, they are based on less formal principles, reflecting shared understandings that states either have not yet sought to codify or have chosen deliberately not to. In spite of this, we can still observe a process of institutionalization occurring, either through acceptance in international fora (such as through United Nations resolutions and other international declarations) or through processes of customary or soft law which still provide clear empirical markers.

For some issues, the lack of codification can be a more advantageous process for normative emergence. As Orchard (2010: 285–6) argues, informal processes can have a number of distinct advantages. Not only do they allow for greater inclusion of non-state actors (Checkel 1999: 555), but they can also help to lower costs associated with a hard law regime, thereby expanding possible institutional arrangements and facilitating compromise (Abbott and Snidal 2003: 434–50). Watson demonstrates such a process in his chapter. He argues that a norm reflecting the desirability of international disaster relief is widely accepted but that, when the norm was first developed in the 1920s, actors contested whether it should be voluntary or a mandatory obligation. The eventual triumph of the voluntary view and a lack of similar contestation within the UN, he argues, reflects "a relatively stable interpretation of humanitarianism, and in turn disaster relief, as a voluntary act" (Watson, this volume, Chapter 13). Thus, principle norms based on informal arrangements can emerge when no agreement on hard law is possible (Shelton 2000: 13). As Orchard argues in his chapter, in the case of the guiding principles on internal displacement, new norms emerged through the reinterpretation or application of existing international law to new issues or groups.

But as a number of the authors demonstrate (see the chapters by Paddon, Orchard, Welsh, and Job and Shesterinina), principle norms are also more likely to be clustered, nested, or "composite" in character than treaty norms. This reflects a developing argument in the literature on regime complexity, which recognizes that institutions may overlap or be nested within one another (Alter and Meunier 2009; Keohane and Victor 2011; Raustiala and Victor 2004). As the chapter authors demonstrate, it is necessary to both acknowledge the complexity of principle norms and unpack them in order to understand how they interact in ways that shape both the institutionalization and implementation processes.

Policy Norms

A third category, policy norms, as Park and Vetterlein (2010: 4) have noted, specifically relate to "shared expectations for all relevant actors within a community about what constitutes appropriate behaviour, which is encapsulated in...policy." These norms, they argue, "emerge, stabilize, and decline within IOs" and are thus primarily subject to internal IO processes (Park and Vetterlein 2010: 13). While they use it specifically in relation to the International Monetary Fund and the World Bank, such a view can equally apply to the internal processes of any large international or domestic organization through which new norms are generated or adapted for use. Importantly, however, this suggests that implementation processes within international organizations or within governments can reflect their own specific dynamics of intra-agency contestation and reinterpretation. Thus Weaver and Peratsakis find that the World Bank's strong implementation of the international aid transparency policy norm was greatly assisted by strong champions in the organization who were able to overcome opposition in part by quickly mainstreaming the policy into the daily routines of Bank staff. Similarly, Milner finds that the UN's integrated approaches policy norm functioned well in Burundi due to the champions within the UN field office who were able to work closely with the government, while similar efforts failed in Tanzania due to contestation. This view that norm implementation can vary across states is echoed by Schmidt's work looking at refugee determination in Uganda and Tanzania, while Paddon finds similar variance even within a single state when examining the implementation of the protection of civilians norm in the Democratic Republic of the Congo.

But, as Aneja argues in her chapter (a point reinforced by Paddon), policy norms may reflect broader treaty or principle norms which are reinterpreted within organizations. Thus, she suggests that a widely accepted norm for needs-based humanitarian assistance was interpreted by international aid NGOs to reflect a duty they owed to ensure that people's rights were secured, leading to the creation of the rights-based approach to humanitarian assistance. Alternatively, vague norms may need to be implemented in the field. Anderson argues that the norm of property repossession was only clearly articulated by the international response in the former Yugoslavia; this norm as institutionalized in the Pinheiro principles reflects that experience and hence will likely be subject to further alteration.

These three different "types" of norms not only indicate different legal and institutional bases for norms, and hence different reasons why a particular norm may have salience or suasion, but also suggests different constellations of actors involved in the implementation process. Treaty and principle norms are more likely to involve disparate actors within government and the domestic policy community in their process towards acceptance at the domestic level, while policy norms are more likely to be focused within a single organization or set of organizations.

A THEORY OF NORM IMPLEMENTATION

Problematizing the implementation process introduces clarity to the existing debates on the way in which international norms take effect within domestic politics and provides for a more complete understanding of normative introduction and change. Where the conceptual relationship between the institutionalization and implementation processes is currently blurred, we argue that clearly distinguishing between institutionalization as a primarily international process and implementation as a primarily state-level or organization-level process opens up an important and fruitful domain of research. Examining implementation in this way enables us to explore a new phase of political contestation for the introduction of a new international norm.

Furthermore, implementation matters because there is nearly always some degree of ambiguity and imprecision in international norms. Rarely can international norms be fully determined at the global level. The nature of law is that it requires interpretation, application, and jurisprudence. Precision will vary on a spectrum across different norms, and rarely will full determinacy be possible. This opens up the analytical challenge to identify the conditions under which the resulting "institutionalization–implementation gap" is significant or epiphenomenal in explaining outcomes.

Focusing on the institutionalization–implementation gap offers particular value-added for a range of research agendas. In particular, it opens up potentially fruitful new terrain in the study of international institutions by offering insights into arguably the three most long-standing theoretical concerns of scholars of international institutions. First, it helps us understand institutional *change*. Rather than simply identifying change as taking place at the levels of international bargaining or institutionalization, it draws attention to a third level at which institutions can change and adapt: implementation. In the words of Schmidt (2006: 30), "change is equally located at the state level." This has important theoretical and practical implications in demonstrating that, even in the absence of formal renegotiation, institutions may be able to adapt to new, unforeseen problems at the national level. Second, it helps us understand institutional *effectiveness*. If "outcome" is defined not in terms of what states sign on to or what they say they will do but in terms of what actually happens "on the ground," then implementation draws our attention to a crucial part of the causal process through which norms are "effective" or not in their outcomes. Third, it contributes to our understanding of institutional *dissemination*. Rather than seeing norms as fully institutionalized once they are accepted by governments, it opens up space for causal analysis of how international norms are then diffused from state capitals through a range of regional and local levels.

CAUSAL MECHANISMS

Given that implementation processes trigger a new phase of political contestation within the state or organization, the same international norm may be implemented through a variety of different causal pathways in spite of its level of institutionalization. Thus, implementation may lead to different outcomes in terms of practice at the national, regional, and local levels and within different organizations. The authors in this volume inductively explore these differing causal pathways in order to better understand how state practice can vary in spite of clear institutionalization of an individual international norm.

Drawing upon and organizing the existing relevant literature, we can identify three broad sets of "structures" that may either constrain or constitute implementation efforts driven by particular actors: these include ideational, material, and institutional factors. These factors provide a basic heuristic framework. They are not strictly mutually exclusive but provide a way of identifying critical implementation mechanisms that can then be examined

Table 1.1 Implementation's causal factors

Domestic structural influences on norms	Constitutive *changing the norm*	Constraining *channelling the norm*
Ideational	Cultural context (e.g. Acharya 2004)	Legal system (e.g. Simmons 2009)
Material	Actor interests (e.g. Krasner 1999)	State capacity (e.g. VanDeveer and Dabelko 2001)
Institutional	Bureaucratic identity (e.g. Checkel 2005)	Bureaucratic contestation (e.g. Deere 2009)

as operationalizable variables via process tracing and in-depth qualitative research.

Each of these sets of factors (see Table 1.1) may in turn play a constitutive role on the norms (changing the norm) or a constraining the norm (channelling the norm) by enabling or limiting its impact and salience within domestic policy and practice. These structural factors may be exacerbated or mitigated through the role of particular actors exerting agency on those structures.

Ideational

On an ideational level, norms may be constituted by the cultural context of domestic politics. Acharya (2004)'s idea of "norm localisation," for example, points directly to how norms are altered at the regional level through their encounters with ideas and culture. Although his work is often identified as a contribution to debates on "institutionalization," it arguably fits better with implementation insofar as it relates to the sub-global level of political contestation of the norm. His work represents a key starting point for our framework. However, we broaden the analysis in at least two respects. First, he focuses mainly on the role of culture and ideas as the mechanism of norms translation, where we also see interests and institutions as central to the mechanisms of translation. Second, despite the use of the word "local" within his core concept, his empirical focus is in practice on the regional level, looking at South-East Asia, rather than drilling down to the national or local levels. Wiener's (2007, 2009) work also emphasizes the role of ideas and culture in constituting international norms at the domestic level. Her notion of "meaning-in-use" highlights how international norms are not simply "grafted" on to national and local contexts but that they can come to mean radically different things when combined with the pre-existing cultural and historical context.

Equally important are the agents who introduce or reinterpret new ideas. Here norm entrepreneurs can play critical roles. These actors are able to "call attention to issues or even 'create' issues by using language that names, interprets and dramatizes them" (Finnemore and Sikkink 1998: 896–7; see also Nadelmann 1990; Price 1998). While the focus has been on the international level, having individuals (including individual leaders: Nye 2008) or organizations with a commitment to "carry" an international norm from institutionalization to implementation can be important in shaping implementation and surmounting potential structural obstacles. Thus, Orchard finds that pressure exerted from international norm entrepreneurs caused the government of Uganda to move forward on implementing what had been a paper IDP policy.

Domestic epistemic communities and designated "experts" play a critical role in translating international norms into implementable policies at the domestic level. Once an international norm is adopted by a state, it still requires a degree of technical "expertise" to carry that norm into practice. Who is designated an "expert" and the "technical" knowledge and understanding of causal relationships that shape implementation will depend on which structures of epistemic knowledge and which epistemic communities are designated as having authority over implementation. In some states, for example, international experts or consultants may play a dominant role; in others implementing actors may be indigenous to the norm-receiving state (Haas 1992; Betts 2010; Ferguson 1990).

Equally important may be the environment these agents operate in, especially if they have access to networks and "small world environments" within the national policy process (Hafner-Burton and Montgomery 2009). In his chapter, Milner finds that senior UN staff were able to successfully play the role of "norm implementers" in Burundi, using their networks and commitment to overcome institutional obstacles.

Further, some norm entrepreneurs may be able to successfully tread between the two levels, while other international actors may serve as "Trojan horses," having a distinct if potentially unrecognized presence within the domestic policy-making process. The Coalition for the International Criminal Court, Schroeder and Tiemessen note, seeks to actively recruit domestic partners and to further their efforts, while adopting a "results not credit" policy to keep their own role in the background (this volume, Chapter 3). But international actors pushing new norms at the domestic level can also have negative consequences. Aneja finds that efforts by international NGOs to undertake rights-based programming in Sri Lanka actually undermined their credibility with the government, leading to their marginalization following the end of the conflict and the government instead to rely on non-traditional donors.

Because some form of international institutionalization sets off the implementation process, this may also have two other effects on norm entrepreneurs. The first is that it may open up new pathways at the domestic level, and hence provide agency or power to actors not previously involved (Lutz and Sikkink 2000: 658), a finding echoed by Schroeder and Tiemessen. Equally, however, a new norm which does not accord with the interests of important domestic actors may create a new and strong opposition movement among them (Jörgens 2004: 256; Bob 2010).

Success, here, will depend at least in part on how these actors frame the new norm, where framing is "the conscious strategic efforts by groups of people to fashion shared understandings of the world and of themselves that legitimate and motivate collective action" (McAdam et al. 1996: 6).[3] Successful framing leads to the new norm resonating with broader public understandings (Finnemore and Sikkink 1998: 897) and, as Busby argues, works "through two causal mechanisms, one informational/ideational and one instrumental. First, frames get the attention of decision-makers and individuals on the basis of ideas and values they already think are important. Based on those frames, citizens and like-minded elites then mobilize political pressure to influence others" (Busby 2010: 51, see also Béland 2005). Thus, Paddon argues that how the protection of civilians norm was framed by key individuals helped to increase its effective implementation.

Finally, the domestic legal system may also either play a constitutive role, or serve as a constraining ideational structure in legitimating (or not) different international norms, and allowing them to take effect. Cortell and Davis (2000), for example, examine the way in which different international norms acquire legitimacy within some domestic contexts but not others. Part of the explanation for this might arise from the fact that norms combine with pre-existing normative and legal frameworks, and the way in which they interact with existing law and jurisprudence constrains and enables their impact in practice. Simmons (2009) identifies variation in national legal frameworks as the most significant independent variable in explaining variation in how human rights norms are implemented in different states. Indeed, the constitutional framework of a state, whether its legal system is based on common law or statute law, or the number of qualified lawyers in a country, might all make a difference to implementation.

Material

Rather than simply seeing norms and interests as distinct and mutually exclusive, a growing number of international relations scholars have recognized that interests shape and change norms (Owens 2009; Jones 2010; Percy 2007a). Krasner (1999)'s notion of "organized hypocrisy" recognizes

---

[3] This is one form of framing. As social objects, frames also reflect existing ideologies, paradigms, standard operating procedures, and shared definitions of the environment. Hence Autesserre (2009: 252) notes they can either "pre-exist action or they can emerge from practice."

that when norms are imprecise or ambiguous they are likely to be adapted by states to fit preconceived interests. While Krasner's framework is applied at the international level, it has equal application at the national and local levels, where imprecise and ambiguous norms are likely to be interpreted (and hence applied) through the lenses of parochial sets of interests and through political processes in which conflicting interests are reconciled through power. In that context, incentives for particular types of interpretation—whether derived from the domestic or the international levels—may play a role in shaping how ambiguous norms are interpreted (Betts 2010). This kind of interest-based normative contestation is likely to apply at every level of government from the federal/national level to the regional and local levels. Interests can also govern the activities of non-state actors, including business coalitions, other non-governmental organizations, and even norm entrepreneurs (Barnett and Finnemore 2004; Barnett and Coleman 2005; Carpenter 2010).

At the level of constraint, capacity is also likely to matter for implementation. In looking at why compliance takes place VanDeveer and Dabelko (2001) argued "it's about capacity stupid," and it may well be the case that state capacity plays an important role in explaining variation in implementation. For example, Orchard finds that Nepal has been unable to implement an IDP policy due to the chronic weakness of the post-conflict government. Capacity can reflect such issues as economic strength—capacity in terms of state GDP per capita or the state's own capacity as an actor (in terms of the state's own revenue as a share of GDP)—but also the broader institutional structure of the state and its (in)capacity to deal with corruption or other forms of rent-seeking behavior.

Furthermore, these kinds of capacity constraints might apply at different levels of governance from national to regional to local. In some states, the distribution of power between core and periphery will vary; some governments may be more centralized than others, and regional authorities may exert different degrees of autonomy in policy-making. VanDeveer and Dabelko (2001) argue that capacity and "capacity-building" remain under-theorized, and few international relations scholars have examined what capacity means for the role of international norms (Urpelainen 2010). State capacity is also likely to matter because it will affect how much pressure other states and international actors can apply at the level of implementation. Different levels of capacity may reflect that developing countries may need more implementation assistance, and thus be more reliant on international support and learning. As Deere (2009: 19) puts it: "National economic circumstances and political factors *within* developing countries shaped the capacity of governments to filter and manage international pressures regarding TRIPS implementation and the influence of global [intellectual property] debates."

Institutional

The type of institutional structures that engage in policy-making and implementation will vary between countries in ways that may shape how a norm changes between the global, national, and local levels.

National history and politics will define important variations in the organizational structure of the civil service, how government ministries divide responsibility in particular policy-fields, and how competences are divided across different levels of government (e.g. federal-state or national-regional-local delegation of authority). Checkel (1999, 2005), for example, shows how variation in norm dissemination across the European Union is explained by the particular institutional, bureaucratic, and organization structures and identities within EU member states. While elected politicians or diplomats may decide upon institutionalization, it is likely to be civil servants working within bureaucracies—or in some cases seconded or contracted external "experts"—who take on the role of developing and implementing policy. In their chapter, Schroeder and Tiemessen note the importance of receptive state agencies (such as the judiciary and prosecutor's office) to further the implementation of domestic legal standards in line with the Rome Statute. These, they argue, can be critical to overcome other state agencies' opposition (such as defence ministries).

Variation in constitutional frameworks may also affect access points through which international norms enter national politics by channelling access to the policy-making environment, privilege certain actors, and create different ways in which to form "winning" coalitions to ensure the new norm is adopted (Risse-Kappen 1995: 16: Cortell and Davis 2000: 66). Importantly, domestic institutions can also play the role of policy gatekeepers or veto players if they have "sufficient power to block or at least delay policy change" (Busby 2007: 254; see also Tsebelis 2002: 442). Different political and institutional arrangements will therefore influence how governments undertake implementation and how permeable they are "to lobbying by domestic interest groups and international actors" (Deere 2009: 15).

In addition to specific bureaucratic identities and roles in changing international norms, bureaucratic contestation is likely to define which aspects of norms are successfully implemented and which fall by the way-side. Such contestation and conflict may take place on an inter-agency level, between branches of government, or across levels of government (federal-state, national-regional-local government). Legro (1997) highlights the role of organizational contestation at the national level in mediating how norms play out nationally. Moreover, this process of bureaucratic contestation may also draw in international actors. It is not the case that the international actors' role ceases with institutionalization. Rather, as Deere (2009) demonstrates in her work on TRIPs, there may be an ongoing "implementation game" in which international actors interact with national actors to contest and shape how exactly those international norms are applied in practice in particular developing countries.

From these three sets of factors, therefore, we can find two sequential signposts to measure the implementation of new norms (Cortell and Davis 2000:70; 2005). The first is marked by its appearance in domestic discourse. The second is changes in domestic institutions, particularly replacement or formal alteration, which provides an indication that a new norm has "achieved more than nominal domestic salience." This process may vary across states, or even within them, since "a range of policy choices can be consistent with a given norm" (Cortell and Davis 2005: 9). These changes also have to be strong enough to actually shift behavior (O'Neill et al. 2004: 165). But they are also neither predetermined nor linear: the state "can change one policy to placate international or domestic pressure but fail to modify a host of other policies and procedures that diminish or undermine the norm's impact" (Cortell and Davis 2000: 71; see also Thomas 2001). Even so, a good marker that the process has ended in the internalization of the norm is that evidence of contestation should decrease (Kelley 2008: 236). But even domestic implementation of the new norm may not end the process. Thus, with respect to the responsibility to protect, both Welsh and Job and Shesterinina find that there has been continued contestation of the norm at the international level.

METHODOLOGY FOR EXPLORING THE "INSTITUTIONALIZATION– IMPLEMENTATION GAP"

Understanding the implementation of international norms relies upon opening up the domestic "black box." It depends upon a methodological approach that traces how the "international" plays out within domestic politics, exploring what international relations has often referred to as "the second image reversed" (Gourevitch 1978). In that sense, an examination of implementation straddles international relations and comparative politics methodologies. It relies upon in-depth exploration of the translation mechanisms through which international norms encounter and are changed within different domestic political contexts.

Significant amounts of work already exist that bridge this methodological and theoretical divide (Jupille 1999; Milner 1997; Haas 1998; Holsti 1996). Furthermore, much of the existing work on norms is inherently at this confluence, given the very nature of its focus on the variation in how international norms affect different states (Finnemore 2001). However, a sizeable proportion of the IR-comparative work is focused on the interaction of the international with particular kinds of states, generally Western liberal democracies such as the European Union (Hurrell 1996; Jupille 1999; Risse-Kappen 1996), leaving open the particular context of how norm implementation works across more "challenging" state environments that do not conform neatly to Weberian ideal-types of the state—such as many of the developing countries analysed in this volume (Jackson 1993; Clapham 1996).

In rare cases, it may be that quantitative datasets are available to enable cross-sectional or time series analysis of the variables that shape outcomes at the level of practice. This might be the case for certain forms of development assistance or electoral norms, for example. More often, however, the absence of adequate quantitative data will mean that explaining variation in implementation will rely upon in-depth qualitative research grounded in process tracing and counterfactual analysis to identify the causal mechanisms that shape implementation. In particular, one of the hallmarks of "implementation research" is likely to be that it goes beyond "armchair international relations" and engages in in-depth fieldwork in order to examine the micro-mechanisms through which international norms adapt at national and local levels.

The most important analytical tool for examining the micro-level processes of implementation is process tracing, which involves inductively identifying the causal pathways that explain how norms are contested and change between institutionalization and practice (Gehring and Oberthur 2004: 272–5). Process tracing offers a flexible methodology which allows the micro-foundations of the relationship between independent and dependent variables to be causally unpacked in a way that is not possible using methodologies designed simply to reveal correlation. Process tracing can be complemented by the use of counterfactual analysis in order to "test" the significance of particular micro-level mechanisms in explaining outcomes. Such counterfactual analysis involves holding constant a particular observed independent variable and enquiring as to whether the observed variation on the dependent variable would have been possible in its absence (Lebow 2011).

One of the core methodological challenges for this kind of micro-foundational level of analysis is access. While there are many different approaches to data collection for processing, one such approach relevant to implementation research is to draw upon the insights of anthropology. In particular, there has been the gradual emergence of an ethnographic turn within international relations that potentially offers complementary insights for implementation research (Autesserre 2009, 2010; Vrasti 2008). Ethnography implies the use of sustained fieldwork alongside a variety of mixed methods, most notably participant observation and semi-structured interviews. Participant observation offers an approach that allows the researcher to be part "insider" and part "outsider" within a research environment, in a way that is particularly useful for understanding how norms are contested at the national and local levels.

Traditionally, anthropology focused mainly on periods of fieldwork of over two years and the study of communities. However, over time, anthropologists have begun "studying-up" to look at organizations, institutions, and policy processes (Schwartzman 1993; Merry 2006).

Meanwhile, international relations scholars have started drawing upon ethnographic methods to examine how norms function at the domestic level. Auteserre's work on peacekeeping norms in the DRC, for example, unpacks how norms play out in a particular local context (Autesserre 2009, 2010). Weiner's "meaning-in-use" approach sets out a qualitative research agenda that, while not ethnographic, directs researchers towards an approach that requires an interpretive analysis of what norms mean at the local level (Wiener 2008, 2009). Authors such as Vrasti (2008) criticize international relations' use of ethnography for being based on an empiricist data collection motive. For Vrasti, using ethnographic insights for international relations risks compromising the "emic" approach of anthropology (looking at the meaning communities themselves accord to concepts on their own terms) by imposing its more "etic" approach (bringing its own organizing concepts and theories to the field). Others take these critiques even further (Rancatore 2010). Yet, there is no reason why international relations should not balance the in-depth insights of ethnography with the broader comparative insights of political science. Indeed, it offers a methodology through which micro-level processes can be traced and understood in order to speak back to macro-level theory. Even if the depth of fieldwork or participant observation falls short of anthropological ideals, these tools nevertheless offer opportunities for explaining variation in norm implementation.

Specific patterns of implementation will emerge for different issue-areas and different norms. The principal means by which an explanation for variation in implementation given constant institutionalization might be derived is as follows. We propose the inductive analysis of particular norms in particular issue-areas, followed by comparative analysis across issue-areas and norms in order to derive deductive hypotheses and generalizable conceptual claims relating to implementation. For a given international norm, this would involve: (1) selection of a particular international norm (or cluster of norms); (2) observation of constant institutionalization across countries with variation in outcomes across those countries; (3) process tracing to identify the causal mechanisms through which implementation leads to diverging outcomes given the same levels of institutionalization; (4) use of existing data and/or the use of fieldwork (including semi-structured interviews and participant observation) to explore these causal mechanisms; (5) the use of a comparative politics methodology to explain variation across different country case studies.

This kind of exploration of the processes that explain variation in patterns of norm implementation for particular treaty, principle, and policy norms then potentially opens up the possibility to explore a number of comparative questions about norm implementation, from which deductive hypotheses might be developed. These might include: What is the relationship between institutionalization and implementation? Are there archetypal patterns that emerge on processes and mechanisms that apply across the cases? What's the balance between structure and agency in determining implementation? Does the nature of the issue-areas make a difference? Does the inherent design of the international institutional framework or the character of the norm itself make a difference? What role can or do international actors play in shaping implementation? Are there potential points of intervention through which international actors can influence the "normative institutionalization–implementation gaps"?

OVERVIEW OF THE BOOK

This volume provides a framework for understanding implementation as a parallel process to norm institutionalization. We posed the questions to the contributors, who were asked to focus on a single norm or set of norms within their individual areas of expertise. While all broadly adhere to a constructivist view of international relations, the contributors were otherwise left to challenge, interpret, and adjust the framework as they saw fit. As noted, we divide the volume into three parts, reflecting the primary nature of norm or norms discussed in each chapter: whether it reflects an international treaty, more informal international principle, or policy norm within a state or organization (or set thereof). In the conclusion, we return to our initial theoretical framework to see how it survived these tests across a range of issues.

Alexander Betts examines the core protections offered to refugees in the Refugee Convention, and argues that individual states understand such core rights as non-refoulement in different ways. He examines the flight of refugees from Zimbabwe into South Africa and Botswana, and argues that the response of these two states was dramatically different due to how they have interpreted and implemented this right of non-refoulement. He argues that South Africa chose to stretch the refugee regime to include a set of survival migrants who had fled Zimbabwe but did not fall within the classic Refugee Convention definition. This was a shift, he argues, that was driven entirely by domestic factors—faced with a similar situation, Botswana made no similar attempt to reframe the right of non-refoulement. Similarly, he finds that the United Nations High Commissioner for Refugees had little influence, or interest, in pushing the issue and instead simply followed the South African government's choices.

Michael Schroeder and Alana Tiemessen focus on the accountability norm: that those "most responsible" for massive human rights abuses *ought to be* held accountable, as codified in the Rome Treaty and with the creation of the International Criminal Court. This would similarly appear to be a well-institutionalized norm, with 139 signatories and 119 ratifications of the treaty. However, they argue that implementing corresponding domestic legislation has been poor in all regions except for Europe, and particularly problematic in Africa due to a mixture of lack of political will and state capacity. Thus, they focus on the role played by an NGO advocacy campaign—the CICC and its efforts to help states to implement the treaty. The CICC, they argue, has successfully switched from a ratification campaign to supporting its domestic NGO partners to push for implementation. The CICC has played a critical role through technical assistance, including low-cost access to research and expertise, but has also assumed a hands-off role, letting domestic NGOs choose their own approach. As such, they find that a mixture of public pressure and working with supportive state actors has been critical to reassure domestic audiences, develop domestically appropriate interpretations of the Rome Statute, and pass complex implementing reforms.

Sarah Percy examines the case of an imprecise treaty norm—the norm against mercenaries. While demonstrating clear signs of institutionalization—including an international Convention signed in 1989 and ratified in 2001—Percy argues that this normative prohibition has never been implemented. Instead, weaknesses in how mercenaries were defined allowed actors to circumvent the treaty; over time this has altered the norm to instead reflect a view that accepts the use of mercenaries in limited circumstances when used by legitimate states and when used defensively. She explains this shift in two ways. First, the weakness of the Convention, she suggests, was due to its long negotiation period, as states contested three different normative issues: the anti-mercenary norm, but also norms about state responsibility and about freedom of movement. Equally important were external shifts—including the relative rarity of true "mercenary" activities, even as organizations emerged which avoided the Convention and the growing use of such private contractors following the war in Iraq—which further undermined the existing normative consensus. Thus the very process of adding precision through formal institutionalization, coupled with the contingency of external factors, has significantly altered state understandings of the norm.

Urvashi Aneja examines the norm of need-based humanitarian assistance established in the Geneva Conventions and Additional Protocols. The norm establishes that need-based humanitarian assistance is to be provided to civilians in conflict, by an impartial actor, in a manner that does not intentionally influence the outcome of the conflict. But she finds that international humanitarian NGOs, the chief operational agencies of the humanitarian system, have translated this norm into policy in different ways. In particular, she argues that a set of NGOs have redefined it as reflecting the notion that all people have rights, and that these organizations have a duty to uphold these rights and ensure they are secured. The outcome of this, the rights-based approach to humanitarian assistance, thereby reinterprets the norm away from need and towards human rights. In examining the case of Sri Lanka, however, she finds that this rights-based approach led indirectly to NGOs privileging the LTTE in order to preserve access and thereby indirectly supporting the rebel movement's attempts at state-building. These actions undermined the credibility and perceived neutrality of the organizations with the government of Sri Lanka, a problem which was accentuated once the conflict ended.

By contrast with the more formal treaty norms, principle norms emerge through several different mechanisms. However, they remain subject to similar implementation problems. Phil Orchard explores domestic efforts to implement the soft law guiding principles on internal displacement. These principles, he argues, forms a foundation for a global internally displaced persons (IDP) protection regime, defining who qualifies, the rights they possess, and the responsibilities of individual states and the broader international community for the protection and assistance of IDPs. The guiding principles appear to be strongly institutionalized at the international level—including widespread recognition within UN fora and other regional organizations. They have also been widely adopted in domestic law, with twenty-five of the sixty-two states with internally displaced populations having passed some forms of legislation or policies to assist IDPs, many of which either enshrine or explicitly note the role of the guiding principles. In spite of this, he finds their domestic implementation has lagged in two ways. First, they have been subject to reinterpretation, as governments narrow the definition of IDP status and their rights. Second, even clear and expansive policies—such as those introduced by the governments of Nepal and Uganda—can stall out due to lack of political will and incapacity. Here, he finds that concerted international pressure reflecting the state's positive rhetorical stance can help reinvigorate the implementation process.

Jennifer Welsh explores how the Responsibility to Protect (R2P) has developed as a principle norm, with the 2005 World Summit Outcome Document as a key moment for its institutionalization. She argues that the R2P represents a hard case for exploring implementation issues as, rather than creating an observable policy or action on the ground, it establishes a duty to consider action in a crisis involving mass atrocity crimes. Whether action occurs and in particular when the international community's remedial responsibility should be activated, she suggests, instead relies on a range of other factors and remains a contested issue. Rather than assuming consistency in responses, therefore, she argues that we should measure the R2P's implementation by examining the duty of conduct held by members of the international community in two forms: whether they identify that atrocity crimes are being committed; and to deliberate on how it applies.

Brian Job and Anastasia Shesterinina similarly examine the R2P as a principle norm, focusing on China's engagement with the emerging norm. Critically engaging with the implementation framework, they argue that the actions of China demonstrate an additional mechanism in the institutionalization–implementation process: that of a bottom–up response in which a state takes their domestic understandings back up to the international level to further modify a norm even after institutionalization. This process, they suggest, is aided by the nature of the R2P itself: it is a composite norm, one in which elements of the norm are nested together and have different points of institutionalization. They argue China supports the R2P, but has sought to shape the norm to reflect their own specific interpretation of the norm which highlights the role of the state and the inviolability of sovereignty. Therefore, China views the implementation of the R2P as a task primarily undertaken by the state, with support from other actors and regional organizations, and has deliberately sought to constrain its scope.

Emily Paddon examines the protection of civilians norm, which establishes that while the primary responsibility for protection of civilians lies with the state, UN peacekeepers also have an obligation to do so. As such, the norm is both a principle norm but also a policy norm implemented within the UN system and in humanitarian agencies. Examining the case of the Democratic Republic of the Congo (DRC), she finds that a mix of material and institutional factors has inhibited the implementation of the norm. In particular, these reflect risks to the UN peacekeeping mission, including the risk of expulsion from the country, of escalating hostilities, and of property damage or personal injury. These risks, however, can be mediated by capacity within the mission—the role of key individuals in either facilitating or impeding the implementation of the norm is crucial—and through strong support from the UN Secretariat and the Security Council.

Scott Watson examines the origins of the norm of disaster relief, which establishes that there is a collective expectation to provide assistance either through multilateral or bilateral means at the request of the receiving state. The norm, he argues, is a robust one, even though it is not formally institutionalized in international law. This lack of institutionalization, he argues, reflects debates held during the 1920s between two sets of actors. One was the American Red Cross and the League of Red Cross Societies it helped to establish which supported a voluntarist approach to disaster relief. The other, led by the Italian Red Cross, sought to create a formal international organization through League auspices, the International Relief Union (IRU). While this period of contestation ended with the creation of the IRU through a formal multilateral convention, the original vision of compulsory funding and fixed financial commitments for states was replaced by the voluntaristic notions which remain paramount today, with the now-International Federation of the Red Cross continuing to play an important implementing role.

With respect to policy norms, these authors focus on norm contestation and reinterpretation within organizations. Catherine Weaver and Christian Peratsakis examine the implementation of the international aid transparency policy norm within organizations, focusing on the case of the World Bank. In 2010 the Bank introduced a new access to information policy resting on the presumption of automatic access to all materials except those on a carefully defined list of exceptions. They argue that this shift was led by critical champions within the organization, who carefully negotiated and implemented the policy in order to avoid many of the pitfalls of a major policy change. This success however has had two major outcomes. The first, a positive one, is that it also triggered an unanticipated change in which the Bank, through its "Open Data" initiative, made much of its data available to the wider public. But they also note that the World Bank's move to champion transparency appears to have shifted the goal line of the norm itself, away from a view of transparency as an end in itself to transparency as a means to greater accountability.

Miriam Anderson explores the implementation of the norm of individual property repossession in post-conflict situations. This norm has been institutionalized within the UN system through the 2005 Pinheiro Principles. She argues that implementation on the ground actually predates this institutionalization process. In different post-conflict situations throughout the 1990s, efforts to address this issue were ad hoc and varied from case to case, a classic example of norm imprecision. The earlier norm—one in which population transfer, and the resulting permanent loss of housing, was accepted—was clearly overturned following the Second World War, and an internationally recognized right of property return for refugees appeared in disparate cases such as Israel in 1948 and Cyprus in 1974, while a similar right for IDPs appears in the 1998 guiding principles on internal displacement. Large-scale implementation attempts in the 1990s and early 2000s, she suggests, brought to the fore a number of issues left undefined by the general norm, which led to a renewed instance of institutionalization.

James Milner examines the policy norm of integrated approaches within the UN system. The policy norm, which had high-level support from the Secretary-General and from member states as it emerged in the mid-2000s, sought increased integration among UN agencies in order to avoid overlap and competition and thereby increase the efficiency and coherence of program delivery. While strongly supported at the headquarters level, Milner finds that implementation varied considerably in the field. In Tanzania, these efforts were constrained by limited government capacity as well as institutional constraints, including different planning cycles and program methods employed by different international development and humanitarian actors. In Burundi, by contrast, there was a high degree of collaboration between the government and international actors. This was enabled due to material factors—particularly a convergence of interests—but also through a shared bureaucratic identity held by key staff members who were committed to the norm and were able to overcome institutional obstacles.

Finally, Anna Schmidt examines how refugee status determination procedures are implemented at the state level. Procedures are critical to refugee protection; and yet there is no clear formal international legal framework to ensure they are applied evenly and consistently across states. Consequently, ambiguities within these procedures tend to be addressed in either formal national policies or in operational practices. These remain highly malleable. She examines the experiences of self-settled refugees in Tanzania and Uganda, and finds that these refugees were frequently excluded from official registration processes, which focused on aid provision. Yet the lack of registration became a crucial issue in both countries as they became subject to refoulement to their own states, a process in which UNHCR was complicit.

CONCLUSION

Although the role of institutionalization is widely understood to play an important role in shaping the impact of international norms, it does not by itself provide a complete explanation for variation in the impact of international norms on practice. In order to account for variation in the effects of international norms across countries with similar levels of institutionalization, there is a need to understand the parallel—and theoretically neglected—process of implementation.

Recognizing the normative institutionalization–implementation gap within IR scholarship, this chapter has attempted to conceptualize the concept of implementation, clearly distinguishing it from institutionalization and compliance. A number of IR scholars have explored how processes of institutionalization extend into domestic politics or organizations; however, there has been little consistency in how the "line" between institutionalization and implementation has been drawn. Although challenging to analyse, highly contingent, and reliant upon micro-level process tracing, we have argued that implementation represents a crucial complement to existing theoretical accounts of the role of international norms in world politics.

Part I

Treaty Norms

2

From Persecution to Deprivation
How Refugee Norms Adapt at Implementation

Alexander Betts

States have primary responsibility for protecting the most fundamental rights of their own citizens. Yet, sometimes, the assumed relationship between state, territory, and citizen breaks down and people are forced to flee across international borders in search of protection (Haddad 2008). The modern international refugee regime, based around the 1951 Convention on the Status of Refugees and the Office of the United Nations High Commissioner for Refugees (UNHCR) was created by states in the aftermath of the Second World War in order to establish a reciprocal basis on which states would mutually commit to allow refugees onto their territory (Loescher 2001; Betts et al. 2012). The core norm within that treaty-based regime is *non-refoulement*: the idea that a state should refrain from forcibly returning someone to a country in which he or she faces a serious level of human rights violation.

The modern refugee regime gave clarity to the norm of non-refoulement by defining the group of people to whom such an entitlement should apply. In both the definition of a "refugee" in article 1a and article 33 on non-refoulement, entitlement would focus on those with "a well-founded fear of persecution." The drafters of the regime envisaged that the meaning and scope of "who is a refugee" would and could adapt to changing circumstances over time, either through jurisprudence or supplementary international agreements. In practice, though, the global definition of a "refugee" as a legal-institutional category focused primarily on people fleeing persecution (Price 2009) the direct discriminatory acts of states towards their own citizens (McAdam and Goodwin-Gill 2007).

Over time, however, the nature of human displacement has changed while the international regime has remained relatively constant. There has been a gradual shift in the circumstances under which people cross international borders in search of protection. Rather than simply fleeing persecution many people cross international border because of a very serious threshold of basic human rights deprivations (Betts 2013; Foster 2009; Shacknove 1985; Shue

1980). In the context of fragile and failed states, a range of threats to rights—including from food insecurity, environmental change, and livelihoods failure—can mean that, as a last resort, people need to cross an international border. Yet people fleeing deprivations rather than persecution fall outside the dominant global interpretation of a "refugee" and are usually denied the right to non-refoulement.

Yet empirical observation reveals that the norm of non-refoulement, and the people to whom it applies, shows considerable variation both across and within regions. Within Africa, for example, responses to Somalis, Congolese, and Zimbabweans fleeing serious human rights deprivations vary considerably in different host states of first asylum (Betts 2013). The same populations can face roundup, detention, and deportation in one country while in others they may be given access to non-refoulement as though they were refugees.

Even states that receive the same populations and have similar levels of institutionalization of global and regional normative frameworks frequently have radically different practices on non-refoulement. This observation represents an apparent paradox for existing literature on international norms and begs an interesting question of wider theoretical relevance: under what conditions do global treaty norms vary (or adapt) at implementation? When is it that a particular norm will stretch or contract in its meaning at the level of implementation, even in the absence of variation (or change) in the international norms or their institutionalization?

Complementing other work on refugees and implementation (see Schmidt 2006; Chapter 14, this volume), this chapter develops the concept of "regime stretching"—which it defines as the *degree to which the scope of a regime at the national or local level takes on tasks that deviate from those prescribed at the global level*—to explore how an international treaty adapts at the national and local levels. The refugee regime serves as a methodologically ideal case study for exploring regime stretching. This is because the adaptation from "persecution" to "deprivation" provides clear benchmarks around which to assess the extent to which regime stretching takes place. It offers a framework within which to identify a clearly defined "global" understanding of the relevant norm, as well as a wider normative benchmark against which to assess deviation from the "global" consensus.

The chapter explains variation in regime stretching in one particular case study: the flight of Zimbabweans from Robert Mugabe's regime between 2000 and 2012. It provides a context in which the overwhelming majority of people were not fleeing "persecution" in the terms of the 1951 Refugee Convention. Instead, the over 2 million people fleeing were seeking sanctuary as a result of large-scale human rights deprivations for which they had not access to a domestic remedy. In order to explain variation in regime stretching, the chapter explores responses to the Zimbabweans in two host states: South Africa and Botswana. The two host states exhibit variation in regime stretching. In

Botswana the norm of non-refoulement fails to stretch and all Zimbabweans outside the "persecution" framework have been liable to roundup, detention and deportation. In South Africa, by contrast, the regime has stretched to some extent, with, for example, a temporary moratorium on deportations for Zimbabweans.

Examining a range of competing explanations for variation in regime stretching, the chapter argues that the variation in practice in the application of non-refoulement between South Africa and Botswana cannot be adequately explained by variation in institutionalization of international norms. Instead, the chapter suggests that, where the international norm of non-refoulement is ambiguous and imprecise, elite interests at the national level define whether and how international norms adapt at implementation.

REGIME STRETCHING

This chapter theoretically builds on the Betts and Orchard introduction to this volume, taking the exploration of implementation in a particular direction. It examines the sub-question of how international institutions adapt and change at the level of implementation, even in the absence of formal renegotiation at the global level. To explore this, it develops the concept of "regime stretching" to highlight the way in which both norms and international organizations can adapt (and vary) at implementation, even given constant international agreements and constant institutionalization of those agreements.

The concept of a regime is often defined by its "consensus definition" of "principles, norms, rules, and decision-making procedures *around which actor expectations converge* in a given issue-area" (Krasner 1982). Yet the definition is unwieldy and almost impossible to operationalize (Goetz 2003). It makes far more sense to see regimes as having just two core elements: norms and international organizations (which can both be subsumed under the notion of "international institutions").[1] Within each of these two areas, adaptation and change may take place. Even in the absence of creating a new regime or formally renegotiating norms or international organizations, change and adaptation can and do take place.

---

[1] Stephen Krasner—as author of the original regime definition—acknowledges in conversation that seeing regimes as norms and international organizations makes more sense, especially in empirical application. Other authors such as Gary Goertz have also argued for a more minimalist concept of a regime. Goertz (2003: 19) states "for my purposes, norms, principles, decision-making procedures, and rules can be seen as synonymous," arguing that the logical form of these norms is broadly reducible to the idea of a norm (as a single standard of behavior)—although it may be useful to distinguish between those norms that define action and those that define organizational procedures.

Yet, in contrast to the comparative politics literature, which has examined processes of institutional change and adaption (Mahoney and Thelen 2010; Pierson 2004; Weyland 2008), international relations has relatively neglected the issue of international institutional adaptation. Regime adaptation—in terms of both norms and international organizations—can be understood to take place at three levels: (i) international bargaining, (ii) institutionalization, and (ii) implementation.[2]

At the first level of *international bargaining*, norms may be changed through inter-state (re)negotiation, and international organizations may be changed through statute (re)negotiation. For example, treaty norms are sometimes adapted through "additional protocols" to a convention, while international organizations may be formally changed through the UN General Assembly choosing to authorize the change in an international organization's mandate. This level of change is widely recognized within liberal institutionalist literature, which implies that when states' demand for international regimes changes (for example, because of a change in preferences, power, or the nature of the problem), they will formally renegotiate the bargain on which the regime is based.

At the second level of *institutionalization*, norms may adapt in the way in which they are disseminated internationally, and, in particular, in how they are signed, ratified, and adopted. For example, if states change their ratification of a regime, or whether or not the regime is incorporated within national legislation, this will represent an adaptation of the regime. This type of change is widely recognized within constructivist literature on institutionalization. International organizations may adapt in terms of the way in which their mandates are institutionalized (and interpreted) by the international organization. Meanwhile, many organizations' interpretation of their own mandates may change at the global level even in the absence of a formal General Assembly Mandate. This type of change within literature on principal-agent theory as applied to international organizations.

At the third level of *implementation*, in relation to norms, the introduction of a norm's precepts into formal legal or policy mechanisms at the national level in order to routinize compliance (i.e. "policy") may vary between different national contexts. For example, even where two countries have the same degree of institutionalization of an international norm, one may observe very different outcomes because of a state's willingness or ability to implement norms. In relation to international organizations, the way in which the organization's national representation interprets its mandate (i.e. "practice") may vary between different national contexts. For example, an IO's national representation in one country may act differently from the same organization

---

[2] These categories broadly follow Ostrom (1990), who has three levels of analysis: constitutional, directive, and operational in looking at collective action.

in a different country. In contrast to the other two levels, this third level of regime adaptation is almost entirely neglected within international relations. Yet, it is important insofar as we observe variation (or change) in outcomes even in the absence of variation (or change) at the levels of international bargaining or institutionalization. The "implementation" stage has been especially neglected by international relations in its consideration of processes of institutional adaptation.

In order to explore how the implementation stage matters for regime adaptation, I develop the concept of "regime stretching," which I define as the *degree to which the scope of a regime at the national or local level takes on tasks that deviate from those prescribed at the global level.* Such stretching may be regime-consistent (taking on tasks that are complementary to the underlying purpose of the regime) or regime-inconsistent (contradicting the underlying purpose of the regime). The concept highlights the way in which a regime may adapt at the national level even in the absence of adaptation at the levels of international bargaining or institutionalization.

This is a particularly important concept in the context of a world in which new problems and challenges are emerging but new formal institutions are created at a much slower pace, and there is often a need for "old global institutions"—both norms and organizations—to adapt to "new national challenges." As problems emerge that were not within the scope of a regime at its creation, the norms and organization may adapt, even without formal renegotiation.

Furthermore, regime stretching adds a spatial dimension to how we think about regime adaptation. Comparative politics has explored temporal explanations of institutional change (Hall and Thelen 2009; Pierson 2004). James Mahoney and Kathleen Thelen's (2010) work in particular shows the range of causal mechanisms (displacement, layering, drift, convergence) through which an institution changes between time period t1 and time period t2. However, exploring the relationship between the global and the local opens up a spatial dimension to the question of institutional change, highlighting how the same global regime can have different national manifestations (in states a, b, and c) at the same time period (whether t1 or t2).

For a formal regime, regime stretching is relatively easy to assess. The dominant "global" interpretation of the norm offers a benchmark against which to assess the default behavioral norm, around which practice may oscillate. So for the refugee regime that default benchmark represents an entitlement to protection (including non-refoulement) for those fleeing persecution. "Stretching" would be considered to take place when the norm and the international organization that comprise the regime adapt to ensure protection for a wider groups of people. In the refugee case, stretching might be measured by looking at the *number* of additional people included within the refugee framework, and the *degree of rights* that they receive.

FROM PERSECUTION TO DEPRIVATION

In the refugee regime, the particular form of stretching that takes place relates to the scope of application of the norm of non-refoulement. Who are the people who have a right not to be forcibly returned home? The dominant "global" interpretation is that the norm applies to people fleeing individualized or group persecution. In other words it protects people who primarily flee the discriminatory acts of states.

However, over time, other people have crossed international borders in search of protection who fall outside the original framework's "persecutory bias." "New drivers" of cross-border displacement—notably around the impact of environmental change, food insecurity, and generalized violence—have emerged and been widely debated. In a state with strong governance, it is unlikely that these threats would come to matter for asylum. Yet in fragile or failed states, they can mean that people need to cross an international border. Ultimately, though, such people are not fleeing persecution;[3] they are fleeing human rights deprivations (Foster 2009). They are fleeing the omissions rather than the acts of the country of origin.

The empirical shift from people fleeing persecution to deprivations has become more marked over the last two decades. During the Cold War, the refugee regime protected people fleeing persecution by ideologically driven governments; a significant amount of refugee movement was in some way East–West. Since the 1990s, the emergence of fragile states has meant that more people are fleeing states that are unable or unwilling to protect their rights. The practical challenge, however, is that, while a relatively high degree of legal precision exists for people fleeing persecution, there is comparative legal imprecision for those fleeing rights deprivations. Consequently, while there is relative consistency in state practice towards those fleeing persecution, there is relative inconsistency in state practice towards those fleeing deprivations (see Table 2.1).

The observation that the existing "global" regime mainly protects only the former of these categories has led to widespread *normative* debate on who, among people fleeing deprivations rather than persecution, should be entitled to non-refoulement. At one extreme, Price (2010) has argued that there is something particular about asylum that means it should focus on those fleeing persecution. At the opposite end of the spectrum, Shacknove (1985) has argued that everyone fleeing a particular threshold of basic rights deprivations should be entitled to asylum.

---

[3] It should be noted that jurisprudence on "persecution" is complex and has gone beyond targeted state persecution to include e.g. non-state-actor persecution. The persecution–deprivation binary therefore offers a stylized framing of a legally complex area of jurisprudence.

Table 2.1 Contrasting causes of, and responses to, cross-border displacement resulting from persecution versus deprivations

	Persecution	Deprivation
State of origin role in rights violations	**Acts** (e.g. civil and political rights violations)	**Omissions** (e.g. inability or unwillingness to mitigate serious threats to human security)
Empirical trend	**Declining number of repressive states** (e.g. Soviet Union)	**Growing number of fragile states** (e.g. Haiti/Libya)
Quality of legal protection	**Legal precision** (1951 Convention)	**Legal imprecision** (regional conventions; human rights law)
Host state practices	**Consistency** (based mainly on law)	**Inconsistency** (based mainly on politics)

Yet what has been missing is a *positivist* analysis, not of who should be a refugee or receive access to asylum but rather of who does receive asylum, non-refoulement, and refugee status, and why. It is that positivist dimension to the issue of "who is a refugee?" that this chapter seeks to explore in complement to the existing normative debate on whether the refugee regime should formally adapt. Irrespective of who *should* be entitled to not be forced home, what determines who *is* given access to the norm of non-refoulement and the sets of corresponding rights that come with it?

In order to set up an analytical basis for assessing regime stretching from persecution to deprivation, this chapter uses the term "survival migration" as a normative concept to include the totality of people who are outside their country of origin because of an existential threat to which they have no access to a domestic remedy or resolution (Betts 2010, 2013). It is an inclusive term that highlights the situation of people fleeing a serious threshold of basic rights violations, irrespective of whether they result from persecution or deprivation. It uses the term "refugee" as a legal-institutional concept to highlight people who are recognized by states as refugees.

It is conceivable that all survival migrants could be recognized as refugees. Indeed, the precise gap between "survival migrants" and "refugees" will vary from country to country. To add conceptual clarity, Figure 2.1 highlights the conceptual relationship of survival migrants to refugees and international migrants. Refugees are survival migrants, but not all survival migrants are refugees, and survival migrants are international migrants, but not all international migrants are survival migrants.[4]

---

[4] Adapted from Trygve G. Nordby, IFRC Special Envoy on Migration, Keynote Speech, High Commissioner's Dialogue on Protection Challenges, Geneva, 11–12 Dec. 2007.

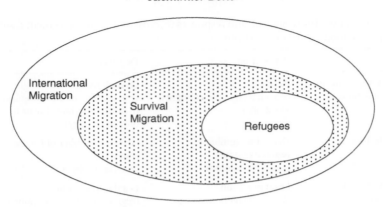

Figure 2.1 Diagram showing the conceptual relationship of survival migration to refugees and international migration

The population that this chapter is primarily concerned with is the middle segment of Figure 2.1, relating to survival migrants who fall outside the refugee framework. The inner dividing line in Figure 2.1 cannot be understood as fixed—either over time or space. Exactly where it is drawn changes over time and is subject to significant variation across different states. In theory, given the organic nature of the "refugee" definition, all survival migrants could be recognized as refugees—either universally or in a specific state. In practice, though, there is a significant global gap and usually some degree of gap in the practice of most states. Usually, as has been argued, the inner circle of "refugees" is limited to those people fleeing persecution, while the middle circle relates to those fleeing other sources of serious human rights deprivations. Nevertheless, there is huge variation and inconsistency in where and how the line is drawn in different states. The questions with which this chapter is concerned relate to when and how the refugee regime stretches such that the "gap" between "refugee" and "survival migration" diminishes or expands.

THE CASE OF ZIMBABWEANS IN
SOUTHERN AFRICA

Since the start of the millennium, Zimbabwe has gone from being one of the most developed countries in Africa to being mired in economic and political crisis. After the government of Robert Mugabe initiated a wave of land invasions to transfer white-owned farms to its political supporters in 2000, the resulting international sanctions, capital flight, declining agricultural productivity, and hyperinflation have conspired to plunge living standards to a level that ranks the country alongside the most fragile and failed states in the world. Simply in order to survive or to provide basic subsistence for their families, millions of people have been forced to migrate within or beyond the borders of Zimbabwe, with nearly one-quarter of the population going into exile in neighbouring countries. The resulting movement has been described as "The largest migration event in the region's recent history" (Polzer et al. 2010). Although there are no accurate statistics available, it is commonly suggested that around 2 million Zimbabweans crossed into neighbouring countries between 2000 and 2012 (Crisp and Kiragu 2010; Polzer 2008; Solidarity Peace Trust 2012), making it by far the largest mass influx situation anywhere in the world since the start of the twenty-first century.

However, despite the fact that the Zimbabweans have left a desperate humanitarian situation in which their most fundamental human rights cannot be guaranteed, the overwhelming majority have not been recognized as refugees. This is because governments and UNHCR have consistently argued that—with very few exceptions—the Zimbabweans could not be regarded as refugees, given that most were not fleeing individualized persecution. In the words of one South African human rights advocate, "most have been escaping the economic consequences of the political situation" rather than political persecution per se.[5] Hence UNHCR described most Zimbabweans as in a "neither/nor" situation, being neither refugees under the 1951 Convention, nor voluntary, economic migrants. The Zimbabwean situation therefore represents an archetypal case of survival migration (Betts and Kaytaz 2009). As UNHCR has acknowledged, "Zimbabwean survival migrants who have left their own country because they cannot sustain themselves and their families at home fall into an important protection gap" (Crisp and Kiragu 2010).

What is particularly interesting for the purposes of this book is that the national responses to the same populations have varied across different host countries of asylum. In particular, the responses of South Africa and Botswana have been very different. In addition to the norm of non-refoulement being applied differently in the different countries, the organization for overseeing that norm—UNHCR—has responded differently to that population. In the theoretical terms just outlined, the refugee regime has partly "stretched" to protect those fleeing deprivations rather than persecution in South Africa but not in Botswana.

This variation provides an empirical basis on which to explore regime stretching as a dependent variable. Why is it that the practice of who receives an entitlement to non-refoulement varies across states? The South Africa–Botswana comparison is methodologically interesting because of what can be held constant and what varies. Importantly, both have received people fleeing for identical reasons and yet there is variation in their response. This offers meaningful

---

[5] Interview with Kajaal Ramjathan-Keogh, Head of Refugee and Migrant Rights Programme, Lawyers for Human Rights (LHR), Johannesburg, 18 Mar. 2009.

variation in the dependent variable. On the independent variable side, both countries have a number of things in common: they are middle-income countries with procedural democracies. Both also have similar levels of border control and deportation capacities to make them capable of exercising choice over whether or not to offer non-refoulement to a particular population.

The two countries have slight differences in their institutionalization of the refugee regime. Both countries have signed and ratified the 1951 Convention and its 1967 Protocol, incorporating it into domestic legislation and policy. They have also signed and ratified the same broad human rights instruments. However, there are two notable differences on institutionalization. First, South Africa incorporates the 1969 OAU Convention within its national legislation while Botswana does not. This is potentially important because the OAU Convention expands the definition of a "refugee" to include "people fleeing a serious disturbance to public order" in ways that potentially move beyond protection for people fleeing persecution to those feeling serious deprivations. Second, the Government of Botswana entered reservations on the elements of the 1951 Convention relating to freedom of movement and the right to work meaning that asylum seekers are required to remain in detention in Francistown during their Refugee Status Determination (RSD) process. If they receive recognition, they are entitled to live in the refugee camp, but then have to apply for a work permit if and when they find work.[6]

However, do differences in institutionalization actually offer an adequate explanation of variation in the practice of non-refoulement towards the Zimbabweans, in the way that much of the existing constructivist literature in international relations might assume? In order to explore this, the chapter sets up the idea that variation in institutionalization explains variation in regime stretching as the null hypothesis:

H0: Variation in institutionalization explains variation in regime stretching.

Against this null hypothesis, the chapter explores whether, beyond institutionalization, political contestation at the level of implementation is significant in explaining some of the variation in regime stretching. And, if so, by what mechanisms does the norm of non-refoulement adapt at the level of implementation? In order to examine this, two alternative hypotheses are explored.

The chapter offers an interest-driven account of the conditions under which regime stretching takes place. It argues that, rather than law and principle shaping whether and how norms adapt to new challenges at the national level, it is the interests of elites in government. More precisely, what matters is whether there are positive or negative incentives for regime stretching emerging from either the international (e.g. money or legitimacy) or domestic levels

---

[6] Interview with Gelafele Beleme, Associate Protection Officer, UNHCR, Botswana, Gaborone, 28 Mar. 2009.

(e.g. electoral gain) that result from regime stretching. More formally stated, this leads to the alternative hypothesis:

H1: Variation in elite interests at the national level explains variation in regime stretching.

In addition to this, the chapter explores a further hypothesis, relating to the mechanisms by which regime stretching takes place. Given that regime stretching as a concept encompasses both normative and organizational adaptation, it seeks to examine which of these elements leads and which follows. Do international organizations drive regime stretching or do states? At the global level, a range of studies have suggested that international organizations, including UNHCR, have independent causal effects on state behavior (Barnett and Finnemore 2004; Loescher 2001). However, this chapter explores whether this is actually the case at the national level, suggesting that it is not, and that UNHCR's role in regime stretching appears to have been epiphenomenal. Formally stated, it examines the hypothesis that:

H2: international organizations are epiphenomenal at implementation.

South Africa

There has been a lack of reliable data on the numbers and changing patterns of cross-border displacement (Crush and Tevera 2010; Polzer 2008). One South African NGO has claimed that estimates of the number of Zimbabweans in South Africa in 2007 ranged between 1 and 9 million (CoRMSA 2008: 17). The South African Department of Home Affairs (DHA) has frequently quoted a figure of around 2 million, based on numbers coming through the asylum system.[7] Most academics, though, suggest a number nearer to 1–1.5 million entering South Africa during the entire period (Polzer et al. 2010). The only official statistics available come from asylum numbers, with new applications being 45,000 for 2007, 250,000 for 2008, and 150,000 for 2009. However, in practice, many Zimbabweans choose to remain outside of formal channels, which offer few economic and social benefits.

Dependent Variable: Regime Stretching

The response of the South African government to the influx can be characterized as ad hoc. However, in contrast to Botswana, incremental adaptation has taken place. Rather than creating a coherent response, existing legislation and institutions have been adapted at implementation to provide some minimum, albeit patchy and inconsistent, forms of protection against refoulement.

[7] Interview with Florencia Belvedere, Dept of Home Affairs, Johannesburg, 1 Apr. 2009.

Two forms of adaptation have taken place at implementation. First, asylum legislation has been implemented (through so-called "asylum seeker permits") in a way that allowed Zimbabweans at least to obtain access to territory and right to work, pending assessment of their asylum claim. Given the backlog in refugee status determination procedures this has often allowed access to territory for a significant period. Secondly, there has been a gradual shift in the political response towards finding alternative ways to enable Zimbabweans to avoid being returned to their country of origin, mainly by drawing upon and reinterpreting existing legislation.

The main legislation in post-Apartheid South Africa relevant to cross-border mobility is the Immigration Act and the Refugee Act. The application of the existing legal framework to address the situation of the Zimbabweans is best understood as divided into two phases pre- and post-April 2009.

Until April 2009, the main policy towards Zimbabweans was "arrest, detain and deport" for all of those outside of formal asylum or labour migration channels. Furthermore, once RSD was complete, the Zimbabweans were no longer able to receive an asylum seeker permit and were liable for arrest, detention and deportation. Until 2009 the refugee recognition rate for Zimbabweans was extremely low. In the early 2000s, there was an informal practice of the Department of Home Affairs rejecting all Zimbabwean applications (Polzer et al. 2010).

Even at the peak of the crisis in Zimbabwe in 2008 and 2009, the refugee recognition rate was only around 10 per cent of Zimbabweans, with refugee status only being made available to people individually persecuted because of direct political links to the opposition MDC.[8] According to the Department of Home Affairs' own statistics around 150,000 people were deported each year between 2001 and 2003, increasing to 175,000 in 2004, 200,000 in 2005, 250,000 in 2006, and 300,000 in 2007 and 2008 (Vigneswaran et al. 2010: 466; Crisp and Kiragu 2010). It has been suggested that the sizeable majority of people recorded in these government statistics are Zimbabweans (Polzer 2008: 8).

After April 2009, there were some attempts to adapt policy and the application of existing legislation. Around the time of the peak outflow in 2008, the government came under increasing international scrutiny and pressure relating to its treatment of the Zimbabweans. A range of policy options were discussed on how existing legislation could be applied to provide formal status. Two options were widely debated. The possibility was discussed of applying the broader refugee definition contained in the OAU Refugee Convention to cover events which "seriously disturb or disrupt public disorder" in his/her country (Polzer 2008). Indeed South Africa's Refugee Act incorporates both the 1951 and OAU Conventions. However, both UNHCR and the government resisted

---

[8] Interview with Belvedere.

this on the grounds that this clause within the OAU Convention "lacks doctrinal clarity" (Crisp and Kiragu 2010). Beyond that, a more serious suggestion was made, based on recognition that section 31(2)(b) of the Immigration Act allows the Minister to "grant a foreigner or a category of foreigners the rights of permanent residence for a specified or unspecified period when [there are] special circumstances." Refugee rights advocates—and UNHCR—began lobbying the government to grant Zimbabweans temporary residence permits under section 31(2)(b).

Emerging from this discussion, and recognition of the inadequacies of the response up until that point, a number of policy proposals were made in April and May 2009. First, in April, the Home Affairs Minister Mosiviwe Mapisa-Nqakula announced a moratorium on deportations and a temporary "special dispensation permit" for all Zimbabweans under section 31(2) (b) of the Immigration Act. Second, in May, the government announced a three-month visa waiver for all Zimbabweans in line with the provisions of the SADC Protocol on the Free Movement of Persons. Third, an additional Refugee Reception Office (RRO) was set up outside Pretoria, reserved for use by people coming from other SADC countries, to take pressure off the other RROs.

These policy proposals had limitations. First, although deportations were formally stopped, there were reports that the South African Police Services (SAPS) continued to deport in the aftermath of the announcement (MSF 2009). Second, the three-month visa waiver applied only to Zimbabweans with travel documents and, in practice, obtaining a passport in Zimbabwe is difficult and can cost up to $820. Third, although the new RRO was opened at Marabastad, the backlog on RSD decision-making remained at around 400,000 and most Zimbabweans in the country continued to lack formal status.

The moratorium on the deportation of Zimbabweans ran only from May 2009 until October 2011. During that period a Zimbabwean Dispensation Project (ZDP) was implemented, which provided a short window (September 2010–December 2010) within which Zimbabweans without status could seek either asylum seeker permits or temporary work, business, or study permits for up to four years. By the time applications submitted during the window were processed in August 2011, it was revealed that just 275,000 of the estimated 1–1.5 m IOM illegal Zimbabweans had applied. One of the biggest weaknesses was that use of the system had required applicants to have a Zimbabwean passport. In the words of the Consortium on Refugees and Migrants in South Africa, "the entire process was held to ransom by the Zimbabwean authorities' ability to make passports available" (CoRMSA 2011).

In October 2011, Home Affairs Minister Nkosazana Dlamini-Zuma proclaimed that "those who have failed to take advantage of this [ZDP] process will in due course face the full consequence of South Africa's immigration laws" (IRIN 2011). The number of documented deportations at the Beitbridge

Border was 7,755 between October and December 2011 and 7,177 between January and March 2012 (Solidarity Peace Trust 2012). The brief moratorium for Zimbabweans was effectively over.

Consequently, the South African response can be considered to be one of partial regime stretching. For the period between May 2009 and October 2011, the norm of non-refoulement was extended to Zimbabweans who fell outside of the 1951 Convention framework. Interestingly, it was not on the basis of South Africa's institutionalization of the OAU Convention but rather through a series of ad hoc measures that the norm of non-refoulement adapted and was extended in scope. Yet, even within that context, the norm's implementation remained patchy due to a range of obstacles and bottlenecks to implementing the new framework—notably capacity (the limitations of the Refugee Reception Offices), joined-up government (the police continuing to deport for bribes), and policy coherence (the unrealistic requirement that Zimbabweans have access to passports).

What of the international organizational response of UNHCR? The protection of Zimbabweans in South Africa has fallen between cracks of different international organizations' mandates. UNHCR's role in relation to the Zimbabweans in South Africa has, by its own admission, "been a subtle and arguably ambiguous one" (Crisp and Kiragu 2010). It has consistently regarded most Zimbabweans as not being refugees. Only the quirk of the South African asylum system—of granting "asylum seeker permits" to all who request them—has designated Zimbabweans as people who fall within the purview of UNHCR's mandate. In the words of one staff member "in South Africa, an involvement with refugees and asylum seekers inevitably means an involvement with migrants because such large numbers of migrants have entered the asylum system" (Crisp and Kiragu 2010: 21). This "asylum seeker" link to UNHCR's mandate has meant that UNHCR has played a practical role in trying to ensure and oversee access to the asylum system at border and at RROs. However, due to its limited staff and presence in both contexts, its significance in relation to this role has been called into question; one member of DHA staff described UNHCR as "largely invisible."

Consequently, UNHCR began to advocate for alternative responses to the crisis that would take responsibility outside of the asylum and refugee framework. In UNHCR's own words: "In advocating for a moratorium on the deportation of Zimbabweans, however UNHCR has unusually asked for the principle of non-refoulement to be applied to a non-refugee group" (Crisp and Kiragu 2010: 21). On the one hand this can be read as an attempt to ensure a more coherent and sustainable response to the problem. On the other hand, it can also been seen as an attempt to take the issue outside of UNHCR's mandate. According to UNHCR, other members of the UN Country Team were "relatively inactive" because "they perceive it as a 'UNHCR problem'" and "irregular migrants constitute a grey zone in the UN system" (Crisp and

Kiragu 2010). In practice, then, UNHCR was a reluctant partner in protecting the Zimbabweans. Most notably, it refrained from any sustained advocacy campaign, and at no point argued strongly for South Africa to apply the OAU Convention clause on people fleeing "a serious disturbance to public order" (Crisp and Kiragu 2010).

Independent Variable: Incentives on Elites

Up until April 2009, South Africa faced strong incentives to refrain from regime stretching. Domestically, the 2000s witnessed a stronger domestic backlash against immigration. The May 2008 xenophobic violence in the townships, in which Zimbabweans were amongst those targeted (Landau and Misago 2009), economic recession, and 27 per cent unemployment led to increasing political pressure to move beyond an earlier pan-African commitment to open borders and towards increasing deportation for illegal immigrants (IOM 2009).

Specifically in relation to the Zimbabweans, there were important international incentives against regime stretching that resulted from South Africa's bilateral relationship with Zimbabwe and its mediating role in the SADC-facilitated Global Political Agreement between ZANU-PF and the MDC (Polzer 2008, 16). The personal relationship between Mbeki and Mugabe for a long time stymied South African criticism of Zimbabwe.[9] The government acknowledges that its response to Zimbabwean survival migrants has been shaped significantly by the Department of Foreign Affairs not wishing its grant of status to Zimbabweans to be interpreted as condemnation of the Mugabe regime.[10] For example, when in March 2009, South Africa was considering some kind of temporary visa exemption status for all Zimbabweans in South Africa, it first discussed the issue with the Zimbabwean Government at a meeting in Victoria Falls.[11]

However, by 2009, a range of countervailing incentives had emerged that pushed the Government of South Africa to consider an alternative position. The handling of the Zimbabwean exodus had been subject to widespread condemnation by human rights NGOs (HRW 2008, 2009a), international organizations (MSF 2009; Crisp and Kiragu 2010), academics (Betts and Kaytaz 2009), and the media (Polzer 2008: 16–17). Furthermore, during the Mbeki regime in particular, the President's own personal relationship with Mugabe placed a strong constraint on the degree to which the country could be seen to be criticizing Mugabe, either directly or through recognizing

[9] Interview with Simon K. Moyo, Zimbabwean Ambassador to South Africa, Zimbabwe House, Pretoria, 30 Mar. 2009.

[10] Interview with Advocate D. Mashabane and Andries Ousthuizen, Humanitarian Affairs, Dept of Foreign Affairs, Pretoria, 18 Mar. 2009.

[11] Interview with G. Burton Joseph, Director of Immigration Policy, Dept of Home Affairs, Pretoria, 19 Mar. 2009.

fleeing Zimbabweans as victims of a failed and human rights-abusing state. As Hammar et al. (2010: 269) put it: "Mbeki's protracted support for ZANU (PF) revealed the importance of solidarity among a cohort of liberation leaders." By 2009, that relationship had partly changed due to the election of Jacob Zuma as President and the new power-sharing agreement in Zimbabwe.

The regime stretching that took place seems to therefore owe more to changing incentives on elites than it does to institutionalization or the role of international organizations. Although South Africa is—unlike Botswana—a signatory to the OAU Refugee Convention, this played absolutely no role in South Africa's policy response to the Zimbabweans. It was never invoked and there was no serious debate about its application. Furthermore, UNHCR's role was one of followership rather than leadership. Interviews with UNHCR staff within the Regional Office highlighted their despair at the pressure created on the organization and their personal workloads in the context of the influx. For example, the Office (i) argued that the majority of Zimbabweans are not refugees; (ii) avoided invoking the OAU Refugee Convention in a way that might have brought the Zimbabweans within the refugee regime; and (iii) advocated for special immigration exemption status as an avenue that would alleviate pressure on the asylum system.

At each stage of the story, UNHCR consistently maintained an almost identical position to that of the South African Government. In its own internal evaluation, it consistently highlights the coincidence of interests with the government: "Like South Africa itself, UNHCR considers the majority of Zimbabweans not to be refugees" (Crisp and Kiragu 2010: 21). The organization was also been compromised in its ability to advocate for Zimbabwean rights in South Africa by needing to preserve diplomatic ties and protection space within Zimbabwe for other groups of refugees, not least the Congolese refugees in the Tongogara refugee camp.[12]

Botswana

After South Africa, Botswana has been the most numerically significant destination for Zimbabweans. Although only estimates are available, at the height of the crisis in 2008 some 1 million individuals crossed the border—although many moved onwards or returned home—and between 40,000 and 100,000 Zimbabweans were believed to have remained resident in a country with an overall population of less than 2 million.

Botswana has been recognized as having "the most exclusionary policy towards Zimbabweans" within the region (Kiwanuka and Monson 2009). In contrast to South Africa, where Zimbabweans have at least had access to

---

[12] Interview with NGO staff member working on the protection of Zimbabweans in South Africa.

territory and a brief period of moratorium against deportation, Botswana's approach has been based on drawing a sharp dichotomy between refugees and economic migrants.

On the one hand, those entering the asylum system have been detained in Francistown pending refugee status determination and then encamped in the Dukwi Refugee Camp if successfully recognized. The number of Zimbabwean refugees in the country has remained constant between 2009 and 2012 at around 900. On the other hand, those who have not entered the asylum system or who have fallen outside the 1951 Convention definition of a refugee have received no assistance and have faced the risk of roundup, arrest, and deportation—despite the virtual collapse of the Zimbabwean state (Betts and Kaytaz 2009).

Dependent Variable: Regime Stretching

The response to the overwhelming majority of Zimbabweans has therefore been one of exclusion. In 2003 Botswana built a 300 mile long, 2 metre high electric fence along the border with Zimbabwe. In 2005, the government reviewed its immigration policy to increase deterrence, including penalties for illegal migration and harbouring migrants, introducing a US$40 fine for unlawful entry. Those who are present illegally or are not recognized as refugees are liable to be detained and deported. The state deported an average of 5,000 Zimbabweans per month in 2008 and 2009 (Monson and Kiwanuka 2009). Botswana puts more money into deportation than any country in the region except South Africa, spending around 2 million pula (approximately US$285,000) per month.[13] Since establishing its Plumtree Reception and Support Centre in 2008, IOM has documented and assisted over 150,000 forcibly returned Zimbabweans.[14]

The international response has replicated the government's approach of starkly dividing between refugees and economic migrants. UNHCR and the other UN agencies have therefore provided support and assistance in relation to the relatively small number of Zimbabwean refugees within the asylum system. UNHCR—with support from UNDP, UNICEF, and WFP—has focused on fulfilling this core aspect of its mandate, working to ensure that Botswana complies with its core refugee obligations. However, the entire UN system has refrained from any protection, assistance, or advocacy in relation to the

---

[13] Quote from the Vice President of Botswana in May 2009. Information provided by Roy Hermann, UNHCR Representative, Gaborone, Botswana, personal correspondence, 25 May 2009.

[14] The total number of forcibly returned people assisted by IOM at the Plumtree Reception and Support Centre between 2008 and Apr. 2012 was 150,151. Between Jan. and Apr. 2012 the number was 5,448. Email correspondence with Natalia Perez y Andersen, Acting Chief of Mission, IOM Harare, Zimbabwe.

much larger group of vulnerable Zimbabwean migrants outside of the asylum system.

Independent Variable: Incentives on Elites

The Botswana Government's approach to immigration in general has been dominated by a focus on internal security and economic nationalism under President Ian Khama. Since the 1990s, the state has been regarded as an economic "success story," implementing austerity measures under structural adjustment programs to emerge with one of the highest economic growth rates and most stable democracies in Sub-Saharan Africa. Yet, as a small state, with a former military President and facing the economic challenge of an HIV/AIDS epidemic, it has focused increasingly on national security.

The international incentives on Botswana have been fairly neutral. It has not faced significant international pressure or incentives to stretch or not. Few arguments have been made to the government that it should recognize Zimbabweans. The international organizations in Gaborone, and especially UNHCR and the UN resident coordinator, have not criticized the government position, either privately or publicly.[15] Instead, they have been passive and accepting of their own non-involvement in the issue and recognized the sovereign right of the government to detain and deport.

Meanwhile, there have been strong domestic incentives against regime stretching. The electorate has strongly favoured deportation, and there has been growing xenophobia towards the Zimbabweans. The numbers of Zimbabweans (40,000–100,000) have been high relative to the overall population (1.8 million), and Zimbabweans in Gaborone have been associated with crime and prostitution.[16] With pressure on the country's own resources and high HIV rates, the electorate has been reluctant to allocate rights to non-citizens.[17]

The incentives on the government have therefore been neutral at the international level but there have been strong domestic incentives against regime stretching. UNHCR's own role has followed the government's decision on non-stretching. In interviews, UNHCR staff have argued that the organization's own work has been constrained by the government position and claimed that it could not get involved unless it was invited to do so by the government.

International organizations have had little response or strategy in response to Zimbabwean survival migration to Botswana. Alice Mogwe of Ditshwanelo

---

[15] Correspondence with Roy Hermann, former UNHCR Representative to Botswana; interview with Khin-Sandi Lwin, Representative (and UN Resident Coordinator), UNDP 24 Mar. 2009.

[16] Interview with Alice Mogwe, Director of Ditshwanelo, Gaborone, 25 Mar. 2009.

[17] Interview with Mogwe, 25 Mar. 2009.

said of the UN response, "I'm not sure how effective they are. They are very governmental and so there are restrictions on them in terms of what they can and cannot do."[18] Across all of the main UN agencies present in the country, there has been no mechanism or advocacy strategy to promote protection or assistance for Zimbabweans outside the asylum system. Furthermore, as a middle-income country, Botswana has little dependence on external assistance, massively constraining UNHCR's bargaining position vis-à-vis the government. This lack of influence was most starkly illustrated when in 2009 the UNHCR representative was expelled by the government for being seen to have adopted a critical stance towards the government on its policies towards Somali refugees.

CONCLUSION

This chapter has applied the Betts and Orchard framework to the refugee context to look at the norm of non-refoulement. It has explored implementation in relation to the specific question of how treaty-based norms adapt at implementation, looking at how the population to whom the norm of non-refoulement applies—"refugees"—sometimes adapts at the national level. In other words, rather than looking at "who is a refugee?" from a normative perspective, the chapter has explored that question from a positivist perspective, assessing not who should be a refugee but who—in practice—gets treated like a refugee.

To explore this question, the chapter has developed the concept of "regime stretching" to look at how norms and international organizations may adapt at implementation to new challenges that were unforeseen by the original creators of an international regime. In the refugee context, such "stretching" relates to the extent to which the regime has adapted from its "global" focus on providing non-refoulement to people fleeing persecution to those fleeing basic rights deprivations beyond persecution, particularly in the context of fragile and failed states.

The refugee context represents a methodologically useful context in which to explore such questions. It offers clear benchmarks against which to assess regime stretching because it offers a "from" and a "to". On the one hand, the regime has a clearly defined "global" consensus definition around people fleeing persecution, as set out in the 1951 Convention. On the other hand, survival migration offers a normative benchmark against which to assess the totality of people fleeing basic human rights violations who have a normative human rights-based case for non-refoulement.

---

[18] Interview with Mogwe, 25 Mar. 2009.

Furthermore, the Zimbabwean exodus within Southern Africa offers an empirical context in which to examine this process, because of the variation in responses exhibited by the host countries of asylum towards the same population at the same time. South Africa showed some regime stretching. Between May 2009 and October 2011, it provided a moratorium on deportations for all Zimbabweans, extending them an entitlement to non-refoulement. Meanwhile, Botswana did not show any regime stretching, instead detaining and deporting Zimbabwean survival migrants throughout the period.

The null hypothesis that institutionalization explains variation in practices of non-refoulement can be rejected. Although South Africa is a signatory to the 1969 OAU Convention and Botswana is not, this did not play a role in the allocation of non-refoulement to the Zimbabweans, never being invoked in South Africa despite existing in legislation. Instead, what defined the degree of regime stretching in both states were the interests of elites in government and particularly the sets of international and domestic incentives on those elites. In South Africa there were domestic and international tipping points at which elite incentives changed—in terms of pressure from civil society and the changing relationship with Zimbabwe—that made the moratorium on deportations more plausible in 2009 than earlier. In Botswana, the international and domestic incentives remained strongly against regime stretching.

Variation in practice has therefore been shaped by political contestation at the implementation phase rather than variation in the institutionalization of international norms. Yet the case study also reveals that international organizations have been epiphenomenal in this process. While international organizations—including UNHCR—have been shown to have independent causal effects on world politics at the global level, they have not been significant in changing implementation in the case study examined. Instead, UNHCR largely followed the position of the host state. This is a pattern replicated across other case studies in Africa (Betts 2013). Overall, then, at implementation, UNHCR and the role of international treaties have mattered far less for practice than domestic politics.

The case study also illustrates barriers to implementation beyond politics. Even in South Africa between May 2009 and October 2011, there was a range of practical barriers to full implementation of the moratorium. First, capacity limits mattered for the government's ability to process all those eligible. Second, there were bureaucratic challenges of joined-up government, with the police, for example, continuing to round up Zimbabweans in order to solicit bribes. Third, there were issues of coherence, with parts of the policy needing complements that were unavailable (e.g. the requirement that Zimbabweans produce passports).

Regime stretching as a concept arguably has relevance beyond the refugee context. In particular, it seems like a useful idea in areas in which old institutions face new challenges. Rarely in global governance do international regimes die and rarely do new ones emerge. Instead, part of the process of adaptation involves incremental change at the national level. Regime stretching helps draw attention to that process, which seems to have parallels across an array of other regimes. However, it is also important to be aware of ways in which the refugee regime can be considered representative or not of other regimes. There are three features of the regime that may be different in other regimes. First, in terms of *regime type*, the regime is a rights-based regime (as with, for example, the humanitarian regime). This means that the "measure" of stretching is likely to be (i) the categories of people to whom a set of rights are accorded and (ii) the numbers of people getting access to those rights. In other regimes, the measure of stretching may be different. Second, in terms of *norms–IO relationship*, the refugee regime is characterized by the presence of an IO which oversees implementation of the regime's norms (as with, for example, the nuclear regime in which the International Atomic Energy Agency oversees the Non-Proliferation Treaty). This may not be the case elsewhere, and hence the IO would drop out of the analysis (as with e.g. "R2P"). Third, in terms of *specificity*, in some regimes there may not be a formally specified regime at the global level which is as easy to identify (e.g. peacekeeping). Hence—although there are direct analogues across all of these features (e.g. the humanitarian regime, in which ICRC oversees implementation of international humanitarian law), some of the characteristics of other regimes may be different, and these differences offer a basis on which to explore hypotheses about how the inherent nature of the regime may or may not be a significant variable in explaining the scope for "regime stretching."

At the level of policy, the chapter highlights the causal mechanisms and hence policy levers through which old institutions can be made to adapt to new challenges. Even where old international institutions cannot be formally renegotiated, they may be made to adapt through structuring and realigning the incentives on national governments to enable adaptation to take place further downstream. It represents an especially important observation for international public policy-makers insofar as it highlights that "making international law work" relies upon recognizing the political translation mechanisms through which it works from the global to the national and down to the local levels. Given that nearly all areas of international law have some degree of ambiguity and imprecision, it is crucial to be aware of how political incentives shape how international institutions are implemented.

3

Transnational Advocacy
and Accountability
From Declarations of Anti-Impunity to
Implementing the Rome Statute

Michael Bluman Schroeder and Alana Tiemessen

Today, the international community expects that those "most responsible" for committing massive human rights abuses ought to be held accountable, irrespective of their political power or potential to spoil a peace process. Since the 1990s, the proliferation of a "justice cascade," in terms of trials and non-judicial measures in international and domestic institutions, suggests a stage of the accountability norm's development that is well beyond the aspirational. Indeed, the norm's most prominent institutional expression, the Rome Statute that constitutes the mandate and jurisdiction of the International Criminal Court (ICC), is a powerful statement about state commitment to international justice for atrocities. The Statute requires States Parties to pay more than lip service to the accountability norm; they are expected to implement a range of legislative and institutional reforms and, in the event of atrocities, comply with the Court's decisions and cooperate with its activities or take concerted legal action domestically.

In practice, implementation of the Rome Statute has met with varied success since it was established in 1998. Most signatories have moved to ratify the treaty (122 out of the 139 signatories) but progress on corresponding implementing legislation is poor in all geographic regions except for Europe. Implementation has been particularly problematic in Africa—the region with the most ratifications of the Rome Statute; among the thirty-three States Parties only a handful of states have completed and enacted implementation laws. Importantly, several States Parties have refused to cooperate with the Court but also failed to hold leaders accountable on their own terms following atrocities.

In this chapter, we join the other contributors in examining the relationship between compliance and implementation and offer illustrative examples of the obstacles to implementing the treaty norm of accountability. However, our primary focus is the NGO advocacy campaign—the Coalition for the International Criminal Court (CICC)—that assists, shames, and persuades States Parties to overcome these obstacles. This campaign is critical because treaties are seldom self-implementing—advocacy is almost always necessary to advance implementation.

For the CICC, advocating for Rome Statute implementation is a natural extension of its earlier work advocating for the treaty. However, the tasks and processes of institutionalization are different than those of implementation, and we examine how CICC advocacy did or did not change as a result of these differences. First, we find that implementation of the Statute requires overcoming a number of the obstacles described by Betts and Orchard, such as a lack of state capacity, technical expertise, and political will. Cooperation with the ICC can be politically costly for some elites, which encourages these elites to delay implementation. Consequently, the CICC has sought ways to reinforce its existing strategy of empowering national campaigns with low-cost access to research and expertise, to the extent that even a small local NGO can sustain a prolonged implementation campaign.

Second, consistent with Betts and Orchard, we find that institutionalization and implementation are parallel processes rather than sequential ones. Where states have not ratified the Statute, the CICC and its local partners often work with government actors to bring key domestic regulations and laws into conformity with the Statute in hopes of reducing the perceived political costs of ratification. Finally, we find that CICC strategies are largely consistent with strategies scholars attribute to other transnational advocacy campaigns, but the CICC also developed organizational innovations to bridge the gap between its internationally focused institutionalization campaign and its domestically focused implementation one. These innovations include policies to recruit and retain local NGOs, and give them more credit for the CICC's work and a platform for championing the Rome Statute without stifling constructive criticism of the ICC.

The Accountability Norm and the Rome Statute: Emerging Advocacy and Institutionalization

The accountability norm prescribes holding accountable, through formal trial and punishment, perpetrators that are considered most responsible for committing the most serious violations of international humanitarian law, such as genocide, crimes against humanity, and war crimes. The ICC, as constituted by the Rome Statute in 1998, is the most prominent institutional, and only permanent, expression of this norm, which stems from a collective response to a history of impunity for atrocities in the Cold War era and precedents set by ad hoc tribunals. The accountability norm has evolved over the past two decades to reflect a hierarchical division of labour. Domestic trials are prioritized over international tribunals to provide accountability while building respect for the rule of law and facilitating reconciliation. International tribunals are thus a last resort when domestic courts have no capacity or political will to provide for fair and effective accountability.

The early institutional expressions of the accountability norm were largely state-led projects (Fehl 2004: 374). First, the various domestic trials, truth commissions, and international ad hoc and hybrid tribunals suggested a "justice cascade" among states and growing, if inconsistent, collective support for institutionalization (Sikkink 2011). Second, the UN General Assembly's Sixth Committee established an Ad Hoc Committee in 1994 to investigate a possible permanent court. This committee created a focal point around which the so-called Likeminded Group (LMG) of states could organize. The LMG— mostly middle powers with multilateralist and liberal foreign policies—wanted a court to backstop a global order that promoted human rights and human security. For the LMG, the atrocities and subsequent tribunals in Rwanda and former Yugoslavia generated, somewhat paradoxically, tribunal "euphoria" and tribunal "fatigue," and created a sense of urgency for a permanent court with universal acceptance (Akhavan 2009: 627; Kirsch and Holmes 1999: 4). In 1995, the LMG orchestrated the Assembly's adoption of the Ad Hoc Committee's report and established a Preparatory Commission to begin work on a draft text for a future treaty conference. As the Commission's work concluded, preparations started for official treaty negotiations to begin in Rome.

In June 1998, 160 state delegations formally opened negotiations on the Rome Statute to establish an International Criminal Court. The negotiations themselves proved controversial and cantankerous at times, and major divisions between and among state delegations and civil society were most prominent on issues of jurisdiction, the Court's relationship with the UN Security Council, and the powers of the chief prosecutor. Nonetheless, the Statute was adopted on 17 July, with 120 votes in favour, 7 opposed, and 21 abstentions, and the Statute came into force four years later when the sixtieth state ratified the agreements.

NGO Advocacy for the Rome Statute: The CICC

When the Rome Statute was signed, it represented a victory for the LMG as well as civil society operating under the CICC umbrella. The CICC had been a reaction to the slow and inconsistent pace of norm institutionalization in the early 1990s (Bassiouni 1996). In February 1995, thirty NGOS formed it to coordinate a transnational campaign for an effective and independent International Criminal Court. A steering committee was established to provide overall campaign guidance, and William Pace of the World Federalist Movement-Institute for Global Policy became the convenor. The steering committee made it a priority to work closely with the LMG, and the focus was "naturally framed and facilitated by the UN and by its procedures" (Pace and Schense 2004: 108). For example, the CICC empowered LMG delegations by accrediting NGOs to the UN and treaty conference, enforcing decorum, lobbying on common positions, researching complex technical issues, and proposing draft treaty language (see Pace and Schense 2004; Welch and Watkins 2011).

CICC membership ballooned to over 800 members when formal negotiations opened in 1998. The membership included human rights NGOs of different sizes, women's groups, peace groups, religious groups, and legal professional groups. Though many members were Western-based, the membership spanned most regions of the world, despite difficulties initially attracting NGOs from North Africa, the Middle East, and Asia.

This membership surge reflected three features of the campaign. First, the close working relationship between the LMG and the CICC leadership meant CICC members enjoyed unique access to Assembly meetings, state delegations, and the Rome negotiations. Second, the CICC asked only that an NGO subscribe to the core mission principle of establishing an "effective and just International Criminal Court" (CICC 2006). Consequently, membership did not require NGOs to change their missions or to work exclusively on ICC issues. Third, the campaign's coalition structure was a mechanism for pooling resources and expertise, coordinating member lobbying, and disseminating information on developments and state positions. At Rome, the CICC "shadowed and tracked" states and created regional and thematic caucuses to coordinate lobbying, optimize monitoring of the official proceedings, and disseminate reports.[1] It is worth noting that this approach did not curtail member autonomy as NGOs self-selected into desirable teams or caucuses (Welch and Watkins 2011).

Many scholars credit the CICC with keeping negotiations on track and securing robust rules despite opposition from states like the US (see Glasius 2006, 2008; Human Rights Watch 2004a). Working with the LMG, the CICC successfully insisted that elite perpetrators should be held responsible via trial and punishment. In this vein, they opposed subordinating the power of the prosecutor to the UN Security Council—a concession that would limit the Court's ability to prosecute heads of state and political and military leaders. CICC members also effectively "channeled their concerns for the addition of victims" rights, reparation, and reconciliation into meetings (Schiff 2008: 39). This work would give the coalition credibility during implementation because it distanced the coalition from power politics, made it a voice for victim communities, and gave it a reputation for insight into local justice demands. Indeed,

---

[1] The CICC notes that its members and its reports were often critical to informing small state delegations on the state of negotiations, other state positions, and complex technical questions (see Welch and Watkins 2011).

with the treaty signing in Rome, the CICC leadership and its members were already turning their attention to the Statute's ratification and implementation.

BEYOND ROME: CAMPAIGNING FOR IMPLEMENTATION

In the post-Rome period, the CICC leadership and its now 2,500 plus members advocate for States Parties to pay more than lip service to international accountability. As Schiff (2008: 151–2) remarks, "the NGOs that had expended such huge energy to create the Court believed further effort would be needed for it to succeed." Successful implementation requires lobbying States Parties to ratify the Rome Statute, adopt appropriate reforms, strengthen their national court system, and when a situation arises, cooperate with the ICC's activities. CICC members are both advocates of accountability and technical assistance providers, and the specific mix of assistance and advocacy depends on an NGO's capacity and expertise as well as domestic political will and the institutional setting. We describe here some of the most common obstacles to implementation and the kinds of work undertaken by the CICC leadership and its members to overcome those obstacles.

Ratification

A significant undertaking post-Rome is the CICC's "Universal Ratification Campaign." The campaign targets one country each month and assists local members with media outreach, organizing local workshops and meeting with government officials and the opposition. The CICC hopes this approach will generate more momentum for ratification in the underrepresented Asia and Middle East and North Africa (MENA) regions (interview, 3 Oct. 2011). This regional variation in ratification presents a significant challenge for advocates (CICC 2011: 16). As of June 2013, 122 of the 139 signatories to the Statute have also ratified it. However, a regional breakdown of ratification offers a more complex picture as signatories in Sub-Saharan Africa (thirty-three), the Americas (twenty-eight), and Europe (forty-two) have largely ratified the Statute while those in Asia (seventeen) and the Middle East and North Africa (MENA) (two) have not.

To be sure, the extent of African state ratifications is important, given that all of the current "situations"[2] before the Court are from that region. However,

---

[2] "Situations" refer to particular events or conflicts that are under the jurisdiction of the ICC and not cases, individuals, or the state itself.

the regional disparities create the perception that the accountability norm is not universally applicable. This concentration has also reinforced criticism that the Court is biased against Africa and is a form of Western judicial colonialism in weak states. CICC advocates work to dispel this perception in hopes of increasing support from domestic civil society (interview, 3 Oct. 2011). Besides Africa, this perception is also prominent among the states in the MENA region where anti-Western sentiment and distrust of international institutions is stronger. In Asia (and among some major powers), CICC members must also convince many audiences that ratifying the Statute would not frivolously weaken state sovereignty by subjecting citizens to a "foreign" court.

To dispel these negative perceptions, the CICC encourages and supports the educational and outreach programs of its members. These programs engage high-level officials as well as offer public forums where citizens can bring their questions and concerns. Interestingly, the CICC leadership does not take positions on the ICC's selection of situations or individual cases and offers its members minimal guidance to disprove accusations of bias in those decisions. Instead, it allows local members to voice their own positions, criticize the Court, or, if they wish, to adopt the secretariat's position that it "is a cheerleader for the Rome Statute, but not a cheerleader for the Court" (interview, 3 Oct. 2011). In other words, the CICC has, to some extent, addressed perception problems by framing support for the Court's prosecutorial strategy and judicial decisions as separate from support for ratifying and implementing the Statute.

These perceptions aside, there are other advocacy challenges when it comes to ratification. In particular, the CICC hopes to persuade or leverage the major powers that have not acceded to the Statute but engage the ICC when it suits their interests, especially the US, China, and Russia who wield vetoes in the UN Security Council. To this end, the Council's decisions to refer Darfur and Libya to the ICC gave advocates some optimism that these states could be persuaded through long-term "constructive engagement." However, the referrals also foment accusations of hypocrisy and selectivity by States Parties, who point out that some of these major powers are themselves outside the Court's jurisdiction and unlikely to refer their allies. Moreover, the CICC leadership argues that the absence of major powers denies the Court critical funding precisely when demands on the nascent court are escalating and it needs to demonstrate that it can meet the goals set out in the Statute (interview, 3 Oct. 2011). Finally, ratification is stalled or unlikely in countries where the ICC would have immediate cause to take action. In countries like Zimbabwe and Sri Lanka, political elites and armed groups engaged in fighting or repression oppose the Rome Statute because perpetrators have no desire to stand trial and non-perpetrators fear undercutting peace or reversing fragile reforms (CICC 2011: 21–2). Alternatively, authoritarian institutions that are closed and repressive make it difficult for Rome Statute advocates to access lawmaking bodies, resources, and the media.

Implementing Legislation

Beyond ratification, the CICC has campaigned for States Parties to implement the requisite legislative and institutional reforms. These reforms improve state cooperation and compliance with the Rome Statute and realize the constitutive and regulative effects of the accountability norm. However, the need for advocates to monitor and press for reform is critical, as the degree of implementation is low in all regions except Europe, and it is especially low compared to the number of ratifications overall. In total, forty-seven States Parties have implemented complementarity reforms and forty have implemented cooperation ones. To shine light on the problem, Amnesty International (2010) published a "Report Card" prior to the ICC's 2010 Review Conference, indicating that less than one third of States Parties had enacted necessary legislation. Furthermore, Amnesty International (2010: 2–3) argues that much of the enacted legislation is "significantly flawed"; for example, some implementing legislation had weak definitions of the crimes, allowed for political control over the initiation of prosecutions, and included provisions that could prevent cooperation with the ICC.

This weak record has multiple sources, and thus CICC members carry out a variety of implementation activities. Implementing the Statute involves complex legislative issues and effective judicial administration and law enforcement. At its extreme, States Parties may require a constitutional amendment—a situation which, if possible, the CICC recommends avoiding with an authoritative reinterpretation of existing constitutional provisions. For example, if a state constitution forbids extradition of a perpetrator, the CICC works with lawmakers to interpret surrender to the ICC (a Statute provision) as legally distinct from and consistent with non-extradition (interview, 3 Oct. 2011). Furthermore, the Rome Statute was designed to operate across diverse legal traditions, thus often leaving unclear exactly what legal and bureaucratic reform should look like for any given country.

The need to increase institutional capacity is critical to give effect to complementarity—the provision that only if a state is unwilling and unable to investigate and prosecute will a situation be admissible for the ICC. In this vein, the Rome Statute prescribes that the ICC is a "court of last resort" so States Parties are expected to develop robust rule of law institutions that take effective action in the event of mass atrocities. Complementarity also reduces the ICC's case load and facilitates victims' access to justice and redress.

For CICC members, support for capacity-building is a major entry point into the implementation process in States Parties. Technical assistance generates less public attention and controversy than advocacy, while allowing transnational NGOs to draw on their expertise and local ones to expand networks and access into government. Indeed, technical assistance is generally welcomed by States Parties who find it an affordable source of resources and expertise. This assistance is particularly necessary for states with a dualist legal system, which treat international and national legal obligations as separate domains. As a result, conflicting legal obligations often arise and addressing these conflicts requires enacting new domestic legislation and ensuring the legislation takes precedence over older conflicting domestic laws (Stone and Du Plessis 2008: 8).

In general, the CICC's local members often work with transnational members who have a particular legal or other technical expertise. Transnational NGOs such as the ICRC, No Peace Without Justice, and Amnesty International all offer legal assistance. For example, the ICRC works with local NGOs and military leaders to incorporate the Geneva Conventions and the Rome Statute into military manuals (interview, 3 Oct 2011). Alternatively, CICC members work with regional organizations, such as the Organization of American States (OAS), to create model legislation that reduces the complexity and burden of adapting Statute obligations to different legal systems. Where model legislation is unavailable or requires additional tweaking, CICC members work with supportive legislators to draft legislation and persuade ambivalent legislators to support it. CICC members meet with Justice and Foreign Ministry officials, urge legislators to present implementing legislation to its congress or parliament, and monitor the legislative process and shame efforts to stall its passage. Finally, if the legislation is contentious, CICC members provide education and outreach to the general public as a counterbalance to any opposition groups.

New legislation, however, adds little without effective institutions to investigate crimes, prosecute perpetrators, and assist victims and witnesses. As a result, CICC members often press government officials and legislators to ensure the police, judiciary and prosecutor have the necessary capacity—including staff and budget—to meet their legislative obligations. Other CICC members support this advocacy by offering training for judges and bar associations, developing best practices, or organizing seminars. Though such institution building can be costly and challenging to NGOs, it also offers unique opportunities; especially where implementation is stalled or ratification has not taken place, as was the case in the Philippines and Nepal.

In these cases, the CICC may advocate for institutionalization (i.e. ratification) while simultaneously pressing for the implementation of domestic legal and regulatory reforms that conform to the Statute. Put another way, the CICC treats implementation and institutionalization as parallel processes. For example, the CICC provides technical assistance to strengthen rule of law institutions that, in turn, will support (or at least acquiesce) to ratification. Even where a state has ratified the Statute, the CICC usually combines technical assistance with political advocacy. Advocacy remains critical during implementation. The public act of signing and ratifying the Rome Statute typically brings a government the domestic and international benefits of signaling its commitment to human rights and the rule of law. However, implementation brings fewer direct benefits as it receives less media attention, can be too technical for the general public to understand, and takes place over a prolonged period. Furthermore, political will may decrease if the government who signed and ratified the Statute is no longer in office and been replaced by sceptics of the ICC. Lastly, those societal interests long opposed to the ICC (particularly the military) often increase their resistance as the Statute moves closer to taking effect.

It is instructive to note that the CICC leadership seldom takes a position on the content of legislation and encourages local members to offer contextual analysis that will fit their institutional and cultural setting (CICC 2011: 23). In the words of the leadership:

> The approach—to decentralize the substantive work, to maintain a low-profile, service-based Secretariat and to maximize the independence of the members to act—has been undertaken in recognition of the fact that local and national NGOs are much better placed to assess political conditions in their own countries, to identify key stakeholders, to assess how to motivate political will to ratify and to evaluate existing laws and legislative processes with an eye towards implementation. (Pace and Schense 2004: 113)

The secretariat thus spends nearly all of its time on helping members and supporters stay updated and disseminating vital communications. The secretariat also conducts research at the request of its members and states, though its policy is to seldom take credit for doing so.

Cooperation and Compliance

Ensuring that States Parties cooperate, and hence comply, with the ICC is highly political and has a patchy record of success. Cooperation with the ICC is required if there is an active prosecutorial investigation, indictments or arrest warrants are issued, or trials are under way. The Rome Statute obligates all States Parties to provide the Court with requested information, share evidence, allow ICC officials access to victims, and permit the travel of witnesses. Furthermore, they are obliged to execute arrest warrants and surrender any accused (nationals or not) to the Court—two obligations that are the most problematic to date.

These latter obligations present several challenges. First, a state's laws must allow the extradition of nationals that, in some countries, can require a constitutional amendment. Alternatively, the state may be unable to locate the accused. For example, the Ugandan situation has not resulted in any trials as the Ugandan and other regional governments have been unable to arrest the indicted members of the Lord's Resistance Army leadership. In other instances, there is little political will to arrest powerful political or military elites indicted by the Court, particularly given their ability to become "spoilers" of peace processes. In the clearest example, many African states and the African Union oppose the arrest of the President of Sudan, Omar al-Bashir, and several States Parties—Malawi, Djibouti, Chad, and Kenya—violated their Statute obligations by permitting him to safely travel in their territory. The Sudan and Libya situations also demonstrate the obstacles to cooperation when an arrest warrant results from a Security Council referral for acts committed in a territory that is not a State Party. In response to such a coercive judicial intervention, domestic authorities in Sudan and Libya have challenged the legitimacy and jurisdiction of the ICC by refusing to arrest or transfer the accused, despite their legal obligations to cooperate with it under the UN Charter.

States Parties are also uncooperative if they invoke the complementarity principle to ensure impunity for the accused instead of meting out accountability in their own courts. Such a challenge is legal and political as it requires interested parties to weigh and contest subjective assessments about whether there is sufficient political will and capacity to pursue accountability. The Uganda and Kenya situations illustrate this challenge. In Uganda, some victim communities and, at times, the Ugandan Government have suggested national trials and local traditional justice are preferable to ICC trials because they advance the peace process without sacrificing standards of justice. In Kenya, the government has repeatedly and unsuccessfully petitioned the UN Security Council and the ICC to drop cases against the accused in favour of allowing domestic courts to handle the cases, citing that it is in the interests of both peace and justice to do so.

These challenges illustrate why implementation and compliance are separate, but interrelated, activities. Compliance is more likely if implementation results in the incorporation of Rome Statute obligations into domestic law, and state agencies and judicial bodies are empowered and authorized to enforce those laws. Parties may face political obstacles to compliance irrespective of the degree of implementation. The Kenya situation is illustrative of a mixed record of compliance in this respect. On the one hand, the government has sought a deferral of its cases with justifications that lack credibility and it failed to execute the ICC's arrest warrant for President Bashir when he was on Kenyan territory in 2010. On the other hand, the Kenyan indictees summoned by the ICC have thus far all appeared voluntarily for their hearings and, despite political pressure, a Kenyan High Court ruled that authorities were obligated to arrest Bashir upon any future visit. Such instances of compliance reflect how the implementation of Rome Statute provisions empowered domestic judicial institutions as well as the ongoing role of advocacy groups in keeping pressure and attention on the Kenyan Government to meet its Statute obligations.

In the long run, the CICC expects that the implementation of legislative and institutional reforms will raise the cost of non-cooperation. In the short run, CICC members are voices of dissent that seek out the media to shame a State Party who permits the travel of an accused onto its territory, refuses to arrest and surrender the accused, or fails to provide access to witnesses and evidence. Moreover, CICC members facilitate cooperation by engaging in outreach activities with victim communities whose cooperation is needed for the ICC to investigate, collect evidence, and carry out trials. In northern Uganda, for example, local CICC members join the ICC and other likeminded civil society leaders to educate and reassure a distrustful victim community, help answer questions and concerns, meet directly with The Hague-based officials, and give them access to victim and witness programs.

Though most CICC activities are domestically driven, some international advocacy still takes place. The CICC lobbies regional organizations as well as the UN Security Council to urge them to pressure resistant states to cooperate. For example, the Kenya deferral request was opposed by a sizeable segment of Kenyan civil society who successfully lobbied against it after coordinating with high-profile CICC members like Human Rights Watch and the CICC steering committee and advisory board. Finally, the CICC participated actively in 2010 Review Conference for the ICC where its members engaged in "stocktaking" and advised on non-cooperation issues. Much of this effort was directed toward encouraging the Court to engage more directly with victims.

THE COALITION AS INDISPENSABLE TO THE ICC

The Court itself is reliant on the CICC because of the membership's continuity, constructive criticism, local knowledge and contacts, and representation of victim communities. Additionally, the reputation of the leadership as a neutral advocate for the Statute and of its members as experts in international justice and human rights allows them to better engage with States Parties and victims communities than the Court itself.

The continuity of CICC leadership and staff since Rome adds to the credibility of their expertise and knowledge of the Statute and the Court's activities and procedures. In contrast, there is a significant turnover in representatives to the Assembly of States Parties and ICC personnel and, therefore, "the long involved NGO personnel would have greater institutional knowledge—and thus be better potential agents of socialization for new members of the ICC community—than many ICC staff" (Schiff 2008: 161). NGOs have an in-depth knowledge of how to interpret the Rome Statute, how the ICC operates, and the consequences of the Court's actions for States Parties and victims.

Another dimension of the CICC's credibility stems from their position as supporters *and* constructive critics of the Court. Members, and to a lesser extent the leadership, express critical views of the ICC's prosecutorial strategy, the progress of trials, and the Court's engagement with victims and witnesses. For example, some local Ugandan NGOs voiced concerns of victim communities regarding the political and security implications of the LRA arrest warrants and assessed the possibility of alternative national justice mechanisms (UCICC 2007). In the trial of the DRC warlord, Thomas Lubanga, NGOs also voiced the outrage of victim communities when the case was almost dismissed. More generally, CICC members monitor and raise concerns about the slow progress of the investigations and trials and bring the Court's attention to crimes. For example, local NGOs in the Central African Republic (CAR) communicated the details of various atrocities and successfully pressed the Prosecutor's office to open an investigation into this situation (Glasius 2008, 2009). While the CAR Government referred its conflict situation to the ICC in 2005, the advocacy and information provided by NGOs was a critical factor that led to the Prosecutor's decision to open investigations two years later.

Furthermore, the ICC's self-advocacy and outreach program is limited compared to local NGOs with greater access and engagement with local communities. The support of these communities is necessary if the ICC hopes to obtain evidence, secure witnesses, and develop its assistance and reparations programs. In fact, the Assembly of States Parties implicitly recognizes the need for NGOs to supplement the work of ICC officials in its Strategic Plan for Outreach which states that such "civil society groups with a broad grassroots base may also assist the Court in reaching out to broader networks" (Assembly of States Parties, ICC 2006: 7).

The CICC uses multiple channels to relay information between communities and ICC officials. First, it participates in bi-annual NGO-ICC roundtable meetings in The Hague; these meetings provide access to the Court for both small and large NGOs and in exchange, the Court's organs benefit from their information and expertise. Second, the Coalition's leadership, and convenor William Pace in particular, engages in high-level diplomacy and communication with Court officials and organs. Third, the Coalition has a formalized role and consultative status with the Assembly of States Parties and the Coalition's contributions and expertise is often acknowledged in ASP resolutions (interview, 3 Oct. 2011). Lastly, the ASP's outreach plan includes holding joint workshops and seminars and arranging visits to the Court for representatives of local NGOs (Assembly of States Parties, ICC 2006: 12).

ANALYSIS: CAMPAIGN RESPONSES TO THE CHALLENGE OF NORM IMPLEMENTATION

Betts and Orchard's framework offers a number of important insights for understanding the implementation of the international accountability norm. First, the norm illustrates the value of differentiating implementation from compliance as implementation has not resulted in seamless cooperation with the ICC. Nor, as Betts and Orchard suggest, has norm development been a linear process. The actions of the ICC create opposition from those, particularly African states, who perceive the Court as applying the norm selectively across the world. Though much of this contestation stops short of outright rejection, governments and populations are asking whether they should have more discretion in applying the norm in a given context.

Furthermore, the structural variables identified by Betts and Orchard have shaped both implementation outcomes and advocacy efforts. Ideational variables, particularly sovereignty, are a barrier against accession or ratification, especially in Asia and the Middle East. In Uganda, political elites and some civil society groups have fused together sovereignty norms and ideas about conflict resolution and proposed interpretations of complementarity that differ from ICC officials. More generally, some actors fail to implement or comply with the norm for political reasons while others have more material interests at stake. For example, political leaders in Sudan, Kenya, and Libya have challenged the ICC's jurisdiction.

Other ostensibly constraining structures have more complicated and uncertain effects. For example, the Statute has led to opposition from some state agencies such as defense ministries. However, other state agencies such as the judiciary and the prosecutor's office have more mixed responses as complementarity increases their budgets and available technical support. Similarly, the complexity of the Rome Statute and the complementarity principle create capacity problems for many States Parties. The institutional burden is particularly high for States Parties with dualist legal systems and weak courts. Yet capacity problems create openings for NGOs to offer technical support, and this technical support deepens ties between advocates and policy-makers and may create more openings to exert pressure for implementation.

Finally, Betts and Orchard's framework rightly suggests that agency can facilitate or obstruct norm implementation. Our study has focused on the transnational advocacy campaign and the campaign's choices in strategy, organizational structures, and policies adopted to advocate for implementation and provide technical assistance. These choices show that the effect of agency on implementation cannot be reduced to the degree that advocates are present or absent. Instead, the influence of agents may depend on the innovativeness of the campaign's leadership and members, not just in overcoming political obstacles to the norm but also organizational obstacles faced by the campaign itself.

A substantial scholarship exists on the evolution and strategic choices of transnational advocacy campaigns organized around principled issues such as addressing a ban on landmines, the protection of civil and political rights, women's rights, and protecting the environment (e.g. Keck and Sikkink 1998; Price 2003). These campaigns, including the CICC, start as voluntary networks of "norm entrepreneurs" and "gatekeeper" NGOs that exchange information to coordinate tactics, recruit new members, and frame the norm to attract support (Price 2003: 584; Bob 2009). Eventually, interaction intensifies, and in many cases like the CICC, the network establishes a coalition with a steering committee and small secretariat for servicing the growing membership and managing and routinizing interactions among members.

A coalition's steering committee and secretariat develop strategic plans to identify target audiences and resonant frames, increase access to intergovernmental forums, engage likeminded states and international civil servants, and secure resources for the campaign. The coalition's leadership also coordinates and manages key resources such as social media platforms like Twitter, Facebook, and the coalition's website—technologies that enhance information flows and keep dissemination costs low (Diebert 1997). For instance, the CICC sends emails to the listserv and updates the website where visitors find member reports, learn about campaign and ICC developments and make donations. In this way, it acts as a "clearinghouse" that can sort, organize, and prioritize information (interview, 3 Oct. 2011).[3]

However, one question inadequately addressed in this scholarship is how a campaign's internal structures and policies change once a treaty is signed. This question is an important one because treaty-making focuses on international outcomes while norm implementation primarily requires changing domestic ones (Betts and Orchard, this volume; Bob 2009: 12). Though some internal features, such as information-sharing structures, may continue to be relevant, campaigns may also find existing features to be inadequate, for example in securing the appropriate technical expertise. To be sure, the international level is not entirely excluded. For example, a treaty may create new international channels for NGOs to distribute information they collect about state practice (Weiss and Gordenker 1996). As such, the coalition's "prodigious information gathering reveal(s) actual implementation of the treaty norms" (Gaer 2003), including the enactment of implementing legislation and bureaucratic reforms.

---

[3] By organize, we mean that it can create categories and links that determine how and where particular information is located. By prioritize, we mean that it can make information more or less visible by placing it in high-traffic webpages or include/exclude from emails.

That said, the coalition structure must ultimately facilitate work at the national level (Khagram et al. 2002: 10). In this way, the CICC's approach is consistent with studies showing that implementation means advocating for and assisting with the reform of national laws and institutions, getting reluctant states to sign the treaty, and pressing States Parties to comply with it (Wapner 1996; Price 2003; Keck and Sikkink 1998; Martens 2005). To a large extent, the coalition structure remains useful by helping to pool expertise and collect and exchange information to shame, cajole, and persuade States Parties.

At the same time, the coalition structure needs to be adapted to address the specific political and organizational challenges of implementation. One of the biggest political challenges is securing access to domestic political systems so they can press for implementation and help states enact robust reforms (Khagram et al. 2002: 16). To this end, the CICC leadership builds up national and regional campaigns that "can more systematically challenge government processes that are closed to outside input" (Pace and Schense 2004). During implementation, "even the largest coalition members could not undertake [implementation activities] on their own; instead they require the sustained coordination of NGOs of all sizes and mandates, from all over the world" (Pace and Schense 2004: 113). As such, the organizational challenge is recruiting and retaining NGOs and integrating them into the CICC's work.

This challenge is made somewhat easier by the treaty itself, which serves as a "rally point" that attracts new members to a campaign (Clark 2001). Since 1998, six hundred new members have joined the CICC, including a number of NGOs from traditionally underrepresented regions like the Middle East and Asia. Today, the coalition's present membership consists of a variety of regional and transnational NGOs, but the "majority" are small, local ones (interview, 3 Oct. 2011). The regional distribution of NGOs includes roughly 1,000 African-based ones, 500 European, 300 Middle Eastern and North African, 450 North and South American, and 400 from Asia Pacific (interview, 3 Oct. 2011). This surge is not solely a result of earlier successes but also more proactive recruitment measures. For example, the CICC occasionally puts out "a bulletin, an active call" to identify NGOs in target states, and to raise a region's profile and the steering committee has expanded from six to sixteen, with more than half of the committee coming from outside of Western Europe and North America (interview, 3 Oct. 2011).

The leadership has also looked for new ways to keep the cost of NGO participation low so small NGOs can join. Since the beginning, CICC membership carries few obligations so NGOs can maintain substantial autonomy. In fact, members are asked only to "be involved at a level they think is appropriate to them." Members do not pay annual membership fees—a policy that requires a growing secretariat to pay the costs of fundraising and soliciting grants (interview, 3 Oct. 2011). The CICC also sustains many of the thematic and regional caucuses created in Rome and members self-select into caucuses that further their missions (for example, victim rights), increase their expertise, and build personal contacts with key government and IO officials. Since the CICC leadership does not decide the make-up of each caucus, the allocation of expertise may not always reflect overall advocacy needs—gaps may develop. The CICC Secretariat addresses this problem by developing (at its own expense) specialized bureaus that support the caucuses and offer research services to members and States Parties. Overall, this membership strategy prioritizes recruiting more widely, not finding NGOs that need to immediately contribute resources or technical expertise. Thus, the CICC is making "a long-term commitment of resources and expertise" to develop national networks who can more readily advocate at the domestic level (Pace and Schense 2004: 114). By 2009, eighty national networks had been established, including fourteen in Asia and the Pacific, thirty-two in Africa, fourteen in Europe, eleven in MENA, and nine in the Americas (www.iccnow.org).

A third organizational challenge is finding ways to empower domestic members so they can sustain a prolonged implementation campaign. Scholars find that a treaty is itself empowering, with "the political terrain being tilted in favor of political challengers (both state and non-state) committed to implementation of the new norm" (Khagram et al. 2002: 20). However, the CICC leadership has adapted its policies to magnify this effect. The regional and thematic caucuses help small members pool their resources and maximize monitoring of important developments. The CICC leadership also increases the visibility of members by following a "results not credit" policy, in that more credit is attributed to domestic NGOs and States Parties and not to the CICC as a whole (interview, 3 Oct. 2011). The secretariat often carries out research on behalf of members or puts experts in contact with domestic members. However, the members are encouraged to take credit and "there are a number of times when the CICC has specifically made the decision to not take credit for it and to work behind the scenes" (interview, 3 Oct. 2011).

The final organizational challenge is addressing intra-coalition conflicts. As Schiff (2008: 144) notes, CICC members "do not speak to the ICC with one voice because they pursue a range of objectives." Some disagreements stem from the varying missions of the membership, which range from transitional justice to human rights, to rule of law reform, to conflict resolution. Moreover, the membership comes from different regional and national backgrounds and has varying organizational needs. As a result, they often take divergent positions on the specific actions and decisions of the ICC. For example, NGOs from different countries pushed for national delegations to support particular judges during the inaugural elections. Similarly, domestic members may disagree with transnational ones about what action should be taken when a situation arises, with some domestic members "maximizing local interests, at least in the short spans of potential victims' lives" (Schiff 2008: 155).

Rather than try to mediate or suppress such disagreements, the CICC leadership accepts, if not embraces, them. Curtailing disagreements is not feasible, at least if the CICC hopes to maintain its large membership. It may also be undesirable as the dissenting voices of local NGOs may actually increase the NGOs' credibility at home, in turn helping them gain access to the domestic policy-making process. To support this view, the leadership policy is one of neutrality that encourages domestic NGOs to express their own concerns. For its part, as Richard Dicker of Human Rights Watch notes, "the Coalition Secretariat quite properly does not get involved in a country situation" (Welch and Watkins 2011: 994). The leadership also does not discourage or punish members who criticize the Court or take positions more consistent with local demands. In return, members agree not to speak on behalf of the CICC or even use its logo without the express approval of the CICC (interview, 3 Oct. 2011). The leadership maintains that, while it serves its members, it does not consider itself an embodiment of the membership as a whole. As such, "the work of the Secretariat and the activities of the Coalition members should be distinguished" (Pace and Schense 2004: 113). It is left to members to decide how best to support the Rome Statute.

CONCLUSION

It has been twelve years since States Parties signed the Rome Statute to give effect to a norm that prescribes holding accountable those most responsible for mass atrocities. Since that time, the implementation of this treaty norm has varied significantly across supporting states. This chapter has highlighted some of the most common political and technical obstacles to implementation—obstacles also highlighted in the volume's theoretical framework. Moreover, consistent with Betts and Orchard, institutionalization and implementation are parallel processes rather than sequential ones in many countries.

The focus of this chapter is on the agency behind implementation and specifically the transnational advocacy campaign—the CICC—that has played a critical role in advocating for the Treaty and assisting States Parties to overcome obstacles to implementation. We find that the CICC's leadership and members provide essential technical and legal assistance to States Parties who are without the capacity to do so alone. The Coalition also plays a leadership role in generating and sustaining the political will necessary for ratification and cooperation. In fact, the members' role as political advocates and technical assistance providers is deeply intertwined as technical cooperation with state officials provides new entry points to advocate for further implementation. Where a state resists ratification, the CICC and local members seek to bring domestic laws and regulation into conformity with the Statute prior to ratification in hopes of reducing domestic uncertainty about the costs of ratification.

These findings about the CICC echo other work on transnational advocacy that highlights the importance of setting strategic objectives, maintaining a coalition structure to coordinate tactics, and relying on the dissemination and framing of information and pooling resources and expertise. That said, the CICC also adopts organizational innovations that explain how it bridged the gap between structures and policies established early on in the campaign and the new political and organizational challenges of Rome Statute implementation. These innovations include policies to recruit and retain local NGOs, give them more credit for the CICC's work, and give them a platform for championing the Statute without stifling their political advocacy and constructive criticism of the ICC. These innovations highlight the importance to advocates that improved norm implementation requires first developing an effective implementation campaign. Overall, the Coalition's strategic approach and commitment to implementation sustained the life of the campaign beyond Rome, to the mutual benefit of the ICC and the Coalition.

4

The Unimplemented Norm
Anti-Mercenary Law and the Problems of Institutionalization

Sarah Percy

The norm against mercenary use is an interesting case to examine in a volume that seeks to consider how norms are implemented after their institutionalization, because it has never been successfully implemented. Assessing the anti-mercenary norm and the process of its institutionalization sheds light not only on the reasons norms may fail to be implemented (which has obvious consequences for future institutional design) but also contributes to a wider debate about whether institutionalization and implementation preserve norms or in fact prompt further change.

Betts and Orchard have asked us to consider implementation as an important next chapter after institutionalization. The anti-mercenary norm affords an additional opportunity: what happens to norms if they are institutionalized but not implemented? A cursory glance at the military stage would seem to reveal that the anti-mercenary norm is either dead or ailing. Private military and security companies (PMSCs)[1] are unquestionably part of the fabric of modern war.[2] It is highly unlikely that the United States has the operational capacity to go to war without contractors, and equally likely that contractors will continue to be used to counter new problems when they arise. For example, the use of private security guards to protect shipping from the predations of Somali piracy is a frequently cited solution to the piracy problem.[3] But in 1994, Janice Thomson argued that "today, real states do not use mercenaries"

---

[1] What to call private companies that provide military service is a vexed and much debated point in the literature. For the sake of simplicity and to avoid academic arguments rehearsed exhaustively elsewhere I will refer to PMSCs when referring to post-2001 companies operating in Iraq and Afghanistan and restrict the term private military company (PMC) to Executive Outcomes and Sandline.

[2] In 2012 there were more contractors among the American contingent in Afghanistan than regular armed forces.

[3] See <http://www.economist.com/node/21552553>.

(Thomson 1994: 96). How, in a very short space of time, did real states seemingly embrace the use of mercenaries? Does the use of PMSCs signal that the underlying anti-mercenary norm has been revised, or has it died? Has a failure to implement an institutionalized norm undermined that norm?

The anti-mercenary norm is an interesting case because its poor institutionalization and the resulting non-implementation might suggest that the norm is unprotected and likely to disappear (or possibly to regress, or to experience what McKeown (2009) bluntly refers to as "norm death"). However, despite all its challenges, the anti-mercenary norm appears to have altered rather than died. The norm has not died, or perhaps not even regressed, but it has unquestionably changed. Accordingly I use the story of anti-mercenary law to probe questions about how institutionalization and implementation can drive normative change, even when that change is not directed or desired by players on the international stage.

Unlike many of the contributions to this volume, this chapter will not examine a particular case. Rather, it will consider the reasons why anti-mercenary law has been impossible to implement and consider the implications. I argue that the anti-mercenary norm has been effectively unimplementable for both intrinsic (related directly to the way the norm was institutionalized as international law) and extrinsic (related to the international environment) reasons. This examination leads me to three resulting arguments. First, institutionalization and even implementation may not preserve a norm at all, but rather act as opening salvoes for further contestation. Second, when a norm is ineffectively institutionalized, this can create channels through which change will occur. In the case of the anti-mercenary norm, states exploited loopholes in the law that have had a noticeable impact on the underlying norm. Third, even when norms are poorly institutionalized and not implemented, they are still robust, and can be best understood as altering rather than regressing.

To make these arguments I proceed in four sections. First, I briefly outline the anti-mercenary norm and its institutionalization as international law. Second, I examine the intrinsic problems with institutionalization that led to an unimplementable norm, considering the question of precision. Third, I probe the extrinsic reasons for implementation problems, and argue that contingency played a crucial role only possible to capture when norms are not considered to be static. Fourth, I consider how the apparent "death" of the anti-mercenary norm in fact signals how institutionalization and implementation do not always have a protective effect on underlying norms and may in fact represent starting points for further contestation.

THE ANTI-MERCENARY NORM AND
ITS INSTITUTIONALIZATION

The norm against mercenary use has deep historical origins (Percy 2007a), reflecting the equally long history of mercenary use. Mercenaries were common in European wars throughout the post-classical period, in slightly different guises. Individual, entrepreneurial mercenaries who shifted from employer to employer, often organizing themselves into bands, were common throughout the medieval period through to the end of the Thirty Years' War. At this time, the nature of mercenary use altered. States began to control the trade in mercenaries and bought and sold groups of soldiers from each other. After the French Revolution and the Napoleonic Wars, European powers stopped using mercenaries and began to use more effective forms of conscription and develop citizen armies (Avant 2000; Thomson 1994; Percy 2007a). Great Britain was the last state to abandon the use of mercenaries, after experiencing humiliating recruitment problems during the Crimean War that required raising mercenary troops. These troops were never sent because the war ended before the process was complete (Percy 2007a; Bayley 1977).

After the Crimean War, mercenaries made a remarkably complete disappearance from the world's battlefields. The importance of this shift is crucial: despite having been commonplace and indeed essential for hundreds of years, mercenaries were not used from the end of the Crimean War until the 1960s. Even when they reappeared, the use of mercenaries was covert and illegitimate (Percy 2007b). In 1994, Thomson was quite correct in arguing that real states did not use mercenaries: in fact, mercenary use was rare and mainly by insurgent groups *against* states, almost exclusively in Africa. Thomson argues that the various mercenary actions of the twentieth century "appear to us as anomalies precisely because they are only marginally legitimate" (Thomson 1994: 97).

The anti-mercenary norm demonstrates how norms shift over time, underlining the contingent nature of norms. If norms are changeable, then both institutionalizing and implementing them may not be "end points" in a norm's life but rather *transformative* points. While objections to mercenaries on moral grounds are longstanding, their specific nature (and so the precise content of the anti-mercenary norm) has altered substantially over time. I have argued that there are two components to the anti-mercenary norm, present in varying degrees at different points: first, the idea that mercenaries are unacceptable because they do not have an appropriate cause for which to fight; and second, that mercenaries are problematic because they are not members of the group that hires them. In the medieval period, the notion that mercenaries had financial motivation was inapplicable, because nearly all fighters were considered to be so motivated; however, fighting without sharing the cause of the hiring army was considered to be problematic. Mercenaries were not necessarily disliked because they were foreign (another concept that was fluid during this period) but because they were at the very least outsiders (Percy 2007a: 69–70).

By the nineteenth century, the idea that a financial motivation was particularly problematic crept in alongside the notion that mercenaries were foreign actors (not just outsiders). The idea that fighting and killing for money was reprehensible was commonly asserted, and this factor has remained common up until the present day. By the 1960s, mercenaries were used mainly to disrupt newly decolonized states in Africa. As a result, the anti-mercenary norm took on a new dimension: mercenaries were also deemed to be morally troublesome because they subverted the growing belief in a right to self-determination. This view was enshrined by the inclusion of condemnation of mercenaries within a series of UN Security Council and General Assembly resolutions relating to national self-determination.[4] The anti-mercenary norm itself demonstrates the ebbs and flows in a norm's content over time, even before that norm is formally institutionalized. Different sets of circumstances and events led to the norm sanctioning different variations of behavior.

THE INSTITUTIONALIZATION PROCESS AND INTRINSIC CHALLENGES FOR IMPLEMENTATION

By the 1970s, in part because of activism among newly decolonized states in the UN General Assembly, there was a strong appetite to create international law to deal with mercenaries. The international lawmaking process worked through four main stages: a Luanda Draft Convention on Mercenaries;[5] the Luanda draft evolved into an OAU (now AU) Convention (1977); Article 47 of Protocol II Additional to the Geneva Conventions (1974–7); and a UN Convention, which was slowly negotiated from 1980 to 1989. I will not discuss the first two of these in significant detail, but it is important to note that all four share a virtually identical definition of a mercenary and calls for control.[6]

These formal legal initiatives reflected international developments elsewhere. There were a series of specific United Nations General Assembly and Security Council resolutions against mercenary activity in general and in relation to specific uses; mercenary use was included in the General Assembly's

---

[4] For details see Percy 2007b.

[5] The Luanda Draft was created at the trial of the mercenaries captured in Angola in 1976. Although the trial itself was criticized for politicization, it was attended by fifty-one commissioners who wrote the draft convention and came from, in addition to Africa, the USA, Canada, Sweden, France, Belgium, the UK, the Netherlands, Italy, Germany, Vietnam, and the USSR (Cesner and Brant 1977: 351).

[6] A key difference is that the OAU Convention includes the crime of "mercenarism," which is the state sponsoring of mercenary activity, and bans mercenary activity against national liberation movements, leaving open the possibility that African states themselves might employ mercenaries (Zarate 1998:75). Attempts to include mercenarism in the other legal instruments were more problematic; it was excluded from Article 47 and its inclusion in the UN Convention has been highly problematic. See Percy (2007b) for details.

Definition of Aggression; and in a variety of UN resolutions relating to self-determination.[7]

Given this flurry of anti-mercenary activity, we might expect that the resulting institutionalization was robust. However, mercenary laws are notoriously useless, primarily because they share an unworkable definition of "mercenary."

Legal Loopholes and Implementation

There is little doubt that states were very keen to create legal instruments that would reflect their concerns about mercenaries (Percy 2007b), reflecting a broad climate of international intolerance for mercenary action. However, states were particularly clear about the type of actor they wanted the law to control: a foreign, financially motivated actor. Creating such a law was problematic, because states simultaneously wished to protect other forms of service in foreign armies, such as longstanding regimental arrangements (like the Gurkhas or the French Foreign Legion or foreign officers on secondment) and recognized the significant issue posed by the fact that it is next to impossible to prove a financial motivation.

However, throughout the four documents outlined, states stuck to a cumulative definition of a mercenary that contained many clauses. Anyone suspected of mercenary activity would have to meet *all* of the proposed criteria in order to be considered a mercenary. The definition used in Article 47 is the most concise and is essentially the same as that used in the OAU and UN Conventions:[8]

Article 47 states in full:

1. A mercenary shall not have the right to be a combatant or a prisoner of war.

2. A mercenary is any person who:
    (a) is specially recruited locally or abroad in order to fight in an armed conflict;
    (b) does, in fact, take a direct part in the hostilities;
    (c) is motivated to take part in the hostilities essentially by the desire for private gain and, in fact, is promised, by or on behalf of a Party to the conflict, material compensation substantially in excess of

---

[7] In total the General Assembly has created more than 100 resolutions criticizing mercenaries since the 1960s and the Security Council made a series of resolutions through the 1970s about mercenary use in specific cases. See Percy (2007b: 373–4) for details.

[8] The OAU Convention (now the AU Convention) is essentially identical while the UN Convention adds a second part related to the crime of "mercenarism," or state support of mercenaries.

that promised or paid to combatants of similar ranks and functions in the armed forces of that Party;

(d) is neither a national of a Party to the conflict nor a resident of territory controlled by a Party to the conflict;

(e) is not a member of the armed forces of a Party to the conflict; and

(f) has not been sent by a State which is not a Party to the conflict on official duty as a member of its armed forces.

While this set of clauses is very precise and reflects the qualities states were trying to control, it is full of loopholes. To avoid being considered a mercenary, all a prospective foreign fighter would have to do is to ensure that he was enroled as a member of the regular armed forces *or* officially paid the same as regular soldiers *or* avoid direct participation in hostilities.[9]

Insisting on enshrining such a problematic definition in international law made it nearly impossible to implement. Article 47 as a document of the laws of war does not have any specific requirements for implementation by states, in the way that other types of treaty law might. Rather, to be implemented, states would have to apply the law during international armed conflict. The fact that the law is so easy to avoid means that it has not ever been implemented on the battlefield. There are no cases of mercenaries being denied prisoner of war status or charged with a crime instead of being considered lawful combatants. [10]

In other words, it is impossible to implement a badly written law, and as I have argued in depth elsewhere, it is not always the case that weak law results from an absence of normative commitment (Percy 2007b). It may only be worth legally institutionalizing norms that have content that allows the possibility of implementation. This may seem to be an obvious point, but one of the fascinating features of the debates leading to the creation of Article 47 is the fact that states *knew* that the resulting law was likely to be unworkable but felt like they could not adjust it without losing the sense of what they found objectionable about mercenaries. A differently worded law would not have reflected the anti-mercenary norm (Percy 2007b).

Consequences of Loopholes

The fact that loophole-filled law was impossible to implement is not as surprising as the impact that the creation of weak law may have had on the underlying

---

[9] It is on this latter point that PMSCs mainly avoid anti-mercenary laws, and I will discuss this in further depth later.

[10] As I will note, the fact that mercenaries were not used in international armed conflict further undermined the norm.

norm. Making loopholes may inadvertently channel behavior as potential vio-
lators seek to make their behavior appear lawful. In turn, if enough violations
of this type occur, it may alter the underlying norm. Potential mercenaries
were very careful to manoeuvre through these loopholes, obeying the letter of
the law, while still violating the norm. I argue that this has caused the norm to
change from one which opposes all types of mercenaries, to one which accepts
the use of private force by states in a limited capacity.

There are two ways in which new types of mercenary actor worked through
loopholes in international law, influencing the underlying norm. When PMCs
first emerged in the late 1990s they utilized the "members of the armed forces"
loophole to avoid being considered mercenaries, by enroling in the local armed
services, especially as they continued to offer combat services. However, the
industry evolved rapidly after the appearance of PMCs and transitioned to one
where companies actively avoided combat *as a way to avoid being considered
mercenaries*. I argue that the use of this loophole has altered the underlying
norm, and that the norm against mercenary use now contains two new provisions: that private force is acceptable when used by "legitimate states" and
when used defensively.

Move away from Combat

In the 1990s, a new type of private force appeared on the international stage: the
private military company (PMC). PMCs were corporate organizations providing a range of military services, including active combat and the command
and control of military operations, and its two exemplars are the companies
Executive Outcomes (EO) and Sandline. EO began its activities in Angola in
1995 and Sandline in 1997.[11] In 1999, the market for their growth was perceived to be "robust and fertile" (Shearer 1997) but later that year, EO went
out of business, and Sandline followed in 2004. Both companies avoided the
mercenary accusation by enroling in the armed forces of the hiring state, thus
allowing them to provide combat services. When Tim Spicer, then head of
Sandline, was asked if his company would go on combat operations, he replied
"of course we will" (Spicer 1999). However, combat services were simply too
controversial and the demand for them was limited. Indeed, distaste for the
open provision of combat helped push EO and Sandline out of business (Percy
2007a: ch. 7).

Spicer's second company, Aegis, was explicitly designed to *avoid* combat
(Percy 2007a: 228). Private security companies operating first in Iraq and now

---

[11] Allegations that EO and Sandline were sister companies, and that Sandline appeared in an
effort to avoid EO's image problems, were rife. See Percy (2007a: 227).

Afghanistan eschew "offensive combat" and many are quick to point out that they provide very few armed services of any type (Percy 2007a: 226). Many PMSCs insist that armed work was only ever a small proportion of their over-all work, and still others have merged with domestic private security com-panies (i.e. security guards), further diminishing the percentage of armed activity they undertake.[12]

States have also provided explicit authorization for PMSCs to operate only if they avoid active combat. US Department of Defense contractors are "authorized to use deadly force when such force appears necessary to exe-cute their security mission to protect assets/persons"[13] (US Department of Defense, 2006) in other words, only in self-defence. Krahmann argues that the use of contractors in this way has also changed the norm that the state has a monopoly on the use of force, and that states have accepted that only an offensive use of force violates this norm (Krahmann 2013: 66). In other words, the mark of what is objectionable about the use of private force is no longer necessarily its foreign character or its financial motivation but rather the type of force used.

I argue that avoiding the "combat" provision of anti-mercenary law has been crucial to avoid being considered a mercenary. As a result, the underly-ing norm against mercenary use has altered. Historically, the norm was silent on the question of combat. After all, mercenaries were only ever hired to fight, and the idea of a non-fighting mercenary makes very little sense in historical context. However, the insistence in international law that mercenaries must actually fight has allowed PMSCs and the states who hire them to manipulate the law and insist that they do not provide active combat, and so they are not mercenaries. The fact that existing law cannot be used against PMSCs rein-forces the idea that combat is the defining characteristic of a mercenary (as opposed to financial motivation and foreign status, which were the qualities states universally agreed upon in the 1970s).

The idea that the use of private force is acceptable only as long as those employed do not use force is increasingly internationally accepted. The Montreux Document, which is the preferred international regulatory instru-ment in the US and the only applicable such instrument in the UK, limits the use of force by PMSCs to self-defence or defence of third parties. In the UK, use of defensive force by PMSCs is quite legitimate (Panke and Petersohn 2011: 12). Combat, or the "offensive" use of force, has become the defining

---

[12] By some measures, in 2008 only 5% of all contractors in Iraq were in protective security (the others were involved in a range of logistical support issues (personal communication, Doug Brooks, International Peace Operations Association, 14 Feb. 2009). In 2008 ArmorGroup was acquired by G4S, best known for its domestic security guard activity. <http://www.telegraph.co.uk/finance/markets/2786738/Troubled-ArmorGroup-secures-sale-to-G4S.html>.

[13] US Dept of Defense, available at <http://www.law.cornell.edu/cfr/text/48/252.225-7040>.

factor of a mercenary, and the anti-mercenary norm is now restricted to those actors who use offensive force.[14]

It is still possible to argue that real states do not use mercenaries, if we are persuaded by the argument that PMSCs are not mercenaries. PMSCs have succeeded in rebranding themselves, and the use of old-fashioned mercenaries, like the group that attempted a coup in Equatorial Guinea,[15] is still frowned upon. Muammar Gaddafi used mercenaries in the last days of his regime, and their use was seen as a signal of his loss of legitimacy, as he required them to fight against his own people.[16] Indeed, even legitimate but weak states have had their authority to use PMSCs in combat challenged. In 2003, a British PMC was blocked from assisting Côte d'Ivoire by the Foreign and Commonwealth Office, and their potential use was condemned by the UN Security Council (Percy 2007a).

The shift in the anti-mercenary norm that allows strong, legitimate states to use private force is an interesting transition. There are practical reasons for this shift. Strong states are involved in conflicts large enough to require PMSC assistance, and retain powerful enough militaries that armed actors do not pose a threat. Moreover, the prospect of an entirely free market whereby all types of actors can hire private force is undesirable for strong states. However, there are also interesting power-related issues at play. It may well be that the anti-mercenary norm has become instrumental and that large states will continue to restrict the acceptable use of private force in a manner that benefits them and prevents the proliferation of private force. The Montreux Document can then be seen as an instrument that reflects the interests of powerful states (by allowing them to continue to use private force in a limited capacity while denying it to other actors) but may not reflect the interests of weaker states. Powerful states have protected their interest in using private force, but they have done so in a way that suggests some adherence to the underlying norm.[17]

---

[14] This is despite the fact that the distinction between offensive and defensive uses of forces is at best difficult or at worst impossible. It is hard to draw the line around defensive actions—e.g. is a patrol operating away from a base that fires in the course of its duties defensive? In addition, force looks the same to its victims regardless of whether or not it is used defensively. It is hard to imagine the Iraqis shot in Nisur Square felt that the force used against them was defensive.

[15] Led by former EO employee Simon Mann. For details see Roberts (2006).

[16] <http://www.time.com/time/world/article/0,8599,2090205,00.html>, <http://www.csmonitor.com /World/Africa/Africa-Monitor/2011/0228/Libya-s-mercenaries-pose-difficult-issue-to-resolve>. While it was initially assumed that the mercenaries were Africans, many of whom were migrants and may have been involuntarily pressed into service by Gaddafi, later it was confirmed that mercenaries from Eastern Europe were employed <http://www.time.com/time/world/article/0,8599,2090205,00.html>.

[17] The US remains the only state to have used PMSCs to support military operations in conflict zones. Other militarily capable states have used PMSCs to guard embassies (e.g. the UK). While other states may well use PMSCs for internal security and policing, the sort of transnational operations discussed in the Montreux Document refers mainly to the US and the UK.

Extrinsic Obstacles to Implementation: Contingency

Price and Tannenwald argue that contingency plays a central part in the evolution of norms. The norm against the use of chemical weapons "owes much to a series of fortuitous events" (Price and Tannenwald 1996: 127). I argue that just as fortuitous events can facilitate the development of a norm, they can challenge it. This highlights the point that changing international circumstances must have an influence on normative content. The institutionalization of the norm against mercenary use experienced four examples of bad luck, which further challenged implementation and led to alterations in the underlying norm against mercenary use.

First, very little mercenary use actually occurred after the norm was institutionalized, and what there was occurred outside international armed conflict. While mercenary activity had been increasing throughout the 1970s, it declined sharply in the 1980s. The only significant incidences of mercenary activity were the attempted coup in the Seychelles led by Mike Hoare and a series of coups in the Comoros Islands led by the French mercenary Bob Denard. Both of these states, particularly the latter, are small and peripheral states even by the standards of the mainly Sub-Saharan African states most enthusiastic about controlling mercenaries. More importantly, neither of these episodes occurred during an international armed conflict so Article 47 did not apply and could not be implemented. Thus, throughout the period after the first flush of legal creation, there were no incidents where the newly created laws dealing with mercenaries could be used. Indeed, in the Seychelles, Hoare and the other mercenaries were charged with hijacking[18] rather than offences related to being a mercenary or of mercenarism (Major 1992).

In fact, mercenary activity had become rare enough that by the mid-1980s it appeared highly irregular and unlikely to continue once colonial conflict ended. Taulbee even argues that the movement to regulate mercenaries in the 1970s and 1980s was essentially an overreaction, stating in 1985 that the "current effort and concern is directed at a phenomenon essentially transitory in nature. The reaction, when compared to the historical record, is out of proportion to the actual threat." He goes on to argue that mercenary use will decline with the increased skill of national armies and the end of decolonization stopping tacit support for mercenaries by former colonial powers (Taulbee 1985: 362).

The slow pace of the UN Convention, which was due to its problematic construction,[19] presented a further challenge to the underlying norm against

---

[18] The mercenaries had hijacked a plane to escape the Seychelles airport after their weapons were discovered.

[19] See Percy (2007a, 2007b) for an in-depth discussion of how the Convention's design delayed its implementation.

mercenary use. States began to discuss the convention in 1980 and only reached agreement in 1989, and it came into force in 2001.[20] Its slow pace meant that, when there were incidences of mercenary activity to which it would apply, it could not be used.

Perhaps most importantly, when private military companies appeared on the international stage, the UN Convention faced two major challenges. First, it did not come into force until 2001. While the PMCs Executive Outcomes (EO) and Sandline received extensive international attention in the late 1990s, this meant it could not be used. EO was particularly controversial because it engaged in active combat. Worse still, however, was the fact that, even if it were in force, the UN Convention's problematic definition excluded EO and Sandline, who were careful to enrol in the national forces of the state that employed them. Even if according to the letter of the law, PMCs were not mercenaries, public perception disagreed. EO and Sandline were constantly dogged by criticisms that PMCs were merely mercenaries in a new guise (Percy 2007a: 216).[21]

Article 47 similarly did not apply to these actors because, once again, they were not involved in international armed conflicts. Arguably, no use of mercenaries or even of PMSCs occurred in an international armed conflict until the US invasion of Iraq in 2003, by which time, as I will argue, the norm had greatly altered (and even so these contractors were enroled in the armed services of the hiring state and/or not actually engaged in combat). The law, in light of these new actors, looked completely toothless (Singer 2004: 531; Percy 2007b: 391).

The fourth and final unlucky blow to the anti-mercenary norm was the invasion of Iraq in 2003. The American military had, in line with a general move towards privatization across government (Dunigan 2011: 9) begun to privatize military support activities. Military privatization in the US has had a relatively long lineage, beginning with the privatization of logistical support in the Vietnam era, a process which gained considerable pace during the 1990s (Dunigan 2011: 11; Stanger 2009: 84). The extensive use of private contractors in Iraq was, in a way, another casualty of the noticeably poor military planning for occupation after the invasion (Rathmell 2005). Had the war in Iraq not become so protracted and so unpopular, it is quite likely that the US would

---

[20] Compare the following Conventions from 1989: Rights of the Child (signed Dec. 1989, came into force Sept. 1990); Basel Convention on Transboundary Waste (Mar. 1989, May 1992). Compared with other conventions dealing with military matters it is also slow: Ottawa Convention (landmines): Dec. 1997, Mar. 1999; Convention on Biological Weapons (1972, 1975); Convention on Certain Conventional Weapons (1980, 1983).

[21] Indeed, the bulk of the literature written about PMCs before 2003 directly called EO and Sandline mercenaries. See, among others: Dorney 1998; Kritsiotis 1998; Nossal 1998; Adams 1999; Arnold 1999; Brauer 1999; Clapham 1999; Francis 1999; Musah and Fayemi 2000; Taulbee 2000.

have needed fewer contractors and that these contractors would not have been held up to so much public scrutiny. In other words, a short sharp invasion followed by the quick creation of a new and stable Iraqi government would have required far fewer troops (and therefore contractors) and provided far fewer opportunities for PMSC personnel to commit human rights abuses, as they did at Abu Ghraib, or fire on civilians, as they did in a market square in Baghdad in 2007. As Iraq was the first conflict that utilized contractors in such large numbers, the failure of the occupation has become entwined with views about contractors (Tiefer 2009).

International circumstances can thus promote a norm or challenge it. Contingency has an impact on the way norms will develop in the international system, but crucially will affect what happens to them after they are institutionalized, while they are being implemented or waiting to be implemented.

Implementation as an Invitation to Contestation

Both institutionalization and implementation present further opportunities for states to contest norms. The anti-mercenary norm demonstrates that institutionalized norms are not necessarily "fixed." Even if the letter of the law is relatively permanent, underlying norms may still change.

Krook and True reject "the assumption that a norm can be equated with a commitment written into international treaties or instruments" and argue that norms evolve over time in response to debates caused by competing meanings of a norm and interaction with the external environment, including other norms (Krook and True 2012: 105). They argue constructivist explanations of norm creation and evolution are dynamic, but once this process has finished the assumption is that normative content becomes static (Krook and True 2012: 106).

However, as Krook and True note, the rest of the world, including states, other actors, and other norms, goes on changing, so the conflict between fixed normative content and changing international environment is jarring. Assuming that normative content remains the same "limits the ability to explain how and why norms change as they diffuse, why they travel so widely across borders, and why they often fail to achieve their intended goals" (Krook and True 2012: 106).

Sandholtz's description of the dynamics of international norm change also describes the changeability of normative content. Sandholtz argues that normative change forms a dialectical cycle whereby arguments about existing norms result in changes (altering some norms to make them stronger or weaker). In turn, these new norms are subject to the same process of contestation, with "the altered norms establish[ing] the context for subsequent actions, disputes, and discourses" (Sandholtz 2008: 105).

In the case of anti-mercenary law, the shifting international environment put pressure on the fixed, institutionalized definition of the norm. The law no longer reflected international reality, and the disjunction between a changed environment and the static norm made it impossible to use or implement anti-mercenary law. The result was, as already discussed, that the underlying norm was altered.

I extend Sandholtz's argument about the international dynamic of normative change and suggest that legal institutionalization can actually create *more* opportunities for contestation, which means that normative change may be *more* likely once legal institutionalization has occurred. Precision and some of the other features scholars consider specific features of international law may actually open the opportunity for debate and create new mechanisms of change. I will consider these arguments as part of a larger discussion about norm death or norm regress.

Norm "Death" or Norm Regression

Understanding that the process of change and contestation is continuing, and that institutionalization is not a static end state for a norm, is essential to understanding why, despite ineffective international institutionalization, the norm against mercenary use did not die. If norms do not have fixed content, then institutionalizing them formally will only ever be a reflection of what a norm means at a particular moment in time. In turn, we would expect norms to change when international circumstances change, or when they come into conflict with other norms. Actors will continue to argue about definitions, content, and prohibitions associated with norms. The "ongoing potential for contestation means, in turn, that co-optation, drift, accretion and reversal of a norm—including disputes over whether it is a norm at all—are constant possibilities" (Krook and True 2012: 104).

Petersohn and Panke argue that the anti-mercenary norm has been "incrementally degraded" by its poor institutionalization and the interests of actors in using PMSCs and therefore violating the norm (Panke and Petersohn 2011). However, the norm against mercenary use has retained significant influence in how the private security industry has evolved. It is both surprising and interesting that the anti-mercenary norm has remained influential despite the fact that powerful states in the system are keen to use private force, and despite the incredibly poor institutionalization of the norm. The anti-mercenary norm prompts us to consider whether or not it is useful to think in terms of norm death and norm regress, rather than norm change. I will make this argument in this section by arguing that the idea of regress or death actually cements some of the teleological problems with the norm life-cycle. Moreover, institutionalization and implementation may actually create more contestation rather than act as a brake against potential norm regress.

The legalization literature in international relations argues that legalization fixes the content of a norm and acts as a "backstop" against normative regression (Goldstein et al. 2000: 163). The anti-mercenary norm suggests there are two related problems with understanding law in this way, which may reveal differences between social and legal norms. First, it may well be impossible, as the critical constructivists suggest, to "fix" the content of a norm, given the constantly shifting international political landscape and competing interpretations of a norm and the processes of institutionalization and implementation which open up avenues of contestation. Second, if norms are constantly shifting, either in a dialectic fashion with their legalized form or because the discourse about them is shifting, can they genuinely regress or are they simply changing form? I will examine each of these in turn.

The notion of norm death, or even of the more gently phrased norm regress, really only makes sense when we assume that the end point of the norm life-cycle firmly fixes a norm by institutionalizing it (in most cases in the form of some kind of law). While McKeown (2009) points out that this understanding of the norm life cycle is teleological, assuming that norms regress down a similar path is just teleology in reverse. For McKeown, the norm life-cycle explains how norms evolve "up" to institutionalization and he attempts to explain how norms regress "down." But the rubric of "up" and "down" does not reflect that fixing an understanding of a norm in a constantly evolving international environment, where unexpected developments cause recalibration and norms can conflict with each other, may only ever be temporary. Some norms may be more "fixed" than others, and their institutionalization and meaning may go unchallenged for longer.

One explanation for why some norms are crystallized by institutionalization in a way that lasts and others are not may simply be luck. McKeown questions how it is that the anti-torture norm, considered to be fundamental by many, was so seriously compromised in such a short period of time by the Bush administration in the United States. One of the great counterfactuals of the early 2000s may prove to be what would have happened if Al Gore had defeated Bush in the 2000 presidential election. Would the torture norm have been so challenged if he had?

Another explanation for the durability of normative institutionalization may be contestation, which in turn goes back to the question of state interests. Some states may disagree with an institutionalized norm, regardless of whether they participated in the institutionalization or not. States may seek to protect their interests at the expense of the norm or alter its content to suit them, and state leaders and domestic constituencies may have different interests. As Krook and True argue, contestation about the norm may go on after it has been institutionalized, either internationally or when the norm hits the domestic implementation phase. While leaders may agree to sign up to a norm, domestic opposition may not, and the process of this debate may alter the content of the underlying norm and challenge the way it has been institutionalized.[22] In other words, as Sandholtz suggests, institutionalization may not be an "end point" at all, but rather the starting point for further contestation. The process of implementation further opens up room for contestation, which in turn can alter the content of a norm.

More specifically, we must consider whether or not providing a norm with the features of legalization—precision, obligation, and delegation (according to Goldstein et al. 2000)—also provides three new opportunities for actors to contest the validity of the law, and to change its meaning via creative interpretations.

An oft-mentioned difference between social and legal norms stems from the idea of precision (Abbott et al. 2000; Brunee and Toope 2010). Turning norms into law forces states and other actors to render them more precise. Implementation is a crucial part of legalization, as states first adopt and then interpret the law. However, just as it is not correct to assume that legalization is an end state for norms and can prevent regression, it is misleading to assume that precision can or will preserve a norm from regress. Petersohn and Panke analyze three cases of norm regress, and argue that the external environment, the precision of the norm, and the presence of actors who challenge the norm will explain whether or not norms rapidly change or incrementally degrade; higher precision makes the process slower (Petersohn and Panke 2011).

Precision may clearly articulate what states and other actors want in the creation of law, and it may, in some ways, strengthen the norm by clarifying what behavior does and does not fall under the norm's sway. However, as I have argued elsewhere (Percy 2007b), precision does not always mean that a law will be effective. I argue that anti-mercenary law is in fact highly precise, but its precision creates weak law that cannot be used. If a law cannot be used, the possibility for contestation rises dramatically. The appearance of PMCs and PMSCs were both accompanied by high levels of concern that there was no effective law to deal with them, which further underlined the problems of existing anti-mercenary law. A great deal of debate about how to regulate them in light of inadequate measures enshrined the alterations to the norm just outlined.

---

[22] Interestingly McKeown's explanation of what happened to the anti-torture norm demonstrates exactly this: Bush and his advisors disagreed with the anti-torture norm and authorized actions that violated it; however, they did so by arguing that torture rules needed redefinition. In other words, they contested the institutionalized version of the norm out of state interest, in an attempt to alter its meaning. Norms remained influential, however, because as opposed to abandoning the norm the administration sought to alter it. The international community has not accepted the Bush definition of torture and nor have many of his domestic opponents. But the contestation of the norm has opened new avenues that may alter its content.

Making norms more precise could, as some scholars suggest, reduce the chances of argument about the rules and therefore prevent regress. However, as we have seen with the anti-mercenary norm, precision can also alter behavior in unexpected ways, as actors choose to interpret the law to further their own interests, however defined. Sandholtz points out that disputes over norms occur when actions "fall within the penumbra of uncertainty surrounding a rule, or into the gap between different rules" (Sandholtz 2008: 106). These same gaps and penumbras are often created by highly precise language. If one category of action is legally acceptable, but another is not, we ought to expect actors to alter their behavior so they fit these rules. The fact that there are unintended consequences to the creation of rules would come as no surprise to domestic legal scholars: laws to control one area can be extended to control another. Precision may well reflect exactly what lawmakers are trying to control, and it may resolve existing disputes via clarification. However, it will *not* end contestation. Higher courts around the world would find themselves with very little to do if writing things down prevented contestation and fixed meanings.

Likewise, the very idea of delegation, or the idea that a third party will undertake interpretation, monitoring, and implementation (Goldstein et al. 2000: 387) includes within it extensive possibilities for underlying norms to be altered and the process of contestation to continue. These processes are a crucial part of implementation. Third parties that "interpret" laws in the domestic context are courts, and courts routinely question the intent of lawmakers or challenge the validity of underlying norms. The process of implementing a norm is widely recognized as a source of considerable contestation. Domestic constituencies have the chance to argue about and challenge the norm, or even to attempt to find ways to opt out of norms formally agreed upon at the international level. States can partially implement norms, fail to implement them at all, or implement them quite quickly.

CONCLUSION

The problematic institutionalization of the anti-mercenary norm meant that it could never be implemented. Loopholes allowed states and other actors to present new forms of private force that did not violate the law, but altered the underlying norm. The anti-mercenary norm now permits the use of private force where that force is defensive and employed by states as a supplement to their own armed forces. It is likely that the norm will change again, as contestation continues and new international events and variants of private force appear.

One of the advantages of studying norms with a long lineage, like the anti-mercenary norm, is the degree to which they demonstrate that normative content is not static. I have argued elsewhere that the norm against mercenary use contains two broad categories (the idea that mercenaries fight without appropriate cause and that they do so for a group other than their own) but within these two categories there has been historical variation. Today, the notion of "appropriate cause" means that we disapprove of a financial motivation for violence; in medieval Europe, mercenaries were problematic because they did not have "just cause" and were not fighting under the direction of the noble classes or the church (Percy 2007a: 72). Mercenaries have always been outsiders, but sometimes the group they stand outside of has been a state, and sometimes it has been a city (as in the Italian city-states). Norms will always change because events change around them; it would be impossible for them to remain static in the face of considerable change. The really interesting questions may be why they alter so little or how they retain their influence in light of this change.

I have argued that the role of norms in identity formation may explain why it is difficult for norms to regress, but also that thinking of norms in terms of life-cycles and progression is problematic. Norms do not move "up" and "down" steps towards institutionalization and implementation. They are not static and their content is always changing slightly.

There are a series of important research questions that stem from the idea of durability of institutionalization. What causes some norms to be durably institutionalized? How much do contingent factors like changing international events matter, and how might we quantify their impact? Does the quality of the institutionalization matter? Does durable institutionalization mean that normative content stays more stable over time?

Another avenue for future research is further probing of the idea of "norm death" or abandonment. How many cases of norm death are there, and did state identity have to alter for the norm to die? Or is normative change more common?

Finally, the anti-mercenary norm reminds us that it is useful to examine the failures as well as the successes of the international system. A norm that was so badly institutionalized that it was unimplementable is an opportunity to probe questions about what makes norms difficult to institutionalize, and what the consequences of problematic institutionalization and a failure to implement are. Some of the points about the anti-mercenary norm may not be generalizable, but others are worth probing so that we have a clearer picture of how norms evolve, why they become institutionalized, and how they change.

5

International NGOs and the Implementation of the Norm for Need-Based Humanitarian Assistance in Sri Lanka

Urvashi Aneja

Emergency humanitarian assistance is often the first, and sometimes the only, international response to civilian suffering in political emergencies. The rules and principles for provision of humanitarian assistance are codified in the 1949 Geneva Conventions and 1977 Additional Protocols, which taken together can be said to constitute the formal legal regime for humanitarian assistance. The Conventions seek to balance military necessity and state sovereignty with the moral imperative of reducing suffering by making provisions for assistance that is of a humanitarian and impartial character, which is extended to civilians suffering excessive deprivation owing to a lack of supplies essential for survival. The key norm underlying the humanitarian regime is that assistance should be based on the sole criteria of "need," and not any other political, social, economic objective or criteria; the scope of such needs covers goods and services essential for the survival of the population, namely food, shelter, health services, and water and sanitation. Limiting humanitarian assistance to essential needs is also intended to ensure that humanitarian assistance will not amount to interference in conflict or contribute to local war economies (Mackintosh 2000; Beauchamp 2008; Jinks 2003; Stoffels 2004). The provisions in the Geneva Conventions, as Neil Macfarlane (1999) argues, are thus intended to keep separate the realms of political and humanitarian action.

The norm of need-based humanitarian assistance can be considered a treaty norm in that states are signatories to the Geneva Conventions,[1] and the rules and

---

[1] The treaties of 1949 have been ratified, in whole or with reservations, by 194 countries. Despite disagreements about some of the provisions in the Conventions, the norm that humanitarian assistance should be need-based is generally undisputed by states.

norms in the Conventions are the basis on which international humanitarian organizations (inter-governmental and non-governmental) operate in political emergencies.[2] However, field-level accounts, and academic and policy literature, highlight tremendous variation in the manner and extent to which this norm is upheld. There is thus a normative institutionalization–implementation gap with regard to the norm for need-based humanitarian assistance. This chapter studies this gap by interrogating the policies and practices of international NGOs during the Sri Lanka conflict, between the Sri Lankan state and the LTTE, from 1990 to 2010. Following the defeat of the LTTE by the Government of Sri Lanka (GoSL) in 2009, numerous reports and studies noted the "failure of humanitarianism in Sri Lanka" (Elhawary 2011; ICG 2010b). However, it was not a clear case of norm compliance or violation as various actors held differing interpretations of what exactly constituted this failure (ICG 2009b; UN 2011a; CPA 2009; Harris 2010).[3] The Sri Lanka case is a good example to study how a norm can mean different things to relevant actors, and how a norm, in practice, does not fall into simple binary categories of compliance or violation.[4] Aside from available secondary literature, the findings presented in this chapter are based on a study of international NGO (or INGO) policy documents (headquarters and country-specific), and fieldwork conducted in Sri Lanka in June 2010 and April 2011.

NORMS AND ACTORS

The existing literature on the functioning of the humanitarian regime tends to explain the institutionalization–implementation gap in the norm for

---

[2] e.g. the provisions of the Conventions are reflected in the Code of Conduct for the International Red Cross and Red Crescent Movement and NGOs in disaster relief, as well as the UN Office for the Coordination of Humanitarian Affairs (OCHA) guidelines for humanitarian assistance.

[3] International and domestic actors have accused the GoSL of subordinating humanitarian assistance to its political and security objectives, and of violating international humanitarian law. At the same time, international humanitarian actors in Sri Lanka have come under increasing scrutiny. On the one hand, the international humanitarian community has been charged with failing to abide by humanitarian principles, and even of having enabled the GoSL's violation of international humanitarian law; on the other hand, the GoSL and a section of the Sri Lankan population have accused the international humanitarian community of violating Sri Lankan sovereignty, operating in line with their own interests and organizational imperatives.

[4] While a single case, studying Sri Lanka provides a number of benefits. First, it allows one to identify and trace in depth the functioning of particular causal mechanisms; the ten-year time period also facilitates the study of implementation as a process rather than a one-time static event. Second, the Sri Lanka case also provides an opportunity to examine in-case variation, as the broad contours of INGO policy have remained the same over the ten year period, though with different outcomes. Finally, Sri Lanka is not a high-profile media emergency like Darfur, or one of high strategic significance like Afghanistan; while there has been some degree of international involvement in the crisis, especially with the Norwegian-led Sri Lanka Monitoring Mission (SLMM), the absence of such overarching external constraints makes it possible to study implementation in Sri Lanka as primarily a domestic process.

need-based assistance in terms of the politicization of aid by donors (Cornish 2008; Donini 2012; Macrae 1998); the manipulation of aid by warring parties and the characteristics of so-called new wars (Hoffman and Weiss 2006; Kaldor 1999); or as a collective action problem characterized by agency competition (Barnett and Ramalingam 2010; Cooley and Ron 2002). These accounts provide important insights into the challenges facing the international humanitarian regime. However, these accounts tend to privilege structure over agency; they neglect the process from institutionalization to implementation; and they do not systematically examine how the meaning of the norm might itself change at practice.

In contrast, this chapter argues that the process from norm institutionalization to implementation cannot be explained in structural terms alone; actors responsible for the implementation of a norm are a key part of understanding this process. Norms, as Betts and Orchard note, are shared understandings of appropriate behaviour for actors with a given identity. Accordingly, a study of norm implementation needs to be seen in the context of specific actors, i.e. how particular actors understand what constitutes appropriate behaviour for them and how it translates to norm-implementation.

This chapter thus examines how a specific set of actors—INGOs, the chief operational agencies of the international humanitarian regime—understand and implement the needs-based assistance norm, and the outcomes it produces. International NGOs are the key implementing agencies of the international humanitarian system; they control the bulk of humanitarian resources and are often the key agents of change in the international humanitarian system (Stoddard 2003). The humanitarian INGO sector is dominated by a handful of giant NGOs—Oxfam, World Vision, Save the Children, CARE, and Médecins Sans Frontières (MSF) (Stoddard 2003). Aside from MSF, each of these "giants" has shifted from being a relief-only agency focused on emergency assistance to a multi-mandate organization concerned with humanitarian assistance, poverty-alleviation, and human rights. The chapter thus draws on illustrative examples from the policies and practices of Oxfam, World Vision, and CARE, to make a broader argument about the process from norm institutionalization to implementation in the international humanitarian regime.

A norm undergoes two phases of contestation: first, as actors responsible for implementing a norm interpret the norm in formulating their own policies, and second, as the norm is implemented in the domestic arena, encountering new actors, interests, and beliefs. These two levels of contestation are interconnected as interpretation at the policy level structures the nature of interaction and contestation at the domestic level. The chapter also suggests that the key factor at the level of interpretation is the identity of NGOs, i.e. "relatively stable, role-specifying, understanding and expectations about the self" (Wendt 1992: 397). At the level of implementation in Sri Lanka, material factors—the interests and capacity—of domestic actors shaped the practice of the norm.

Implementation however is also found to be a path-dependent process in Sri Lanka, involving ongoing negotiation and contestation, that must take into account the identity and beliefs of actors.

TREATY NORMS TO POLICY NORMS

In the introductory chapter, Betts and Orchard distinguish between three kinds of norms—treaty, principle, and policy norms. While they note that the line between these three kinds of norms might be blurred, the relationship between these norms is unpacked here as part of the explanation of how norms move from institutionalization to implementation.

Betts and Orchard argue that "nature of law is that it requires interpretation...and rarely will full determinacy be possible"; moreover, norms once adopted may continue to mean different things to different actors, as norm adoption may simply usher in "a new phase of battle over the norm itself" (Van Kersbergen and Verbeek 2007: 218–19). This suggests that even a treaty norm with constant institutionalization has first to be interpreted by the actors responsible for implementing the norm. Actors, in this case INGOs, must translate a treaty norm into a policy norm and this process can result in reinterpretation of the norm itself.

The reinterpretation of the norm is an important step in explaining both the process from institutionalization to implementation and, in the case of the humanitarian regime, the institutionalization–implementation gap. The formulation of policy norms, as Betts and Orchard note, is a reflection of internal organizational processes; this point is borne out here as it is found that INGO reinterpretation is primarily a reflection of INGO self-understandings of their role and function.

From Needs to Rights

Since the 1970s, INGOs have interpreted the treaty norm for need-based humanitarian assistance in terms of existing human rights frameworks (Chandler 2001; De Chaine 2002; Heerten 2009; Brauman 2006). They have argued this is necessary to move humanitarian assistance from being an act of charity to a duty and obligation of responsible actors. Oxfam, CARE, and World Vision, along with a majority of multi-mandate INGOs, all follow a rights-based approach (RBA) to humanitarian assistance. CARE argues, for example, that people have rights, and there is therefore a corresponding duty to ensure that those rights are secured (CARE 2010: 8; Henry 1999). Its RBA approach to humanitarian assistance focuses on "people achieving the minimal conditions for living with dignity... [which] are not only civil and political rights, but also social, cultural, and economic rights" (Peter Bell, former CARE president, 2001, cited in Barnett 2009: 644).

Oxfam uses the concept of "Basic Rights," arguing that its "commitment to responding to humanitarian suffering—the most extreme form of poverty—goes to the core of its values as an organisation, that is taking a rights based approach to poverty to provide the basis for conceptually integrating its relief and development practices" (Oxfam policy cited in Rehman 1999: 92; Eade and Williams 1995). Oxfam's RBA approach encompasses a "full range of rights" which for Oxfam include the right to a decent livelihood, essential services, a voice in decision-making, and an identity free from discrimination (Oxfam International 2009). Using a rights-based approach, World Vision "works to prevent conflicts and maintain peace by supporting civil society through dialogue, mediation, advocacy, and building awareness and tolerance among the groups in conflict" (World Vision 2012b).

An RBA reinterprets the norm for need-based humanitarian assistance in two crucial ways. First, the scope of humanitarian needs is no longer defined in terms of emergency assistance items, but in terms of human rights. Defining the scope of humanitarian assistance in terms of rights expands the range of goods and services that can be argued to fall under the ambit of humanitarian assistance. Thus, for example, sustainable livelihood, conflict resolution, and rule of law programs can fall under the ambit of need-based humanitarian assistance when needs are defined through a rights framework. Second, an RBA shifts attention from the needs of civilians to the duties and responsibilities of external actors, whereby the former are defined in terms of the latter. In other words, RBA suggests that people have rights, and therefore there is a corresponding duty to provide for those rights; by linking rights with duties, the focus of an RBA effectively becomes the duties of actors. The scope of intervention is defined not in terms of the existing needs on the ground, but what external actors, here INGOs, define as the scope of their responsibility and duty. As O'Callaghan and Pantuliano (2007: 8) note,

> understanding assistance as a right, rather than as charity, moves the humanitarian endeavour beyond the voluntary provision of assistance to the provision of assistance on the basis of a legitimate claim for it on the part of its beneficiaries. This involves a conceptual shift whereby victims of beneficiaries become rights holders, and humanitarian agencies become their advocates.

Moreover, under an RBA, as addressing rights concerns is framed as necessary for meeting the basic needs of civilians, these rights-based activities are also seen as morally necessary (Whitaker 1983: 29–30). Thus, even while a focus on rights concerns can amount to inference in the domestic affairs of the state or in the conflict, once framed as needs and thereby morally necessary, they can be justified as non-political programs distinct from the conflict itself. Chandler thus argues that "the humanitarian NGOs were the first international organisations that sought to use the terminology of human rights in an attempt to justify political policy choices in the language of ethics" (Chandler 2001: 683).

Betts and Orchard's framework identities the three kinds of causal mechanisms shaping implementation: ideational, material, and institutional. INGO interpretation of the treaty norm in terms of an RBA is a result of ideational factors, namely INGO identity and self-understanding of their role and responsibility as particular kinds of actors. The key "test" for this is that INGO ideas about RBA predated material incentives offered by donors or policy shifts within the UN and other international organizations. The shift from needs to rights-based humanitarian assistance began during the latter years of the Cold War, at a time when Western states were keen to limit and scale back their involvement in Third World states. Equally, during that time, the UN was still constrained by the rules of a sovereignty-bound international order (Duffield 1994, 2007; Collinson et al. 2010). INGO reinterpretation of the norm for needs-based humanitarian assistance through a rights framework can therefore not be explained only in terms of material incentives from donors or the broader normative and institutional structures in which they were embedded. On the contrary, in the case of CARE for example, its shift towards a rights-based approach cost it both financially and symbolically (Barnett 2009: 641); the former CARE President noted, for example, that "We would do info commercials for RBA on TV and it was a complete loser. We were told by consultants to go back to the starving baby and emergencies. We decided to swallow the lost dollars" (Peter Bell cited in Barnett 2009: 642). INGOs can in fact be considered norm entrepreneurs in introducing an RBA to humanitarian assistance. As Goodhand (2006: 79) argues, INGOs have played a key role in the "progressive incorporation of human rights and humanitarian values into the international political and normative structure." Chandler (2001: 385) similarly notes that the sphere of NGO "goal-oriented rights-based humanitarianism set up crucial practical precursors for more direct and invasive government-led, human rights-based interventionism of the late 1990s."

Factors internal to INGOs better explain this shift to a RBA. A key component of an RBA is that needs are defined in terms of the duties and responsibilities of external actors. INGO interpretation of the treaty norm for need-based humanitarianism through a RBA reflects their identity and self-understanding of their role and purpose. Multi-mandate INGOs such as Oxfam, CARE, and World Vision see themselves as moral agents concerned with alleviating human suffering; this is the belief on which they were founded, and the basis of their public legitimacy and legal validity. This necessitates a concern not only with goods and services essential for survival, but a more long-term transformative approach that ensures that human rights of civilians are restored and upheld. INGO policy documents and field-based accounts are replete with the justification of an RBA approach not only in terms of humanitarian needs, but also in terms of INGO "responsibility" and "added value" as humanitarian actors (CARE Strategic Plan; Oxfam Note on Humanitarianism; World Vision's Response). As moral agents concerned with alleviating human suffering, INGOs cannot turn a blind-eye to human rights violations. Moreover, as organizations founded and embedded in a liberal and democratic normative structure, a basis in human rights is seen as a necessary and perhaps the only available emancipatory framework.

INGO adoption of an RBA can also be argued to be an attempt to increase their influence and relevance at the global-policy level and the operational level. Barnett points out, for example, that Oxfam's decision to provide aid in Cambodia in 1975 and comply with the regime's demand to withhold assistance to camps on the Thai border was motivated, at least in part, by "more earthly temptations...as...[Oxfam] imagined that it would become a leader of a consortium of NGOs in this high profile event" (Barnett 2011: 151). A similar argument is made about INGOs in Afghanistan post-2001, where INGO concern for contracts and visibility led to organizational goal displacement (Cooley and Ron 2002). However, organizational interests such as influence and visibility cannot be separated from INGO identity and their perception of their role and responsibility, as INGOs sought influence and visibility as particular kinds of organizations, with specific beliefs and values. Thus, INGO "ideas" about their role and purpose "gave material factors such causal effect" as they sought to define and maintain themselves as organizations with a particular identity (Tannenwald 2005: 21). The identity of multi-mandate NGOs such as Oxfam, CARE, and World Vision, as actors concerned with restoring and upholding the rights of civilians, is now institutionalized in their mandates and structures the manner in which they engage in domestic contexts, such as Sri Lanka.

IMPLEMENTING RBA TO HUMANITARIAN ASSISTANCE IN SRI LANKA

INGOs operational in Sri Lanka have attempted to implement the policy norm of RBA rather than the treaty norm of need-based humanitarian assistance. The meaning of the norm thus has already been reinterpreted at an international policy level, before entering into the domestic context, and has structured the implementation and contestation of the humanitarian regime in Sri Lanka. In Sri Lanka, the RBA approach legitimated a concern with extending humanitarian assistance to development and peace-building activities, and engaging in advocacy to an international audience on human rights abuses by combatants. The ability of INGOs to implement such programs shifted with the extent to which programs coincided with the interests and capacity of the GoSL and LTTE. Yet INGO implementation of the policy norm of RBA placed them in opposition to the GoSL, creating a climate of mutual suspicion and distrust and complicating thereby the provision of humanitarian assistance.

War for Victory, 1990–2000

By the mid-1990s, the LTTE had established control over most of northern Sri Lanka. The final blow for government forces came in 2001, when the LTTE took over Sri Lanka's only international airport, destroying half the air fleet. Despite the ongoing conflict, the GoSL maintained a skeleton administration in the so-called "uncleared" LTTE areas; this signalled continued control over its territory and an acceptance of its obligations towards the war-affected populations. As it had the capacity to provide assistance, the GoSL was the primary provider of food and other essential assistance items. The GoSL resisted international involvement in the conflict, arguing that it was an internal matter. International donors also had limited geopolitical interests in Sri Lanka, and the dominant approach was to work around the conflict, with most donors putting development assistance to the north on hold until the fighting was over (Goodhand 2001; Goodhand and Klem 2005; Bastian, 1999; Mayer et al. 2003).

In the 1990s, there were approximately eight major INGOs operational in the northeast, including Oxfam, CARE, Save the Children (SCF), and MSF. During the first half of the 1990s, agencies tended to focus primarily on the provision of assistance items in "cleared" areas, i.e. areas formerly under LTTE control but reclaimed by the GoSL. By the mid-1990s however, reflecting a shift in the policy norm from need-based to RBA, INGOs began to work more directly "in conflict." INGOs argued that a rights-based approach necessitated developing a more long-term view to humanitarian programming, focusing on livelihood strengthening and peace-building (Goodhand 2001). In 1996, Oxfam and SCF conducted a field-based study, "Listening to the Displaced," to identify humanitarian needs; based on interview data, the needs identified included education, self-reliance, and peace (Harris 2000). The fact that such a broad set of needs was identified highlights how humanitarian needs assessment was based on an RBA (Demusz 2000).

The needs identified are also quite a general list of programs that people faced with similar circumstances might demand; however, this does not in itself make it the responsibility of INGOs to provide for these needs. The INGO focus on addressing these needs arguably reflected their own self-understandings of their role and responsibility, their identity institutionalized through their self-assigned mandate. Yet, the adoption of RBA is justified in terms of needs identified through exercises like Listening to the Displaced. The former Oxfam

Program Director and Country Representative, Simon Harris, described the shift in Oxfam's programming as follows:

> As an NGO working with people affected by conflict, and accepting that such conflict prevents sustainable development, Oxfam in Sri Lanka believes it has a responsibility to help bring about the conditions for a just, equitable, and sustainable peace. It aims to contribute to this by supporting the activities and initiatives of people and organisations aimed at preventing, mitigating, and positively transforming violent conflict. (Harris 1999, cited in Harris and Lewer 2002: 12)

Oxfam also began to put more emphasis on international advocacy within the framework of its definition of basic rights. In 1995, Oxfam employed two staff to ensure that information about the situation was fed into the offices of critical policy-makers in the international community (Harris and Lewer 2002).

In practice, however, INGOs faced considerable difficulties in getting development and peace-building programs off the ground. The GoSL sought to restrict the scope of humanitarian assistance and the nature of INGO engagement in the north to ensure that humanitarian assistance did not benefit the LTTE materially or symbolically. It thus placed an economic embargo on goods entering LTTE areas. The blockade made longer term aid programming aimed to support sustainable livelihoods difficult (Goodhand 2001). The GoSL interest in limiting humanitarian assistance was backed by its institutional capacity to provide humanitarian assistance, as the primary provider of assistance.

Contestation between INGOs and the GoSL over the functioning of the humanitarian regime did not end there however. Keeping with an RBA, INGOs began to engage in advocacy to an international audience. In practice, this advocacy came to be perceived as support for the LTTE by the majority Sinhalese population and the GoSL, and placed INGOs in opposition to the GoSL. This was because "ethical positions are applied selectively...INGOs may make a public statement about the lack of humanitarian assistance for war widows, but are reluctant to 'go public' on human rights abuses by the Tamil militant groups" (Goodhand and Lewer 1999: 82). Lakshman Kadirgamar, the former Sri Lankan foreign minister, argued, for example, with reference to an INGO discussion paper on the human rights situation in Sri Lanka that, "the discussion paper...on human rights contains many statements which are not acceptable, which are not polite, which is not the way a foreign organisation of this kind should deal with matters in our country" (Kadirgamar quoted in Goodhand et al. 1999: 72). In addition, INGO advocacy also had the effect of making them participants in the conflict; a local NGO humanitarian worker argued, for example, that INGO advocacy had contributed to the internationalization of the peace process in the years to come. He argued:

> Because of the NGO community, information started to go out...The government did not sign the ceasefire because it thought it was necessary...it was imposed on the government by the international world. But who gave the information to the international world? Officials in the government feel that INGOs were primarily responsible.[5]

The implementation of the INGO policy norm took place in a context of conflicting interests, which was then reconciled by the GoSL power and capacity. Yet, as INGOs jostled to find space to implement their policy norm in practice, the norm came to mean that INGOs placed themselves in opposition to the GoSL, and were perceived as being supportive of the LTTE. This had important consequences for the reputation and legitimacy of INGOs in Sri Lanka, influencing the subsequent implementation of the humanitarian regime in Sri Lanka.

Peace Negotiations and the Internationalization of the Conflict, 2001–2006

By 2001, the GoSL, under Ranil Wickremesinghe, wanted breathing space in which to reinvigorate the economy and was keen to negotiate some kind of interim settlement with the LTTE (ICG 2006). A ceasefire agreement (CFA) was signed in February 2002 under the auspices of the Norway-led Sri Lankan Monitoring Mission (SLMM). At the Tokyo Conference in 2003 Western donors pledged $4.5 billion towards reconstruction and development assistance; assistance, however, was tied to progress in the peace talks. The GoSL also sought to use development and reconstruction assistance to create a peace dividend, and the Tokyo conference thus "marked a point of convergence between international and domestic actors, both of whom were operating with an ideological framework of the liberal peace" (Goodhand and Klem 2005: 79).

However, as Sriskandarajah argues, the peace dividend approach blurred the lines between the political (conflict resolution) and economic (reconstruction and development) aspects of peace-building, with the risk that the "development cart was being put before the conflict resolution horse" (Sriskandarajah 2003: 32). Moreover, as Goodhand and Klem argue, there was "no seismic shift in the tectonic plates underpinning the conflict...the peace that followed the signing of the CFA had the effect of freezing the structural impediments to conflict resolution" (Goodhand and Klem 2005: 7).

---

[5] Author interview with INGO staff, Vavuniya, Sri Lanka, June 2010.

INGOs saw the signing of the CFA as an opportunity to implement develop-ment and peace-building programs, following from an RBA. The *Practitioner's Kit* developed by the Consortium of Humanitarian Agencies in Sri Lanka states:

> the provision of humanitarian assistance should go hand in hand with efforts to advocate for and protect the physical safety and human rights of civilians...Relief programs should be designed to lay the foundation for development...It is important those who provide aid and those concerned with political negotiations coordinate closely to make certain that aid interventions support the negotiating process (CHA 2003: 7).[6]

CARE's programs during this period provide a good illustrative example. CARE sought to implement two programs: the Transition to Reconciliation and Community Action for Development. The purpose of Transition to Reconciliation was to "enhance CARE's peace-building capacities in order to ensure that its efforts are sustainable by ensuring a long term program-matic and financial foundations for reconciliation" (Interaction 2007: 25). The Community Action for Development program sought to "rebuild and empower civil society to engage in local development initiatives...[creating] organisations that are functional, democratic, and accountable to their mem-bers and civil society" (Interaction 2007: 24). Similarly, Oxfam's programs in the northeast focused on community participation, social awareness, empow-erment, capacity building, gender justice, and institutional strengthening (Kelly et al. 2004: 699–70). INGOs also argued that "human rights could and should be used to promote reconciliation in Sri Lanka. This should be done through the institutionalisation of key political rights and the promotion of pluralism" (CPA 2003: 12).

INGOs and Western donors, however, had a different understanding from the GoSL about how a peace-dividend approach would play out. The donor community "was of the view that not enough was being achieved with regard to rehabilitation and reconciliation issues at the grassroots...through bottom up peace-building strategies" (Barakat et al. 2002: 22). However, the GoSL hoped that large-scale development and infrastructure projects would help create "social buy-in" among the Tamil people and de-legitimate the LTTE (Government of Sri Lanka 2000). Similarly, INGOs sought to implement transformational development programs that would also address issues of rec-onciliation and peace-building through community-level development pro-grams, capacity building, livelihood support, and community empowerment. This was a different vision of development from the GoSL's focus on top-down,

---

[6] The Consortium of Humanitarian Agencies (CHA) is an association of agencies working in, and supporting work in, Sri Lanka. Oxfam, SCF, Care and World Vision have all been part of CHA.

state-led, reconstruction and development to "regain Sri Lanka." Arguably, the INGO and GoSL strategies were even contradictory: while the use of economic levers aims at normalization and increased support for the government in LTTE areas, the INGO approach aims at community level mobilization and transformation that might result in a greater questioning of the government approach and a more aggressive push for a transformative peace that constitutionally addresses Tamil grievances. In other words, the interpretation of development as necessary for facilitating "social-buy in" to a state and as facilitating ethnic reconciliation through a strengthened civil society are not necessary reconcilable in practice, and can exert competing push and pull pressures. The GoSL was thus suspicious of the INGO programming; the Sri Lankan representative to the UN, P. Kohona, questioned INGO community empowerment programs, asking, "[do they aim to] empower the community to look after itself, or to empower the community to become a thorn in the side of the government?"[7] Despite these differences in interpretation, the GoSL had limited capacity to restrict INGO operations. It required international funds and backing, and needed to demonstrate progress in the peace talks and a commitment to creating a peace dividend.

INGOs also had to negotiate implementation of their programs with LTTE commanders. The LTTE welcomed the focus on community-level development and capacity building activities; it sought to use the INGO operations to help it state-build and legitimize itself among the Tamil population under its control. The LTTE placed taxes on goods entering the northeast and thereby increased its revenue stream; the LTTE also relied on INGOs to provide social services to the population, allowing it to focus its resources and energy on building up its military capacity (Morais and Ahmad 2010; Stokke 2006). As pointed out by an INGO member, "we were careful to design our programs so that they wouldn't help the LTTE...but, whatever activity we did, strengthened civil structures in the Vanni, and thus indirectly the LTTE."[8] Stokke thus notes that there was a genuine process of state formation under way in the east and INGOs enabled this process through their community development, civil society strengthening, and rehabilitation projects (Stokke 2006: 1024). Flanigan also argues that the LTTE was interested in "building legitimacy as a governing authority" and was keen to "harness the resources of the non-profit community and portray these services as coming from the Tamil Tiger 'state'" (Flanigan 2008: 503). The LTTE also required INGOs to work through local NGOS, which it then coordinated. These local NGOs, as Morais and Ahmed argue, served as part of the social-welfare system of the LTTE administration and were essential pillars through which LTTE augmented its local legitimacy and engaged in a process of "state building" in the Vanni (Morais and Ahmad 2010).

---

[7] Author interview with P. Kohona, New York, Sept. 2011.
[8] Author interview with INGO staff, Colombo, June 2010.

The adoption of an RBA also led to INGO advocacy to an international audience about human rights violations by combatants. However, as INGOs were concerned that condemnation of the LTTE's human rights record would result in them losing access to civilians in LTTE areas, the advocacy tended to be more critical of the GoSL. Advocacy, INGOs argued, was necessary to ensure freedom from fear, address the needs of civilians, and protect their dignity.[9]

In practice, however, the function of advocacy shifted from what was intended by INGOs as the LTTE sought to use the organizations as a conduit to voice their aspirations for an independent Tamil Eelam to the international community, highlighting the state's discriminatory policies and human rights violations by the Sri Lankan armed forces. It also created the impression among the Southern Sinhalese population that INGOs were LTTE sympathizers.[10] This once again placed INGOs in opposition to the GoSL. P. Kohona, argued, for example,

> our image was characterised improperly by many NGOs. When something went wrong, even when it was like a breach in law, these INGOs tended not to go to police or local authorities, but straight to their embassies. This is intolerable; you are running a parallel administration to the government which cannot be allowed.[11]

In addition, the overlap between INGO RBA programming and donor emphasis on bottom-up peace building and reconciliation also created the impression that INGOs were operating on behalf of Western donors, as a clandestine effort to influence the outcome of the conflict. Rajiva Wijesinha, the former secretary general of the GoSL Secretariat for Coordinating the Peace Process, argues INGOs that engage in advocacy are mostly " 'Johnny come lately' . . . they belong to an era in which the West suddenly realized that if we start telling people what to do, we might cause resentment. But, if we pretend it's not us, and fund other agencies, then it will be okay."[12]

War for Victory, 2006–2010

In July 2006, the GoSL launched a sustained air and ground campaign against the LTTE, eventually leading to the defeat of the LTTE in May 2009. The GoSL was accused of committing war crimes with the intentional shelling of civilians, hospitals, and humanitarian operations. Once the LTTE was defeated,

---

[9] Author interviews with INGO staff, Colombo, June 2010.
[10] This point is widely made in the secondary literature, as well as being mentioned by almost all interviewees in Sri Lanka.
[11] Author interview with P. Kohona, New York, Sept. 2010.
[12] Author interview with Rajiva Wijesinha, Colombo, June 2010.

the GoSL was also accused of illegally detaining civilians in IDP camps in the north by the UN, Human Rights Watch, and other organizations (ICG 2010b; CPA 2007; United Nations 2011a). Civilians emerging from the conflict zone in the north were sent to an IDP camp outside Vavuniya—Menik Farms. It is estimated that at its peak, Menik Farms housed between 250,000 and 290,000 IDPs, making it one of the largest IDP camps in the world (United Nations 2011a). Menik Farms was a "closed" camp guarded by the military and surrounded by barbed wire, contributing to charges that it was actually a detention centre, with inadequate provisions for food, shelter, sanitation, and medical support (ICG 2010b). However, as Simon Harris points out, "faced with a time critical period in which to act decisively, the mass internment of IDPs was probably the most effective and efficient strategy open to the Sri Lankan government in responding to a very real security threat which, if left unchecked, could have resulted in the prolonging of an already protracted violent conflict" (Harris 2010: 9).

These actions affected the GoSL's international reputation. In April 2009, the US opposed a $1.9 billion emergency IMF loan to Sri Lanka; in May 2009, the European Union tried to have a resolution passed, unsuccessfully however, at the Human Rights Council calling for an international investigation into the GoSL's military campaign (Commission of the European Communities 2009). While Western donors have been critical of the GoSL, the GoSL has strengthened ties with "non-traditional donors": China, India, and Pakistan. China was one of largest donors to Sri Lanka, providing weaponry and technical assistance during the final stages of the war (*Sunday Times* 2009); India also provided over $100 million in assistance (*Asian Tribune* 2009).

Following the defeat of the LTTE in the east, the GoSL initiated an "Eastern Re-awakening" program to generate a peace dividend. The program called for industrial development and infrastructure projects, and projects to provide economic opportunities, build housing, and resettle and rehabilitate those displaced by fighting in areas formerly held by the LTTE (ICG 2009a). Provincial elections were held soon after and intended to signal to international and domestic audiences the official end of the conflict and a transition to post-conflict. Arguably, however, the GoSL sought "to enforce a 'victor's peace', an exercise in stabilization and power-building rather than peace-building" (Goodhand 2010: 351).

The GoSL instructed international agencies, including the ICRC, to close their offices in the east; as the war had ended, the government argued, there were no longer humanitarian and protection concerns for these agencies to address. UN agencies and INGOs thus shifted the focus of their programs in the east from humanitarian relief to early recovery and development assistance (Goodhand 2010; Harris 2010; United Nations 2011a), scaling down their relief programs and launching new projects focusing on housing, roads, livelihoods, and community-level peace building (ICG 2009a). This shift from humanitarian assistance to development coincided with the interests of INGOs as it allowed them to implement their RBA policy norm, giving them greater operational space to implement their mandates and access available donor funding. Moreover, it coincided with the GoSL's interest to demonstrate that the war was over and Sri Lanka was now in a post-conflict state under the authority of the GoSL. The overlap between INGO and GoSL interests thus was key in the implementation of an INGO RBA approach in the east.

INGOs sought to apply a similar approach in Menik Farms. They argued that relief or "hardware" assistance must be accompanied by "software" or rights-based programs, such as "gender, child protection, community mobilisation, vocational training... as these were necessary to have a community re-established."[13] The GoSL however placed strict controls on such software programs, and insisted that all INGO relief assistance was coordinated and supervised by governmental authorities. As Goodhand argues,

> The government is very clear about what kinds of activities do and do not fit with its stabilisation agenda: humanitarian aid should be limited to the emergency phase and quickly transitioned to "early recovery"; reconstruction should focus narrowly on economic development and the delivery of "hardware," particularly infrastructure; and "softer," participatory development/social mobilisation activities are seen as potentially subversive, because of fears that they will create organisations and spaces that may lead to political opposition. (Goodhand 2010: 363)

The implementation of the INGO policy norm was thus being shaped by the GoSL's political and security interests and its perception of INGOs. However, there was also a change in the GoSL's capacity, compared to the CFA period, in light of the material and symbolic support it received from China, India, and other non-traditional donors. Reconstruction and development assistance from these donors reduced the negotiating power and leverage of Western agencies in Sri Lanka (Human Rights Watch 2009b; Harris 2010). It enabled the GoSL to tell UN agencies and INGOs that if they "are unhappy, the airport is there... no [one] is stopping [them] from leaving. Every single penny is helpful, but if it comes with a price on our independence and sovereignty, we can do without it."[14]

The constraints placed on INGOs by the GoSL also highlight that implementation is a path-dependent process. Once the LTTE was defeated, the perception that INGOs were not neutral actors and were enabling the LTTE state-build contributed to a trust deficit between INGOs and the GoSL and a climate of mutual suspicion. This was at least part of the reason for restrictions on agency access to the IDP camps and resettlement sites.[15] INGOs were also

---

[13] Author interview with INGO personnel, Colombo, June 2010.
[14] Author interview with P. Kohona, New York, Sept. 2010.
[15] Author interviews with INGO and UN staff, local and international, Colombo/Vavuniya, June 2010.

believed to have passed on information to the international community about
the GoSL's violation of international humanitarian law, contributing to the UN
Secretary General's appointment of a special panel to investigate war crimes in
Sri Lanka.[16] This again placed INGOs in opposition to the GoSL, and shaped
the GoSL's interest in restricting INGO operations. The path-dependent functioning of the regime highlights that actor reputation and legitimacy is a key
factor shaping implementation of a norm over a period of time.

CONCLUSION

This chapter has sought to examine the process from norm institutionalization
to norm implementation, with reference to the treaty norm underlying the
Geneva Conventions and Additional protocols, that humanitarian assistance
should be need-based. Existing literature on the functioning of the humanitarian regime has noted variation in what this norm means at the level of practice
and across operational contexts. The chapter began by arguing that Betts and
Orchard's framework does not consider how even treaty norms have to be
translated to policy norms for specific actors; actors responsible for implementing, supervising, coordinating the implementation of a treaty norm first
have to translate and interpret it into a policy deemed appropriate for that
actor. This point ascribes a critical role to actors and their agency in the process from norm institutionalization to implementation, and highlights how
the process of interpretation can shift the meaning of the norm itself. Thus,
the treaty norm that humanitarian assistance should be based on need alone
has been reinterpreted to mean a rights-based approach to humanitarian assistance by INGOs. This reinterpretation has been shaped by INGO identity, or
their self-perceived and self-assigned role and responsibilities. In the domestic
context, implementation is shaped by the interests of actors, where conflicting
interests are reconciled through differences in power and capacity. In practice,
the norm can thus come to mean or signify something different than what
was intended by the norm implementers. In Sri Lanka, the RBA policy norm
came to mean support for the LTTE, and placed INGOs in opposition to the
GoSL. The Sri Lanka case also highlighted how norm implementation is a
path-dependent process, as the reputation and legitimacy of INGOs created a
climate of mutual suspicion and distrust.

---

[16] The panel found "credible allegations" which, if proven, indicated that war crimes and
crimes against humanity were committed by the Sri Lankan military and the rebels. The panel
concluded that "the conduct of the war represented a grave assault on the entire regime of international law designed to protect individual dignity during both war and peace" (United Nations
2011a).

Finally, while this chapter has focused on material interests as the key determinant of the implementation of a policy norm, these interests cannot be understood in the absence of identity and beliefs. As Wendt notes, "Actors do not have a 'portfolio' of interests that they carry round independent of social context" (Wendt 1992: 398); rather actors ascribe meaning to their external environment, or context, on the basis of the meanings they ascribe to their own identity.

During the CFA period, for example, the LTTE's interests shaped the implementation of the INGO policy norm, with the effect that INGO policies and practices ended up benefitting the LTTE. This dovetailed with INGO interests, in that INGOs were keen to secure available donor funds available for reconstruction and peace-building programming. However, the availability of funding in itself did not shape the content of INGO policies and goals; these policies and goals were identified prior to the CFA period and followed from INGO conception of their role and responsibility in a particular context. While the LTTE might have instrumentally used INGO assistance to further its own goals, the social welfare programs that INGOS sought to implement were in fact consistent with their own perception of their role and responsibility as particular actors, institutionalized in their mandates. This also explains why INGOs did little in way of adjusting programs or protesting about the manipulation of aid by the LTTE to the international community during the CFA period. Similarly, INGO emphasis on software programming in Menik Farms following the defeat of the LTTE was also justified in terms of their responsibility as particular kind of actors. As an INGO member argued,

> if we are a humanitarian community, then we need to be maximizing our utility as a humanitarian community, and I think our role is more than just providing things...that's a part of our work, but we have a lot more to offer and its worth fighting for access to provide people with the empowerment they need.[17]

Similarly, the GoSL's sensitivity to international involvement in the conflict must also be understood in the context of Sri Lanka's identity as a post-colonial state; this identity facilitated the GoSL in whipping up national sentiment against INGOs and making INGOs a scapegoat for any criticism about international involvement in the conflict. Interests might thus be thought of as necessary, but not sufficient to explain the institutionalization–implementation gap for need-based humanitarian assistance in Sri Lanka.

---

[17] Author interview with INGO personnel, Colombo, June 2010.

Part II

Principled Norms

6

Implementing a Global Internally Displaced Persons Protection Regime

Phil Orchard

Over the past twenty years, a global regime has emerged which focuses on protecting internally displaced persons (IDPs). IDPs find themselves in situations analogous to those of refugees—coercively displaced from their own homes—but unlike refugees they do not have clear international protection since they have not left their own state. While they continue to possess rights as citizens, the state may be unable or unwilling to protect these displaced persons, or it may even be the direct cause of their displacement. In 2012, there were 28.8 million IDPs in some fifty-nine countries (Internal Displacement Monitoring Centre 2013).

This IDP protection regime is based around a set of guiding principles on internal displacement which provide the normative underpinning to the regime. The principles define who IDPs are, establish that they continue to possess legal rights in spite of being displaced, and acknowledge that the state and international community both hold responsibilities towards IDPs. There is substantial evidence that the principles are widely accepted and hence institutionalized at the international, regional, and state levels, where a number of states have sought to implement domestic policies or legislation to protect their own internally displaced populations in line with the principles.

Implementation, as defined in the introduction, focuses on the "steps necessary to introduce the new international norm's precepts into formal legal and policy mechanisms within the state or organization in order to routinize compliance." With respect to IDP protection, however, this implementation process has proven to be problematic in two ways. First, there has been a level of discordance between the principles and these domestic laws and policies which are frequently narrower in providing rights to IDPs and in defining IDP status. Second, in some cases, such as Nepal and Uganda, initially clear and expansive IDP policies have either stalled or threatened to stall out due to problems of capacity or support.

What explains the dramatic difference between the successful institutionalization process and the much slower implementation process? Given the clear institutionalization of the IDP protection regime, the onus is on states which have internally displaced populations to adopt the normative understandings embodied within it. This leads to three possible courses of action for would-be adopters.

1. The *unproblematic* course of action is that a state supports the regime and implements policies which conform to it.

2. Alternatively, a state supports the regime and seeks to implement an IDP policy, but the implementation process is unable to proceed due to domestic opposition or a lack of capacity.

3. Finally, a state may *not* support the regime; rather, it provides rhetorical support by creating a policy due to reputational concerns or pressure, but lacks the incentives to then follow-through with implementation. Such rhetorical action does link the implementation process to the international-level institutionalization process. Hence, it may leave a state open to a process of rhetorical entrapment and shaming by international and domestic actors whereby the government becomes obligated to proceed forward with implementation in response to its critics.

My argument proceeds in four parts. The first examines how the guiding principles on internal displacement have created a set of normative elements and responsibilities for both states and the international community. I then examine the successful institutionalization of the principles at the international, regional, and domestic levels, before shifting focus and critically interrogating the domestic laws and policies within these states. Here, I find that the implementation picture is more ambiguous. At one level, within these laws and policies there is frequently a disconnect with core elements of the principles. IDP status may not be clearly defined, the rights of IDPs not clearly developed, and bureaucratic structures assigned the responsibility to assist the internally displaced lack capacity, resources, and authority. I conclude by examining briefly two cases of stalled implementation. In Nepal, limited international pressure has not shifted the government position, with the result that the policy has not been adopted. By contrast, in Uganda, a concerted pattern of international pressure was enough for the government to move forward on implementing their policy; however this remains limited due to ongoing capacity problems.

THE IDP PROTECTION REGIME

While non-binding, the guiding principles use as their foundation existing international human rights law (including the UN Charter, the Universal

Declaration of Human Rights and the International Covenants on Civil and Political Rights and on Economic, Social and Cultural Rights), humanitarian law (including the four Geneva Conventions of 1949 and Protocols I and II of 1977), and refugee law (including the Refugee Convention of 1951 and the Refugee Protocol of 1967). As Walter Kälin (2005: 29–30), the former representative of the Secretary-General for the human rights of internally displaced persons, has argued: "it is possible to cite a multitude of legal provisions for almost every principle...".

States have provided strong rhetorical support for the principles, and they have gained widespread international recognition. Within the United Nations, Secretary-General Kofi Annan argued in 2005 that the principles should be accepted as "the basic international norm for protection" of IDPs (UN Secretary-General 2005: para. 210) while the 2005 World Summit declaration recognized the principles as "an important international framework" for IDP protection (UN General Assembly 2005: para. 132). The General Assembly, the Security Council, and the Commission on Human Rights/Human Rights Council have all acknowledged or recognized the principles (Orchard 2010: 294). Regional and sub-regional organizations have also recognized the guiding principles and have disseminated and made use of them (Mooney 2005: 166).

There has also been a move to adopt the principles into binding legal instruments, particularly within Africa. The 2006 Protocol on Protection and Assistance to Internally Displaced Persons, adopted by the eleven member states of the International Conference on the Great Lakes Region, obliges those states to accept the principles and incorporate them into domestic law.[1] The 2009 African Union Convention for the Protection and Assistance of Internally Displaced Persons in Africa (the Kampala Convention), ratified in 2012, deliberately replicates the normative structure introduced by the guiding principles (Abebe 2010: 42). This includes the factual definition of IDP status (Art. 1.k), the need to adopt domestic legislation (Art. 3.2.a); to create an authority to coordinate activities aimed at protecting and assisting IDPs (Art. 3.2.b), and to cooperate with "international organizations and humanitarian agencies, civil society organizations and other relevant actors" (Art. 5.6). It also establishes a monitoring provision (Art. 14.1), and disputes between state parties can be referred to the African Court of Justice and Human Rights (Art. 22.1).

Finally, a number of states with internal displacement problems have adopted domestic legislation or policies which reflect the principles (see Table 6.1). The UN General Assembly has encouraged "states to continue to develop and implement domestic legislation and policies with all stages of displacement."[2]

---

[1] See also Beyani (2006: 187–97).
[2] UN General Assembly Resolution A/RES/62/153: Protection Of and Assistance to Internally Displaced Persons, 6 Mar. 2008, 4.

Table 6.1 Adoption of national legislation or policies

State	Number of IDPs (2012)*	Nairobi Protocol Signatories	Kampala Convention Signatories/ Ratifications ***	Policy on internal displacement and year first passed	Explicitly cites Guiding Principles
Africa					
Algeria	Undetermined				
Angola	20,000	S	R	2001/2	Yes
Burundi	78,800^	S	S	2001	Yes
Central African Republic	132,000	S	R		
Chad	90,000		R		
Congo	7,800#		S		
Côte d'Ivoire	Undetermined		R		
Democratic Republic of the Congo	2,700,000	S	S		
Eritrea	10,000#		S		
Ethiopia	Undetermined		S		
Kenya	300,000	S		In preparation	
Liberia	Undetermined		S	2004	Yes
Libya	50,000				
Mali	227,000		R		
Niger	Undetermined		R		
Nigeria	Undetermined		R	In preparation	
Rwanda	Undetermined	S	R		
Senegal	20,000		S		
Sierra Leone	0		R	2001	Yes
Somalia	1,100,000		S		
South Sudan	240,000		S		
Sudan	2,230,000	S		2009	
Togo	Undetermined		R		
Uganda	30,000^	S	R	2004	Yes
Zimbabwe	Undetermined		R		
Asia and the Middle East					
Afghanistan	492,000			2005	Yes

(*Continued*)

Table 6.1 Continued

State	Number of IDPs (2012)*	Nairobi Protocol Signatories	Kampala Convention Signatories/ Ratifications ***	Policy on internal displacement and year first passed	Explicitly cites Guiding Principles
Armenia	8,400#			1998	
Azerbaijan	600,000			1999	
Bangladesh	Undetermined				
Georgia	280,000			2007	Yes
India	540,000			2003	
Indonesia	170,000^				
Iraq	2,100,000			2008	Yes
Israel	Undetermined				
Kyrgyzstan	164,000				
Laos	Undetermined				
Lebanon	44,600				
Myanmar	450,000				
Nepal	Undetermined			2007	Yes
Occupied Palestinian Territory	144,500#				
Pakistan	758,000				
Philippines	1,200			In preparation	
Russia	29,000			1993	
Sri Lanka	93,000			2002	Yes
Syria	3,000,000				
Tajikistan	0			1994	
Thailand	Undetermined				
Timor-Leste	Undetermined			2007	Yes
Turkey	954,000#			2005	Yes
Turkmenistan	Undetermined				
Uzbekistan	Undetermined				
Yemen	385,000			In preparation	
Other					
Bosnia-Herzegovina	103,000			1999	

(Continued)

Table 6.1 Continued

State	Number of IDPs (2012)*	Nairobi Protocol Signatories	Kampala Convention Signatories/ Ratifications ***	Policy on internal displacement and year first passed	Explicitly cites Guiding Principles
Colombia	4,900,000			1997	
Croatia	0			1993	
Cyprus	210,000				
Guatemala	Undetermined			1994	
Kosovo	18,000			2006	Yes
Macedonia	600^				
Mexico	160,000				
Peru	150,000#			2004	Yes
Serbia	225,000			2006	
62 States	**28,800,000**	**8**	**19 (12 R)**	**25 (4 in preparation)**	**13**

Adapted from Orchard (2010).
* Internal Displacement Monitoring Centre 2013. All figures rounded to the nearest thousand. Where IDP figures are represented by a range, I have used the low estimate. Undetermined reflects no recent figure available. ^2011 data. #older data.
**Wyndham, "A Developing Trend," 8–9; Brookings Institution-University of Bern Project on Internal Displacement, "National and Regional Laws and Policies on Internal Displacement Database", 2008, <http://www.brookings.edu /projects/idp/Laws-andPolicies/idp_policies_ index.aspx.>, accessed Feb. 2011.
*** Brookings Project on Internal Displacement "Kampala Convention Signatories" http://www.brookings.edu/~/media/projects/idp/kampala/mapausignedratifiedcountrieswithnumbers%20feb%202014.jpg, accessed 20 March 2014.

The widespread recognition of the principles at the international level, and the moves to incorporate them into law at the regional and state levels, provides strong evidence that the principles have been institutionalized by a large number of states at the international level (see also Muggah 2008: 58).

The guiding principles help form the basis for an IDP protection regime. By regime, I am referring to a structure composed of a bundle of norms which serve as a behavior guide for states and other international actors (Orchard 2014; Goertz 2003).[3] The principles introduce three normative elements. First, they limit the scope of the regime by providing a *constitutive definition* of IDPs as

persons or groups of persons who have been forced or obliged to flee or to leave their homes or places of habitual residence, in particular as a result of or in order

[3] The standard definition of regimes proposed by Krasner (1982: 186) as being composed of "implicit or explicit principles, norms, rules, and decision-making procedures around which

to avoid the effects of armed conflict, situations of generalized violence, violations of human rights or natural or human-made disasters, and who have not
crossed an internationally recognized State border. (Office for the Coordination
of Humanitarian Affairs 1999: 1)[4]

The second normative element is that the principles restate the international
legal rights that IDPs are entitled to; hence they establish a norm that *IDPs
are entitled to the same legal protections as other citizens.*[5] The principles, Kälin
(2005: 28) notes, are critical in making this link as IDPs "are faced with the
fact that no specific international convention exists for the protection of their
rights and that none of the innumerable provisions of international human
rights, humanitarian, and refugee law treaties explicitly addresses their plight."

The third normative element is that the principles introduce *a set of responsibilities*[6] for both the concerned state and the international community writ
large. They establish (in principle 3) that "national authorities have the primary
duty and responsibility to provide protection and humanitarian assistance to
internally displaced persons within their jurisdiction." Principle 25 further
establishes that "the primary duty and responsibility for providing humanitarian assistance to internally displaced persons lies with national authorities"
but that "appropriate actors have the right to offer their services... Consent
thereto shall not be arbitrarily withheld..." (Office for the Coordination of
Humanitarian Affairs 1999: 13).

THE CONTENT OF DOMESTIC LAWS
AND POLICIES

Based on the norms embodied within the IDP protection regime, we can identify three signposts which, if present in domestic laws or policies, would signal accord with international normative understandings. First, the principles'

---

actors' expectations converge in a given area of international relations" has been widely critiqued
(Orchard 2014). While I argue that a regime exists, it remains weak with key elements of how
states address IDP problems remaining underdeveloped. For example, while the principles establish that IDPs have a right to durable solutions—including to return voluntarily to their homes of
resettle in another part of the country (principle 28), there is no equivalent to the refugee cessation clause, with Mooney (2003: 4) arguing that "decisions on when internal displacement ends
are made, if at all, on an ad hoc and arbitrary basis."

[4] While this is a universal definition in the sense that it applied worldwide (Kälin 2008: 1), it is
not a closed definition limited to the specified events (Luopajarvi 2003: 678).

[5] These rights include that IDPs shall not be subject to discrimination; that they shall be free
from arbitrary displacement; and that they should enjoy a broad range of civil, political, economic, social, and cultural rights. They should also have access to a durable solution to displacement, including safe return, resettlement, or reintegration (Office for the Coordination of
Humanitarian Affairs 1999; Kälin 2008).

[6] By responsibility, I follow Erskine that "to be responsible for some act, event or set of circumstances is to be answerable for it" (2003: 7).

definition of who constitutes an IDP should be clearly reflected. Second, the fact that IDPs—as citizens—remained protected by international and domestic law should be noted, as should the principles as a restatement of their international legal rights. Third, there should be a tangible shift in domestic institutions. At a minimum, law or policy should identity the bureaucratic agencies responsible for assisting and protecting the internally displaced. Beyond this, the level of authority, the capacity, and whether or not a bureaucracy is newly formed to deal with the problem are also important factors. There is also a temporal factor—we should expect increased conformity with the guiding principles as time passes since their creation in 1998.

Do the various legislation and policies countries have passed reflect these signposts? As Table 6.2 shows, this pattern is mixed. The table lists some thirty-nine laws and policies passed by twenty-five states until the end of 2012 (minor policies and amendments are not included). It also lists whether the definition from the guiding principles (*GP DEF*) is used, whether IDP rights included in the document refer to domestic sources of law (*D*), the guiding principles (*GPs*), or other international law (*IL*) and whether the document accepts a right of the international community to provide aid (*AID*). Finally, it lists the governmental bureaucracy given responsibility for assisting the displaced, and whether or not this is a new entity.

Within the domestic laws and policies themselves, there is clear acceptance that IDPs require some form of international protection. Not only do a majority provide for the provision of international assistance (twenty-nine policies), but twenty-four policies also note explicitly that IDPs are protected by international law, while slightly less (twenty-one) note that they are also protected by some form of domestic law such as a state's constitution. Most policies or laws also clearly indicate which government bureaucracies are responsible for IDP protection, and in many cases new bureaucracies have been established to fulfill this role. By contrast, only seventeen explicitly mention the guiding principles, and only seven explicitly endorse its IDP definition. In fact, most of these laws and policies either do not provide a definition or introduce a more restrictive definition than that of the principles (Carr 2009: 39).

PROBLEMS IN THE IMPLEMENTATION PROCESS

Beyond their content, there is the question of whether or not these policies and laws are actually implemented. Here, too, the record is problematic. In 2002 Francis Deng argued that "while the Guiding Principles have been well received at the rhetorical level, their implementation remains problematic, and often rudimentary" (UN Commission on Human Rights 2002: 26). A recent survey of fifteen countries with IDP problems found that "nearly half...had adopted some preventive measures on paper. However, efforts to mitigate the

Table 6.2 Conformity between domestic laws and policies and international norms

State	Year	Law/Policy	GP DEF	IDP Rights			AID	Change in domestic institutions (Italics denote new bureaucracy created)
				D	GPs	IL		
Afghanistan	2005	IDP National Plan			Yes	Yes	Yes	Ministry of Rural Rehabilitation and Development; Ministry of Refugees and Repatriation; Ministry of Frontiers and Tribal Affairs
Angola	2001	Council of Ministers Decree No. 1/01- Norms on the Resettlement of Internally Displaced Populations			Yes		Yes	Reactivated Provincial Subgroups on Displaced Persons and Refugees,
	2002	Council of Ministers Decree No. 79/02	Yes				Yes	*National Commission for Social and Productive Reintegration of Demobilised Personnel and Displaced Populations*
Armenia	1998	Law on Population Protection in Emergency Situations		Yes		Yes	Yes	Republic of Armenia Government has monitoring role
Azerbaijan	1999	Presidential Decree "On status of refugees and forcibly displaced (persons displaced within the country) persons"		Yes		Yes-RC	Yes	Executive authorities of the Republic of Azerbaijan.
	1999	Law "On social protection of forcibly displaced persons and persons equated to them"		Yes		Yes	Yes	State Committee on the refugees and forcibly displaced persons
	2004	Presidential Decree "State Program for the Improvement of living standards and generation of employment for refugees and IDPs"					Yes	Implementation assigned to Cabinet of Ministers, updates to President
Bosnia Herzegovina	1995	General Framework Agreement for Bosnia and Herzegovina, Annex VII				Yes	Yes	*Refugees and Displaced Persons Property Fund*

(Continued)

Table 6.2 Continued

State	Year	Law/Policy	GP DEF	IDP Rights			AID	Change in domestic institutions (Italics denote new bureaucracy created)
				D	GPs	IL		
	1999	Instruction on the Return of Bosnian Refugees and Displaced Persons to/within the Territory of Bosnia and Herzegovina					Yes	Department for Refugees
	2005	Law on Displaced Persons and Returnees in the Federation of Bosnia and Herzegovina and Refugees from Bosnia and Herzegovina		Yes			Yes	Federation Government/ Ministry for Human Rights and Refugees
	2005	Law on Displaced Persons, Returnees and Refugees in the Republika Srpska		Yes		Yes	Yes	Ministry for Refugees and Displaced Persons
Burundi	2000	Arusha Peace and Reconciliation Agreement for Burundi, Protocol IV				Yes-RC	Yes	*National Commission for the Rehabilitation of Sinistrés; National fund*
	2001	Protocol for the Creation of a Permanent Framework for Consultation on the Protection of Displaced Persons		Yes	Yes	Yes	Yes	*Committee for the Protection of Displaced Persons; Technical Group for Follow-Up*
	2004	Programme National de Réhabilitation des Sinistrés					Yes	*Ministry for Repatriation, Reinstallation and Reinsertion of Displaced and Repatriated Persons*
Colombia	1997	Law 387 on internal displacement		Yes		Yes	Yes	*National Council for Comprehensive Assistance to Populations Displaced by Violence*
Croatia	1993	Law on the Status of Displaced Persons and Refugees		Yes				*Regional Center for Displaced Persons*
Georgia	2006	Law of Georgia on Internally Displaced Persons		Yes		Yes	Yes	*Ministry of Refugees and Accommodation of Georgia*
	2007	Law on Property Restitution and Compensation for the Victims of Conflict		Yes		Yes	Yes	Commission on Restitution and Compensation

State	Year	Law/Policy	GP DEF	IDP Rights			AID	Change in domestic institutions (Italics denote new bureaucracy created)
				D	GPs	IL		
	2007	Decree #47 on Approving of the State Strategy for Internally Displaced Persons		Yes	Yes	Yes	Yes	As above
Guatemala	1994	Agreement on Resettlement of the Population Groups Uprooted by the Armed Groups		Yes		Yes	Yes	*Technical Committee*
India	2003	National Policy on Resettlement and Rehabilitation for Project Affected Families (development only)		Yes				*National Monitoring Committee*
Iraq	2008	National Policy on Displacement	Yes	Yes	Yes	Yes	Yes	Line ministries and institutions; *IDP Ministerial Committee*
Kosovo	2006	Protocol on Voluntary and Sustainable Return			Yes	Yes		
Liberia	2002	Declaration of the Rights and Protection of Liberian Internally Displaced Persons		Yes	Yes	Yes	Yes	*Liberia Refugee Repatriation and Resettlement Commission*
	2004	National Community Resettlement and Reintegration Strategy	Yes		Yes	Yes	Yes	*Results Focused Transitional Framework Working Committee*
	2004	Guiding Principles on Internally Displaced Persons: Instrument of Adoption			Yes			
Nepal	2004	Relief Program for Internally Displaced People Due to Conflict for FY 2004/05	Yes	Yes		Yes	Yes	*Central Legal Coordination and Directives Committee*
	2007	National Policy on Internally Displaced Persons	Yes	Yes	Yes	Yes	Yes	*Central Steering Committee, Chaired by Ministry of Home Affairs*
Peru	2004	Law No. 28223 Concerning Internal Displacements		Yes	Yes	Yes	Yes	various State entities and services

(Continued)

Table 6.2 Continued

State	Year	Law/Policy	GP DEF	IDP Rights			AID	Change in domestic institutions (Italics denote new bureaucracy created)
				D	GPs	IL		
Russia	1993	Federal Law on Forced Migrants (1993, amended 1995 and 2003)		Yes		Yes	Yes	The migration service
Serbia	2002	National Strategy for Resolving the Problems of Refugees and Internally Displaced Persons				Yes	Yes	*Coordinating Centre for Kosovo and Metohija, Task Force for Monitoring the Implementation of the National Strategy*
	2006	Protocol on Voluntary and Sustainable Return			Yes	Yes		
Sierra Leone	2001	Resettlement Strategy	Yes	Yes			Yes	Resettlement Steering Committee, chaired by National Commission for Reconstruction, Resettlement and Rehabilitation
Sudan	2009	National Policy on Internal Displacement	Yes *	Yes				All levels of government; Humanitarian Aid Commission; *High Committee*
Sri Lanka	2002	National Framework for Relief, Rehabilitation and Reconciliation			Yes		Yes	*National Coordinating Committee on Relief, Rehabilitation and Reconciliation*
Tajikistan	1994	The Law of the Republic of Tajikistan on Forced Migrants		Yes		Yes	Yes	Central Department for Refugees of the Labour and Employment Ministry
Timor-Leste	2007	"Hamutuk Hari'i Futuru" A National Recovery Strategy			Yes		Yes	Vice Prime-minister
Turkey	2005	Integrated Strategy Document			Yes			Ministry of Interior
Uganda	2004	The National Policy for Internally Displaced Persons	Yes	Yes	Yes	Yes	Yes	Office of the Prime Minister—Department of Disaster Preparedness and Refugees
25	39		7	21	17	24	29	

* Definition used, but Guiding Principles not explicitly cited. RC Refugee Convention alone referred to.
Sources: <http://www.brookings.edu/projects/idp/Laws-and-Policies/idp_policies_index.aspx>; <http://www.idpguidingprinciples.org>; <http://www.refworld.org>.

adverse effects of displacement varied, and all fifteen fell short of actually preventing displacement in practice" (Ferris et al. 2011: 23).

Given the widespread support for the guiding principles (and their normative properties) at the international and regional levels, how can we explain the varying content of these laws and policies, and how implementation may stall out at the domestic level? Given the soft law nature of the principles, governments which make a commitment at the international level to protect their own IDPs have only done so rhetorically. This necessarily needs to be followed by changes in domestic legislation and/or policy that embed the commitment into practice at the domestic level (Checkel 1999: 87, see also Cortell and Davis 2000: 73). Creating such legislation and policy is costly, both in financial terms (often requiring the creation of new bureaucratic actors at the national and local levels and the provision of direct assistance to IDPs) and symbolically in that it binds subsequent government action. Since most IDP situations occur within the context of intrastate conflict this can be a substantial impediment.

There are four paths a government may take: (1) adopt and implement national legislation or policies around IDP protection which reflect the international normative consensus; (2) not take any action; (3) endorse the norms through national policies, but fail to successfully implement them due to opposition or lack of capacity; (4) endorse the norms through national policies for reputational or pressure reasons, but deliberately fail to then implement them. In the first two paths, there is no disconnect between acceptance of the norms and implementation: either both processes occur or neither do. Only in the latter two paths does a disconnect occur, either due to government incapability or unwillingness to match their rhetorical action with implementation. Thus, on these paths stalled implementation is more likely.

I propose three possible explanations to explain implementation stalling out. The first is that the government does commit to the norms embodied within the guiding principles, but is unable to proceed in the implementation process. This may be due to a *lack of state capacity* whereby the government lacks the necessary financial, practical and symbolic resources to ensure implementation: "in many cases, governments have been too weak to prevent displacement and mitigate its effects" (Ferris et al. 2011: 25). This can also happen due to *domestic opposition* within and outside of the government.

Alternatively, the IDP policy may reflect the government having decided to make a strategic rhetorical commitment to the norms embodied within the guiding principles with no plan to follow through on implementation. Two alternatives exist here. The first reflects the widespread international support for norms around IDP protection. Due to this, governments which have internally displaced populations may be driven by *reputational concerns* (Finnemore and Sikkink 1998: 903) to rhetorically support these norms. As Schimmelfennig (2001: 48) has argued, states may engage in such rhetorical action even when they may have no interest in engaging in actual compliance.

Therefore, by introducing domestic policies or laws, these states seek to signal their support for the regime at the international level without consummate changes at the domestic level (Hyde 2011: 359).

States may also be responding to advocacy efforts from IOs and NGOs. This may reflect a process of persuasion which shifts the government's or key decision-makers' views on the issue, leading to a normative commitment. Alternatively, the shift in behavior may reflect these organizations' influence on governments through conditionality policies which provide international actors with direct influence over the internal affairs of developing states on a range of issues (Williams 2000; Whitfield and Fraser 2009). For example, UNHCR advocates with governments in favour of the "implementation of a national policy and plans of action that would enhance the protection of IDPs" and also provides government support to do so (UNHCR 2007: 110). This institutional involvement may cause governments to create policies or laws where they otherwise may not have taken action; absent further pressure, however, there will be little follow-through implementation.

In either case, the decision to take rhetorical action by introducing either national legislation or policy around IDP protection opens up governments to the possibility of rhetorical entrapment. While they may lack incentives to undertake concrete actions, a government's public stance may open them up to international shaming efforts based on the legitimacy and widespread acceptance of the norms around IDP protection. Such efforts may lead the government to subsequently take actions in order to ameliorate or reduce pressure (Schimmelfennig 2001: 64, Krebs and Jackson 2007).

How can we determine which of these explanations is at play in explaining a government's failure to implement? If an implementation effort fails due to opposition or capacity, there should be evidence that the government did make an effort to move forward with the policy. Thus, in these cases we are more likely to see examples of stalled implementation—early efforts to move, then protracted non-action. It should also be possible to identify the constraints that the government was under which led to non-implementation. When the government is engaging only in rhetorical action, we may witness the reverse: initially little implementation effort at all. However, international shaming efforts based on the legitimacy of the norms within the guiding principles may lead to rhetorical entrapment, following which the government will respond with (at least some) implementation efforts.

Nepal

In Nepal, a strong initial commitment by the government to an IDP policy has been stillborn. The government fought a civil war with Maoist guerrillas for a decade until a peace agreement was signed in 2006, following the reintroduction of a democratic parliament. The war had created between 200,000 and 400,000 IDPs, the majority fleeing insecurity as well as "forced recruitment and harassment by the Maoists and intimidation by the security forces" (Singh et al. 2007: 105–6). The peace agreement triggered large-scale spontaneous and supported returns. By 2010, the internally displaced population of the country had fallen to 50,000 (OCHA 2010: 3).

In the peace agreement, both sides made a formal commitment to allow the displaced to return voluntarily "without any political prejudice," a finding that Kälin (2010) noted "certainly contributed to finding durable solutions for many IDPs." This followed commitments towards IDP return made by both the Maoists and the Nepalese government in two earlier documents, the 2005 twelve-point agreement and the 2006 ceasefire code of conduct (Adhikari and Joshi 2008: 30). However, the commitment was also driven by local pressure—the Maoist Victims Association staged a number of protests in 2005 to recognize the status of IDPs and to ensure their protection (Human Rights Without Frontiers International 2005: 10)—and by international pressure, including from Walter Kälin, who provided the negotiators with a list of items he thought necessary to "ensure that the human rights of IDPs were taken into account" (Koser 2007: 28).

This led the government to create a policy the following year, which was seen as "comprehensive in scope" and which explicitly referred to the guiding principles. It laid out a clear administrative structure led by the Ministry of Peace and Reconstruction. It also removed a former discriminatory standard in which only those people displaced by the Maoist insurgency were recognized as being internally displaced. However, the policy had several limitations. Notably, while it recognized the need for either return, reintegration, or resettlement of the IDPs, it provided assistance only to those who sought to return to their homes (Ferris et al. 2011: 79; Pandit 2008: 6), with the joint secretary of the Ministry arguing that it did not have "the money to integrate and resettle uprooted families" (Kshetry 2009). In addition, it had only limited applicability in the event of natural disasters.[7] While directives were formulated to implement the policy, the Nepalese Cabinet has not moved to approve them for over four years (IRIN 2010; Internal Displacement Monitoring Centre 2010a). This has been reflected in the help provided to IDPs. One survey found that few government officials were aware of the policy, even when they were nominally directly responsible for its implementation. Similarly, only 35 per cent of IDPs and returnees surveyed were aware of it (Nepal IDP Working Group 2009: 34). Thus, the IDMC has concluded that "the absence of government approval is undermining return and rehabilitation efforts and preventing IDPs from enjoying their full rights" (2010a: 15).

---

[7] Email correspondence with UN official, Kathmandu, Nepal, 16 Mar. 2012.

The government's failure to implement the policy appears to have occurred due to a mixture of incapacity and government structure. The post-conflict government has struggled to move forward on key issues. Not only has the country had four prime ministers since the comprehensive peace agreement was signed, but the drafting of a new constitution has been repeatedly delayed as competing political parties have focused on political manoeuvring rather than governance (Shneiderman and Turin 2012: 141; IRIN News 2011). Not surprisingly, these issues within government have affected the legislative process. By one account, of 439 recommendations forwarded by the National Human Rights Commission to the government, only 8 per cent had been fully implemented and 32 per cent partially implemented (Informal Sector Service Center 2011). Similarly, other major elements of the CPA, including Commissions on Disappeared Persons and Truth and Reconciliation, have not been formed (Informal Sector Service Center 2012: 5).

This is coupled to a widespread culture of impunity for violent crimes and continued insecurity within the country (Shneiderman and Turin 2012: 143)—an independent human rights organization reported some 377 killings in 2011, and 3,039 other gross human rights violations (Informal Sector Service Center 2012: 5). The ongoing level of violence has also led to concerns that humanitarian space in the country is narrowing, with individual agencies increasingly facing access restrictions, extortion, and strikes (Ferris et al. 2011: 170; OCHA 2010: 7).

International pressure has been applied unsuccessfully by both the NGO community and the United Nations. With respect to the NGO community, the Norwegian Refugee Council (NRC) had sought to apply pressure, including commissioning the mentioned study with an NGO consortium. However, the dramatic decline in IDP numbers meant they closed their office in the country in 2009, noting that "NRC believes that the needs of IDPs can be addressed by the government of Nepal with the support of the donor community" (Norwegian Refugee Council 2009). However, the NRC itself flagged that the "government lacked political will" to take action on the issue, while their departure was seen by nationals as being driven in part by "the lack of [a] conducive political and bureaucratic environment" (Wyckoff and Sharma 2009: 45–6).

The UN has remained conscious of the importance of the policy. The 2011 UN Peace-Building Strategy for Nepal flags "implementation of the comprehensive national IDP policy and guidelines" as a "critical peace-building benchmark" (United Nations 2011c: 9). In addition, in 2010 a senior advisor from the UN Protection Standby Capacity Project (PROCAP) arrived in Nepal to support the government in revising and disseminating the policy. However, in spite of the advisor's efforts and those of the broader Protection Cluster in Nepal, the Cabinet has not approved the policy's procedural directives and consequently the policy has not been disseminated.[8]

---

[8] Email correspondence with UN official, Kathmandu, Nepal, 16 Mar. 2012.

While the Nepalese Government supported a strong IDP policy within the context of the 2006 peace agreement, its implementation has been stillborn due to incapacity and ongoing political infighting within the government. This does not appear to reflect a concerted effort to avoid implementing the policy, but rather the policy being caught up in a broader pattern of inaction, coupled with a decline in IDP numbers that has reduced a sense of urgency. International pressure—from both the NRC and the UN—has therefore been unsuccessful in driving the government towards adoption.

Uganda

In Uganda, government support for the norms embodied within the guiding principles was tempered by strategic interests to defeat the Lord's Resistance Army, an insurgency in Northern Uganda active since 1988. At its height, the conflict created 1.8 million IDPs, though all but some 200,000 have returned to their areas of origin since a Cessation of Hostilities Agreement was signed in August 2006 (Internal Displacement Monitoring Centre 2010b: 7). The government has been a champion of the guiding principles at the international level, including being the first to request international training on the principles in 1999 and drafting an IDP policy in 2002, which was adopted two years later. It was also the first government to ratify the Kampala Convention.

Even as the policy was developed, the government engaged in two large-scale operations (dubbed Iron Fist and Iron Fist II) which attempted to destroy the LRA. Beginning in 1996 the government forcibly moved civilians into "protected villages" close to military cantonments (Weeks 2002: 1). Between 2002 and 2004, however, displacement more than doubled from 700,000 to 1.8 million. While large-scale movements of individuals for their own security in emergency situations are allowed under both Protocol 2 of the Geneva Conventions and the guiding principles, the principles note that the authorities have a requirement to try to avoid displacement. Rather, Human Rights Watch suggested displacement was being used "to allow free UPDF movement and operations...as well as to remove the social base in which the LRA might find food and support" (2005: 69). In the camps, the civilian population faced "a brutal cocktail of physical violence, coercion, and sexual exploitation. An estimated 1,000 people die in these camps each week" (Bigombe and Predergast 2006).

While only a small set of international actors were present throughout the 1990s, (Dolan and Hovil 2006: 6) this changed following a 2003 visit by Jan Egeland, the then UN Under-Secretary General for Humanitarian Affairs, who called it the "biggest forgotten, neglected humanitarian emergency in the world today" (Agence France-Presse 2003). However, humanitarian actors were pressured to "remain silent on issues of government responsibility" (Dolan and Hovil 2006: 12) and the government remained focused on increasing the military budget. One UN official was quoted as saying: "Uganda is a functioning state. There are structures in place, but they are ineffective in the case of the north" (Brown 2006: 3).

Dolan suggests that the IDP policy was one of several frameworks "imposed by the international donors" which "were something of a straitjacket for the government" (2011: 66). Certainly, there was substantial international involvement in the policy's drafting, with the government working in close cooperation in particular with the office of the Representative of the Secretary-General for Internally Displaced Persons and with the UN Office for Coordination of Humanitarian Affairs' IDP Unit (Brookings-Bern Project 2006).

The policy was strong on paper—it was based explicitly on the guiding principles, created an inter-agency technical committee which included government ministries, UN agencies, NGOs, and donors, and the Department of Disaster Preparedness and Refugees was identified as the lead ministry to implement the policy (Republic of Uganda 2004). However, there were concerns that the IDP policy was designed primarily to "placate international interests rather than as a forum to address the real situation of the internally displaced" (Brookings-Bern Project 2006: 12; Ferris et al. 2011: 77). Local actors also felt that a new set of governance structures was being imposed on districts which were already "over-stretched and under-resourced" (Internal Displacement Monitoring Centre 2006: 17).

A shift in the government's position occurred following the UN Security Council calling on the government to "renew its commitment to end the conflict and respond to the humanitarian situation."[9] The Uganda Government pointed to the IDP policy as clear evidence that the government had taken action.[10] Following this, the government undertook several concrete implementation steps. These included creating a joint monitoring mechanism between the government and the UN. This was launched by Ugandan President Yoweri Museveni in May 2006, signaling a major commitment. In addition, the government dedicated new financial resources to the initiative, including US$32 million to compensate war victims, which included $10 million from the government and $22 million from the donor community (Cohen 2007: 3; Hovil and Okello 2006).

Government support has since lagged. A year later, this structure was subsumed within a broader Peace, Recovery and Development Plan for Northern Uganda, designed to restore law and order and to enable development. This

---

[9] UN Security Council (UNSC) Resolution 1653: "The situation in the Great Lakes region," 27 Jan 2006. This followed the 2005 Secretary-General's Report which discussed the high mortality and violence rates in the camps and criticized the government for effectively eliminating the right to freedom of movement through the establishment of "free fire zones." UNSC S/2005/740, 28 Nov. 2005, *Report of the Secretary-General on the Protection of Civilians in Armed Conflict*, 5–6.

[10] UNSC S/2005/785, 13 Dec. 2005, "Situation of Internally Displaced Persons in Northern Uganda, Annex" (Hovil and Okello 2006).

suffered from similar issues, including "insufficient funding, incoherent project selection and widespread confusion across sectors, districts and local communities about how implementation is supposed to proceed," leading one analyst to argue that it was "a continuation of politics as usual" (Marino 2008: 8–9; Internal Displacement Monitoring Centre 2010b: 6; Klein 2012).

In the case of Uganda, unsuccessful implementation of an IDP policy triggered sustained international pressure, including from the Security Council and other UN organizations. The government quickly shifted to providing additional resources to ensure the implementation of the policy. Once the pressure declined, however, it appears that similar problems have continued to bedevil successor policies.

CONCLUSIONS: SUCCESSFUL IMPLEMENTATION?

The global IDP protection regime, anchored in the guiding principles on internal displacement, is clearly institutionalized at the international level. I have examined a sub-grouping of states that have IDP problems and that appear to support the international regime, in that all have passed legislation or policies to assist their displaced populations.

While these polices suggest governments take assisting and protecting their internally displaced populations seriously, variation from the international norms embodied within the IDP protection regime are widespread, including around IDP status, incomplete provision of IDP rights, and, most notably, while new or existing bureaucracies are assigned roles, their operations are frequently circumscribed.

Implementation of these norms can be hampered because of environmental factors over which the government has little control—insecurity has hampered IDP assistance in both Iraq and Afghanistan—or by a lack of capacity. Critical, however, are cases in which government implementation has stalled out, as in Nepal and Uganda. As these brief case studies illustrate, while concerted international pressure can overcome some of these failures, as in the case of Uganda, there is a limit. In particular, the case of Nepal demonstrates that fundamental government incapacity can be debilitating for implementation.

Even so, this suggests that government acceptance of the guiding principles on internal displacement through national legislation and policies, a process which should be accelerated by the Kampala Convention, provides an opening to domestic and international actors to pressure governments to conform to the legislation. Consequently, further legalization may provide a pathway towards improved domestic implementation of these measures.

7

Implementing the "Responsibility to Protect"
Catalyzing Debate and Building Capacity

Jennifer M. Welsh

Almost a decade has passed since member states of the United Nations endorsed the principle of the "responsibility to protect" (R2P) in the Outcome Document of the 2005 World Summit (UN 2005a: paras. 138–40). Since that time, there has been a series of efforts to operationalize the principle, based on the implementation plan drafted in 2009 by the UN Secretary-General, Ban Ki-moon (2009a). Most notable among these efforts have been the creation of a "joint office" in New York for the Special Advisor for the Prevention of Genocide and Special Advisor on R2P, the development of a "convening mechanism" that would allow these two officials to bring Under-Secretaries-General of the UN together in crisis situations, and the establishment of a UN-wide "contact group" on R2P (Luck 2012). In addition to these institutional developments, the principle has been invoked in a variety of concrete crisis situations—most notably in March 2011, in relation to the Security Council-authorized military action against Libya, which many regarded as a successful invocation of R2P's key precepts. Gareth Evans (2011), one of the most conscientious advocates for the principle, called the intervention in Libya "a textbook case of the R2P norm working exactly as it was supposed to."

By the autumn of 2011, the Secretary-General was confidently proclaiming: "By now it should be clear to all that the Responsibility to Protect has arrived" (Ban Ki-moon 2011a). Yet, at the same time, there is continuing contestation within international society about how and to what degree R2P should be operationalized, and—more fundamentally—about the legitimacy of R2P's content. In addition, Ban Ki-moon has encountered some resistance in his efforts to "mainstream" R2P within the UN system, both from particular states, which express reservations about the potentially intrusive measures associated with implementing R2P, and from different agencies within the

United Nations, which are sceptical about the value which an "R2P lens" really adds to their ongoing work in development, peace-building, refugee protection, and humanitarian affairs (Bellamy 2012; Kikoler 2008).

Furthermore, at the same moment that proponents of R2P were heralding a breakthrough for the norm in the Libyan context, others were predicting a backlash against the principle from significant corners of international society. In an article titled "R2P, R.I.P.", David Rieff (2011) argued that the morphing of the civilian protection mission into a campaign for regime change in Libya "has done grave, possibly even irreparable, damage to R2P's prospects of becoming a global norm." The statements of key non-Western states in the Security Council in May 2011, which alleged that the NATO air campaign had been both disproportionate and irresponsible (due to civilian casualties), are further evidence of the scepticism that lingers about the trajectory of R2P. As the representative of China proclaimed during this Council debate, "there must be no attempt at regime change... under the guise of protecting civilians" (UN Security Council 2011).[1] Partly as a result of this disquiet, the Brazilian Government in November 2011 launched an initiative—called "Responsibility While Protecting"—to reinterpret R2P by emphasizing the international community's non-military options for exercising the principle, limiting the recourse to force as a "last resort," and strengthening the accountability of those who act militarily on behalf of the Council (Ribeiro Viotti 2011).

This chapter critically analyses the implementation of the norm of R2P, as it was articulated in the 2005 Summit Outcome Document (SOD), drawing on the framework set out by Betts and Orchard in the Introduction to this volume. It begins by arguing that while the SOD—as a moment of "institutionalization"—provided greater precision about the source, scope, and bearer of the responsibility to protect, there is continuing substantive contestation about when the international community's remedial responsibility to protect can and should be activated, and procedural contestation about the forum in which the norm of R2P should be developed. The text agreed to in 2005 does not, in itself, create any new legal obligations, but rather authoritatively interprets states' *existing* obligations to prevent and respond to atrocity crimes.[2] In short, following the terminology set out by Betts and Orchard, R2P is a "principle norm," rather than a "treaty norm." I also suggest that it should be considered a "complex" norm, given that it contains more than one set of prescriptions.

The following section then engages directly with the Betts/Orchard norm implementation framework in two ways. First, with reference to crises such as those in Darfur (2004–6), it questions whether the effectiveness of R2P can be judged by what happens, in their words, "on the ground." In particular,

---

[1] See also the statements by the Permanent Representatives of Brazil, Russia, and South Africa during this debate.

[2] For the purposes of this chapter, "atrocity crimes" will be used as a short-hand for the four acts covered by R2P; genocide, crimes against humanity, war crimes, and ethnic cleansing.

I challenge the view that the successful implementation of R2P can or should be measured in terms of whether military intervention occurs. Instead, I argue that the norm of R2P is primarily a responsibility to *consider* a real or imminent crisis involving atrocity crimes (or what in legal literature is sometimes called a "duty of conduct"); whether international action actually occurs (particularly action involving military force) depends on a series of other factors, such as agreement on the facts (and what they signify) and the likelihood that military tools will have a positive effect. This raises questions for how scholars should measure the strength or success of what Betts and Orchard call "principle norms." This section also demonstrates that—contra their framework—the implementation process with respect to R2P occurs not only at the domestic level (through efforts such as the recently created Atrocities Prevention Board in the United States), but also at the regional and international levels. Given that a core element of R2P is *the international community's* remedial responsibility to act, the creation of international capacity is also critical to implementation. The chapter then goes on to examine international efforts to establish more robust "early warning" capacity to both identify and mobilize a response to developing atrocity situations. It will be shown that, while the causal mechanism for R2P implementation is primarily material—capacity-building at national, regional, and international levels—the impetus has come from a combination of non-governmental advocacy, "experts" (such as the Genocide Prevention Task Force), and the leadership of particular national governments and UN officials.

FROM ICISS TO THE WORLD SUMMIT[3]

The responsibility of individual states to protect their populations has been a recurrent theme in political theory, particularly in formulations of the social contract (Glanville 2010; Welsh forthcoming). Since the end of the Second World War, it has also been recognized in both international human rights law and the law of state responsibility (Rosenberg 2009; Brunnee and Toope 2010). However, the proposition that the international community might have not only a right but also a responsibility to protect individuals inside the jurisdiction of a particular state is more novel and controversial. This more expansive idea was at the heart of the ICISS report, The Responsibility to Protect (ICISS 2001a), which developed a novel case for the use of force on humanitarian grounds, in exceptional circumstances. The Commissioners' argument was based on a more fundamental claim that state sovereignty was no longer about undisputed control over territory, but rather had become a conditional right dependent upon a state's adherence to minimum standards of "good" behavior

---

[3] This section draws on my discussion in Welsh (2013).

(ICISS 2001a: 8).[4] From this premise, the Commissioners went on to assert that where a population of a state was suffering serious harm (from internal conflict, repression, or state failure), and that state proved unwilling or unable to halt such harm, the rights of sovereignty—such as non-intervention—could be overruled by the international responsibility to protect (ICISS 2001: p. xi; Thakur and Weiss 2009).

While the original ICISS report supplied a conceptual framework and rationale for R2P, the unfortunate timing of its release in December 2001—soon after the terrorist attacks of September 11th—meant that it was not accompanied by sustained attention from the international community. Key norm entrepreneurs, such as Commissioner Gareth Evans and then Secretary-General Kofi Annan, worked with friendly governments such as Canada and core members of the EU to push for a General Assembly resolution embracing the concept and for the development of explicit criteria to guide the Security Council in its use of force in situations of humanitarian crisis. With respect to the latter proposal, however, there was very little take-up by key powers such as the United States, Russia, and China, who expressed reluctance about agreeing to criteria that might tie their hands in advance and limit their capacity to decide upon policy on a case-by-case basis, or to employ their veto if they believed core national interests were at stake (Welsh et al. 2002). Moreover, the subsequent war against Iraq in 2003—which eventually used humanitarian justifications after the original case, based on weapons of mass destruction, fell apart—almost killed support for the fledgling principle of R2P, by confirming the suspicions of many developing countries that R2P was a new label for the old practice of great power intervention (Bellamy 2011: ch. 1; Thakur and Weiss 2009; Welsh 2007).

In addition to these challenging contextual factors, the formulation of R2P in the original ICISS report contained three ambiguities that made implementation more difficult (Welsh 2012). First, the trigger for international action was, in the words of the Commission, "large scale loss of life, whether real or apprehended". This left unclear, however, exactly what circumstances the label of R2P was intended to cover. Did it encompass only intentional killing or also, for example, widespread human rights violations short of violent death or deaths that occurred through natural disasters? Second, the source of the international responsibility was not clearly defined. Did it derive from law, or from broader precepts of morality? Members of ICISS expressly avoided the idea of legal obligation when discussing the remedial role for the international community, suggesting that R2P was for them predominantly a moral imperative, deriving from our "common humanity." Finally, the ICISS report did not distribute or allocate the international responsibility to any particular agent,

---

[4] The move toward this more conditional reading of sovereignty had been developed almost a decade earlier in the work of Kofi Annan's former Representative on Internally Displaced Persons, Francis M. Deng (who subsequently served as Ban Ki-Moon's Special Advisor on the Prevention of Genocide). See Cohen and Deng 1998; Deng 1993.

referring only generally to the so-called international community. But this left unclear who, precisely, bears the remedial responsibility of the community—thereby creating a collective action problem in which states and international organizations might shirk their obligations (Pattison 2010: 9).[5]

2005: The Moment of Institutionalization

While the international environment in 2001 appeared inhospitable to the advancement of R2P, the norm entrepreneurs continued to promote the principle. Evans, for example, championed R2P in his role as co-chair of the Secretary General's 2004 UN High Level Panel, ensuring that it appeared in the final text of the panel's report, *A More Secure World*, along with recommended criteria to guide the Security Council's deliberations on the use of force (UN 2004). A commitment to embrace R2P was subsequently incorporated by Kofi Annan (2005: para. 135) in the document on UN reform that he prepared for consideration by heads of state and government at the 2005 summit marking the sixtieth anniversary of the organization.

After intense negotiation, during which at different moments it looked as though R2P language might be dropped (Bellamy 2011: 21–5), government representatives agreed to endorse the principle in the Summit Outcome Document (UN 2005a: para. 139). Article 138 of the SOD acknowledges the responsibility of individual sovereign states to protect their own populations from genocide, crimes against humanity, war crimes, and ethnic cleansing, and to prevent both their commission and incitement. The subsequent paragraph, Article 139, declares the readiness of the international community (working through the UN) to take collective action, using diplomatic, humanitarian, and—if necessary—forceful means in situations where national authorities "are manifestly failing to protect their populations" from such crimes. This paragraph also affirms the commitment of the international community to assist states in building the capacity to protect their populations, and to act before crises fully develop. Finally, the SOD calls upon the General Assembly to consider the further development of R2P, in keeping with principles set out in the UN Charter and international law.

The text of the SOD appears to confirm the belief expressed by some constructivists that institutionalization (and particularly legalization) provides greater specificity to norms, helping both to dampen contestation and facilitate states' adherence (Finnemore and Sikkink, 1998). Indeed, Florini

---

[5] The ICISS report was also ambiguous in leaving open the possibility that intervention for humanitarian purposes might be legitimately carried out without the explicit authorization of the Security Council. The Commissioners' solution to the problem of a politicized and dead-locked Council—which had occurred during the Kosovo crisis in 1999—was to establish procedures that would still privilege Chapter VII-authorized intervention but not forbid action if the Council was paralyzed (ICISS 2001a: p. xiii).

(1996: 364) describes the process of institutionalization as akin to Darwinian evolution: the "better" norm (in this case, R2P) is "selected" to become dominant over previously strong norm (in this case, non-intervention), as beliefs and expectations about appropriate behavior converge. During the 2005 negotiations, states agreed to circumscribe the scope of R2P, expressly limiting it to four specific *crimes*: genocide, crimes against humanity, war crimes, and ethnic cleansing. This list was similar to those crimes which had been identified in both the 1998 Rome Statute and the 2001 Constitutive Act of the African Union, and therefore reflected a reasonably robust consensus on the acts that constituted the kinds of circumstances that R2P was designed to address.

The formulation in Articles 138 and 139 therefore added greater precision to the original ICISS notion of "large scale." This narrow reading of R2P, while still controversial to those who believe that other violations of human rights or natural disasters should also trigger the principle, has quickly become the settled interpretation within the United Nations system.[6] As Evans (2008c: 64–5) argued:

> to use the responsibility to protect too broadly, in non-mass-atrocity contexts, is to dilute to the point of uselessness its role as a mobilizer of instinctive, universal action in cases of conscience-shocking killing, ethnic cleansing, and other such crimes against humanity....if R2P is about protecting everybody from everything, it will end up protecting nobody from anything.

The 2005 Summit also addressed the ambiguities surrounding the source and bearer of the international responsibility to protect. With respect to the former, R2P is now grounded in a *political* commitment expressed by states in the SOD, rather than a new legal obligation. This interpretation rests on two considerations. First, since the UN General Assembly is not a lawmaking body with powers under the Charter to pass legally binding rules, its statements or declarations are not sources of law per se (Strauss 2009; Stahn 2007). Second, it is clear from the diplomacy surrounding the Summit that states did not intend to create additional legal obligations. Indeed, Annan himself insisted that his goal was not to develop new law, but rather to strengthen states' existing legal commitments to protect their populations and to further implementation of international humanitarian law (Jones 2005). Annan's understanding of R2P resonated with a variety of states which, for very different reasons, opposed the crystallization of the principle into a new law of responsibilities to prevent and respond to atrocity crimes. This included several developing countries that were consistently wary of R2P—for fear that it could erode sovereignty and permit excessive intervention—as well as the United States (under the leadership of the Bush administration's Ambassador to the UN, John Bolton), which was uneasy about creating new legal obligations that might reduce America's

---

[6] For a discussion of the debate over R2P's applicability to the aftermath of Cyclone Nargis in Myanmar case, see Bellamy 2011: 56–8; Thakur 2008; Evans 2008a.

sovereign right to decide upon the use of force. In a statement on the draft text for the Summit, Bolton maintained that the US did "not accept that either the United Nations as a whole, or the Security Council, or individual states, have an obligation to intervene under international law" (Bolton 2005).

As a result of these misgivings about creating more demanding obligations, Article 139 does not explicitly articulate an *international* responsibility to protect, which would be automatically activated if the state's primary responsibility to protect its population from atrocity crimes is not fulfilled. Instead, it speaks of states being "prepared to take collective action," on a "case-by-case basis." When negotiating parties turned their attention to R2P in the late stages of summit diplomacy, they sought to circumscribe the scope and character of the international role, thereby ensuring that R2P would not go beyond the prevailing mechanisms of collective security set out in the UN Charter—including the political negotiations among the Permanent Five (P5) members in the Council—in responding to mass atrocity situations.[7] The Article 139 formulation also appears to exclude the possibility of the use of force in the name of R2P without Council authorization, thereby addressing the lingering ambiguity of the ICISS report on this question of "proper authority."

Thus, as I have suggested elsewhere, the most that can be said of the SOD is that it represents a form of "soft law" (Welsh and Banda 2010), which does not create precise legal rights and obligations, but rather helps to shape interpretation of existing rules by emphasizing particular normative understandings about domestic and international conduct. To use the language of Betts and Orchard, R2P is a "principle norm" rather than a "treaty norm." Because of their unanimous backing, Articles 138 and 139 can be taken as an authoritative interpretation by states of key elements of the Charter's provisions on human rights and the use of force, and as a significant reminder to states of the obligations they already have to their own citizens as part of international human rights and international humanitarian law. However because, like other forms of soft law, these paragraphs are written in general and in some ways qualified language, they leave interpretation open to political contestation (Chinkin 1989).

From Institutionalization to Contestation

Beyond the question of the SOD's legal status is the more fundamental issue of whether this moment of institutionalization has catalysed efforts to improve, in concrete ways, upon the international architecture for preventing and responding to atrocity crimes. The views on this broader question are mixed. Many of the principle's advocates, such as Annan, have described the agreement on Articles 138 and 139 as a "historic breakthrough" (UN 2005c) and one of the

---

[7] For a detailed analysis of the different texts which emerged during the negotiation process, see Pollentine (2012: ch. 5).

Summit's "most precious achievements" (Annan 2006: 8) marking the ascendance of R2P as a key norm in international society. Evans (2008b: 284) has been even more euphoric: "Within just four years of the first articulation of the concept—a mere blink of an eye in the history of ideas—consensus seemed to have been reached on how to resolve one of the most difficult and divisive international relations issues of our, or any other, time." Nonetheless, a vocal group of countries, including India, Egypt, and Pakistan, not only expressed unease about the implications of the SOD, but also went so far as to suggest that the precise formulation of the two articles (which did not contain the broader ICISS reconceptualization of sovereignty) had meant that the world had actually rejected the concept of the R2P in 2005 (Steinberg 2009: 433).

On one reading of post-Summit developments, the view of the norm entrepreneurs appears more accurate. In 2006, the Security Council reaffirmed Articles 138 and 139 in a thematic resolution on the Protection of Civilians in Armed Conflict (UN Security Council 2006b: para. 4). In 2007, the UN Secretary-General Ban Ki-moon appointed a Special Advisor on the Responsibility to Protect, Edward Luck, to develop a strategy for implementing the principle, and in 2009 the General Assembly discussed and accepted the Secretary-General's plan to build the capacity necessary to both prevent and respond to the commission of atrocity crimes (United Nations 2009a).[8] More broadly, R2P has become part of the world's diplomatic language, invoked by a variety of international actors (including governments, international institutions, and NGOs) to both explain and demand action in cases such as Darfur in 2004–6, Kenya during its post-election violence in 2008, and more recently the crises in Libya, Syria, South Sudan, and the Central African Republic. This picture would suggest that, following the life-cycle model of norms set out by Finnemore and Sikkink (1998), R2P has successfully passed through the stages of "norm emergence" (during which entrepreneurs such as ICISS lobbied states and key individuals to promote R2P) and "institutionalization" (during which the norm's meaning was clarified by the SOD), and has now entered the phase of norm "cascade" and "diffusion," during which states and other actors will begin to consistently act on the norm's precepts.

However, as the editors of this volume suggest, institutionalization does not necessarily represent a moment of triumph for norms. By contrast, public endorsement of a norm in an international statement or agreement may lead to renewed arguments about both the norm's desirability and the norm's scope, thereby affecting the willingness of norm followers to embrace implementation and in some cases leading to backsliding or differential interpretations of the norm's meaning (Wiener 2009: 176; see also Van Kersbergen and Verbeek 2007; Sandholtz 2008). While earlier scholars, such as Finnemore and Sikkink, acknowledge that contestation might occur between norms (new and old)

---

[8] During this debate, only four governments (Cuba, Venezuela, Sudan, and Nicaragua) explicitly challenged R2P by suggesting that the 2005 SOD should be renegotiated.

during the process of institutionalization, they have not considered the possibility that: (a) contestation between norms can continue after formal adoption; and (b) a different form of contestation—about the meaning of a new norm—can persist into the implementation phase, particularly as new circumstances and crises (different from those surrounding the norm's genesis) arise (Wiener 2008: 6). In short, it cannot be assumed that a norm such as R2P means the same thing to all actors once institutionalized. As I will show, the implementation phase of R2P is encountering contestation of two kinds: procedural and substantive.

Procedural Contestation

The first form of contestation relates to the appropriate forum in which to develop the norm. Recall that the SOD calls upon the General Assembly, rather than the Security Council, to continue consideration of R2P. This text reflected a deep discomfort among some states about the possibility of the Council, with its powerful members and veto rights, producing politically or strategically motivated action or inaction (Brunnee and Toope 2010: 211). While, as suggested, the Security Council officially endorsed R2P in its 2006 thematic resolution on the Protection of Civilians in Armed Conflict (Resolution 1674), it took almost half a year of diplomatic energy to achieve this affirmation. In addition, the Resolution masked serious divisions over the appropriateness of discussing this norm within the Council chamber. Russia and China, joined by three non-permanent members (Algeria, the Philippines, and Brazil), reminded the Council that the SOD had given the General Assembly the mandate for continuing discussion of R2P and that the Council should therefore avoid invoking the principle (UN Security Council, 2006a).

As Bellamy notes, this experience persuaded some R2P advocates to refrain from pushing the Security Council to make greater use of the principle, for fear of creating opportunities for backsliding on the 2005 commitment (Bellamy 2010; see also UN Security Council 2006d). As a result, between 2006 and 2009, the Council referred to R2P only twice, in a resolution concerning the situation in Darfur (on which China abstained) and in another resolution on the protection of civilians in armed conflict (UN Security Council 2006c, 2009). It is also noteworthy that concerns about the Council's frequent politicization over issues that divide the great powers, and its capacity for consistency, resurfaced during the General Assembly debate on Ban Ki-moon's report in the summer of 2009. In fact, some states linked their comments about the implementation of R2P to the broader debate about Security Council reform.

Since 2009, however, the Security Council has explicitly referred to R2P in a number of resolutions, relating both to specific country situations (for example, Resolution 1996 on South Sudan) and to more general themes (for example, the unanimous adoption of Resolution 2150 on the 20th anniversary of the Rwandan genocide).

Substantive Contestation

In spite of the institutionalization of R2P at the 2005 World Summit, international actors have continued to debate what situations are relevant for the application of the norm and what precise actions are entailed by the responsibility to protect. To fully understand the parameters of this substantive contestation, it is important to unpack the three-pillar conceptualization of R2P that was presented to the General Assembly by Ban Ki-moon in his 2009 report on implementation. Pillar one, drawing on pre-existing legal obligations, is the responsibility of individual states to protect their own populations (whether nationals or not) from genocide, war crimes, ethnic cleansing, and crimes against humanity (Rosenberg 2009). Pillar two calls upon the international community (acting through the UN system and partner organizations) to help states fulfill these responsibilities (for example, by helping to build capacity for the prevention of these crimes). Finally, following the logic of Article 139 of the SOD, pillar three specifies that, if the state in question is "manifestly failing" to protect its population, UN member states have a residual role and can respond collectively, in a "timely and decisive manner," using the full range of political, economic, and military tools (Ban Ki-moon 2009a: paras. 10–12). The report goes on to insist that all three pillars are of equal weight, and that the implementation of R2P is a multi-layered agenda including consensual and coercive means.

R2P in its three-pillar form thus represents what I call a "complex" norm, containing more than one prescription. This complex structure also creates a situation in which the *breach* of one of the components of R2P (failure on the part of a national government to protect its population) is meant to act as a trigger for *fulfillment* of another component (the international community's role in protection). This formulation of R2P is particularly vulnerable to contestation, given that states can debate whether certain pillars should have greater emphasis—despite the Secretary-General's claim about equality—and when the international community's remedial role has been activated (i.e. when the national government can be said to have "manifestly failed" to fulfill its protection responsibilities). In addition, despite the efforts of both the SOD and the Ban Ki-moon report to narrow the scope of R2P, there remains significant disagreement about the meaning and appropriate application of the norm.

Two brief examples illustrate how these possibilities for substantive contestation can affect the implementation of R2P. First, in terms of the timing of the so-called third pillar, some states have consistently adhered to a hierarchical reading of R2P, in which national protection responsibilities are paramount and possibilities for international intervention are severely constrained.[9] Thus,

---

[9] See e.g. the statements of Russia, China, Brazil, China, Egypt, and Russia during the Dec. 2005 Security Council debate on the Protection of Civilians in Armed Conflict (UN 2005b).

in the case of Darfur in 2004–6, those that opposed the application of sanctions against the Government of Sudan insisted that states had to be given sufficient time to live up to their responsibility, and that Sudan had not yet demonstrated "manifest failure" (Williams and Bellamy 2005). Similarly, after the release of UN Human Rights Council report on Sudan in 2007, which claimed that the government was failing in its responsibilities to protect the people of Darfur, a series of Arab and Asian states (most notably Algeria, Pakistan, Egypt, Indonesia, and Bangladesh) mounted a campaign to delegitimize the report's findings (UN Human Rights Council 2006, 2007). Their action reflected the continuing concern about R2P's potential to act as a "Trojan horse" for forceful, colonial-style interference in the affairs of sovereign states.

Second, substantive contestation has continued over what situations should be identified as, to use Evans' (2008c: 71) phrase, "countries of R2P concern": cases where atrocity crimes are occurring or imminent, or where circumstances might deteriorate to produce crisis in the medium to longer term. While some criteria might be used to inform such a judgment—including a past history of atrocity crimes, sharp cleavages between ethnic groups, or formal discrimination against a particular group, the strength of a country's institutions to address tension and grievance (Krain 1997; Harff 2003; Bellamy and McLoughlin 2009)—there remains some scope for disagreement. So, for example, in the spring of 2009, at the height of the Sri Lankan Government's military assault against the Tamil Tigers, advocates of R2P engaged in a lengthy debate as to whether the approximately 150,000 civilians caught up in the fighting in the jungle area near Mutulivu were being subjected to atrocity crimes. On the one hand, actors like the NGO Global Centre for the Responsibility to Protect (2009) called on the Security Council to place the situation on its agenda and act upon its responsibility to protect civilians in Sri Lanka by dispatching an envoy to the region and considering the imposition of sanctions.[10] This view was supported by some UN member states, which also asserted that the crisis should be characterized in R2P terms. Others, however, insisted that the Sri Lanka Government was engaged in an existential battle with terrorists that had threatened all its citizens for decades, and that its actions were therefore both necessary and proportionate. One of the ICISS Commissioners, Ramesh Thakur, accused Western states of hypocrisy in their critique of Sri Lankan officials and calls for a ceasefire, given the intense focus that they had given to counter-terrorism in their foreign policy post-9/11. "Given the Tigers' nature and record," he wrote, "it was not unreasonable for the government to acquire the capacity and demonstrate the determination to defeat the Tigers as part of its responsibility to protect" (Thakur 2009). In the end, Sri Lankan diplomacy

---

[10] The letter was signed by, among others, the former UN Coordinator for Humanitarian Affairs, Jan Egeland, and the former Special Advisor on the Prevention of Genocide, Juan Mendez.

was successful in making its case and preventing the crisis from being considered by the Security Council under the banner of R2P.[11]

IMPLEMENTING THE RESPONSIBILITY TO PROTECT

For scholars such as Theresa Reinold, the level of contestation surrounding R2P's scope and content suggests that an intersubjectively shared standard of appropriate behavior does not exist. As a result, norm internalization will not and cannot occur (Reinold 2010: 74). I argue, however, that norms by their very nature as social facts are open to contestation and evolution in meaning *as they are used*. R2P, as a complex norm with layers of prescription, is particularly susceptible to these processes, requiring a different approach to the analysis of implementation.

A False "Test" for the Norm

Other analysts of R2P focus not so much on whether or not it constitutes a norm, but rather on whether it is a strong and effective catalyst for action. Here, cases such as Darfur are viewed as particularly troubling. If the responsibility to protect is to mean anything, such critics contend, then surely it should have generated the will to intervene in a timely and decisive way to halt the mass atrocities committed being perpetrated by the *Janjaweed* militia against the civilian population (Waal 2007; Badescu and Bergholm 2009)? This expectation seems all the more warranted, given the significant amount of attention paid to the crisis by various governments, non-governmental organizations, and by the Security Council itself.

There are two problems with such an approach to assessing the robustness of R2P. First, as outlined earlier, R2P is a complex norm, with various prescriptions. These prescriptions not only apply to different actors (in the case of pillar one, national governments, and in the case of pillars two and three, to various international actors), but also exist at different levels of specificity. As is evident from the text of the SOD, the remedial role of the international community under pillars two and three is less clearly defined than the legal commitments that states have an obligation to uphold as part of pillar one, thereby weakening their "compliance pull." As Bellamy explains, this indeterminacy stems from both the bargaining that took place during the 2005 Summit (and which was

---

[11] As Bellamy (2011: 61) notes, however, reference was made by India—an important player in this crisis—to the Sri Lankan Government's "pillar one" responsibilities to protect its citizens.

repeated during the 2009 General Assembly debate) and genuine differences in assessment about "the most prudential courses of action" (2011: 86).

Second, whether or not military intervention occurs is not an appropriate "test" for effectiveness. Norms only create what Friedrich Kratochwil calls "zones of permissibility" for appropriate behavior, rather than clear, causal pathways (Kratochwil 2001). One of R2P's core functions, as a norm, is therefore to emphasize what is appropriate and to shine a spotlight on what is deemed inappropriate. In this respect, the argument that R2P is best thought of as a policy agenda, rather than a "rallying cry" for action (Bellamy 2011: 80–3), takes an overly minimalist view of the norm's function. Its strength can also be measured, to a certain extent, by the degree to which notions of protection are invoked by international actors during times of real or imminent crisis. In other words, R2P should serve as a catalyst for debate. But exactly what *type* of action follows on from its invocation will depend on a host of factors, *including* other important international norms. At a minimum, then, what the second and third pillars of R2P demand is a "duty of conduct" by members of the international community: to identify when atrocity crimes are being committed (or when there is threat of commission) and to deliberate on how the three-pillar framework might apply. As I will suggest, this duty of conduct is particularly demanding for bodies such as the UN Secretariat, or the UN Human Rights Council, which do not have the same level of politicization built into their structures as a body such as the Security Council.

In the case of Darfur, the Security Council did remain "seized of the matter" and explicitly invoked R2P; it also responded with a range of measures, including sanctions, referral of the situation to the International Criminal Court, and authorization of a peacekeeping mission with a civilian protection mandate (which had the consent of the government in Khartoum) (Bellamy 2011: 52–4). The slow pace of the Council's response, and the relatively limited nature of the military deployment, was partly a function of the opposition of key states such as China, but also of doubts on the part of Western states as to whether a successful military effort could be mounted, given competing missions in Iraq and Afghanistan and the difficulties associated with the terrain in Sudan. There was also genuine concern as to whether such an intervention would have destabilizing effects for neighbouring countries. Given this balance of consequences, Evans concluded, an intervention could not be justified: "It will be the case that some human beings simply cannot be rescued except at unacceptable cost—perhaps of a larger regional conflagration, involving major military powers" (Evans 2008: 145). These words, written in 2008, were also used to characterize the humanitarian crisis in Syria in 2011–12. Despite mounting evidence of atrocity crimes, and frequent invocation of R2P by a variety of actors, a few key powerful states (such as Russia) remained adamantly opposed to the use of coercive measures to resolve the crisis and therefore blocked any attempt by Western members of the Council to pass a resolution under Chapter VII.

This outcome does not mean, as some critics of R2P suggest, that only pragmatism and self-interest, and not normative considerations, affect state behavior (Hehir 2012). Instead, it suggests that the precepts of R2P exist alongside other considerations—both normative (such as the Just War notion of "reasonable prospects of success") and non-normative (such as military overstretch). How these factors work together in decision-making to produce outcomes will differ from case to case. Indeed, in a certain sense, inconsistency is built into the very fabric of R2P, since the 2005 Outcome Document calls upon states to act on *a case-by-case basis*, and not all crises involving the commission or threat of atrocity crimes will be at the same level of severity. As a result, both whether and how each "pillar" applies will vary. The duty of conduct demands only that atrocity situations be identified and considered—not that there will be consistent or uniform outcomes from that consideration. In some situations, such as Libya in 2011, military action will be deemed both possible and legitimate; in other instances, such as Kenya following its post-election violence in 2008, targeted sanctions and meditation measures will be deemed more appropriate. But in both cases, the norm of R2P can be said to be "at work."

Building National Capacity for Preventing and Responding to Atrocity Crimes

Given the indeterminacy of aspects of R2P, a more promising approach to assessing implementation is to examine what Betts and Orchard call the "material" causal pathway: the degree to which concrete capacity is being built to prevent and respond to atrocity crimes. In keeping with their framework, we can observe a variety of capacity-building efforts at the domestic level since the release of the Secretary-General's 2009 report on R2P implementation.

To begin, it is worth reiterating that R2P, in its first pillar, contains a core domestic-level prescription: each state has the responsibility to protect its population from genocide, crimes against humanity, war crimes, and ethnic cleansing. The complex norm of R2P has thus always been built on an effort to remind states of their core function and responsibility—to provide security for their citizens—rather than to undermine their sovereignty. Viewed in this way, implementation of the norm could involve actions ranging from a public reaffirmation of this commitment, to the establishment of law and bodies to address racism and exclusion, to renewed efforts to become parties to the relevant treaties of international human rights law and international humanitarian law, as well as the Rome Statute of the International Criminal Court. As a corollary, Ban Ki-moon has suggested that, as part of pillar one implementation, states should do more to assist the ICC and other international criminal tribunals in apprehending those who have been indicted for crimes (2009a: paras. 16–21). But while these measures are indeed part of R2P implementation, they very closely resemble more specific norms of human rights and criminal accountability, which have been explored extensively by constructivist scholars.

Of greater interest here are the efforts being taken to implement pillars two and three of R2P: the international responsibility to assist states to fulfill their protection responsibilities, and to respond in a timely and decisive way when they have manifestly failed to do so. This international responsibility, however, also has a domestic dimension. It is in particular states that we witness efforts to build an extra-territorial capacity to prevent and respond to atrocity crimes, through the creation of what Koh (1997) calls "symbolic structures" and "standard operating procedures." So, for example, since 2005 a number of countries have explicitly integrated atrocity response into their foreign policy strategy and architecture.

A prominent example is the 2011 decision by the Obama administration, in Presidential Study Directive 10, to create a standing inter-agency Atrocities Prevention Board (APB) to coordinate a "whole-of-government approach" to atrocity prevention and response (Office of the Press Secretary 2011).[12] This directive built upon the recommendations of two important initiatives, both of which highlight the role of the "ideational" pathway to norm development. The first, the 2008 Genocide Prevention Task Force (co-chaired by former US Secretary of State Madeline Albright and former Secretary of Defense William Cohen), convened an epistemic community of officials that called for concrete measures to be taken to build capacity in the US Government to prevent and respond to mass atrocities. This high-profile body clearly timed its deliberations and recommendation to influence the incoming Obama administration (Norris and Malknecht 2013). The second initiative was the 2010 Quadrennial Diplomacy and Development Review, led by then Policy Planning Director Anne-Marie Slaughter, which for the first time created an integrated foreign policy strategy between the State Department and USAID. The QDDR represented both an ideational shift—towards an elevated role for development and "civilian power" in US foreign policy, to better match the stature of and resources given to the US military—and an agenda for structural reform, in which different branches in government would create integrated teams to enhance the country's ability to prevent and respond to conflict (US Dept of State 2010; Stanley Foundation 2011). The QDDR's particular focus on conflict prevention was also a deliberate response to a non-binding Congressional Resolution (S. Con. Res. 71), passed in 2010 with bipartisan support, which recognized genocide prevention as a core US interest and called upon the

---

[12] The APB brings together high-level representatives of eleven agencies of the US Government, including the Dept of Defense, USAID, the Depts of Treasury and Justice, and the State Dept.

administration to build internal capacity to respond to risk of atrocities (US Congress 2010).

The new Atrocities Prevention Board, which came into being in April 2012, has four main functions: (1) to provide a locus of resources, attention, and cross-agency dialogue for responding to situations of mass atrocity; (2) to "give voice" to the executive branch's concern with atrocity issues, when in potential conflict with other competing interests; (3) to serve as a repository for training, doctrine, and contingent planning; and (4) to proactively develop doctrine on atrocity prevention and response, including enhancement of the range of tools (coercive and non-coercive) that the US Government may use to respond to immediate crisis or situations of risk. Situated within the National Security Council and run directly out of the White House, the new APB signals that atrocity prevention and response has become a core objective of US foreign policy, and can therefore be seen as an important indicator of at least senior-level internalization of the norms associated with R2P.[13]

The new board seeks to ensure that atrocity prevention becomes a consistent focus, rather than an ad hoc response to successive crises, by developing both new tools for agencies to employ and tailored training programmes for civil servants on atrocity prevention. Chaired by President Obama's Special Advisor on Multilateral Affairs,[14] the APB has also sought to enhance the ability of the US Government to work with allies and partners in responding to early warning signs.

A second example of domestic implementation involving capacity-building is the move to create "National Focal Points" for R2P within governments, so as to enhance the capacity to respond to the commission or threat of mass atrocities either domestically or in other states. This initiative, launched in 2010, was the result of activism on the part of the Global Centre for the Responsibility to Protect, in association with the governments of Denmark, Costa Rica, and Ghana (all of which have been consistent supporters of the R2P norm). Focal points are senior officials explicitly earmarked and mandated to enable national efforts to improve atrocity prevention and response. Since a variety of government departments are involved in this agenda, states have thus far appointed different kinds of individuals to fulfill these roles (including from the Interior Ministry, in the case of Ghana, or the Ministry of Foreign Affairs, in the case of Costa Rica). The initiative seeks to expand the number of these officials (as of January 2014, over thirty had been appointed) and to embed them within a Global Focal Points Network

---

[13] Given that the APB remains an inter-agency process, rather than an independent entity without its own funding, some argue that it may not have sufficient institutional and Congressional support to survive a change in administration. See Norris and Malknecht (2013).

[14] From Apr. 2012 to Feb. 2013, the APB was chaired by Samantha Power, a well-known advocate of the need for more timely and effective response to mass atrocities. Power was subsequently appointed US Ambassador to the United Nations.

designed to facilitate international cooperation and coordination in pursuit of protection-focused objectives. Ultimately, the core objective is to create a "community of commitment" that increases and integrates state capacity to implement R2P's three-pillar framework (Global Centre for the Responsibility to Protect and Stanley Foundation 2012).

Building the International Capacity to Protect

The dual nature of the focal points agenda, both national and international, illustrates the limits of viewing implementation of a norm such as R2P purely through a domestic lens. As defined by Betts and Orchard, implementation involves "the introduction of a norm's precepts into formal legal or policy mechanisms at the national level in order to routinize compliance." With respect to R2P, as we have seen, national governments can engage in this kind of implementation either by passing legislation that outlaws these crimes, or by creating foreign policy strategies and structures that give explicit attention to the prevention of atrocity crimes (as in the case of the United States). However, because R2P contains prescriptions at various levels, implementation cannot be understood without consideration for *international* capacity-building and coordination. To put it another way, the diffusion of R2P is not from the international level to state and local governments, but primarily across states and within international and regional institutions. This process applies both to pillar two, in terms of providing assistance to other states to fulfill their protection responsibilities, and to pillar three, in terms of creating the tools and procedures necessary to fulfill the international community's remedial role in protection.

Given that implementation of R2P can involve a range of political, economic, and military tools, international capacity-building also stretches across these domains. It could entail, for example: the development of stronger capacity for effective mediation among conflicting parties so as to end violence against innocent civilians; the creation of expertise and technology to impose and implement financial sanctions and embargoes against potential perpetrators of crimes; the training and equipping of armed forces for atrocity-prevention missions (including, for example, safe havens and no-fly zones); or the development of technology to block radio transmissions inciting violence or to provide surveillance that deters perpetrators (Welsh et al. 2012). For the remainder of this chapter, I will focus on efforts to enhance the capacity of regional and international organizations for so-called early warning, including the development of the "joint office" in New York for the Special Advisors on R2P and on the Prevention of Genocide.

In its own internal reports on the tragedies in Rwanda and Srebrenica, the UN had identified gaps in early warning and assessment as important factors in the failure of the organization to respond in a timely way to atrocity crimes. The former case had identified institutional weaknesses in analytical capacity and in the procedures for the transmission of information within the UN system (UN 1999), while the latter had revealed "the reluctance of Member States to share sensitive information with an organization as open, and from their perspective, as 'insecure' as the United Nations" (Annan 1999: para. 486). After the release of both in these reports in 1999, the UN implemented a number of steps to enhance its capacities for early warning and assessment, most notably through its Interagency Framework for Coordination on Prevention Action (known as the "Framework Team"), an informal forum at which twenty-one different agencies, departments, and programmes share information and analysis on situations of concern. In addition, regional organizations, such as the European Union and the Economic Community of West African States (ECOWAS) have significantly enhanced their early warning infrastructure.

Nevertheless, in spite of these initiatives, the 2005 SOD called explicitly for an expansion of the UN's capacity for early warning and assessment (Article 138). The signatories committed themselves to assisting those societies deemed to be "under stress" (Article 139) *before* conflicts and crises development, and in Article 140 pledged support for the Office of the Special Advisor to the Secretary General on the Prevention of Genocide (OSAPG)—whose duties include collecting information from across the United Nations on serious violations of human rights and international humanitarian law, and acting as a mechanism of early warning for the Secretary-General (and ultimately the Security Council). Given the continued contestation about other aspects of the SOD, such as the use of Chapter VII measures, the Secretary-General (working with his new Special Advisor on R2P) made the prevention of atrocity crimes, and particularly the enhancement of early warning, a particular focus in his 2009 report on implementation.

As a result, the first follow-up discussion of Ban Ki-moon's report, held in the General Assembly in August 2010, centred on the issue of early warning and assessment (Ban Ki-moon 2010). While recognizing the efforts that had been made to prevent atrocity crimes through the gathering and sharing of information on developing crises, the Secretary-General identified a series of gaps and deficiencies that needed to be remedied in order to ensure more timely response. The first was the insufficient sharing of information and analysis among streams within the UN system. The second and related problem was the need to regularize and facilitate a two-way flow of information between the UN and regional organizations concerning those countries where risk factors for atrocity crimes are present and intensifying. A third area identified by the Secretary-General was the need to distinguish between conflict prevention and atrocity prevention, which—while often related—do not involve exactly the same kinds of tools and strategies. Given that R2P crimes are not always committed in the context of armed conflict, a particular atrocity perspective is needed in order to interpret actions and events that might be precursors to such crimes. Finally, the discussion underlined the importance of seeking input about countries of concern from a variety of independent sources, beyond states and inter-governmental organizations, and, where necessary, ensuring confidentiality.[15]

The General Assembly dialogue also discussed two concrete capacity-building efforts related to R2P that flowed directly from the Secretary-General's office. The first was the development of a new internal procedure, within the UN, to "expedite and regularize" the process by which the organization responded to atrocity situations. Essentially, the mechanism involved the convening, by the Special Advisors on the Prevention of Genocide and R2P, of key Under-Secretaries General within the UN to identify and evaluate policy options and recommend a course of action for the SG.

The second initiative was the creation and funding of the "joint office" of the Special Advisors on the Prevention of Genocide and the R2P, whose primary function is not to generate more information on emerging crises involving mass atrocity crimes, but rather to collect, collate, analyse, and disseminate information. Two sets of concerns have been raised about this initiative. To begin, as was evident during the General Assembly debate, some states fear that centralized early warning efforts might place certain states under permanent surveillance, and that the process for interpreting information might be politicized by major powers (Welsh 2010: 153). In short, contestation and concerns about infringements of sovereignty are also relevant with respect to this aspect of R2P implementation. In addition, some within the UN worry about the duplication of intelligence-gathering and assessment functions, and therefore about the potential for mixed messages to emerge from different parts of the organization (Bellamy 2012). There is also concern that, if early warning reports are publicly available, rather than remaining part of the Secretary-General's strategy of "quiet diplomacy," they run the risk of being denounced by both the state in question and foreclosing the possibilities for fruitful early action (Stanley Foundation 2010: 12–15). Despite these concerns, Ban Ki-moon has successfully built support for the augmentation of the UN's early warning and assessment capacity, partly by focusing efforts on doing more with existing sources of information (for example, the creation of an inventory) rather than on gathering new information. While the implementation of processes for information monitoring within the joint office is ongoing, it represents, in Bellamy's words, "the UN's best chance of finally establishing an early warning capacity" (2011: 140).

Throughout these efforts to improve upon the international community's capacity for early warning, the leadership of the Secretary-General and his

---

[15] For summaries of the dialogue in the General Assembly, see Global Centre for the Responsibility to Protect (2012b).

Special Advisor was critical. Luck's consultative approach, and his insistence that R2P implementation remain focused on what states had expressly committed to in 2005 (and not on what some advocates of the norm wished it to be), was instrumental in ensuring that the principle did not wither and die during the difficult moments of contestation over its scope and meaning (Bellamy 2011: 33). Ban Ki-moon and his Special Advisor also insisted that the General Assembly, rather than the Security Council, should remain the primary organ for debating various aspects of R2P—thereby allowing for all states to contribute to developing the concept and enhancing its overall legitimacy. Consequently, the dialogue on early warning was followed a year later by a General Assembly discussion on the role of regional organizations (Ban Ki-moon 2011b) and more recently by dialogues on "Pillar Three" (Ban Ki-moon 2012) and "Pillar One" (Ban Ki-moon 2013).

CONCLUSION

R2P is a key "principle norm" in contemporary international society, from which we can learn a great deal about the dynamics of norm implementation. As this chapter has shown, despite the principle's institutionalization at the 2005 World Summit, where key ambiguities about the scope and nature of the international community's responsibility to protect were addressed, contestation over the meaning and implications of R2P has continued through its first decade of implementation. Rather than calling into question the existence of the norm, I have argued that contestation (both procedural and substantive) should be seen as part and parcel of normative evolution, and that R2P—as a complex norm—is particularly susceptible to these processes. As a result, we cannot judge its effectiveness in terms of whether specific actions, particularly military intervention, occur in every instance involving atrocity crimes.

Institutionalization of R2P has led to various forms of implementation at the domestic level, often led by particular individuals or groups of individuals with a commitment to the normative ideas underpinning R2P, all of which have sought to build structural capacity to address real or potential atrocity situations. In addition, however, this chapter has demonstrated that implementation and norm diffusion are not solely domestic-level phenomena. To track the development of a norm, analysts should look beyond legal or policy mechanisms at the national level when assessing the degree to which that norm might have taken root. In the case of R2P, the "material pathway" for implementation also requires capacity-building at the regional and international levels, so that the so-called third pillar of the norm, which involves the *international community's* remedial role in protection, can become a reality rather than just a slogan.

8

China as a Global Norm-Shaper
Institutionalization and Implementation of the Responsibility to Protect

Brian L. Job and Anastasia Shesterinina

This chapter reflects upon and extends Betts and Orchard's theoretical frame-work by considering the case of China's engagement with the emerging international norm, the Responsibility to Protect (R2P).[1] We follow China's engagement with R2P through the three stages of its evolution to date: preliminary debate and framing, institutionalization, and ongoing contestation despite isolated attempts at implementation. Having attacked the norm within the International Commission on Intervention and State Sovereignty in 2001 and accepted it as institutionalized at the UN World Summit in 2005, we argue that China has consistently advanced a particular interpretation of R2P, impacting the evolution in the understanding of the norm and conditioning its implementation. While not accepting an expansive interpretation of R2P, nor has China sought to reject it. Instead, China's agenda has been as a norm-shaper.

This case challenges and opens opportunities for broadening Betts and Orchard's framework. We seek to show that by incorporating what we term a "bottom-up-and-back" process of norm-shaping adopted by China regarding R2P, we can theorize a more dynamic and complex relationship between norm institutionalization and implementation, especially in "principle norms" such as R2P. To this end, the chapter first reviews Betts and Orchard's framework, followed by a charting of the phases of the evolution of R2P and a detailed analysis of China's norm-shaping behaviour throughout these phases.

[1] The support for research and writing from the University of British Columbia Security and Defence Forum Program (both authors) and from the Social Sciences and Humanities Research Council (Shesterinina) is acknowledged. Ashley Bowron, Dept of Political Science, UBC, provided valuable editorial assistance.

BETTS AND ORCHARD'S FRAMEWORK: CAVEATS AND EXTENSIONS

Betts and Orchard argue that understanding the extent to which international norms "make any difference or not in terms of outcome" requires attention to if and how the precepts of a norm, or set of norms, are translated into prescribed actions at the national level. Their framework involves two processes: institutionalization, "an international process" through which agreement is negotiated accepting the precepts of a norm, or set of norms, and reflected in international law and organizations as specific policy changes to be undertaken; and "implementation," a "primarily state-level or organization-level process" concerning policy changes warranted in response to states' international commitments. Additionally, to account for the diversity of international norms, Betts and Orchard set out a typology of three categories of norms—treaty, policy, and principle norms—and envisage differing dynamics of institutionalization and implementation for each.

Betts and Orchard's framework adds considerable nuance to the accepted, standard formulations of norm development offered, for example, by Finnemore and Sikkink (1998), and facilitates fruitful empirical research on the implementation of treaty and policy norms (as demonstrated in the chapters of this volume).

However, their formulation does not fully account for the complexity of norms, especially those concerning human rights, protection of civilians, and humanitarian crises (Betts and Orchard's stated priority areas). Most of these fall into the category of "principle norms" that lack the precision of commitments in legal agreements, i.e. treaties, or specific institutional mandates of largely accepted, "settled," i.e. policy norms. Betts and Orchard struggle to define principle norms, characterizing them as "bundles" of norms brought to bear over such matters as humanitarian intervention. These "composite norms" (our term of reference) are more complex.[2] They combine competing norms; replace existing norms; and create new standards of responsibilities and obligations for individual and collective action. Such norms, including R2P, bring into contestation the fundamental principles of sovereignty and state responsibilities—the "metanorms" of the international order—which makes their institutionalization and implementation more intricate (Sandholtz 2007; Weiner 2007).

---

[2] In a similar vein, Jennifer Welsh (Ch. 7, this volume) characterizes R2P as a "complex norm" due to "its containing more than one set of prescriptions." We believe that referring to principle norms, such as R2P, as "composite norms" better describes their distinctive characteristics, i.e. in simultaneously advancing new principles of behavior, selectively encompassing existing norms, and implicating or negating the standing of others. The complexity of prescriptions represent one of the resulting outcomes of such composite norms.

Related, while Betts and Orchard acknowledge that, in principle, institutional-ization and implementation are parallel, dynamic processes that feed each other, their tendency is to treat them as separate and static, in effect under-appreciating the imprecision of norm development. In practice, international norms are sel-dom articulated definitively through institutionalization. Especially for principle norms that challenge traditional notions of state authority, states are likely to engage in a continual contestation with the aim of (re)shaping these norms to suit their national interests and cultural contexts (Acharya 2011).

This implies, finally, that a greater range of norm engagement processes needs to be considered. For Betts and Orchard, the institutionalization to implementation dynamic is a top-down process, moving from a normative shift at the international level to a domestic alignment with international norms and contestation over implementation ("localization" for Acharya 2004). However, many norms such as "prohibitory norms" (Legro 1997) man-date non-action, rather than action, domestically. Furthermore, implementa-tion is often realized not through domestic, but rather international action. Thus, R2P calls upon states to refrain from committing specific crimes against their populations and, if they fail, mandates international action in response. This complicates an assessment of implementation.

A top-down perspective, we find, ignores a significant complementary, bottom-up dynamic that reflects what the powerful agency states and domestic forces can assert to influence the (re)interpretation of international norms to better represent their "local" views. Prantl and Nakano (2011) describe these processes as following a "feedback loop" from the national to the international level. Acharya (2011) has referred to a dynamic of "subsidiarity," in which local actors seek to "preserve their autonomy" by aligning international norms to reflect their preferred normative frameworks. We believe, however, that a more complex dynamic of norm formation and evolution is involved with simultane-ous top-down and bottom-up processes, what we label a "bottom-up-and-back" dynamic. While specifically applied to a consideration of China and R2P, we find that this dynamic better reflects the tensions in contemporary contestation over international norms, especially the complex principle ones.[3]

RESPONSIBILITY TO PROTECT AS A "PRINCIPLE NORM"

Since the International Commission on Intervention and State Sovereignty (ICISS) launched its report in 2001, the Responsibility to Protect has been

---

[3] Our perspective therefore resonates with Sandholtz's (2007) "cycle theory of international norm change."

the focal point for international debate about the core norms that should animate state behaviour and the international community. R2P attempts to reconcile the conflicting principles and norms of state sovereignty, equality, and non-interference, as centred in the UN Charter, with the protection of human rights, and protection of civilians under duress, also as centred in the Charter, the UN Declaration on Human Rights, UN Development Reports, and international humanitarian and criminal law—advancement on one dimension interpreted as at the expense of the other.[4]

Within Betts and Orchard's typology of norms, R2P sits firmly as a principle norm. From its initiation, R2P has been defined and refined through reports, statements, and resolutions, but has not been codified in any form akin to a treaty or convention. By its very nature, R2P cannot be articulated in a straightforward or singular fashion. It functions as a composite norm, a rubric under which interpretations of its various subcomponents are "nested." Instead of proceeding from a clear statement of agreement about its purpose and commitments (as with treaty norms), the evolution of R2P involves a contention between its norm entrepreneurs, seeking to strike new norms and reorient existing ones, and those who resist challenges to traditional understandings and priorities, playing roles (often shifting from one to another) of norm-rejecters, norm-resisters and constrainers, and norm-shapers (Prantl and Nakano 2011; Badescu and Weiss 2010). Indeed, the extent to which R2P qualifies as an international norm—a widely accepted standard of expected behaviour—has been debated by such states as China who classify it as a "concept" with undecided terms, and certainly not a "principle," as applies to international law (Bellamy 2009: 4–7; 2010: 160–2; Brunee and Toope 2010: 323–42).

Evolution of R2P has involved three stages in Betts and Orchard's terms. Chronologically, these include preliminary debate and framing commencing in the 1990s and leading to the seminal statement of the ICISS Report in 2001, institutionalization over the next five years culminating in the World Summit Outcome Document of 2005 and UNSC 1674 (2006) soon after, and implementation from then on demarcated by the 2009 and subsequent Secretary-General reports and the authorization by UNSC Resolution 1973 (2011) of intervention in the Libyan conflict under R2P. The sequential benchmarks in this timeline should not be seen as implying clear distinctions of institutionalization and implementation. Instead, as Betts and Orchard admit "institutionalization and implementation processes are dynamic, with one feeding into the other and vice versa." As Welsh outlines (Chapter 7, this volume), contention surrounding R2P has prevailed over all three of these stages, with contestation

---

[4] The R2P story has been charted in detail by, among others, Evans 2009; Thakur 2011; Bellamy 2009.

over institutionalization remaining a vital agenda for key players (including China) in the post-World Summit "implementation" period.

R2P Preliminary Debate and Framing

The 1990s saw international attention seized by controversies surrounding humanitarian intervention, ethnic conflict and cleansing, genocide, and war crimes. In this context, the series of regional consultations with the launching of the ICISS in 2000 became a focal point for the genesis and framing of the conceptual foundations of R2P. Strong objections were raised, mainly by developing states, to any Western effort that would erode Charter guarantees of sovereignty and permit non-consensual, non-UN sanctioned intervention. However, a general realization of the need to provide avenues for redress for the killing of civilian populations, often by their own governments, prevailed. The resolution of this tension, for the ICISS, was to reorient thinking around two key premises: first, that state sovereignty entailed a primary positive responsibility for a state to provide for the well-being of its civilian populations; and second, that the international community bore a responsibility to protect these populations (through prevention, rebuilding, and reaction, i.e. intervention) should states fail to do so (ICISS 2001: passim).

Institutionalization of R2P

The ICISS Report in 2001 was a critical first step toward institutionalization of R2P. The four years following its release were ones of vigorous contestation by both supporters and critics—some seeking abandonment of the entire notion, others prohibiting the norm from going beyond Charter provisions. Both they and the UN Secretary-General sought to bring R2P into the institutional ambit of the United Nations, a strategy that came to fruition with the UN World Summit in 2005.

The Summit Outcome Document (SOD), in paragraphs 138 and 139 (A/Res/60/1 2005), and a follow-up reaffirmation in UNSC Resolution 1674 (2006) provide the "precision" of R2P that Betts and Orchard associate with the international institutionalization of a norm. R2P, as originally advanced by the ICISS, is affirmed with formal recognition that sovereignty places a primary responsibility on the state to protect its population—"an important milestone in normative development of international society" (Bellamy 2009: 91). However, the effects of the critics' resistance are also apparent. Protection and response are exclusively delimited to four specified crimes (genocide, war crimes, ethnic cleansing, and crimes against humanity), all of which were previously covered by international law. The authority to respond is exclusively reserved for the UNSC; there is no positive obligation for the Council to act, only to consider, what Welsh (this volume) terms a "duty of conduct." Any debate concerning R2P provisions is delegated to the General Assembly, requiring international consensus for any decision. As a result, on the one hand, R2P advocates, dissatisfied with the watering down of the World Summit's institutionalization, regard it as "R2P lite." On the other hand, states wary of any infringement on sovereignty (such as China) view this interpretation as providing the protections they sought, while at the same time affirming a concern for the need to act to prevent mass killing in failed states—in effect, a positive outcome of their efforts to shape and reorient R2P in a manner consistent with their perspectives and interests.

R2P: Continued Contestation over Institutionalization and Implementation

From 2005 on, two processes of contestation prevail—over institutionalization and implementation of R2P at both national and international levels. While the World Summit's endorsement clarified R2P's scope and constrained it within the Charter parameters, it did not silence resistance by a minority of states to the very existence of R2P. R2P was challenged by such states as Cuba, Venezuela, Sudan, and Nicaragua (the General Assembly president in 2008). However, with the vast majority of states reaffirming their support for R2P, in response to the Secretary-General's reports,[5] and as recently as in the General Assembly's dialogue on R2P in 2012 (GCR2P 2012a), institutionalization of the norm has been reinforced by debate, rather than weakened.

Controversies continue, however, on several specific fronts. Welsh (this volume) characterizes these as "procedural contestation," or debate over the appropriate forum—General Assembly or Security Council—for R2P consideration; and "substantial contestation" over which situations and actions are covered by R2P. The former centres on the efforts of states, including Permanent Members such as China,[6] to ensure that the Council does not broaden the latitude for R2P interventions and that any refinement of R2P occurs through the Assembly, thus effectively blocking change by requiring broad-based consensus.

"Substantial contestation" continues over R2P's applicability to a variety of situations where states endanger their populations, e.g. the Burmese regime's denial of humanitarian assistance to victims of the 2008 Nargis flood (R2PCS 2008) and the North Korean Government's imposition of starvation on its citizens, in addition to its brutal human rights violations (Park 2011). R2P has

---

[5] Ban Ki-Moon 2009, 2010, 2011b, 2012.
[6] See UN Security Council Verbatim Records S/PV.5577 2006.

never been envisaged to extend beyond the circumstances where civilians suffer immediate and extensive violence and death (Thakur 2008). Yet, even with state's "manifest failure" to protect its citizens from the four crimes, "strong," centralized, repressive states, such as Syria (at time of writing in 2013), do not see UNSC action under R2P. In part, this is due to a sovereignty protectionist stance against non-consensual intervention; in part, it reflects the political "protection" extended by Permanent Members to their allies, clients, and proxies.[7]

Implementation of R2P, as a principle and composite norm, is necessarily complex: at the domestic level it functions as a prohibitory norm, and at the international level it does not prescribe specific action, instead suggesting a responsibility to consider. Concerning the former: while individual states have a positive responsibility to protect their populations, there are no agreed upon minimal standards of provision of safety and security. The state's obligation is to not subject its population to the four R2P crimes. Compliance, thus, may be viewed as states' non-action on these fronts.

At the international level, the Secretary-General's report on R2P implementation[8] reformulated R2P around three pillars, the first two—prevention and capacity building—given priority over the third—provision of timely and decisive measures to halt atrocities. This relative emphasis reflects a deep concern of states of the South, regarding the location (mainly Africa) and conduct of peace operations. Brazil's efforts to restrict R2P implementation, through an advancement of its Responsibility while Protecting (RwP), constitute a notable step in this direction (Kenkel 2012; Benner 2013). The Security Council, too, has been reluctant to invoke the term.[9] UNSC Resolution 1973 (2011) on Libya was the notable exception.

In sum, charting the course of R2P demonstrates the difficulty in any straightforward effort to delineate institutionalization and implementation phases concerning the evolution of international norms. These processes cannot be compartmentalized at the international and national levels respectively, as Betts and Orchard suggest. They flow as much, or more, horizontally across states and within institutions as they do vertically, from the international to the national. Further reinforced is the appreciation that institutionalization and implementation of a principle norm like R2P cannot be treated as static. Norms "remain flexible by definition," and not surprisingly the most contested norms, such as R2P, are those that concern fundamental understandings of international relations (Weiner 2007: 6).

---

[7] Consideration of the "precautionary principles" of "reasonable prospects" and "proportional means" set out by the ICISS also play a role. See e.g. Gareth Evans (2003: 71–2) on Iraq.

[8] Ban Ki-Moon 2009.

[9] e.g. UNSC Resolution 1706 (2006) on Darfur mentioned R2P, but further Darfur resolutions dropped the reference.

CHINA AND THE RESPONSIBILITY TO PROTECT

China has actively participated in all three stages of the evolution of R2P. China fiercely opposed the idea of R2P during the preliminary debate in 2001; endorsed the limited version of R2P in its institutionalization in 2005; and has subsequently engaged in an ongoing norm-shaping agenda, involving both institutionalization and implementation.

During the ICISS consultations, the Chinese attacked the concept of humanitarian intervention implied in the idea of R2P as a "total fallacy" lacking a legal basis (ICISS 2001: 392). They argued that permitting the use of force for moral reasons, such as civilian protection, as opposed to national defence or the maintenance of international peace and security, as stipulated in the Charter, would invite chronic unilateral intervention and imperil the primacy of peaceful mediation. Distinguishing humanitarian intervention from humanitarian assistance, they suggested, would preclude a politicized, double standard treatment of human rights issues and ensure precedence of the principles that, according to China, guide contemporary international relations. These principles include sovereignty, host state consent, and UNSC authorization. Steps for humanitarian assistance, the Chinese maintained, should be drawn from these principles.

China abided by this position throughout the 1990s, in its response to the situations in Iraq, Yugoslavia, Somalia, Rwanda, Haiti, and Kosovo, where it opposed non-consensual, unauthorized intervention even in light of massive civilian suffering (ICISS 2001). China called for peaceful mediation in Israel/Palestine, Afghanistan, and Africa's conflicts and argued that economic development should be pursued in attainment of peace (cf. Permanent Mission 2001). Up to this point, China's reaction to R2P was one of a norm-rejecter.

In 2005, however, China endorsed R2P at the World Summit. Ambassador Yishan (Permanent Mission 2005c) accepted that "States have the primary responsibility to protect their own citizens" and that the international community "should provide constructive assistance." He added that "further comprehensive and in-depth discussions" were necessary and that "[a] cautious approach should be taken in determining whether a Government is able or willing to protect its citizens."

Next year, China endorsed UNSC 1674 (2006) that reaffirmed the Summit provisions. Ambassador Zhenmin said this resolution established a "legal framework" for the Council's consideration of civilian protection in armed conflict,[10] but maintained that the General Assembly should continue exploring R2P and that "it is not appropriate to expand, wilfully interpret or even abuse this concept."[11] Thus, R2P, for China, was established as a concept, rather

---

[10] S/PV.5476 2006.   [11] S/PV.5577 2006.

than a norm or a principle of international relations (Bellamy 2009). Lacking the force of international law, it had to "be interpreted and applied in a prudent and accurate manner."[12]

China reiterated its position on R2P in 2009, underlining that the concept applies only to the four crimes and should not be arbitrarily or unilaterally interpreted or extended; and that state consent and UNSC authorization are required for taking action, as set out by the Charter. China further stressed the importance of dialogue and cooperation, and especially the role of regional organizations.[13]

China endorsed this critical and restrictive view of R2P in its support for UNSC 1894 (2009) that once again reaffirmed the World Summit provisions. Shortly after, the Secretary-General clarified R2P implementation around the three pillars. China, however, continued to insist that "Governments bear the primary responsibility for protecting their own citizens" and that civilian protection must be pursued "in line with the Fourth Geneva Convention, international humanitarian law, and the principle of respect for State sovereignty, political independence and territorial integrity as enshrined in the Charter."[14]

China's response to the crises in Darfur, Burma, and more recently, Syria, followed this logic (Teitt 2008; Grono 2006; Shukla 2008; APCRP 2008). An important exception was its abstention on UNSC 1973 (2011), authorizing a no-fly zone and the use of "all necessary means" to protect civilians in Libya. This decision, the Chinese argued, was impacted by regional organizations' endorsement of such action and the urgency of the situation; the vast presence of Chinese nationals in Libya also played a role (Shesterinina 2012).

Explaining China's Response

China's stance on R2P has varied over time and appears to harbour inconsistencies, giving rise to a number of alternative explanations. These lie along a continuum from full commitment to the norm to vocal and active rejection. Neither of these extremes applies with regard to China. Instead, analysts have debated China's adoption of three intermediary positions: (a) rhetorical support but rejection in practice, (b) dual commitment (albeit contradictory) to both R2P and sovereignty, and (c) norm-shaping involving bottom-up and top-down processes. We consider each of these in turn, but conclude that China's engagement with R2P involves a complex "bottom-up-and-back" process of norm-shaping.

Some view China's position on R2P as merely a rhetorical front suggesting acceptance, but an actual policy of rejection (Focarelli 2008; Stahn 2007). This

---

[12] S/PV.5781 2007.   [13] A/63/PV.98 2009.   [14] S/PV.6427 2010.

explanation is grounded in the principles underpinning China's foreign policy and traced back to China's domestic human rights issues and fears of intervention in Taiwan, Tibet, or Xinjiang.

For China, sovereignty is a central "principle" of international relations—the right of a state to be free from interference in internal affairs, broadly defined. This strict understanding of the principle appears to be at odds with R2P view of sovereignty entailing state responsibility and international obligations (Bellamy and Davies 2009: 556). In contrast to sovereignty, R2P is a "concept" and implies no obligations (Bellamy 2009).

Thus, regardless of its rhetorical endorsement of R2P, China has been unwilling to support action against states failing to protect their populations. Its powerful position in the Security Council has guaranteed that the use of force under R2P will in most cases not be pursued. Advocates of this logic find that this is likely to prevail unless extremely serious violations take place in failed states and China's interests converge with those of other members of the Council (Focarelli 2008: 212). China's response to the situations in Darfur, Burma, and Syria illustrate this logic.

The view of China's position as merely rhetorical is overly simplistic. China's active engagement in the evolution of R2P, as evidenced by a change in its position from initial rejection in 2001 to official endorsement in 2005 and thereafter, contradicts it. Indeed, in 2005, China went on record (in its paper on UNSC reform), stating "[w]hen a massive humanitarian crisis occurs, it is the legitimate concern of the international community to ease and diffuse [it]" (Xinhua 2005). Subsequently, China has supported UNSC resolutions reaffirming the World Summit provisions on R2P (Foot and Walter 2011: 47–8).

But neither can it be argued that China has been fully committed to R2P, that is, committed to all of its components as a principle norm. China has very selectively given support for R2P action at the implementation stage. For example, China supported the establishment of UNAMID, the joint UN-African Union peacekeeping mission in Darfur, yet opposed resolutions on Burma. Recently, China supported a UN mission in Libya, but later objected to one in Syria. These actions suggest a more complex picture.

An alternative view sees China's statements and actions as dual commitments, first, to non-intervention, but also to R2P (Teitt 2009; Bellamy and Davies 2009; RSIS 2010). For advocates of this position, this apparently contradictory stance reflects China's evolving management of sovereignty and intervention. Continuing to advance a strong conception of sovereignty, particularly concerning its territorial claims, China's view on intervention in conflict situations has become more flexible and pragmatic (Davies 2011).

China has been willing to pressure governments to solve their humanitarian crises or secure consent to intervention. This may be because stability in its areas of influence is seen as important to the advancement of China's interests abroad (see Evans and Steinberg (2007) on Sudan; Banda (2007) on Africa).[15] Thus, China has engaged in multilateral humanitarian interventions, where state consent and UNSC authorization were secured, as with UNAMID in Darfur (Davies 2011). It initially abstained on resolutions lacking the Sudanese consent[16] but, as the situation deteriorated, participated in securing consent for a deployment of the joint UN-AU force (Davies 2011: 269) and contributed a unit in support of the mission.[17]

Indeed, China has become one of the major contributors of troops to the UN peacekeeping, with contributions ranging from engineering units in Darfur, to civilian police in East Timor, or military observers in Western Sahara (Teitt 2009; Gill and Huang 2009). Its rising contributions reflect China's view on its role in the international system, which advocates of the dual commitment explanation argue invites China to balance its stance on sovereignty and intervention to protect civilians.

Finally, throughout the evolution of R2P, China has stressed the importance of regional organizations.[18] It strongly supported the AU's leadership role in Darfur,[19] arguing that the 2006 Abuja Agreement "would not have been possible without [this] leadership."[20] Since 2006, regional organizations' support has emerged as crucial for China's decisions regarding R2P-related situations, such as Libya (Shesterinina 2012; Teitt 2008, 2011).

Thus, the principal conclusion for scholars looking at China's dual commitment is that China's evolving understandings have shaped its "cautious and contained" approach to R2P (Teitt 2009, quoted in Bellamy and Davies 2009: 31). While more complex than the rhetoric—and full commitment-based arguments—this explanation is also incomplete. It suggests that China is comfortable advancing an inherently inconsistent dual policy and does not recognize the dynamic whereby China actively seeks to shape the emerging norm.

A third view on China's engagement with R2P, one that significantly adds to our understanding of this relationship, sees China as an active norm-shaper. Chin and Thakur (2010) and Foot (2011), for example, find that China has not simply reacted to R2P with its evolving understanding of the norm and its components. It has been actively engaged in seeking to shape the emerging norm, "find[ing] a way to make...intervention more palatable to it and more compatible with its preferences" (Foot and Walter 2011: 48).

---

[15] International pressure, e.g. regarding the 2008 Beijing Olympics, which China was preparing for as the events unfolded in Darfur, may also play a role (Davies 2011: 269).
[16] S/PV.5519 2006.   [17] S/2007/596, 2007.
[18] S/PV.4980 2004; S/RES/1631 2005; S/PV.5649 2007; A/63/PV.98 2009.
[19] S/PV.5015 2004; S/PV.5423 2006.   [20] S/PV.5434 2006.

Advocates of this account accept that China's views on sovereignty and intervention have changed. "[T]he speed with which Beijing adapted to the rise of [R2P]" demonstrates this evolution (Chin and Thakur 2010: 129). They argue that socialization, influenced by China's responsiveness to the weight of international support for R2P (Banda 2007: 26), softened China's position on the norm (Prantl and Nakano 2011: 11). In this explanation, China's official endorsement of R2P since 2005 represents China's "learning" of new global norms (Chin and Thakur 2010: 129).

This explanation does not stop with a top-down logic of socialization—it adds a bottom-up norm-shaping dynamic. In particular, it is found that China has aimed to shape R2P so as to preclude R2P-related breaches of the principles of sovereignty and non-interference by accentuating the preventative aspect of the norm (Foot 2011). "This interpretation [of R2P] is one way that China is shaping global norms and rules, interpreting Western Enlightenment principles through a Confucian lens of governance that stresses an essential unity between citizens and state, rather than giving primacy to human rights as claims against the state" (Chin and Thakur 2010: 130).

"Bottom-up-and-back": Added Complexities of China as a Norm-Shaper

All the explanations presented here apply in important part to the ways in which China has addressed the tensions embedded in R2P. Of these, the strongest alternative is that of norm-shaping. Having rejected R2P initially, yet subsequently accepted its key elements, China has persistently advanced a specific interpretation of R2P, impacting the evolution in the institutionalization of the norm and its components and significantly conditioning its implementation. Advocates of the norm-shaping argument emphasize a top-down process of "localization," or, in the case of China and R2P, making R2P compatible with China's local beliefs and practices, and a bottom-up process of "subsidiarity," or aligning R2P to reflect China's preferred normative frameworks (Acharya 2004: 245; 2011: 97–8). We advance a closely related, but more complex reading of China's engagement with R2P.

Our view does not privilege either top-down or bottom-up logics, but sees both as intrinsically involved. Looking closely at China's engagement with R2P, we see what we term the "bottom-up-and-back" dynamic of norm-shaping involving several simultaneous processes. It is triggered at the international level at t1 with norm entrepreneurs seeking to advance acceptance of new norms, such as R2P. States may straightforwardly reject or accept these at t2, but more usually engage in contestation involving the newly advanced and existing domestic and international norms. As advancements in the norm development are made internationally at t3, they once again go through the process of adjustment on the domestic scene. This process then feeds back to states' attempts at (re)shaping the norms as wholes or their specific components at the international level at t4 and continues from t2 on as long as these norms are on the states' agenda.

Thus, China has pursued its norm-shaping agenda prior to and following the 2005 institutionalization of R2P to ensure: first, that its key principles of international relations are upheld in any consideration of R2P; second, regarding the specific components of R2P, that there is no expansion or encroachment upon the 2005 World Summit statement; and third, that prevention and cooperation with regional organizations continues to be central in R2P.

With regard to the first point, China has insisted that host state consent and UNSC authorization are necessary for intervention under R2P.[21] This "green light" requirement precludes general abuse of R2P and its application for the purposes of non-consensual, unilateral intervention, China's serious and long-standing concern (ICISS 2001b: 170).

Furthermore, China has maintained that any intervention be pursued only with an aim of the "maintenance of international peace and security" in accordance with a strict reading of the Charter's Chapter VII, Article 39.[22] Efforts were made during the 1990s to broaden the interpretation of Article 39 to extend to cases where civilian populations were under serious attack (ICISS 2001: 10), for example with UNSC 688 (1991) condemning the repression of the Iraqi population as a threat to international peace and security (ICISS 2001a: nn. 13, 12), and later with regard to Burma.[23] China, however, regarded both as strictly internal problems.

Finally, China has called for "all peaceful means [to] be exhausted," even in R2P situations, before considering the use of force (A/63/PV.98 2009). Thus, for China, the Sudan regime's killing of civilians in Darfur itself was not sufficient. It was only when the crisis spread to the Sudan's neighbouring Chad that China acted to secure the Sudan's consent to a deployment of the peacekeeping force (S/2006/341 2006; Davies 2011: 269). Overall, given its fears that intervention will become a one-size-fits-all solution, China has asked the Security Council to "make its...decisions in light of specific circumstances, and act prudently."[24]

A second element of China's norm-shaping strategy has been insistence on "a very cautious representation of the [R2P]" as adopted at the World Summit (Permanent Mission 2006).[25] This has meant strictly limiting consideration of the scope of R2P to the specified four crimes and maintaining that any

---

[21] A/63/PV.98 2009; Chin and Thakur (2010).	[22] A/63/PV.98 2009.
[23] S/PV.5619 2007.	[24] A/63/PV.98 2009.	[25] A/63/PV.98 2009.

consideration of R2P be restricted to the General Assembly.[26] Given the need for consensus in the Assembly, China can be assured that no changes to R2P will ensue—thus avoiding the Security Council and prospects of China's having to wield a veto to protect its position.

Subsequent to the Secretary-General's 2009 report, China's engagement with R2P has assumed an additional agenda. China has advanced the implementation of R2P emphasizing the first two pillars—prevention and state capacity. It has asserted that "priority must be accorded to prevention," particularly through preventative diplomacy and longer-term economic development, rather than coercive engagement with states-violators of R2P.[27] Furthermore, Ambassador Guofang (Permanent Mission 2000b) said stability of other states, especially those in Africa, is "a common task of the international community", this being implemented primarily through assistance for state capacity-building.[28]

China has also insisted on cooperation with regional organizations in implementing R2P.[29] China's calls to seek the backing of and collaboration with the relevant regional organizations have been reflected in the implementation of R2P. In the recent crisis in Libya, Arab Council and African Union support for UN action was a crucial factor in China's decision not to veto the non-consensual, UN-sanctioned action against the Libyan Government (Shesterinina 2012).

In these ways, China has shaped both the cautious interpretation of R2P at the institutionalization stage at the World Summit, and its interpretation at the implementation stage thereafter, so as to align R2P within China's broader conception of international relations. China has succeeded in its "policing" efforts to see R2P constrained to the four crimes. China has, moreover, added a number of dimensions, particularly the importance of prevention and the necessity of support from, and cooperation with, regional organizations, which are continuing to affect the implementation of R2P. Contrary to the "localization" and "subsidiarity" logics, in shaping R2P in ways consistent with its foreign policy goals and views on the contemporary international system, China has used international, rather than exclusively local normative frameworks. These have involved engaging the principles of the contemporary international system that China endorses, particularly those of the UN Charter, as these align with specific components of R2P.

---

[26] S/PV.5577 2006; S/PV.5476 2006.
[27] S/PV.4980 2004; S/PV.5577 2006; S/PV.5898 2008; see also Foot (2011); RSIS (2010).
[28] See also S/PV.5655 2007.
[29] S/PV.5282 2005; S/PV. 5529 2006; S/PV.5649 2007; S/PV.5735 2007; S/PV.5868 2008; S/PV.6092 2009; A/63/PV.98 2009; S/PV.6206 2009; S/PV.6257 2010.

INSTITUTIONALIZATION AND IMPLEMENTATION
OF PRINCIPLE NORMS: CONCLUDING THOUGHTS

Reflection on the broader implications of the China and R2P case suggests three insights relevant to Betts and Orchard's efforts to advance an understanding of the institutionalization and implementation of international norms. These relate, first, to the complexities inherent in principle norms; second, to the particular role of states, such as China and other rising powers (the so-called BRICS), who resist roles as norm-takers and instead function as norm-shapers, resisters, and containers; and third, to the multi-faceted strategies and processes of norm-shaping that states adopt in their attempts to reconcile the relationship between their institutionalization and implementation of new norms.

The normative foundations of global and regional economic, political, and security institutions are today under intense scrutiny, as the international community struggles to adjust to ongoing crises of legitimacy, capacity, and governance. Existing norms and sets of norms, e.g. those associated with sovereignty, are being challenged in whole or in part. New and revised standards of responsibility and obligation are under contention. The critical norms at issue in the international system today are what Betts and Orchard have labeled principle norms, and what we further characterize as composite norms. For such norms, including the R2P, there is little prospect of definitive institutionalization at the international level or any direct relationship between institutionalization and implementation (at both systemic and domestic levels). Gaining a better understanding of principle norms will require further research to "unpack" the various components of these norms and to chart the lines of complementarity and contention with existing norms and principles.

Much of the research on the evolution of norms has been cast on a stage involving norm entrepreneurs who seek, through various strategies, to secure adoption of a norm (and acceptance of associated appropriate standards of behaviour) by a sufficient number of states to set in motion a "cascading" effect that establishes a new norm (e.g. Keck and Sikkink 1998; Finnemore and Sikkink 1998). In this framework, states are seen to be norm-adopters or norm-resisters and rejecters (concerning international institutionalization) and compliers or non-compliers (concerning domestic implementation). This categorization of states does not adequately reflect the current reality that certain states withstand, as a matter of principle, the adoption of norms and institutions which they did not play a role in creating. In essence, the substance of a norm, per se, may be less at issue than its embedded normative and institutional framework. This is increasingly apparent in the stance taken by rising powers from the developing world, like China, Brazil, and India, who challenge the legitimacy of institutions such as the UN Security Council, the IMF, and the World Bank. Consideration of this broader context that may shape the reaction of states to any effort at normative change needs to be taken into account. Although only beginning to be apparent in contention over global governance on environment, financial, and security dimensions, researchers will need to be attentive to the strategies adopted by such states as they seek to advance norms that reflect their interests in establishing new global regimes. Needless to say, contestation over implementation and monitoring of compliance will take on whole new dimensions of complexity.

Finally, scholars studying the paths of norm evolution—especially those focused on regional contexts such as Southeast Asia (Acharya 2004, 2011) and Europe (Checkel 2005)—have realized that processes of norm transfer are not unidirectional, particularly no longer exclusively top-down from the systemic to regional and national levels, as in the initial theorizing of norm adoption and "localization." Further study has demonstrated states' adoption of increasingly sophisticated strategies to advance into regional and systemic institutions, and interpretations of norms that reflect their own interests and national political cultures. The contestation within and across institutionalization and implementation involves combinations of top-down and bottom-up processes (Acharya 2011), feedback processes (Prantl and Nakano 2011), and associated efforts at norm-shaping (Foot and Walter 2011). Indeed, states like China may evidence all of these in their adept manoeuvring concerning principle norms such as R2P. Further investigation of these combined and nuanced strategies is warranted, as this will yield important insight into Betts and Orchard's perplexing questions as to when and how norms matter.

9

Peacekeeping in the Congo
Implementation of the Protection of Civilians Norm

Emily Paddon

The protection of civilians (POC) in armed conflict has become a central norma-tive ambition of the post-Cold War era and a consistent objective of responses to the worst of today's crises. While primary responsibility for POC lies with the state, the conviction that peacekeepers also have an obligation to protect civil-ians in areas of deployment has gained credence, such that the United Nations asserts that protection now forms part of peacekeeping's "core business" (UN DPKO 2008: 24). However, as UN Secretary-General Ban Ki-moon laments, "[a]ctions on the ground have not yet matched the progress in words and the development of international norms and standards" (UN 2009c: 1; Ki-moon 2011c). There is, as with other norms explored in the contributions to this vol-ume, a significant gap between institutionalization and implementation.

This chapter analyses the disconnect between normative commitments and actual practice in the realm of civilian protection, through examination of the UN peacekeeping mission in the Congo, the Mission de l'Organisation des Nations Unies en Congo (MONUC). The UN's largest and most expen-sive mission to date, MONUC was first deployed in 1999 just as POC was institutionalized at the UN. Over its decade-long deployment, the putative "robustness" of the mission steadily increased to support implementation of the POC norm: its Chapter VII mandate expanded to encompass the entire country, POC was designated the mission's highest priority, and officials devel-oped novel protection tools and strategies for use in the field (Holt and Taylor 2009: 261–304; Reynaert 2010).

These developments did not, however, translate into greater compliance with the POC norm by UN forces. Instead, the Congo case illustrates, as Betts and Orchard note in their introductory chapter, how the process of implementa-tion may "open up a new arena for interpretation and contestation" of a norm, leading to significant variation and inconsistencies in its operationalization.

At times, peacekeepers in the Congo engaged in some of the most combative enforcement action in the UN's history in order to protect civilians. At other times, glaring inaction in the face of civilian insecurity resulted in casualties and charges of the mission's ineffectiveness and cowardice. To account for this variation, I focus largely on dynamics at the organizational level; i.e. on normative political contestation within MONUC.

The chapter proceeds in three substantive sections. The first provides background on the POC norm. It specifies POC's relationship to other established peacekeeping norms and illuminates areas of conceptual ambiguity that persist despite POC's institutionalization. The next section engages in a "within case" analysis of the norm's implementation in Congo by peacekeepers (Bennett and Checkel forthcoming). Specifically, it considers MONUC's response in four contexts of civilian insecurity. These cases are selected to investigate variation and include two instances of inaction in which force was not used to protect civilians (the Kisangani Massacre, 2002; the Bukavu Crisis, 2004), one of repeated direct action (the Ituri Campaign, 2005–6) and one that is more mixed (Operation Kimia II in 2009). Drawing on the Betts and Orchard heuristic framework, I explain this variation as the result of a combination of material and institutional factors, highlighting the central role played by risk. I define risk as the perception of potential harm or loss that influences and informs decision-making in contexts of uncertainty. Unlike hazards, which are naturally occurring events that can produce harm, risks, as sociologist Ulrich Beck asserts, may be understood as man-made and inextricably linked to the interests of an actor or group of actors; in other words, what one stands to lose is tied to one's interests (Beck 1999; see also Hameiri and Kühn 2011). The analysis demonstrates how risk perceptions, moderated by capacity, varied significantly within MONUC, reflecting the diversity of actors that comprise contemporary peacekeeping missions. This heterogeneity engendered contestation and meant that certain individuals had greater influence to determine when and how the POC norm was implemented. The final section discusses the implications of the findings of the Congo case for the Betts and Orchard framework and for the study of norm implementation more broadly.

THE PROTECTION OF CIVILIANS IN ARMED CONFLICT

The protection of civilians in armed conflict is a broad and multifarious norm that cuts across the "treaty, principle, and policy" typology put forward by Betts and Orchard, suggesting that this distinction may not hold for all norms. The conceptual origins of the norm can be traced back to the just war tradition and the notion that civilians should be treated humanely based on the principle of distinction between combatants and non-combatants during armed conflict (Roberts 2011). As a treaty norm, POC has a long history of formal standing under international humanitarian law (IHL) and international human rights law (IHRL). It falls under the legal mandate of both the International Committee of the Red Cross (ICRC) and the Office of the High Commissioner of Human Rights (OHCHR), and, as concerns specific vulnerable peoples, the United Nations High Commissioner for Refugees (UNHCR) and the United Nations Children's Fund (UNICEF). More recently, in response to the targeting of civilians during armed conflict in the 1990s, POC has proliferated as a policy norm. Today, many, if not most, humanitarian organizations and UN agencies regard protection as an overarching policy priority that is to be "mainstreamed" across all areas of their programming (Barnett and Weiss 2008; WVI 2012).

As the number of actors involved in protection work has increased, so too have the various understandings of the norm (Ferris 2011). At a minimum, protection entails some idea of ensuring physical safety from violence and the supply of assistance to meet basic needs, but more frequently it has come to entail broader objectives such as the provision and safeguarding of legal rights (Caverzasio 2001). This chapter focuses on the first, narrower, conception of protection in the area of peacekeeping, namely the immediate physical security of civilians, and the action taken by UN forces to address this need.

Peacekeepers as Protectors

While many peacekeeping missions of the 1990s were involved in human rights monitoring, the safeguarding of assistance corridors, and escort of humanitarian convoys, the protection of civilians as an explicit activity and objective of UN peacekeeping—and one in which peacekeepers are authorized to use force to realize—is relatively recent (Wills 2009; Bellamy and Williams 2011; Hultman 2013).[1] It arose out of events in the 1990s and in particular the failure of blue helmets to shield civilians from slaughter in places like Bosnia and Rwanda (UN Secretary-General 1998a, 1998b). As Jean-Marie Guéhenno, the former head of the UN Department of Peacekeeping Operations (DPKO), remembers: "There was a deep embarrassment with what happened; a sense of shame amongst the Secretariat and member states—amongst everybody really—and so you had to reconceptualize [peacekeeping]."[2]

The genesis of POC as a core norm of peacekeeping can be traced to Secretary-General Kofi Annan's *Situation in Africa* (UN Secretary-General 1998) report in which he identified POC in conflict as a "humanitarian

---

[1] The explicit authorization to protect civilians under Chapter VII was first mandated in 1999 by the Council with respect to the situation in Sierra Leone. United Nations, S/RES/1270 (1999).
[2] Interview with Jean-Marie Guéhenno, Former Under-Secretary General of UN Peacekeeping, New York, June 2011.

imperative," and called for the Council to pay greater attention to areas of concern. The following year, his bulletin on the *Observance by the UN of IHL* (1999c) merged and reinforced the provisions within the Geneva Conventions and the two Protocols, giving peacekeeping forces a proactive obligation under section 5 to "take all necessary precautions to protect the civilian population" in areas of deployment. Further evidence of the norm's institutionalization is found in the Secretary-General's periodic reports on POC, the Security Council's thematic debates and resolutions, doctrine and policy reform, and the explicit injunction for peacekeepers to use force to protect civilians under Chapter VII, which has been applied in the overwhelming majority of peacekeeping mandates since 1999.[3] It is in this latter context of specific mission mandates that the norm of POC is instantiated and the area of implementation for peacekeepers is specified. In some countries this has entailed provisos such as the protection of civilians only "within the capabilities and areas of deployment" of the force or "without prejudice to the responsibilities of the government."[4] In other cases, such as in the Congo, protection has been designated a priority in relation to other mandated tasks, and in particular in decisions about the use of available resources.[5]

As a relatively recent priority for peacekeepers, POC interacts with other established and institutionalized norms of peacekeeping—what are commonly referred to as the "holy trinity" of peacekeeping: *impartiality, consent,* and the *non-use of force* except in self-defence and defence of the mandate (James 1990; Bellamy et al. 2010). The adoption of POC and its specific focus on physical protection has resulted in the reinterpretation of this trinity. Building on previous reform efforts, the DPKO document *Principles and Guidelines*, which serves as a touchstone for peacekeeping practice, articulates these doctrinal foundations, and more broadly the nature and scope of contemporary operations. Impartiality, no longer construed as passive and now clearly differentiated from neutrality, means that "UN forces should implement their mandates without favour or prejudice to any party" (UN DPKO 2008: 33). Consent, while still necessary, is now qualified. Specifically, consent at the strategic level (obtained from the "main parties," including the host state) is differentiated from consent at the tactical level (obtained from non-state actors, including local groups or factions on the fringe of a peace or political process).

---

[3] For all UN documentation on POC see: <http://www.un.org/en/peacekeeping/issues/civilian.shtml>. As of Feb. 2013, 88% of all UN forces deployed under the aegis of DPKO were explicitly mandated under Chapter VII to use "all necessary means" to protect civilians at risk of imminent harm (calculation based on United Nations, *Peacekeeping Factsheet—February 2013,* DPKO: <http://www.un.org/en/peacekeeping/resources/statistics/factsheet.shtml>). In addition to UN-led peacekeeping missions, the Council has also delegated authority to regional peacekeeping arrangements to protect civilians in contexts such as Somalia and the Congo.

[4] e.g. United Nations Security Council (UNSC), S/RES/1270 (1999).

[5] e.g. UNSC, S/RES/1856 (2008), discussed later.

The former is stated as a requirement of any peacekeeping mission, while the latter is no longer deemed necessary—forceful action should be taken against those who imperil civilians (UN DPKO 2008: 34).

Despite institutionalization of POC and the reinterpretation of the holy trinity, ambiguities and tensions persist in the relationship between POC and the established norms of peacekeeping. Missions authorized under Chapter VII contain the procedure for enforcement action and legally allow the use of force without the consent of the host state. This is incongruent with DPKO's stipulation that consent from the main parties is still required. Moreover, who constitutes a "main party," beyond the state, is underspecified and the possibility that actors may be internally fragmented or may use proxy forces has received little consideration. Similarly, tensions and confusions persist around impartiality, the use of force, and POC over what forms of action are permissible (e.g. pre-emptive action) and whether force can be used against one party without the mission being regarded as distinctly partial.

As the analysis of MONUC in the following section evinces, realities on the ground impinge upon the norms of peacekeeping and bring these tensions to the fore, engendering contestation among those actors involved in the implementation process. In this respect, the Congo case affirms the assertion made by Betts and Orchard that ambiguous and imprecise norms are more likely to be "interpreted (and hence applied) through the lenses of parochial sets of interests and through political processes in which conflicting interests are reconciled through power" (Introduction to this volume).

PEACEKEEPING IN THE CONGO: PROTECTION IN PRACTICE

The Congo has a long and tragic history of plunder and predation, first under Belgian colonial rule and then under the thirty-two-year rule of President Mobutu. The country's more recent history is also one of intractable armed conflict and deep civilian insecurity. Between 1996 and 2003 the Congo War killed some five million people, making it the deadliest conflict since the Second World War (Reyntjens 2009; Prunier 2009; Stearns 2011). It was amidst the war that MONUC was first deployed in 1999, three years before the formal cessation of hostilities. The mission was initially conceived as an observer force to oversee the Lusaka Ceasefire Agreement.[6] However, as it quickly became apparent that the parties had no intention of upholding the agreement and that widespread human rights abuses continued, MONUC was

---

[6] UNSC, S/RES/1279 (1999).

authorized under Chapter VII to "take the necessary action, in the areas of deployment...and as it deems it within its capabilities...to protect civilians under imminent threat of physical violence."[7] MONUC was the second UN mission to receive such a mandate.

The mission evolved in a fluid and dynamic political context, which greatly affected peacekeeper perceptions of risk and their capacity to protect civilians. Throughout the first two years of MONUC's deployment, the war continued unabated as ten foreign armies continued actively to fight each other on Congolese soil, each one supporting one or more domestic armed groups. Uganda and Rwanda were amongst the most active belligerents during this period (UN 2002). The consequences for civilians were dire. However, during this same period, MONUC's role was greatly circumscribed, as member states were reluctant to commit resources and to provide the political backing necessary for the mission to take a stand and protect civilians (Hawkins 2003).

Things began to change in 2001 when President Laurent Kabila was assassinated. The appointment as president of Joseph Kabila, Laurent Kabila's seemingly more amenable son, marked a turn in the war that paved a path to a series of new peace deals (Stearns 2011: 312–13). In 2002, both Rwanda and Uganda signed bilateral accords with the Congo, leading to the formal withdrawal of their forces from the country. These accords allowed for the Global and All-Inclusive Agreement and the eventual signing of the Sun City Agreement in 2003, which established a Transitional Government (TG) and ushered in a more active and committed phase of international engagement (Winter 2012).[8] The TG lasted until 2006 when the country held landmark elections, during which incumbent President Kabila won the vote. MONUC continued to be deployed until 2010 when it was replaced by the Mission de l'Organisation des Nations Unies de Stabilisation en Congo (MONUSCO).

In what follows, I analyse implementation of the POC norm by MONUC in four specific instances where civilians faced imminent protection threats or were actually harmed. All four cases took place in the volatile eastern region of the country and collectively they span the pre- to post-transition periods. The analysis reveals how the perceived risks of using force to protect civilians figured prominently during the implementation process.

This included (1) the risk of *property damage* or *personal injury*; (2) the risk of an *escalation of hostilities* by alienating parties on the ground, causing an intensification of conflict or prompting retaliation; and (3) the risk of *expulsion*, the withdrawal of consent for the mission and its activities. Risk perceptions were in turn moderated by capacity—i.e. the hardware and software deemed necessary to protect civilians, as well as "top cover," or political backing from

---

[7] UNSC, S/RES/1291 (2000).

[8] The TG was based on a "one-plus-four" model in which President Kabila was supported by four vice presidents, each of which represented one of the main belligerents during the war.

the UN Secretariat and members of the Security Council.[9] As risk perceptions varied, within each case, and where relevant, I highlight contestation among actors and offer an explanation for how and why certain courses of action were ultimately pursued over others.

Each case begins with an overview of events that highlights contestation over the appropriate role for MONUC. This is followed by an analysis of the various factors that explain variance in peacekeeper implementation of the POC norm. The conclusion synthesizes the findings across the four cases and considers the implications for the study of norm implementation.

Kisangani Massacre (2002)

On 14 May 2002, violence broke out in Kisangani, Congo's third largest city. Following a suspected mutiny, members of the Rwanda-backed Rassemblement Congolais pour la Democratie (RCD) "went on a rampage," killing roughly 180 people and injuring many more (HRW 2002a). Young women were rounded up and raped, and hundreds of homes were pillaged. The 1,000 or so peacekeepers stationed in the area, who had knowledge of the violence under way, did not use force to halt the massacre or patrol to deter abuses (HRW 2002b: 23).

The mission's weak-kneed response to the Kisangani massacre stemmed largely from the fear that, by confronting the aggressors, peacekeepers would endanger themselves; a fear based in part on their inadequate resourcing. From its inception, MONUC lacked the funds, personnel, and logistical hardware necessary for the tasks authorized by the Council. By February 2001, only 200 UN military personnel had arrived in Congo, and an additional two years passed before the original size of the force authorized by the Council was realized.[10] During the crisis, senior military leadership expressed concern about potential casualties, given the paltry resources available to them and the threat posed by the RCD militia (HRW 2002b: 24). As an analyst on the region asserted, "[t]he mission was terrified of the RCD and their [Rwanda] backers... It was a brutal incident. The RCD were ruthless and very powerful and the UN was in way, way above its head. It was serious fighting and not the business of the mission."[11]

In addition to the perceived threat to peacekeepers, senior UN officials were also worried that use of force would derail the rapidly progressing peace

---

[9] Hardware includes personnel, weaponry, mobility assets, and information-gathering capacities. Software includes such intangibles as training, language skills, technical expertise, and local knowledge.

[10] UN Secretary-General 2001: para. 76.

[11] Phone interview with former analyst and senior UN official, Mar. 2010.

process. Mere months away from signing the Sun City agreement, UN officials were reluctant to do anything that would risk alienating the RCD and thereby jeopardize a potential settlement.[12] Moreover, senior officials in the mission questioned whether, despite their Chapter VII mandate, forceful action would in actual fact garner wider support, given that Anglophone and Francophone interests over Great Lakes policy were at odds in the Security Council (Cilliers 2001; Gegout 2009; Cumming 2011). Both these sets of factors meant that there was little agreement within the mission and across the UN as to whether action was possible or indeed advisable in Kisangani, as well as in other incidents during the war where civilians were imperilled. As Jean-Marie Guéhenno, then Under-Secretary-General for Peacekeeping, warned, "[t]he risks are tremendous. We are taking a gamble" (2002: 78).

While the Kisangani massacre became a hallmark of MONUC's passivity during the war, it was also a watershed event. POC was once again explicitly called for in Resolution 1417 of June 2002, and reaffirmed thereafter in every subsequent resolution for MONUC. In addition, international engagement in Congo and support to the mission increased significantly following the massacre, as tensions in the Security Council dissipated and member states were galvanized by the creation of the TG and the promise of elections. The number of uniformed personnel more than doubled from roughly 4,000 troops during the Kisangani massacre to over 10,000 troops by early 2004. As demonstrated in the analysis of the two cases that follow, this increase in capabilities during the transition enabled the effective implementation of POC in certain contexts, but not in others; for senior UN officials, safeguarding the transition and avoiding any possible escalation of hostilities took precedence over immediate protection concerns.

Bukavu Crisis (2004)

While the Sun City Agreement succeeded in reuniting the country under the TG, it did not bring an end to the violence. The political calculus that underpinned the transition was skewed in favour of President Joseph Kabila. This alienated certain groups, in particular the Rwandan-backed RCD, which faced a precipitous decline in power after controlling nearly two-thirds of the country throughout much of the Congo War (ICG 2005).

In May 2004, fighting broke out in Bukavu, the capital of the province of South Kivu, as ex-RCD officers disputed the terms of their integration into the national army, the Forces Armées de la République Démocratique du Congo (FARDC). The situation quickly escalated when Laurent Nkunda, a

---

[12] Interview with former MONUC official in Kinshasa, Feb. 2011.

renegade ex-RCD general based in North Kivu, launched an attack in support of the dissidents in Bukavu and allegedly to prevent a genocide against the Tutsi community (HRW 2004b). As Nkunda approached the city, FARDC troops fled, unprepared to defend Bukavu from Nkunda's better-equipped force. Emboldened by their flight, Nkunda took Bukavu on 2 June without resistance. The militia raped civilians and pillaged the city, killing more than 100 people and displacing an estimated 24,800 civilians in the region before retreating under international pressure.[13]

While MONUC staff evacuated civilians and provided assistance to those displaced by the crisis, peacekeepers refrained from using force. This occurred despite the fact that, at the time, MONUC had a Chapter VII mandate to protect civilians, had roughly 800 troops stationed around Bukavu, and also had access to attack helicopters and heavy weaponry. According to several military and civilians officials deployed in the east during the crisis, MONUC could have contained the belligerents in Bukavu and "stare[d] down Nkunda's forces had it wanted to."[14] But material capabilities were not the critical issue.

MONUC's failure to defend Bukavu and protect its inhabitants was, rather, the result of conflicting perspectives and directives within the mission at various levels. Unlike during the Kisangani massacre, MONUC officials disagreed greatly on the appropriate course of action. From the beginning of the crisis, MONUC's military leadership and civilian field staff favoured a robust posture to protect civilians. They issued ultimatums to the renegade militia, and a directive reminding UN troops that the mission was operating under a Chapter VII mandate and that force was to be used to "deny entry into the town of non-government forces."[15] Their efforts, however, were undermined in two ways. The first was by a contingent of Uruguayan peacekeepers who, charged with defending the airport on the outskirts of Bukavu, took direction from their own government and capitulated to Nkunda, giving over the facility. Sources say they were instructed by their superiors in Montevideo not to take action that would risk their own bodily harm.[16] Second, and more critically, plans to defend Bukavu were thwarted by the political leadership of the mission in Kinshasa, who ordered the retraction of the ultimatums that had been issued to the militia in Bukavu and transmitted a message to the brigade commander that force was not to be used against Nkunda. When pressed to explain their decisions, the political leadership expressed concern that the use of force by MONUC could have derailed the transition by provoking Rwandan intervention and/or the withdrawal of the RCD from the TG.[17]

---

[13] United Nations, DPKO (Best Practices Unit). 2005. *MONUC and the Bukavu Crisis 2004* (Internal). New York, 2005.

[14] Interview with MONUC official in Goma, Jan. 2009.

[15] United Nations, DPKO 2005: 18.   [16] United Nations, DPKO 2005: 47.

[17] United Nations, DPKO 2005: 18.

The mission's inaction during the Bukavu crisis incurred great opprobrium. A groundswell of public protest and violence towards the government and MONUC rose up across the country. Millions of dollars of UN property was destroyed and staff members received death threats. An internal UN report condemned the mission for failing to uphold its Chapter VII mandate and censured the political leadership for having "undermined the military chain of command and the military concept of operations during the crisis."[18] The report also argued that the threat to the TG was precisely the reason *for* a forceful response. It concluded that "MONUC's failure to use force during the Bukavu crisis smeared the Mission with the taint of impotence and cowardice. It made UN military and civilian personnel objects of contempt to the Congolese people they were supposed to be helping. It emboldened potential enemies of MONUC and of the Transition."[19]

In response to the Bukavu crisis, the Security Council strengthened the "robustness" of MONUC's mandate. Resolution 1565 of October 2004 increased the number of MONUC personnel to 16,700, a number which would grow to nearly 20,000 personnel by the elections in late 2006. Furthermore, MONUC was authorized to "use all necessary means within its capacity and in the areas where its units are deployed" to build "confidence", "discourage violence," and "protect civilians under imminent threat of physical violence".[20] Six months later, in Resolution 1592, MONUC's mandate was strengthened further with the specification that the mission "with all necessary means . . . may use cordon and search tactics to prevent attacks on civilians and disrupt the military capability of illegal armed groups that continue to use violence in those areas."[21] Both resolutions allowed for pre-emptive action.

The Ituri Campaign (2005–2006)

With their new mandate, UN forces launched a military campaign between early 2005 and late 2006 to protect civilians and pacify the country's eastern region so that elections could be held. Ituri, a district of Province Orientale, was the epicentre of this enforcement activity. Employing a carrot-and-stick approach, peacekeepers coerced militias to disarm and used considerable force if they failed to do so. At the peak of the campaign, MONUC conducted an average of fifteen operations per day, most of them supported by attack helicopters.

To oversee the campaign, Secretary-General Annan deployed his own military advisor, Major General Patrick Cammaert, as the Division Commander in eastern Congo. Of Dutch origin, Cammaert had served with the United

---

[18] United Nations, DPKO 2005: 20.   [19] United Nations, DPKO 2005: 22.
[20] United Nations, S/RES/1565 (2004).   [21] United Nations, S/RES/1592 (2005).

Nations Protection Force (UNPROFOR) in Srebrenica. Past UN inaction in
the face of violence greatly informed his approach to peacekeeping. According
to Cammaert, "MONUC [was] obliged to act when directly confronted with
any force attacking/threatening civilians" (Cammaert 2008: 4). Cammaert's
stern command was also bolstered by Dominique McAdams, the head of the
UN's Ituri Office, whom many in the UN itself feared and revered. Her "no
nonsense" approach led some to call her "General" McAdams. "She was her
own SRSG", as one former official described, "she walked into a room and the
military would quiver. There were no two ways about it, she expected us to
take action."[22]

Unlike the Bukavu crisis, there was little contestation within the mission
over the campaign in Ituri, and it was widely trumpeted a success. Under the
direction of Cammaert and McAdams, the leaders of several armed groups
were arrested, entered the DDR process or integrated into the FARDC.
Without these key individuals at the helm, many of the groups dissolved and
roughly 18,000 militia members were demobilized in the lead-up to elections.

A confluence of factors explains why a robust approach to peacekeeping
was realized in this case. First, the risk that military action taken to protect
civilians would result in either an escalation of hostilities or the expulsion of
the mission was largely irrelevant in Ituri. The armed groups against whom
operations were conducted were not party to the Sun City Agreement or to
the TG. Consequently, confronting them did not pose a threat to the stability of the transition; if anything, UN officials asserted that it guaranteed that
the transition stayed on course. Moreover, the possible withdrawal of consent
was not an issue since the armed actors in Ituri had not consented to the mission's deployment or to the peace agreement it was tasked with overseeing.
Second, the concern that robust operations to protect civilians would imperil
peacekeepers themselves did not stymie enforcement action as it had at other
points during the mission. This was in spite of twenty-five peacekeepers losing
their lives in active combat during the campaign—the highest level of fatalities
throughout MONUC's entire deployment.[23] Officials contend that the willingness of troop-contributing countries to sustain such casualties was partly due
to the Council's strong support for the campaign. Between 2003 and 2006,
Ituri figured prominently on the Council's agenda, the resources available to
the mission increased exponentially, and, as several officials noted, the deployment of Cammaert, the Secretary-General's own military advisor, to oversee
the operations conveyed the seriousness of the Council's intent.[24]

---

[22] Interview with UN Official in Kinshasa, Feb. 2011.
[23] United Nations, DPKO, "Fatalities by Year, Mission and Incident Type," <http://www.un.org/en/peacekeeping/resources/statistics/fatalities.shtml>.
[24] Interview with senior UN official in New York, Mar. 2010.

That the POC norm was not implemented universally across the mission during the transition is likely due to the fact that these factors were unique to Ituri. In the Kivus, as in other parts of the country, MONUC remained passive towards those actors either party to or backed by others who were party to the Sun City Agreement. As a senior MONUC official reflected: "Dealing with the Ituri rebels was feasible because they were of secondary importance. The same thing would never have been possible in the Kivus. There was no Rwandan involvement in Ituri and the parties MONUC was using force against were not critical for the transition. In the Kivus they were."[25] Out of the public eye, Nkunda continued to carry out human rights abuses, and in 2006 he produced the Congrès national pour la défense du peuple (CNDP), an armed group that would wreak ever-greater havoc on the population of North Kivu following the elections (Stearns 2008; Scott 2009).

Operation Kimia II (2009)

Despite the high hopes of the international community, elections in Congo did not bring about stability, and in 2008 the Security Council issued Resolution 1856, which acknowledged continued and widespread violence. The resolution was unprecedented in two respects. First, it was the first mandate to designate POC as a mission's highest priority. Second, and in direct response to the influx of abuses committed by government forces, Resolution 1856 specifically authorized the use of force to ensure the protection of civilians "under imminent threat of physical violence... from *any* of the parties engaged in the conflict."[26] While the importance of protection relative to other mission tasks was implicit and action against the FARDC legal under the mission's previous Chapter VII mandate, the explicit injunction in the resolution added an important emphasis and demonstrated the political backing for the mission to take action.

Resolution 1856 was quickly put to the test. In early 2009, a political rapprochement between Rwanda and the Congo led to the CNDP's integration into the FARDC, and the launch of several large-scale offensives by the FARDC against remaining rebel groups in the east (ICG 2010a) These operations were conducted jointly—first with Rwandan forces under Operation Umoja Wetu, and then with the support of MONUC under Operation Kimia II. During Kimia II, MONUC provided significant material, logistical, and operational assistance to the FARDC. However, no sooner had Kimia II commenced, than evidence began to surface of widespread FARDC abuse of civilians and repeated human rights violations, particularly in operational areas where the

---

[25] Interview with senior MONUC official in Kinshasa, Feb. 2011.
[26] United Nations, S/RES/1856 (2008): 4, emphasis added.

newly integrated ex-CNDP forces were deployed (HRW 2009a: 85). These abuses, in addition to those committed by other armed groups, contributed to a precipitous deterioration in security throughout the region. One million people were displaced in 2009 alone. In the words of Philip Alston, UN Special Rapporteur on Extrajudicial, Summary or Arbitrary Executions, the political and humanitarian consequences of the operations were "catastrophic."[27]

MONUC's support to the FARDC during Kimia II was strongly encouraged by Western diplomats in Kinshasa and members of the Council who praised the regional rapprochement, and who now competed to win favour with Kabila's administration in the hopes of securing lucrative mining contracts. To senior UN officials, MONUC's participation precisely suited its mandate. In addition to outlining the mission's protection function, Resolution 1856 affirmed MONUC's commitment to assisting the nascent government, including providing support to the FARDC in operations aimed at disarming foreign and domestic armed groups. Moreover, Alan Doss, the Special Representative of the Secretary-General (SRSG) in Congo, maintained that the mission's protection mandate was precisely why peacekeepers should be involved in the operations, as they would be better placed to ensure that civilians were protected (Doss 2010: 99). Last, and more generally, there was a fear among Congo's international donors that failure to meet the government's request for military support could jeopardize consent for the mission. Kabila had made it clear on several occasions following his election, as one official recounts, "that anyone who dared so much as question his authority was not welcome" in Congo.[28]

These competing interests meant that throughout Kimia II, implementation of the POC norm by UN peacekeepers was highly selective and occurred in a wider context of impunity, in which the mission leadership proved reluctant to confront and condemn the government about human rights abuses committed by or those affiliated to state institutions. When UN forces witnessed abuses by the FARDC, action was not taken. An internal UN report noted that when confronted about their inaction, peacekeepers claimed "that [they] could not stop FARDC who were committing human rights violations against civilians because they were partners."[29] Similarly, suggestions to senior UN officials that force be used to address FARDC violations provoked fiery protestations that such action would never have the backing of the Council. In this respect, "resolution 1856 was disingenuous," as one Western diplomat remarked: "[t]here wasn't the appetite for any action against the FARDC. Everyone knew government forces were a big part of the problem but the use of force against them was unthinkable."[30]

---

[27] United Nations. 2010: 1.

[28] Interview with senior UN official in New York, Mar. 2010.

[29] United Nations, MONUC (Civil Affairs Section), *A Preliminary Assessment of the Impact of the Joint Protection Teams* (Internal), Oct. 2009.

[30] Interview with senior UN official in New York, Mar. 2010.

The leadership's decision to participate in Kimia II, and its uncritical stance towards the government, were virulently contested within the mission. Several officials working within the Civil Affairs and the Human Rights sections of MONUC opposed their superiors' decision to engage in the joint operation from its inception. They cited the FARDC track record of civilian abuse, and argued that the potential backlash and retaliatory measures by other armed groups were likely to be significant. Moreover, in March 2009, civil affairs staff brought forward concerns about the mission's possible complicity in human rights violations by the FARDC and the need for conditionality measures, given that MONUC's operational support was not contingent on the FARDC's adherence to IHL. These concerns echoed formal legal advice given to the mission by the UN Office of Legal Affairs (OLA) in January 2009.

The initial objections of a few within the mission became more widespread as the consequences of Kimia II, as well as abuses by the FARDC, came to light. Civilian and military staff in the field and close to the frontline were amongst the most ardent critics. However, MONUC's leadership gave little weight to their concerns. Specifically, staff complained that their field analyses of the humanitarian and political implications of the operation were regularly dismissed by senior officials in Kinshasa, and that they were sidelined from decision-making forums in which their objections could be raised. Tense relations between field offices and the mission's national headquarters developed, with the former being expected to toe the line of the latter.

MONUC to MONUSCO

After eight months of reinforcing government troops during Kimia II, MONUC eventually limited its support to one FARDC unit, after it was found to be responsible for the slaughter of no fewer than sixty-two civilians.[31] This withdrawal of assistance set a wider precedent. In late 2009, the Council renewed MONUC's mandate in Resolution 1906 and introduced the UN's first-ever conditionality policy, in which the mission's support to Congolese army units was to be contingent on human rights verification and respect for IHL. Days following Resolution 1906, Kimia II was terminated and a new set of operations called Amani Leo ("Peace Today") began.

Amani Leo incorporated the conditionality policy and reiterated POC as a key objective of the operations. However, FARDC abuses continued and, as during Kimia II, peacekeepers did not respond with force. Moreover, challenges in the enforcement of the conditionality policy meant that the UN continued to work alongside miscreant elements of the FARDC, which only

---

[31] Relief Web, "UN Peacekeeping Chief Concludes his Visit to the DRC," 6 Nov. 2009.

further tarnished the mission's credibility. In April 2010, it was reported that General Ntaganda Bosco, an ICC-indicted war criminal, was serving as deputy coordinator of the joint operations despite the government's and MONUC's assurances to the contrary (Smith 2010; McCrummen 2010). In mid-2010, in what many opined was a "rebranding" exercise, MONUC was replaced by MONUSCO. The new mission's emphasis on stabilization has arguably aligned the UN even more closely and compromisingly with the Congolese government (Paddon and Lacaille 2011).

CONCLUSION: IMPLEMENTING POC

The purpose of this chapter has been to analyse the POC norm within UN peacekeeping as an example of the "institutionalization and implementation gap." The Congo case offers several insights for the Betts and Orchard framework and for the study of norms more broadly. I will highlight four contributions before concluding.

First, this chapter introduces and develops the concept of risk, which, with few exceptions, has been largely unexamined by constructivists (Price 2008). While closely related to the structural factors of Betts and Orchard's framework, the formative role played by risk in the Congo case suggests that the character of norms and specifically what normative practice entails warrants greater attention in order to more fully comprehend processes of implementation. An examination of the risks or "costs" associated with certain norms is particularly important given that constructivists tend to work on people-centred issues where the human risks are indeed great, as the contributions by several authors in this volume illustrate.

Second, and closely related, the case study presented in this chapter underscores the need for institutional disaggregation and analysis of the different decision-making pathways during the process of implementation. While Betts and Orchard argue that structural differences and bureaucratic contestation within and across national institutions may mediate how norms play out within particular domestic contexts, the Congo case shows how similar dynamics may shape implementation by international organizations. Peacekeepers do not form a homogeneous group. Contemporary UN missions encompass a diversity of actors that operate at multiple levels (e.g. field, national headquarters, organizational headquarters) with differing bureaucratic and operational identities and interests, capacities, and capabilities. In the Congo, such diversity gave rise to contestation at various levels within the organization as differences arose over what should be the appropriate course of action, based on perceived risks and attendant capabilities.

For example, senior officials in the operational headquarters of the mission were reticent to take any action that could jeopardize consent or risk an escalation in hostilities. This reticence is possibly explained by the close proximity of such actors to the host state and to key stakeholders, and given their seniority, their involvement in formal peace and political processes. Conversely, civilian officials, and in particular those working in the civil affairs and human rights sections, in often-remote field locales, where the day-to-day activities of peacekeeping take place close to violence, were more compelled to engage armed actors when they believed it was within their capacity and when the adverse effects on the population did not outweigh the benefits. By the same token, on several occasions—specifically during the Bukavu crisis—military personnel deployed in the field were unwilling to protect civilians for fear that action could pose risks to themselves. In a country such as the Congo, where mission headquarters and areas of deployment are separated by thousands of miles, these differences were all the more stark.

Third, contestation within the mission revealed a hierarchy of structural factors that shaped implementation. The perceived risk of both escalation of hostilities and the possible revoking of consent and therefore expulsion of the mission provided the dominant explanation for inaction to protect civilians. The former was most evident during the transition period, and stemmed largely from the fear of a possible Rwandan re-invasion and/or the derailing of the TG. The latter issue of consent was of greatest consequence during the post-election period when President Kabila, as elected sovereign, repeatedly threatened expulsion and thus limited what action could be taken against government forces and their allies. Other factors such as risk of casualties also played a role in shaping implementation but were secondary to the other two forms of risk. As indicated by the example of the Ituri campaign, at times peacekeepers from the same countries did use force at considerable risk to themselves.

Perceived risk was moderated by an actor's attendant capacities. While capacity in terms of the resources necessary to implement POC grew steadily over the course of the mission, the cases revealed that such capacity was a necessary but not sufficient condition for action. Without political backing or "top cover" from mission headquarters and New York, often in the form of explicit directives over and above the mandate, action to protect civilians was unlikely. Several factors potentially explain the need for political backing over and above the mandate. (1) The relative "newness" of the norm likely made the need for top cover all the more pressing. MONUC was the second mission to receive a mandate to protect civilians and thus actors may have been more reluctant to undertake implementation without the certainty of political support. (2) The ambiguity of POC and its relationship to other established norms of peacekeeping was also surely a factor. With the exception of Resolution 1856, POC was not explicitly prioritized relative to other mission tasks in the mandate, nor were specifications given as to the type of force to be used and against which parties. Additional assurances and directives from authorities within the institution served as a means to clarify objectives and more precisely what implementation should entail. (3) The risks associated with implementation, particularly of such a new norm, undoubtedly strengthened the need for greater oversight and backing. As one peacekeeper exclaimed "when you fire a shot that has the potential to kill, you want to make sure your superiors have your back."[32]

Last, while structural variables—based on risk and capacity—were central to explaining the variation in peacekeeping practice, the Congo case study underscores the importance of agency; i.e. the ways in which specific individuals or groups within an institution can play a critical role during the process of norm implementation such that certain structural constraints are either further entrenched or overcome. For example, at several junctures, particular individuals in the mission impeded POC's implementation by filtering information that contributed to strategic decision-making and therefore to political backing, and by explicitly blocking action. This form of obstructionism was visible both during the Bukavu crisis and Kimia II, when particular sets of actors exerted their influence to limit the scope of POC's implementation.

In contrast, at other times, individuals figured as "enablers of implementation." For example, the role played by Cammaert and McAdams in Ituri demonstrates how individuals can alter the risk calculus by optimizing the use of resources, by motivating mission personnel, and by garnering the necessary political support to take action. In this respect, Cammaert played a key role in framing POC as commensurate with what it is to be a peacekeeper and used persuasion at various levels of the institution, including beyond the immediate context of implementation, to overcome structural obstacles. This entailed direct communication with troop-contributing countries to obtain assurances of support for implementation, particularly with regard to casualties. These efforts allowed Cammaert to overcome certain structural constraints such as the risk of physical injury and limited resources. Nevertheless, implementation of the norm was to a certain extent still delimited by the risk of escalation and consent, as the campaign in Ituri was not replicated in other areas, such as the Kivus.

In sum, an examination of peacekeeping practice in the Congo reveals how the interplay of both structure and agency explains the puzzling and still problematic variance in the implementation of the POC norm. Protection continues to be illusory for many, if not, most civilians in the Congo.

---

[32] Interview with military official in Goma, Mar. 2011.

Part III

Policy Norms

10

Engineering Policy
Norm Implementation
The World Bank's Transparency Transformation

Catherine Weaver and Christian Peratsakis

Open data is arguably the most prevalent policy norm today, shaping the rules and practices of international aid organizations. Since the 2005 Paris Declaration on Aid Effectiveness, the 2008 Accra Agenda for Action and launch of the International Aid Transparency Initiative (IATI), and the Busan Partnership for Effective Development Cooperation in November 2011, aid donors have committed themselves to the principle of opening access to information on their activities. Advocates view this as a right of citizens and key to aid accountability and effectiveness. Transparency empowers citizens to hold donors and governments accountable for the use of aid funds, reduces information asymmetries that hinder coordination between donors, and improves the predictability of aid flows (Publish What You Fund 2009; Collin et al. 2009; Mulley 2010; McGee and Gaventa 2010, 2011). Aid transparency promises much for a global industry beleaguered by crises of legitimacy, relevance, and effectiveness.

In this chapter, we seek to understand the evolution of the *international aid transparency policy norm*, defined as the shared expectation in the global development aid regime complex that donor agencies make public comprehensive, timely, comparable, and accessible information on their activities, budgets, and other relevant data. We unpack the causal mechanisms of *norm implementation*, defined here as the process through which aid organizations translate the principles of transparency into organizational policies and practices to not only ensure compliance with new rules, but also to engender the internalization of the policy norm's precepts and to incite meaningful and sustainable changes in organizational behaviour. Analyzing the opportunities and constraints on policy norm implementation enables us to examine pervasive cynicism about the capacity and willingness of international organizations to change, or more simply to determine if aid institutions are just talking the transparency talk or walking the transparency walk.

We are thus interested in teasing out the reasons why aid organizations have now—after many decades of incremental steps towards openness—signaled a strong commitment to transparency norms. More critically, we seek to understand the conditions under which aid agencies are willing and able to *implement* policies that uphold this norm. This requires going beyond a story about the agency, institutional processes, and structures that converged to produce the "donor transparency norm cascade" that we have recently observed and beyond a checklist or scorecard of agencies' compliance with transparency norms.[1]

As Betts and Orchard argue in their framework chapter, the process of implementing policy norms in states or international organizations often opens up opportunities for the reinterpretation, fragmentation, and even rejection of the underlying norm. At the same time, policy norm implementation may unfold in a fairly rapid and uncontested manner. This may result from effective advocacy and policy design, which strategically addresses issues of norm imprecision, contestation, and capacity constraints prior to implementation. Such issues can be effectively sorted out during the "policy norm negotiation phase," wherein the nature of negotiation (particularly, decisions regarding who is consulted or included in defining the scope of the policy) matters. Also significant is the preparation period between the signaled commitment to a policy norm and the formal operationalization of those policies. Careful preparation for the implementation phase can even lead to unanticipated *expansion* and *diffusion* of the underlying norm beyond its original objectives.

Indeed, quite to our surprise, we observe the latter instance of negotiation, implementation, and subsequent policy norm expansion in the case study we present here of the implementation of the transparency agenda at the World Bank (hereafter Bank). In late 2009, the Bank was the first organization in the international aid regime to overhaul its information disclosure policy and to take the dramatic steps of publishing extensive information on its projects, development data, and budgets. While previous incremental steps toward transparency were certainly present, in 2009 the Bank shifted from a "positive list" of limited materials available for disclosure to a "negative list" resting on the presumption of automatic access to all materials except those on a carefully defined list of exceptions. This represented a "transformative change" in the Bank's culture and approach toward organizational transparency.[2] According

---

[1] See Publish What You Fund's *Aid Transparency Index* (2011) and the Center for Global Development and Brookings Institution's *Quality of Official Development Assistance* (QuODA) (Birdsall et al. 2011).

[2] Interviews with Caroline Anstey, World Bank Managing Director (2012); Jeff Gutman, former World Bank Director of Operational Policy and Country Services (2011), Chad Dobson (2011), Director of the Bank Information Center; and Owen Barder (2011), Senior Fellow at the Center for Global Development.

to Barbara Lee, Manager of the Aid Effectiveness Unit at the Bank, the Bank shifted "from a hush-hush place to an era of openness" as the result of this policy.[3]

The Bank's embrace of transparency was by no means spontaneous, but rather the result of a protracted debate over its information disclosure policy that surfaced in the early 1990s. The timing of the Bank's long awaited reversal of its information policy reflects, in some sense, a dramatic alignment of ideational and material pressures for greater transparency in the mid-2000s. But it also reflects the fact that those championing transparency at the Bank were well aware of the potential pitfalls of pushing transparency too far, too fast. Advocates inside and outside of the Bank aligned and worked to ensure the passage of an "airtight [access to information, or AI] policy"[4] by the Bank's Board of Executive Directors that would minimize internal and external resistance to the AI policy. They also sought to cultivate an environment for nervous staff wherein compliance would be strictly enforced, while recognizing that "mistakes will happen."[5] Likewise, they pushed for sufficient time for Bank management to establish operational policies, in-house resources for managing public access to and requests for newly released information, and oversight and compliance measures to ensure the policy was quickly mainstreamed into the daily routines of Bank staff.

As a result, we discover here that the effective implementation of the AI policy can be attributed to the careful manner in which the new policy was negotiated, prepared, and executed. Specifically, what strikes us as significant to this outcome is the participatory design of the AI policy and implementation plan; which included the extensive involvement of key actors inside the Bank as well as some of its most vocal external critics. Second, we note the importance of the management of the seven-month implementation preparation period between the end of 2009, when the Board passed the new AI policy, and July 2010, when the policy went into effect. During this preparation period, there was a conscious effort to identify and preempt capacity constraints and potential points of political resistance. The ensuing integration of the AI policy into Bank standard operating practices was both more rapid and smooth than its architects, advocates, and even critics expected.[6]

Furthermore, we find evidence that the successful engineering of the implementation process of the AI policy led to an unexpected expansion of the transparency agenda from a narrow focus on increasing access to information to a broader set of principles now embodied in the Bank's prominent Open Data and Open Development agendas: initiatives that strive to make the Bank's vast storehouse of development data, analytical tools, and research production

---

[3] Quoted in Harris 2011.   [4] Interview with Gutman (2011).
[5] Interviews with Anstey (2012) and Gutman (2011).
[6] Interviews with Anstey (2012), Gutman (2011), Dobson (2011), and Barder (2011).

open, free, and easily accessed by a wider public. From the perspective of many Bank staff and managers we talked to, the surprisingly unproblematic implementation of the AI policy "opened the door" for a broader transparency agenda and "set the ball rolling down the hill"[7] for the "democratization of development" (Zoellick 2010). In turn, the Bank's transparency agenda has started to diffuse to other aid agencies, which are now seeking to adopt similar AI and open data policies in response to changing public expectations regarding aid transparency (Mulley 2010). In other words, the AI policy seems to have spurred, or at least set the stage for, a host of other policies and initiatives that we can broadly construe to constitute an aid transparency norm complex in the international aid regime.

In this chapter, we draw insights regarding the dynamics of policy norm implementation by focusing on what we see as the *successful* story of the AI policy at the Bank. We do not do so naively. We recognize that the AI policy itself is not free of criticism. Some may dispute our view that this is a successful case of policy norm implementation, pointing to instances where the Bank has resisted releasing information or put limits on the scope of disclosure. Watchdog organizations, for example, lament the rules against simultaneous disclosure of important Board documents (such as transcripts of Board meetings) and other areas of exceptions in the new AI policy. Moreover, the policy is also quite new. It may well be that as vigilant oversight of implementation and enforcement of the AI policy wanes, behaviour in the Bank may "revert to the mean." But most experts with whom we have spoken confidently assert (and we agree) that "this is one genie you cannot put back into the bottle."[8]

More provocatively, what we also note in our case study is a more critical discussion of the transparency agenda and what "implementation" actually means. As we will discuss in the conclusion, transparency is embraced not just as a goal in itself, but as essential for improving aid accountability and impact. As such, much attention has now shifted from "Phase I" of the transparency agenda (the supply and implementation of aid transparency policies) towards "Phase II," which entails demonstrating how and when more open information actually leads to enhanced aid accountability and effectiveness. For many involved in the Bank's open development initiative and the global aid transparency movement, full implementation of the transparency agenda requires evidence that transparency policies are in fact facilitating the achievement of this deeper objective. As norm implementation progresses, the goal line appears to be shifting.

In this chapter, we use qualitative process tracing and draw extensively on primary and secondary materials from inside and outside the Bank. We also use evidence from interviews with several key actors central to the design and

---

[7] Interview with Gutman (2011).   [8] Interview with Anstey (2012).

execution of the Bank's new AI policy and the subsequent open data initiative. We further draw insights on aid transparency from over 100 interviews we conducted in Africa and the US in 2011 as part of our work tracking and mapping climate change aid. Finally, we also benefit from both non-participant and participant observation in aid transparency efforts, facilitated by our ongoing collaboration with AidData, Development Gateway, and the World Bank Institute's Open Aid Partnership.

THE TRANSPARENCY TRANSFORMATION AT THE WORLD BANK: A PERFECT NORM STORM?

In 1985, the Bank established its first set of staff guidelines on public information disclosure. This was in response to demands of activists concerned about the impact of Bank programs on the populations and environments of developing countries. In the next twenty years, three significant revisions in the Bank's information disclosure policies were made. The first was in 1994 (the year of the "Fifty Years is Enough" campaign), when the Bank established its first official disclosure policy. This coincided with the creation of the Independent Inspections Panel and the opening of the Bank's Public Information Center (Bissell 2009). The 1994 policy ostensibly worked on a presumption of disclosure. But in fact not all Bank data and documents were eligible for disclosure, unless they were on a short list of permissible items—a so-called "positive list." For example, in 1993, it was nearly impossible for an interested party to obtain through official channels timely and detailed information on lending agreements, individual projects, or even announcements (much less minutes or transcripts) of Board meetings.

In response to shifting demands regarding informational disclosure, the World Bank incrementally revised its "positive list," roughly every two years. For example, in 1998, the Bank made Country Assistance Strategy papers public, albeit only with the permission of the country in question. In 2001 the Board expanded the list quite substantially, and also revised the archival policies to make it slightly less difficult to access historical materials (World Bank 2005).

By 2002, partially in response to mounting external pressure for greater transparency (see below), the Bank's management began to discuss deeper policy changes.[9] In 2003, the Board of Executive Directors debated the disclosure of Board minutes and other deliberative process materials. However, the "presumption in favor of disclosure" remained limited by the existence of the

---

[9] In 2002, the Bank also established a global network of Public Information Centers to enhance public access outside of the US, by filling requests for information when documents could be disclosed.

cumbersome positive list, which many within the Bank felt to be ambiguous and difficult to interpret.

The third and most substantial change in the Bank's informational disclosure policy—the subject of our more detailed analysis—began to percolate in the mid-2000s. By this time, there was a near perfect storm of internal and external pressures pushing for deeper change in the Bank's policies.

External Pressures for Bank Transparency

The first external factor generating pressure for greater transparency was the *iRevolution*. The iRevolution refers to the explosion of widely accessible technological tools, such as the internet, GPS, and social media. These technological tools dramatically changed the ease of physically accessing information, as well as people's expectations regarding the availability of data (Mulley 2010). The rapid global expansion of mobile phones in particular generated new ways to reach intended aid beneficiaries, and spurred the growth of open government (or "Government 2.0") movements in both the developed and developing world.

The influence of technological change on the Bank's transparency was reinforced by a parallel movement in extractive industries, a sector that frequently involved Bank lending. In 2002, UK Prime Minister Tony Blair launched the Extractive Industries Transparency Initiative (EITI) to fight pervasive corruption, human and labour rights violations, and systemic non-compliance with environmental and social safeguards. EITI had a notable influence on the later inception of the International Aid Transparency Initiative (IATI) and the Bank's own efforts to be more transparent in two manners. First, member states and organizations in EITI voluntarily signed onto a transparency initiative in which their own activities were under scrutiny. Secondly, EITI provided guidance on how civil society and governments could operate together to increase transparency. The Bank, which endorsed the EITI principles in 2003, saw EITI as integral to not only its own extractive resource tracking, but also as complementary to its own Governance and Anti-Corruption Strategy (World Bank 2007; Haufler 2010). A year later the Bank assumed responsibility to oversee EITI's managed trust fund.

A third external factor was the growth in domestic *access to information policies* (or Freedom of Information Acts, FOIAs) and *open government* movements around the world. By 2007, over seventy countries had passed some form of a FOIA (Calland and Neuman 2007). The influence of this was evident in the Board's discussion of the Bank's information disclosure policies between 2001 and 2009. Both internal documents and our interviews emphasized that Executive Directors from countries with strong FOIA traditions—particularly India, Mexico, and the United States—were vocal proponents of similar freedom of information policies at the Bank. At the same time, these countries advised the Bank to approach freedom of information slowly and incrementally, as if "peeling an onion," in order to build broad support and develop the institutional capacity to manage a robust freedom of information system.[10]

Overall, the evolving discussions of transparency and AI policies at the Bank took place in the context of increasing scrutiny of aid accountability and effectiveness by donor and recipient states, as well as a groundswell of NGO campaigns for fundamental reform of the entire international aid system. Stagnating economies in Europe and North America dampened the enthusiasm of taxpayers and politicians alike for spending on aid. Likewise, the post-9/11 era revealed a marked decline in demand for Bank loans, particular from middle income countries, such as Brazil, India, and Mexico, which had high growth rates and easy access to international commercial markets. This general shift in the supply and demand side of aid spurred efforts to address underlying weaknesses in the aid system, starting with the United Nations International Conference on Financing for Development in Monterrey, Mexico in 2002.[11] The Bank and other aid organizations faced pressure to demonstrate their legitimacy and performance-based results. Internally, this was closely entangled with discussions of transparency.[12]

The final and most prevalent external factor was the cumulative pressure of NGO campaigns. For decades, NGOs led a concerted and sustained campaign against the Bank's secretive culture. NGO demands for greater transparency were especially prominent at the Gleneagles G8 Summit in 2005 (Mulley 2010). The following year, the Global Transparency Initiative (GTI), a network of civil society organizations promoting openness in the international financial institutions (IFIs), was established. Its focus was to "promote people's right to information from public institutions and a right to participate in the development policies and projects that affect their lives." GTI went so far as to draft a model policy for the World Bank's Access to Information Policy in early 2009, many parts of which later appeared in the real policy adopted by the Bank (GTI 2009).[13]

The Bank Information Center (BIC), a leading NGO aid watchdog group within the GTI, was a central player up to and during the 2009 AI policy negotiations. For years, BIC had ardently pushed the Bank to move from a positive to negative list, and also advocated for the disclosure of particularly sensitive materials such as draft country programming plans, project appraisal

---

[10] Interview with Gutman (2011) and Anstey (2012). See also World Bank 2012.

[11] Monterrey was followed by a series of High Level Forums on Aid Effectiveness, in Rome in 2003, Paris in 2005, Accra, Ghana, in 2008, and Busan, South Korea, in 2011.

[12] Interview with Gutman (2011).

[13] In addition to the NGOs and campaigns already mentioned, some of the most prominent watchdog NGOs with respect to the aid transparency and accountability movement include AidInfo, Aid Watch, BetterAid, Bretton Woods Project, EURODAD, and Reality of Aid Initiative.

and policy documents, and access to Board documents (Jenkins 2009). In late 2007, the Bank reached out to BIC to help coordinate the Bank's external consultations in thirty-three countries of its new draft AI policy paper. Carolyn Anstey, one of the key architects of the new AI policy and (as of June 2013) one of the three Managing Directors of the Bank, argues that having an NGO partner, like BIC, as a standard bearer was helpful to the Bank's evolving stance on its own AI policy and building external support for the policy.[14] BIC later became a member of the AI Working Group, in charge of preparing for the Bank's policy implementation in 2010–11.[15]

Internal Pressures for Bank Transparency

The intensification of external pressures converged with internal pressures for reform. Foremost amongst the internal factors was the Bank's ongoing Governance and Anticorruption (GAC) agenda, which started under President James Wolfensohn (1995–2005) and gathered momentum under President Paul Wolfowitz (2005–7).[16] The GAC agenda demanded that aid-receiving countries publish information about their procurement processes, budgets, and other public spending. In 2011, shortly after the passage of the AI policy and the launch of the Open Data Initiative,[17] President Robert Zoellick gave a speech on freedom of information in developing countries, in which he asserted that the Bank "will not lend directly to finance budgets in countries that do not publish their budgets or, in exceptional cases, at least commit to publish their budgets within twelve months" (Zoellick 2011).

Such expectations for transparency and accountability on the part of borrower governments naturally rebounded on the Bank. The Bank's 2007 strategy paper on implementing the GAC agenda specified the need for more transparency and accountability in the Bank's own internal conduct in order to set an example for others and to demonstrate that the Bank lived up to its own ideals (World Bank 2007, 2009, 2012; Volcker et al. 2007). In the words of Shaida Badiee, Director of the Bank's Development Data Group, "if we are going to support Open Data and Open Government in countries, the World Bank must not only preach it, but also do it."[18]

---

[14] Interview with Anstey (2012).

[15] Jenkins 2009; World Bank 2012; interviews with Jenkins (2009), Dobson (2011), Gutman (2011), and Anstey (2012).

[16] Interview with Gutman 2011. See also Weaver 2008; World Bank 2011a, 2012.

[17] In April 2010, as a part of the Bank's new AI policy, President Robert Zoellick announced the launch of the Open Data Initiative. It is an effort to make data at the Bank, including the World Development Indicators, free and publicly available.

[18] Remarks at "Putting Open Government into Action" event at the World Bank, Washington, DC, 23 Feb. 2012.

In addition to the momentum of the GAC agenda, the *role of internal advocates and leadership* at the Bank helps explain the timing and substance of the AI policy shift in 2009. The ongoing debate in the Board of Executive Directors is especially pertinent here. There is substantial evidence that by 2004 some Executive Directors were making the case for more open access with respect to policy and strategy papers related to operations (World Bank 2005). Of particular importance were the internal discussions over disclosure of documents related to Board deliberations. In a series of meetings between 2004 and 2005, the Executive Directors discussed the disclosure of Board minutes, drawing on the experience of other international financial institutions (such as the Inter-American Development Bank and Asian Development Bank).

Informal notes between the Executive Directors in 2005 indicate "an emerging consensus to move toward greater transparency in this respect, with the understanding that the content of Board minutes would not change from its present form" (World Bank 2005: 4). The proposal to increase the transparency of Board discussions was approved, but with several caveats: material deemed by the Board to be too sensitive would be redacted prior to disclosure, and Board transcripts, summaries of discussion, committee minutes, and reports to the Board (called "green sheets") would not be disclosed. The Board also solicited a cost-benefit study of simultaneous disclosure, designed to assess the possibility of further disclosure creating opportunities for "undue pressure from special interest groups" or risks of "loss of candor." Despite some evident reluctance on the part of Board to go the distance on the release of deliberative documents, the progressive discussion of disclosure reform attracted some much desired praise from external watchdog groups (Kovach et al. 2003). Momentum was building, ever so slowly, at the level of the Board.

Arguably, the final and most important impetus for the 2009 AI policy shift came from Bank management, especially then President Robert Zoellick. Arriving in the wake of the Wolfowitz scandal (Weaver 2008), Zoellick signaled that the Bank's transparency and accountability would be his key priority. He quickly and quietly set about to revitalize the Bank from the inside out (Mallaby 2012).

Interviews with Bank staff reveal that Zoellick was keen to solidify the Board's support for the transparency agenda and willing to exercise his authority to overrule reticent managers and staff. During the implementation stage, Zoellick made it clear that the new AI policy would be put into place quickly and effectively. Resources needed for this (and later for the Open Data Initiative) would be reallocated from existing budgets, already suffering from seven years of zero per cent growth. Moreover, there would be no tolerance for non-compliance. Vice-presidents would report directly to Zoellick on the progress of the AI policy implementation and would be held responsible for lax enforcement within their units.

Zoellick was supported by a cadre of Bank managers in External Affairs (EXT) and Operations Policy and Country Services (OPCS). Carolyn Anstey was especially important in mobilizing internal resources for the AI policy reform and later the Open Data Initiative. Anstey formerly served as a country director for Haiti, where she worked extensively with NGOs on the monitoring of government budget transparency. That experience made her keenly aware of the power of involving citizens in transparency and accountability movements, and is one reason she reached out to BIC and supported an extensive external consultation process during the drafting and implementation of the AI policy.[19]

IMPLEMENTING THE ACCESS TO INFORMATION POLICY AT THE WORLD BANK

According to the World Bank's 2009 Approach Paper, "the disclosure policy and its effective implementation rank[ed] high in the Bank's corporate agenda" (World Bank 2009: 1). The paper concisely summarizes the strong consensus that had emerged over the previous several years:

> the existence of such a positive list has limited the Bank's ability to implement the expressed presumption in favour of disclosure. The policy is also not clear about what cannot be disclosed, and there are many ambiguous and overlapping rules that cumbersome and difficult for Bank staff to implement, and for the public to understand. At the same time, public interest in transparency has been growing. Many countries have adopted freedom of information legislation and the transparency standards of international financial institutions are subject to increased public scrutiny. Both within and outside the Bank, many feel that the Bank's disclosure policy framework still does not go far enough. (World Bank 2009: 1)[20]

The resulting policy, renamed Access to Information,[21] was passed by the Board in December 2009. The new policy maintained critical exemptions to disclosure that reflect continued concerns over the need to protect client confidences and preserve candour in key deliberations (see appendix 2). Many of the exemptions, particularly related to Board documents,[22] were not warmly

---

[19] Interview with Anstey (2012), Gutman (2011), and Dobson (2011).

[20] The 2009 approach paper provides extensive detail on the ambiguity of procedural rules, the lack of institutional resources to serve request for information, and general confusion over which documents and data were eligible for disclosure. See World Bank 2009: 2–6.

[21] Several people we interviewed noted that the term "information disclosure" was considered out of fashion by 2009. "Access to information" is considered to be better aligned with democratic principles, insofar as it highlights citizens' rights to information, not only governments' (or organizations') obligations to provide information.

[22] Specifically, the old policy barred the simultaneous disclosure of confidential information pertaining to Board proceedings, verbatim transcripts of Board and committee discussions, and

received by external critics, but were largely seen as a necessary compromise in order to "strike an appropriate balance between the need to grant maximum public access to information in the Bank's possession, and its obligations to respect the confidentiality of its clients, shareholders, employees, and third parties" (World Bank 2009: 2).

Overall, the proposed policy was characterized as nothing less than a "paradigm shift" (World Bank 2009, 2010a). It moved the Bank away from the infamous "positive" list to a "negative" list, consciously limited to narrow set of items exempted from automatic disclosure. The policy was intended to align the Bank with its espoused commitment to the "presumption of disclosure" and make publicly available vast numbers of hitherto closely guarded documents, including those related to ongoing aid projects (e.g. Implementation Status Reports). It was also designed to mirror disclosure policies adopted in numerous countries through FOIAs, and "put the Bank at the forefront of other multilateral agencies with respect to disclosure" (World Bank 2009: 15).

Importantly, the background papers on the policy revisions and our interviews indicate that the ultimate scope and content of the AI policy was the result of learning from past policy revisions. It was also an exhaustive and inclusive process for designing the revised policies that gave voice and influence to critical groups inside and outside of the Bank. This participatory negotiation process generated widespread political support for the new AI policy prior to its formal adoption, while also allowing for careful consideration of where the policy might meet resistance during its implementation.

The architects of the AI policy approached the process of implementation in a very cautious and strategic manner.[23] This was actually against the preferences of President Zoellick, who wanted the policy immediately implemented after the Board approval in December 2009. Instead, the new constructed Disclosure Policy Committee insisted on a period of six to seven months to prepare for implementation.

The preparation period was consciously designed to give the Bank time to put into place sufficient institutional resources, oversight mechanisms, and compliance measures. Strategic planning for the policy implementation included extensive consultation with NGOs (especially the aforementioned BIC) and their participation in testing the new system to identify unforeseen bottlenecks in accessing the vast amounts of newly disclosed information (World Bank 2010a). In addition, the new AI policy established an appeals

---

documents prepared by staff for the Board. The new policy presumes that Board papers will be disclosed at the end of the deliberative process, but any materials classified as confidential or strictly confidential will not be disclosed unless the Board specifically provides authorization. World Bank 2009: 7–8. Classified materials are subject to disclosure after twenty years.

[23] These architects came from within the Bank's External Affairs Office (EXT), Operational Policy and Country Services (OPCS) and the Legal Department (LEG), among other units.

process that insured continued NGO participation in the Bank's development and initial implementation of the policy (World Bank 2010a).

The preparation period between December 2009 and September 2010 further focused on securing Board approval to declassify more than 17,000 documents. In addition, the 2010 AI policy moved the locus of the Bank's documents from the Public Information Centers to the World Bank's external website, using the preparation period to build and strengthen its technical infrastructure and in-house information management systems.

Predictably, there was considerable anxiety regarding how the Bank staff and management would respond to the new policy. The implementation architects were quite concerned that staff would resist the new policy. This was not because staff did not believe in making the Bank more transparent, as there was very little dissent on this general principle. Instead, staff reluctance stemmed from concerns regarding resources, candour, and uncertainty.

Some Bank staff feared that opening the Bank would mean a loss of revenue in instances where the Bank charged for access to information and data. This was particularly the case within the Development Economics vice-presidency (DEC) and its Development Data unit, who used the sale of development indicators (now accessible through the Open Data Initiative) to help offset the cost of collecting, compiling, analyzing, and reporting data. Zoellick, however, assured DEC that the Bank would suffer no revenue loss (and would even experience a revenue gain) by releasing the data.[24]

There was also concern that public exposure would compel staff to be less candid in key project documents like Implementation Status Reports, which were critical for mid-course corrections in lending programs. The AI policy team defended the disclosure by arguing that disclosure would *improve* candour by promoting greater accountability and access to third-party information and incentivizing staff to produce higher quality reports. But more compelling was the built-in oversight mechanism:

> the main indicator of candour is the "realism index" which measures the extent to which the current ratings of projects in the portfolio reflect the average rating of projects at exit over the recent past. But, at any point in time, the number of operations classified as being in "problem" status is well below the average for the

---

[24] A similar debate occurred within the context of the Zoellick's effort to "democratize development economics" (Zoellick 2010) by not only opening public access to key development databases like the World Development Indicators, but also by supporting the creation of open source analytical tools (such as PovcalNet and ADePT) that would empower people outside of the Bank to access datasets and draft publications, and replicate the Bank's analytical work in areas such as calculations of global poverty figures. Martin Ravallion, Senior Economist at DEC, calls this the "wholesale retailing" of development economics. Bank economists feared this would interfere with their first mover advantages in publishing the results of their data collection and analysis and run up against copyright rules in peer-reviewed journals where they are encouraged to publish: Ravillion 2010; interviews with Anstey (2012) and Gutman (2011).

projects that exit the portfolio. During the first 18 months following the adoption of the revised policy, Management [will] closely monitor the implications of the changes in the policy on candour, including the realism index. (World Bank 2009: 20)

Arguably, the most important part of the implementation plan focused on preparing staff for the policy change. This was a daunting task in an organization that includes over 15,000 staff, with high turnover, with a large DC headquarters and over 100 mission offices worldwide. To prepare staff, upper Bank management enacted a series of measures to educate and train staff on the new AI policy. For example, numerous materials were compiled and disseminated, and an internal AI website with helpdesk was created. Training sessions were held on how to classify and declassify materials. Bank vice-presidents designated 189 staff to serve as AI focal points to provide staff support as well as provide feedback on implementation challenges.

Rigorous oversight and compliance measures were put in place. Most prominent was the *mandatory* AI e-learning program during the first few months after the formal adoption of the AI policy. Completion reports were compiled and distributed every two weeks to all the vice-presidents, who publicized a list of those who had not yet completed the training. Severe sanctions were threatened: staff were repeatedly told that failure to complete the e-learning program would result in the loss of their email privileges.[25] This proved extremely effective. One staff member we spoke with said, "I can confirm the seriousness with which the staff awareness of the policy was approached. Within my VPU, we were regularly reminded of the need to do the training module, lists of non-complying staff were circulated on several occasions and the VPs office did pursue staff who had not done the training module. The threat to cut off email access was taken seriously. The training module was actually not bad either."[26]

Overall, the preparation for the implementation period involved an impressive amount of foresight and attention to detail. The AI Working Group (now AI Committee) established vigilant monitoring mechanisms and the published detailed progress reports every quarter during the first year and annually thereafter. The progress reports, produced by the Bank's Legal Department and published online, provide extensive information on internal compliance rates with the mandatory e-learning program (now near 100 per cent) as well as a precise list of all public access requests (with time taken for the requests to be filled) and all appeals (with data on which appeals were granted and reasons provided for those that were not) (World Bank 2010b, 2010c, 2011b, 2012).

---

[25] Interviews with Gutman (2011) and Anstey (2012). See also World Bank 2011c.
[26] Email correspondence with Jeff Chelsky, 10 Mar. 2012.

Thus, by the time the 2010 policy was formally adopted, everything was in place for a smooth transition. Opportunities for policy norm contestation or rejection in the implementation phrase were effectively preempted. A strong consensus was built, reinforced by oversight and control mechanisms and a clear delegation of responsibilities regarding policy enforcement. The architects of the AI implementation plan were nonetheless surprised a year later to see how smoothly and quickly the AI policy took hold.[27] According to one staff member we interviewed, "change does not usually come that quickly in the Bank!"

CONCLUSION: THE DIFFUSION—AND LIMITS?—OF AID TRANSPARENCY

When governments democratize their data, magic happens.

(Vivek Kundra, Executive Vice President of Emerging Markets, SalesForce; formerly Chief Information Officer, USA)

We've seen that magic happen at the World Bank.

(Shaida Badiee, Director of Development Data, World Bank[28])

The Bank's 2011 Access to Information Annual Report opens by calling the AI policy a "radical policy shift" which "has heightened the World Bank's interaction with the public...and positively impacted the development community by broadly encouraging other development institutions to adopt similar public access policies, which has helped to push forward the objective of aid transparency and accountability" (World Bank 2012: 1; see also BIC 2010). The report goes on claim that in FY2011, the Bank's Documents and Reports database received more than one million visits, 4.5 million page views, and 795,000 downloads (World Bank 2012).

Since 2010, the Bank has placed on its website almost all of its project and program documents (the first aid organization to do so). The Bank has also made a concerted effort to facilitate access to the Bank's financial data through an open access website and a mobile application (World Bank 2011b). These steps, in turn, have earned the Bank top scores on many external transparency indices and aid performance scorecards (Publish What You Fund 2011; Birdsall et al. 2011; Easterly and Williamson 2011; Ghosh and Kharas 2011).

---

[27] Interviews with Gutman (2011), Dobson (2011), and Anstey (2012). See also George 2012 and World Bank 2011b (quoting Neil Fantom, head of the World Bank's Open Data Initiative).
[28] Remarks at Putting Open Government into Action, event at the World Bank, Washington, DC, 23 Feb. 2012.

Once seen as the bastion of secrecy, the Bank is now held up as a model of best practice.[29]

The Bank's embrace of transparency through its AI policy has contributed to the growth of other major aid transparency initiatives. The most prominent of these agendas is the aforementioned Open Data Initiative, which makes available to the public—at no cost—the Bank's immense collection of development data, including the once pricey World Development Indicators. The World Bank also initiated a data visualization campaign by mapping all of its active aid projects worldwide through its "Mapping for Results" program. This is an unprecedented exercise in transparency, widely lauded in the press, and has spurred a virtual "geomapping" race between international aid agencies aspiring to attract similar accolades.

To our minds, there is clear and persuasive evidence of the diffusion and expansion of the transparency norm within World Bank, with the successful implementation of the AI policy appearing to have a catalytic role or "multiplier effect." However, it also appears to have incited a broadening of the norm itself. More critically, we observe a new discourse on transparency norms, focused not on the principle or means of transparency, but rather on the relationship between transparency and accountability.

In this sense, the aid transparency policy norm is shifting from seeing transparency as the end to seeing it as a means to greater accountability. Inside the Bank, this is discussed as a shift from "Phase I" of the Open Development agenda to "Phase II," moving beyond information access to ensuring that this information enables citizens to hold their governments—and the Bank itself—accountable for the impact of development assistance. Moreover, transparency is expected to empower citizens by arming them with the data and tools to produce their own development knowledge and innovative development solutions.

It is here, in Phase II of the policy norm implementation, that norm precision starts to fall apart. Thus far, there is little evidence of transparency's causal effects on aid accountability and effectiveness (Fox 2007; Manning 2010; Mulley 2010; McGee and Gaventa 2010, 2011). Very few studies to date test whether increased transparency results in effects such as increased aid predictability, improved coordination between aid donors and between donors and government, or more "stakeholder ownership" of the development process (Fox 2007; McGee 2013; Joshi 2011).

In Phase II, we also anticipate areas of normative contestation and fragmentation. We have already observed public discussion on whether the "supply side" of the aid transparency movement has in fact moved ahead of

---

[29] According to Chad Dobson, Executive Director of the BIC, "the World Bank's Access to Information Policy continues to set the standard for other institutions to strive for" (quoted in George 2012).

the "demand side." As Sarah Mulley argues, "more progress been made on transparency and accountability *of* than transparency and accountability *to*" (Mulley 2010: 5; italics added). Vivek Kundra observes: "how do you make sure we're measuring impact, and not just the number of datasets?"[30]

A final question concerns how much the transparency transformation at the Bank will be emulated by other aid institutions, leading to the policy norm's implementation throughout the global aid regime complex. Pressures for adoption and implementation of aid transparency policies at other aid agencies are very similar, but constraints vary, leading to considerable differences in the degree of openness between aid agencies today. There are several factors which may influence whether and how other multilateral or bilateral organizations implement transparency agendas, including donor state pressure, recipient state interests, bureaucratic politics, the commitment of organizational leaders, institutional structure (especially degree of decentralization and autonomy of mission offices), diffuse or focused civil society and NGO pressure, and peer pressure from other aid agencies. There are also likely to be pervasive technical and resource capacity constraints on implementation. While such material constraints were certainly present at the Bank, they were not insurmountable, and the World Bank is a relatively wealthy and well-endowed institution compared to its peers.

It is also not clear that the aid transparency policy norm, while similarly institutionalized across institutions, will be similarly implemented and enforced. The International Aid Transparency Initiative (IATI) tries to ensure that this does happen, by constructing a common set of rules and expectations for aid reporting. Yet getting aid agencies (or more accurately their states, in the case of bilateral aid agencies) to sign on to IATI is just the first political hurdle. The deeper challenge is getting the signatories to actually input data into IATI's platform. For many agencies with different data collection and reporting procedures, the transaction costs of adhering to the IATI standard may be quite high, requiring significant institutional investment in converting complex raw data into a simple, "digestible," form for the general public. This in turn requires reallocation of scarce staff time and resources, and a difficult culture change in the organization's reporting habits.

At this point, what we observe in terms of the rather remarkable story of the successful engineering of transparency norm implementation at the Bank may not tell the whole story of the policy norm's life-cycle in the broader international aid regime complex. Yet it does seem to be the case that, even in the face of implementation challenges in different international organizations, this is one policy norm whose underlying principles and practices have indelibly shaped the contemporary global governance of development.

---

[30] Remarks at Putting Open Government into Action, event at the World Bank, Washington, DC, 23 Feb. 2012.

11

From Principle to Policy
The Emergence, Implementation, and Rearticulation of the Right to Post-Conflict Property Repossession

Miriam J. Anderson

For much of history, those who lost their homes during war had little hope of ever returning to them. This has begun to change since the Second World War, however, culminating in the 2005 establishment of universal principles in favour of repossessing one's home following armed conflict. The norm of post-conflict property repossession has evolved interactively between institutionalization and implementation between 1945 and the present through three key stages: *initial* institutionalization, implementation, and *informed* institutionalization. It was first institutionalized during the Cold War by calls from UN bodies for those displaced during particular conflicts to return to their homes, such as in Israel and Cyprus, as well as by the establishment of international principles such as non-expulsion and private property protection. The first attempts at implementation occurred, beginning in the 1990s, in jurisdictions including: Bosnia-Herzegovina, Croatia, Georgia, Guatemala, Kosovo, and Rwanda, among others. These implementation attempts brought to the fore various inconsistencies in practice across cases such as: varying types of sub/ownership rights, inheritance, secondary occupation, and a time limit on return.

The attempts at post-conflict property restitution in the 1990s spurred the articulation of principles regarding property and housing rights relevant to refugees and internally displaced persons (IDPs) by the UN Sub-Commission on the Promotion and Protection of Human Rights in 2005, in the form of the United Nations Principles on Housing and Property Restitution for Refugees and Displaced Persons (the Pinheiro Principles). Prior to the Pinheiro Principles, the norm of post-conflict restitution existed, though it was diffusely distributed across a range of international instruments and repossession regimes. However, the norm remained underspecified, as the problems that occurred in the large-scale restitution regimes established in the 1990s indicate. In particular, the norm was vague; specifying only that those displaced from their homes as a result of conflict had the right to return to them, leaving unspecified in which cases the norm should apply, during which time period, and how return and repossession should be undertaken.

The national restitution regimes, particularly in Bosnia-Herzegovina and Croatia, triggered recognition that clear guidelines were needed at the international level to define the right of return specifically to one's home of origin. The Pinheiro Principles mark informed institutionalization of the right of refugees and internally displaced persons to repossess their properties lost during conflict. They reflect an attempt to resolve a number of problematic issues that were encountered during various efforts at repossession worldwide and especially in the former Yugoslavia. As a policy formulated by an international body, the Principles represent a significant milestone in the institutionalization of the right to post-conflict property repossession. However, the Principles were formulated based on repossession regimes that had particular characteristics. For example, the respective populations who had lost their homes had been displaced shortly before the establishment of the repossession programs. Additionally, the repossession regimes had taken place in environments where, by and large, a Western conception of property prevailed. The norm as currently articulated, then, is limited by the various attributes of previous attempts at implementation. Therefore, implementation regimes in post-conflict states with different characteristics will be required in order to enable a more detailed articulation of the norm. Such attempts might include cases such as Israel/Palestine, Cyprus, and Kashmir, where repossession claims have been outstanding for decades.

This chapter argues that the evolution of the norm of post-conflict property repossession follows a trajectory where implementation and institutionalization have an interactive relationship: Institutionalization allows for implementation, which, in turn, spurs greater precision in norm articulation. To demonstrate that relationship, this chapter is organized into the following three sections. The first section discusses the establishment of the general principles of human rights in the aftermath of the Second World War and the advent of calls for post-conflict property repossession which marked *initial* institutionalization. The second section provides an overview of the first major attempts at large-scale post-conflict property repossession following the break-up of the former Yugoslavia, indicating implementation. The final section discusses the creation of the Pinheiro Principles, which can be understood as *informed* institutionalization.

STAGE I: GENERAL PRINCIPLES AND INITIAL NORM INSTITUTIONALIZATION

The emergence of the right for refugees and internally displaced persons to return to their homes following a conflict marked a clear departure from previous international norms and practice (Anderson 2011). Refugee flows were historically a feature of state formation (Zolberg 1983) or the result of "pathological homogenization," more generally (Rae 2002). Aristide R. Zolberg (1983) suggests that refugees are produced by the transformation of empires into nation-states. This is because while empires require "only minimal involvement on the part of the subject population [which is limited to] obedience and material tribute," the nation-state requires that "the population...be transformed into individuals who visibly share a common nationality; the process entails an actualization of the myth that they are quite literally 'born together,' that they constitute a natural community" (Zolberg 1983: 36).

Examples of minority expulsion occurred in medieval Spain, for instance. In 1492, Spain expelled between 120,000 and 150,000 Jews, about 2 percent of its total population (Rae 2002: 31–2). Spain expelled its Muslim population, beginning in 1609 and continuing for several years, deporting 275,000 to North Africa (Rae 2002: 32). Between 1577 and the 1630s Spain expelled about 115,000 (about 14 percent of the total population of the Low Countries) Protestants (roughly equivalent to present-day Belgium) (Rae 2002: 32). Rather than exceptions, these cases exemplify a persistent pattern in nation-building.

Rae suggests that "pathological homogenization" has been an "enduring feature" of international history (2002: 1), which has been attempted by a variety of strategies, including legally excluding minority groups from citizen rights, and forced conversion or assimilation, or expulsion and extermination (Rae 2002: 5). Although the practice of expulsion has continued, the difference between the international concern for or view of refugees has changed during the past century. The first attempts to protect minorities were introduced by the League of Nations. However, it operated on a "racial conception" of the nation and the League itself approved of population exchanges (Rae 2002: 302). It was not until following the Second World War that clearly articulated norms that prohibited "pathological homogenization" were introduced in the form of various human and minority rights conventions, as well as in the Genocide Conventions (Rae 2002: 302).

"Population transfer" was previously seen as a legitimate means of nation-building (Jackson-Preece 1998: n. 41) and there are numerous examples to be found in the twentieth century (Anderson 2011). In fact, it was believed that the transfer of ethnic minorities was a viable solution to "nationality problems" (Schechtman 1962: p. ix) and that creating ethnically homogeneous communities would ease existing or potential ethnic tensions (Rosand 1998: 1096). Population transfers were included in the 1913

Convention of Adrianople between Bulgaria and Turkey which called for the voluntary exchange between Bulgarians in Turkey and Muslims in Bulgaria (Schechtman 1962: 22). As well, the 1919 Treaty of Neuilly between the Allied and Associated Powers, on the one hand, and Bulgaria, on the other, envisaged the transfer of 46,000 ethnic Greeks and 96,000 ethnic Bulgarians living in Greece and Bulgaria (Schechtman 1962: 22). Sanctioned by the League of Nations, the 1923 Treaty of Lausanne provided for the exchange of over two million ethnic Greeks and Turks between Turkey and Greece (Rosand 1998: 6–7). During the Second World War, the 1941 Soviet–German agreement foresaw the transfer of Germans from Lithuania, Latvia, and Estonia to German-controlled territory (Schechtman 1962: 27).

Of those treaties mentioned in the previous paragraph, only the Treaty of Lausanne made provisions for compensation to those who lost property as a result of the population transfer, but these provisions were never implemented (Jackson-Preece 1998: 824). Other examples abound of nationally and internationally permitted confiscation of property during conflict. In 1920, the Canadian Government, for example, enacted legislation which permanently confiscated all property of "enemy nationals" that had been taken over by the state as a result of the First World War (RG 2, PC 755, 14 April 1920, as cited in Roberts-Moore 1986: 96). This was sanctioned by the Treaty of Versailles which entitled Canada to "keep and liquidate any German property in Canada."[1] During the Second World War, the Canadian Government decreed that 22,000 Japanese Canadians were obliged to register for evacuation and sign "voluntary" declarations turning over their properties to the Custodian of Enemy Property for safe-keeping (Roberts-Moore 1986: 101). The state subsequently liquidated most of the properties, ostensibly because of the difficulties in protecting them (Roberts-Moore 1986: 102). At the end of the war, those whose property had been confiscated received the proceeds from the sales minus administrative fees and any outstanding debts against the property (Roberts-Moore 1986: 102). The Japanese Canadians' only option for recovering their original properties was to repurchase them.

In addition to justifying property deprivation for reasons of ethnic origin, collective punishment has also served as a justification for property confiscation. For example, the fifteen million ethnic Germans expelled without individual trial throughout Europe following the Second World War were assumed to have collaborated with the Nazis and thus deemed collectively responsible for the Nazis' atrocities (Torpey 2003: 729). In the case of expulsions from Czechoslovakia, the decrees, which called for the expulsion of three million Germans and the confiscation of their property, were explicitly based on the concept of collective guilt (Hayden 1996: 728). In challenging their

---

[1] By 1924 the custodian held over $490,000 worth of enemy property in Canada and $7.3 million in enemy-owned securities (Roberts-Moore 1986: 96).

expulsion and deprivation of property a Czech court ruled that the expulsion of the Sudeten Germans and confiscation of their property had been legitimate because of their assumed collaboration with the Nazi regime (Hayden 1996: 729). This illustrates the perceived acceptability of collective punishment. Due to the assumed guilt of the German nation, the Czechoslovak government deemed paying reparations unnecessary (Hayden 1996: 729).

Justifications underpinned by norms of ethnic nationalism and collective guilt were possible because of the salience that ethnic identity held in international relations. The concept of the individual as a subject of international law grew out of a response to the German atrocities against subnational groups such as Jews, the Roma, homosexuals, and the handicapped (Torpey 2003: 4). The purpose of various post-war international human rights treaties were "to ensure that human beings would not, in the future, exercise their barbarous impulses on others without the latter having a juridical leg to stand on—especially when the perpetrator was the victim's own government" (Torpey 2003: 5). The concept of human rights, which asserts that each individual has inalienable rights, is a significant paradigm shift. The human rights paradigm legitimizes claims of individuals, and does not allow their negation in the name of state interests.

The post-Second World War era featured a series of international human rights treaties which laid the foundation for consideration of individual rights regardless of group membership. This focus on the rights of the individual and the protection of these during conflict, in general, provided a basis for the protection of individual property rights. Various references prohibiting expulsion, protecting the right of peaceful enjoyment of possessions, and calling for refugees to have the option of returning home appear in a number of international documents following the Second World War. Regarding expulsion, a specific example is the 1950 Fourth Protocol to the European Convention for the Protection of Human Rights that prohibits the individual or collective expulsion of citizens and the collective expulsion of aliens. Regarding protections for property, Article 17 of the 1948 Universal Declaration of Human Rights grants the right to own property and prohibits the arbitrary deprivation of such property. Property rights are clearly articulated in regional conventions, such as Article 23 of the 1948 American Declaration on the Rights and Duties of Man, Article 21 of the Organization of American States Convention on Human Rights, Article 21 of the American Convention, and Article 14 of the African Charter.

Regarding refugee return to their homes, this principle was first expressly articulated in the 1948 General Assembly Resolution 194 on Israel which states that:

Refugees wishing to return to their homes and live at peace with their neighbours should be permitted to do so at the earliest practicable date, and that compensation should be paid for the property of those choosing not to return and for loss of or damage to property which, under principles of international law or in equity, should be made good by the Governments or authorities responsible.[2]

This principle was reiterated in the case of Cyprus. The 1974 General Assembly Resolution 3212 states that: "all the refugees should return to their homes in safety and calls upon the parties concerned to undertake urgent measures to that end."[3] Clashing ideological views during the Cold War prevented strong protection for property rights within international conventions, and the UNHCR Statute adopted by the UN General Assembly in 1950[4] used language advocating return to the country of origin rather than to one's home specifically.[5]

More recently, two key documents governing the return of displaced people called for the right of those displaced to repossess their homes. The 1998 Guiding Principles on Internal Displacement and the 2000 International Law Association Declaration of Principles of International Law on Internally Displaced Persons both include general statements on the rights of IDPs to repossess their properties (Paglione 2008: 400). For example, Principle 29 of the Guiding Principles states that:

> Competent authorities have the duty and responsibility to assist returned and/ or resettled internally displaced persons to recover, to the extent possible, their properties and possessions, which they left behind or were dispossessed of upon their displacement. (As quoted in Paglione 2008: 398)

The post-war human rights regime, coupled with specific calls for both the protection of individuals from expulsion and their right of return in case of displacement, marked the *initial* institutionalization of the norm of post-conflict repossession of property. However, the specifics of how repossession would be conducted remained unsettled.[6]

STAGE II: IMPLEMENTATION

The ethnic conflicts of the post-Cold War period resulted in the displacement of millions of persons. The general principles which had developed following

---

[2] UN General Assembly (UNGA) A/RES/194 (III)(1948), adopted 11 Dec. 1948, as cited in Leckie 2001.

[3] UNGA A/RES/3212 (XXIX) (1974), adopted 1 Nov. 1974 as cited in Leckie 2001.

[4] UNGA A/RES/428 (V) (1950), adopted 14 Dec. 1950 as cited in Leckie 2001: 27.

[5] The resolution pledged member states to "[assist] the High Commissioner [for refugees] in his efforts to promote the voluntary repatriations." UNGA A/RES/428 (V) (1950), adopted 14 Dec. 1950, as cited in Leckie 2001.

[6] As noted in Ch. 8 by Brian Job and Anastasia Shesterinina, a number of the post-war human rights conventions had no enforcement mechanisms.

the Second World War were applied unevenly across a number of post-conflict cases. These cases included Bosnia-Herzegovina, Croatia, Georgia, Guatemala, Kosovo, and Rwanda. Prior to the large-scale repossession attempts that began in the latter half of the 1990s, the norm of return and repossession was vague and articulated inconsistently across cases. For example, the 1991 Final Act of the Paris Conference on Cambodia allows for "return to the place of...choice" and the "return to [the] homeland." Likewise UNHCR Executive Committee conclusions on Afghanistan, Angola, Tajikistan, and Myanmar "extend...the right to return to the whole country of origin" (Albert 1997: 10–11). It was unclear whether individuals had the right to return to their homes of origin or simply to their country of origin.

The establishment of the right of return to *one's home* in the 1990s was made possible by the end of the Cold War. For political reasons, asylum had been preferred over return. In the context of the Cold War, "refugee law focused on the right of people to leave their home country and to seek asylum in another state. The right of return was generally not a true option" (Rosand 1998: 1119). Additionally, "the vast majority of refugees find asylum in developing countries, which often cannot absorb them [therefore] repatriation...has become the most viable option" (Rosand 1998: 1119). Sadako Ogata, former UN High Commissioner for Refugees, noted that in the post-Cold war world "refugees [were] victims of civil war and political conflict, rather than persecution" (Rosand 1998: 1119). The Cold War also brought the end to frequent stalemate in the Security Council. This allowed for robust action to be taken to end the war in Bosnia-Herzegovina (BiH) as well as to establish international missions in post-conflict Bosnia. Therefore, the combined factors of a preference for return and the possibility for coordinated action allowed for the creation of property repossession regimes in the aftermath of the mass displacement that occurred during the break-up of the former Yugoslavia.

The break-up of the former Yugoslavia resulted in the large-scale displacement of up to four million people between 1991 and 1995[7] (Weiss 1998: 184). Although massive displacement occurred continuously throughout the conflict, it can be divided roughly into three periods. From June 1991 to November 1992, precipitated in part by Croatia's and Slovenia's declarations of independence on 25 June 1991, Serb paramilitary and Yugoslav National Army (JNA) forces took control of almost 30 percent of Croatia's territory, declaring it the *Republika Srpska Krajina* or the Serbian Republic of the Krajina (Weiss 1998: 185). This initial phase of the conflict resulted in the expulsion of about 200,000 ethnic Croats, Hungarians, and others from the Serb-occupied territory (Weiss 1998: 185). The United Nations High Commissioner for Refugees

---

[7] Official estimates vary between three and four million.

(UNHCR) estimates that by February 1992 there were a total of 605,000 displaced persons throughout the former Yugoslavia (Weiss 1998: 185). From March 1992 to August 1995, the wars in BiH resulted in the displacement of a total of 2.6 million persons: 1 million internally displaced persons within BiH; 1.1 million refugees who left BiH, but remained on the territory of the former Yugoslavia and approximately 500,000 people who emigrated out of the former Yugoslavia (Weiss 1998: 185). Finally, from August to November 1995, the offensive launched by Croatia and the Bosnia-Croatian Federation, together with NATO air strikes against Croatian and Bosnian Serbs, resulted in the displacement of over 750,000 (Weiss 1998: 185–6).

During the conflict and after the cessation of hostilities, political officials, military, and paramilitary personnel, as well as individuals belonging to the ethnic majority of an area allocated "abandoned" housing to refugees, internally displaced persons, and others of the majority's ethnicity (OSCE 2001: 6). In many cases those who occupied properties were not refugees or Internally Displaced Persons (IDPs), but individuals from surrounding communities who sought to profit from the conflict (OSCE 2001: 6). The take-over of "abandoned" property involved at least 220,220 properties in BiH (OHR et al. 2003) and at least 70,000 properties in Croatia (OSCE 2001: 6–7). In part, this served to ameliorate the imminent humanitarian crisis of the vast numbers of people displaced from their homes, but also served to consolidate ethnic cleansing.

The international community's response to ethnic cleansing was to call for the norm of refugee/IDP return to their homes. For example, prompted by reports of ethnic cleansing, the UN and the EC convened the London Conference on 26–27 August 1992 in London (Allcock et al. 1998: 160). The conference established the Steering Committee chaired by Lord David Owen, representing the EC presidency, and Cyrus Vance, representing the UN Secretary-General. The Steering Committee also comprised an EC troika, a CSCE troika, the five permanent members of the UN Security Council (P5), a representative of the Organization of the Islamic Conference (OIC), and two representatives from neighbouring states. The Steering Committee's task was to supervise six working groups on issues ranging from humanitarian to ethnic to economic concerns. The working groups would meet in continuous session at the UN in Geneva.

The conference resulted in all Yugoslav republics recognizing the territorial integrity of BiH and pledging guarantees for minorities. Other outcomes were the establishment of an international peacekeeping force (UNPROFOR), the establishment of the permanent International Conference of the Former Yugoslavia (ICFY), and the declared right of return for all displaced persons and refugees (Allcock et al. 1998: 160). The right of return entailed the right of all displaced persons to return *to their homes*, and if they chose not to return they were entitled to receive compensation for their properties (Rosand

1998: 1107). The establishment of UNPROFOR, it was hoped, would put in place conditions which would allow return to occur.

There was also a strong condemnation of the possibility of partitioning BiH along ethnic lines. At this conference, the Bosnia Working Group presented a paper on "Options for BiH" which eventually evolved into the Vance-Owen Peace Plan (Gow 1997: 235). It envisaged seven to ten multi-ethnic regions, constitutionally designed as multicultural with a federal government (Gow 1997: 235). Although this proposal envisaged "cantonization" based upon majority ethnicity, it also involved the right of individual return and respect for minority rights within each canton.

The ICFY convened in Geneva in September 1992, meeting in continuous session, to provide a framework for ongoing peace negotiations (Allcock et al. 1998: 124). In October 1992, the conference called for the "reversal" of ethnic cleansing (Rosand 1998: 1107). That is, the conference not only condemned forcible expulsions, but called for their undoing. The conference produced the Vance-Owen Plan from 1992 to 1993. The plan sought to ensure territorial integrity of BiH, to resist "ethnic purification," and to deny the Bosnian Serbs contiguous territories (Gow 1997: 309). It comprised three components: military, political, and a map (Gow 1997: 235). The map envisaged the administrative division of a federal BiH into ten provinces governed by proportional representation, based on the 1991 census (Gow 1997: 235). Nine of the ten would have a governor who belonged to the majority ethnicity and a vice-governor belonging to the ethnicity of the second largest ethnic group (Gow 1997: 235). The tenth, Sarajevo, would have a separate status. The Vance-Owen Peace Plan ambitiously envisaged that the local police would be responsible for ensuring that the reversal of ethnic cleansing was carried out and that the UN Civilian Police would be responsible for monitoring the local police's fulfillment of this requirement (Rosand 1998: 1107–8).

The Contact Group, comprised of France, Germany, the UK, the Russian Federation, and the US, was established in 1994 to take the lead in reaching a peace settlement (Allcock et al. 1998: 124). Within the Contact Group, the US and Russia played a greater role and its establishment signified the failure of European leadership and the necessity of US leadership (Allcock et al. 1998: 124). The Contact Group developed a proposal which adhered to the principles set out since the beginning of the conflict—including the right of return and restitution of property—and proposed that BiH be divided into two "entities"; the Muslims and Croats would share the Bosniac-Croat Federation, comprising 51 percent of the territory, and the Bosnian Serbs would have the Republic of Srpska which comprised 49 percent of the territory of BiH (UN 1995: 553).

Proposals that advocated partition and the acceptance of ethnic homogeneity received little currency throughout the conflict. For example, at the 1992 London Conference, the Dutch Presidency proposed that any solution to the conflict would be acceptable if it resulted from a peaceful process and was based on the consent of all parties, even if that process meant partition based on ethnic boundaries (Owen 1995: 33). This proposal was rejected by the eleven other EC members because it was believed that it would open a "Pandora's box" of border disputes, that the various pockets of ethnic minorities would make redrawing boundaries difficult, and that "it was considered out of date to draw state borders along ethnic lines" (Owen 1995: 33).

Throughout the conflict, a host of Security Council Resolutions condemned the practice of ethnic cleansing and called for its reversal through the voluntary return of all those who had been displaced to their homes. For example, 18 April 1993 Resolution 820 (S/RES/820, reproduced in Bethlehem and Weller, 1997: 36) sponsored by nine SC members, including P5 members France, the UK, and the US, stated in the preamble that "any taking of territory by force or any practice of 'ethnic cleansing' is unlawful and totally unacceptable, and insisting that all displaced persons be enabled to return in peace to their former homes." And in point 7: "The Security Council reaffirms its endorsement of the principles that all statements or commitments made under duress, particularly those relating to land and property, are wholly null and void and that all displaced persons have the right to return in peace to their former homes and should be assisted to do so." Resolution 1009, adopted on 10 August 1995 states in point 2:

> The Security Council demands further that the Government of the Republic of Croatia, in conformity with internationally recognized standards... respect fully the rights of the local Serb population including their rights to remain, leave or return in safety... and create conditions conducive to those persons who have left their homes. (S/RES/1009, as cited in Leckie, 2001: 15)

Other Security Council resolutions, such as 752, 757, 771, 787, and 819, demonstrate the consistency of the absolute denunciation of ethnic cleansing throughout the conflict. Language in these resolutions and statements made during Security Council debates reveal the widespread revulsion of ethnic cleansing, and the adamant resolve for its reversal through return.

There were also calls for the older norms in preference of ethnic homogeneity. For example, in 1993 John Mearsheimer advocated the partitioning of BiH into three ethnically homogeneous states with mandatory population transfers under UN auspices. This would have allowed minority populations trapped within the new state borders to join their respective "kinstates" (Mearsheimer 1993). The Serb and Croat statelets, in turn, would be free to join Serbia and Croatia respectively—creating the Greater Serbia and Greater Croatia that both Croatia and Serbia sought to achieve through the war. Mearsheimer further proposed that the UN establish a "Balkan Population Exchange Commission" modeled after the Refugee Settlement which managed the transfer of over 1.5 million people between Greece and Turkey between

1923 and 1931 (Mearsheimer 1993: 26). Proposals such as these gained little traction with the international actors.

The norm of the right of return to *one's home* won out over the previous norms that favored ethnic homogeneity. The right to return remained a norm that was general and somewhat imprecise, however. This changed significantly with implementation attempts in the 1990s. The Dayton Peace Agreement, signed by the Croatian, Bosnian, and Yugoslavian Governments on 14 December 1995 states:

> All refugees and displaced persons have the right freely to return to their homes of origin. They shall have the right to have restored to them property of which they were deprived in the course of hostilities since 1991 and to be compensated for any property that cannot be restored to them. ("General Framework Agreement for Peace in Bosnia and Herzegovina" 1995: annex 7, chapter 1, article 1)

The agreement establishes the Commission for Displaced Persons and Refugees to implement property claims whose mandate it is to

> Receive and decide any claims for real property in Bosnia and Herzegovina, where the property has not voluntarily been sold or otherwise transferred since April 1, 1992, and where the claimant does not now enjoy possession of that property. Claims may be for return of the property or for just compensation *in lieu* of restitution. (Bell 2000: 253)

The post-conflict property repossession regime in Bosnia was the first extensive and comprehensive attempt by the international community to restore property. It also served to establish a precedent of the right of return for a mass group (Rosand 1998). The restitution regime in BiH effected the repossession of over 200,000 properties, virtually 100 percent of those lost as a result of the conflict, which included both private and "socially-owned" properties by 31 December 2003 (OHR et al. 2004). The scale of property loss in Croatia was smaller than that in BiH. In total, about 50,000 households lost control over their properties as a result of the conflict (about 20,000 privately owned and about 30,000 socially owned) (OSCE Croatia 2005: 6, 8). While virtually all private properties were repossessed by their owners, the Croatian Government did not establish any remedy whereby title holders to "socially-owned" properties had the right to repossess them and accordingly none were restored to their former occupants as of 1 November 2005 (OSCE Croatia 2005: 8).

A number of key disparities emerged in the repossession regimes established in the former Yugoslavia, demonstrating the imprecision of the norm regulating post-conflict restitution. For example, many of the properties left empty due to their abandonment by their owners/occupants were subsequently inhabited by "secondary occupants," many of whom had been displaced themselves. BiH and Croatia took differing positions on the issue (Anderson 2011). While Croatia's procedure for return stipulated that secondary occupants could not be evicted without the prior provision of alternative accommodation, owners/occupancy rights holders could repossess their homes within ninety days of submitting an application, regardless of whether the current occupants had alternative accommodation (Anderson 2011). The need for the provision of alternative accommodation served as a major impediment to return. As discussed in the third section of this article, the Pinheiro Principles sought to establish guidelines on how this issue should be dealt with in repossession regimes.

The issue of occupancy/tenancy rights was also dealt with in a dramatically different fashion in both states (Anderson 2011). About 80 percent of all housing in urban areas of the former Yugoslavia was socially owned (Cousens and Cater 2001: 80). The occupancy/tenancy right was a socialist institution that may be considered a "sub-ownership" right: individuals could pay minimal fees to maintain tenancy rights over a property as long as they did not leave it uninhabited for unjustified reasons (OSCE 2001: 8). In post-conflict BiH, former OTR holders had the right to reclaim their apartments, whereas in Croatia that option was not possible since the Croatian Government had not established any claims procedure. This difference in practice signals, at least in part, the imprecision of the norm.

Another disparity between Croatia and BiH on the one hand and Kosovo on the other was the point in time to which the respective repossession programs sought to restore property (Anderson 2011). In the cases of Croatia and BiH, the regimes sought to restore property to the deprivations that occurred due to the conflict. In Kosovo, however, the immediate conflict which resulted in dispossession began in 1999, however, the property restitution mechanism sought to restore property to those who had lost it due to discriminatory policies prior to the outbreak of fighting in 1989 (Arraiza and Massimo 2009). This indicates an imprecision of the norm, which still persists, regarding to which point in time property should be restored.

The practice of restitution differed across other post-conflict states as well. For example, Rwanda's 1993 peace agreement stipulates that Rwandan refugees are entitled to property restitution, provided they have not been absent from the country for longer than ten years (Commission on Human Rights 2003: pt 31). Likewise, women were unable to inherit property in Rwanda until after the passage of legislation in 1999 (Commission on Human Rights 2003: pt 34), which limited the claimants of dispossessed properties to male heirs in cases where the owners had died. Dispossession of property affected over 53,000 refugees and IDPs due to the conflict in South Ossetia in Georgia between 1990 and 1992 (Commission on Human Rights 2003: pt 34), which saw biased application of the 1983 Housing Code which obstructed repossession for a number of those displaced (Commission on Human Rights 2003: pt 35). In Guatemala, the return of housing to returning refugees and IDPs was complicated by the government's decision to "redistribute land and issue new deeds" which led to numerous competing claims (Commission on Human Rights 2003).

These disparities in practice illustrate that the presence of general human rights principles prohibiting expulsion and advocating return did not translate into uniform application. Rather, uneven practice emerged that raised a number of questions regarding the right of return. For example, was there a time limit on the right of return? How should property rights other than *private* property rights be dealt with? What role were states obliged to play in facilitating return? How far into the past should repossession regimes be concerned?

The collective set of practices observed within various post-conflict states demonstrates two points. First, the international community has shown an interest in facilitating refugee return through establishing costly repossession mechanisms. In other words, political will has existed. Second, inconsistent practices suggest that the norm was insufficiently specified so as to allow for repossession regimes to adhere to the same principles.

STAGE III: INFORMED INSTITUTIONALIZATION

The various attempts at property repossession in the 1990s highlighted various ambiguities as to how it should be carried out. As discussed, these regimes drew on a broad principle that those displaced during armed conflict should have the right to return home. This resulted in the emergence of varying practices, leaving a more precise articulation of the norm wanting. Accordingly, the Pinheiro Principles were created in 2005 as a set of universal standards that would provide guidance for governments and international organizations in implementing post-conflict repossession of property.

An attempt at creating international standards for post-conflict property repossession was undertaken at the United Nations in the late 1990s. In 1997, the Committee on the Elimination of Racial Discrimination (CERD) requested that Paulo Sérgio Pinheiro, Sub-Commission[8] Expert, create a "common operational framework on restitution mechanisms" (Paglione 2008: 401). As a result, Pinheiro and his team produced a working paper in 2002 and a preliminary report in 2003 prior to the creation of the final Principles. The Principles were produced in 2005 outlining the norm of post-conflict property repossession and specified how that should be accomplished.

---

[8] The Sub-Commission on the Promotion and Protection of Human Rights is a sub-commission of the Commission on Human Rights, which, in turn, falls under the auspices of the Economic and Social Council. The role of the Sub-Commission is inter alia to provide the Commission on Human Rights with "independent expert studies."

The working paper, preliminary report, and the Principles themselves are explicitly informed by restitution regimes established throughout the 1990s, particularly that of Bosnia. This would be expected as a number of those engaged in the project had worked on the issue of property restitution in Bosnia. The preliminary report states that it seeks to "identify[] best practices...and...some of the more common obstacles to restitution [to] clarify some of the more difficult practical issues surrounding housing and property restitution" (Commission on Human Rights 2003: pt 13). As such, the documents discuss certain problems that arose in other restitution regimes. These include, for example, the destruction of property-holding records (Commission on Human Rights 2002: pt 53), the inability of judicial bodies to function with objectivity in polarized societies (Commission on Human Rights 2003: section III; 2002: pt 45), secondary occupation (Commission on Human Rights 2003: section III; 2002), and the discriminatory application of property abandonment legislation (Commission on Human Rights 2002: pt 49). The preliminary report notes that "restitution programmes have been implemented in varying situations with varying results [which] is at least partly attributable to the lack of a comprehensive and universal approach to restitution policy, informed by international human rights law" (Commission on Human Rights 2003: pt 71). The goal of the documents, then, was to standardize practice, which requires an overarching set of principles with specified procedures for implementation.

The preliminary report depicts the exercise as "a unique convergence between international human rights law, international humanitarian law and local-level implementation" (Commission on Human Rights 2003: pt. 12). This is an apt characterization of the relationship between implementation and institutionalization. The Pinheiro Principles sought to standardize the practices already ongoing, while providing an explicit foundation of general principles of international human rights and humanitarian law. In this vein, the preliminary report identifies six points that should underpin the future policy on protection of property rights during and after conflict. These are (1) the principle of non-discrimination and equality; (2) the right of displaced persons to participate in the establishment of restitution regimes; (3) consideration of the rights of secondary occupants; (4) the right to access independent tribunals; (5) the right to compensation in case restitution cannot be effected; (6) that restitution should be seen as a key component of post-conflict peace-building (Commission on Human Rights 2003: pt 75).

The Pinheiro Principles mark a new phase of institutionalization. They address many of the former ambiguities regarding implementation and crystallize the right of property restitution following conflict. Promulgated by a UN body, the Principles have the legitimacy and potential to impact post-conflict repossession regimes worldwide. Seven years after their passage, they have been discussed in academic literature (see e.g. Anderson 2011; Ballard 2010; Barber 2008; Paglione 2008; Smit 2012; Sweeney 2012; Unruh 2008); championed by groups and individuals in transnational civil society; referenced in policy documents (e.g. the 2008 Iraqi IDP strategy and the 2006 Great Lakes Protocol on the Property Rights of Returning Persons: Williams 2010); and in international and national judicial rulings (e.g. a 2007 Constitutional Court decision in Colombia and a 2010 European Court of Human Rights decision in the case of *Dokic v. Bosnia*: Williams 2010). As well, key humanitarian organizations have produced a Principles implementation handbook (see FAO et al. 2007). The Principles, then, have become essential in discussions and decisions regarding property repossession.

CONCLUSIONS

This chapter has argued that the current norms governing post-conflict property repossession for refugees and IDPs required prior attempts at implementation before they could be framed in their current form. As outlined, there are three phases in the life-cycle of the norm of post-conflict property repossession. The first phase—initial norm institutionalization—based on general principles of human rights can be seen during the period between 1945 and the end of the Cold War. During this period, a host of international human rights instruments articulated the rights of individuals during peace and conflict, prohibiting expulsion and weakening norms of ethnic nationalism and collective guilt. The first calls were heard for those displaced due to conflict to be able to return to their pre-war homes. The end of the Cold War brought with it a new phase of cooperation in the Security Council which resulted in UN involvement in post-conflict reconstruction. The creation of a number of property repossession regimes ensued, demonstrating that returning home following conflict was not simply an aspirational norm, but that the international political will existed to help finance and implement the regimes. These implementation attempts also served to expose a number of difficulties involved in large-scale repossessions and disparities in implementation across cases. The creation of the 2005 Pinheiro Principles marked the third phase of *informed* institutionalization which provided a clearer articulation of the right to repossess property following conflict, offering a more precise articulation of the norm and the mechanisms for ensuring its implementation. As cases of implementation increase, likely new issues will come to the fore, propelling further norm refinement.

This case study suggests that norm institutionalization and implementation can be seen as interactive processes whereby initial institutionalization allows for implementation attempts. In turn, these attempts highlight imprecision in the institutionalized norm, spurring norm refinement or "informed institutionalization." In the course of norm evolution, this process may occur repeatedly. As suggested by the Betts and Orchard framework, institutionalization does not mark the end of the norm life-cycle, but rather is a stage that may be revisited repeatedly, alongside or following implementation.

12

The Implementation of "Integrated Approaches" in the UN System

Lessons from Tanzania and Burundi

James Milner

This chapter considers the policy norm of "integrated approaches" within the United Nations (UN) system as an example of the process of norm implementation, as detailed by Betts and Orchard in their introduction to this volume. Building from the work of Park and Vetterlein (2010: 4), who define policy norms as "shared expectations for all relevant actors within a community about what constitutes appropriate behavior," this chapter considers how the policy norm of "joined-up" or "integrated" approaches emerged within the UN system in the mid-2000s. This policy norm, articulated by member states and the UN Secretary-General as the new standard of appropriate behavior expected for UN agencies and programs, specified that UN agencies and programs working in a common issue area or geographic location should more closely integrate their programs to avoid overlap and competition between agencies, while enhancing the efficiency and coherence of their program delivery.

This chapter details how this norm of "integrated approaches" was institutionalized in various ways, including through the creation of the UN Peace-Building Commission (PBC) in 2005 and the establishment of the One UN development initiative in 2006. This chapter outlines how both examples of institutionalization were motivated by the understanding that a range of actors was currently engaged in peace-building and development activities, but that these actors should adopt more integrated and collaborative approaches to their work. Following the argument of Betts and Orchard in their introduction to this volume, however, this chapter argues that the meaning, significance, and nature of this policy norm is best understood not only by considering its institutionalization through declarations and resolutions at the "global" level, but also through its attempted implementation in a "domestic"—or field—context. In fact, this chapter draws on fieldwork in Tanzania and Burundi to suggest that many of the ideational, material, and institutional dynamics that Betts and Orchard identify as enabling or constraining the implementation of a norm may help explain variation in the implementation of this policy norm at a "domestic" level, notwithstanding its clear articulation at a global level.

To support this argument, this chapter considers the implementation of the norm of integration within two UN field operations: development in Tanzania and peace-building in Burundi. In both instances, conventional UN operations were challenged to adopt more integrated approaches with actors traditionally working in the *same issue area*, while also adopting new approaches to integrate their activities with an established actor from a significantly *different issue area*. Development actors in Tanzania and peace-building actors in Burundi were required to work with humanitarian actors—specifically the Office of the United Nations High Commissioner for Refugees (UNHCR)—to adopt new approaches to respond to the challenges of solutions for the prolonged presence of Burundian refugees in the region.

As detailed in this chapter, there was significant variation in the initial implementation of the norm of integrated approaches in these two locations. In particular, findings from Burundi indicate that strong leadership at a field level and the sustained engagement of the local state helped overcome a number of institutional divisions and gaps that initially frustrated an integrated response. Conversely, findings from Tanzania illustrate how efforts to integrate solutions for refugees into UN development activities in Tanzania prior to 2010 were constrained by differences in institutional approaches, a lack of resources, and differences in expectations. Overall, this chapter suggests that, while future research could more fully explain variation between these and other cases, preliminary results indicate that integrated approaches to development in Tanzania were largely *constrained* by issues of capacity and bureaucratic contestation, while integrated approaches to peace-building in Burundi were *enabled* due to the interests of key actors and the bureaucratic identity created by senior institutional leaders.

The chapter concludes by outlining how the example of UN integrated approaches provides a useful empirical context for understanding the causal mechanisms suggested by Betts and Orchard that determine the outcome of norm implementation, while suggesting a number of new elements that may usefully be highlighted in our theoretical understanding of norm implementation. First, as Betts and Orchard argue in the Introduction, "the implementation process itself can open up a new arena for interpretation and contestation of the norm by relevant actors," the cases of Tanzania and Burundi suggest that pilot programs play an important role in the articulation of policy norms and that the role of pilot programs could be more systematically understood as a mechanism through which policy norms are not only implemented but interpreted. Second, efforts to implement the policy norm of integrated action in Tanzania and Burundi suggest the important role that individuals play in explaining the transition from the emergence to the stabilization of a policy norm, as outlined in the norm circle proposed by Park and Vetterlein (2010: 19–23). In fact, just as norm entrepreneurs are understood by constructivists as playing critical roles in the early stages of the norm life-cycle (see the Introduction to this volume), similar actors play an important role in the implementation process. As such, this chapter concludes that additional research could usefully develop our understanding of the role of individuals not only as "norm entrepreneurs" but as "norm implementers."

METHODOLOGY

As suggested by Betts and Orchard, the process of examining the norm implementation poses important methodological challenges. Given that this chapter is intended to help develop a relatively new area of research on norm implementation, it was decided that the use of "plausibility probes" would be an appropriate approach, given the utility of these "preliminary studies" to consider "relatively untested theories and hypotheses" (George and Bennett 2005: 75). As such, the objective of this study is to consider the presence and possible importance of the factors identified by Betts and Orchard in specific instances where attempts have been made to implement the policy norm of integrated UN action. Given the recent development of this policy norm and the limited number of pilot programs, however, the range of candidate cases was limited.[1] Also, the limited literature on these cases beyond country reports and UN resolutions suggested that fieldwork was required to "examine the micro-mechanisms through which international norms adapt at national and local levels" (Betts and Orchard, this volume).

Given the limited number of available cases and the importance of fieldwork, this chapter employs the cases of peace-building in Burundi and development in Tanzania. Specifically, this chapter draws on a review of UN policy documents and fieldwork conducted in Tanzania and Burundi in July to August 2009.[2] Fieldwork included a total of forty-six interviews with representatives of UN agencies, non-governmental organizations, local and national government and donor governments in capital cities (Dar es Salaam and Bujumbura) and in field locations (Kigoma, Kasulu, Makamba, Mpanda, Nyanza-Lac, and Rumonge). In addition, this chapter builds on the author's past work on Tanzania (Milner

---

[1] When this chapter was first drafted in 2011, there were six cases on the agenda of the UN Peace-Building Commission (Burundi, Central African Republic, Guinea, Guinea-Bissau, Liberia, and Sierra Leone), while there were only eight pilot countries for the One UN initiative (Albania, Cape Verde, Mozambique, Pakistan, Rwanda, Tanzania, Uruguay, and Vietnam).

[2] This research was supported by a grant from the Dean of the Faculty of Public Affairs and the Office of the Vice President (Research and International), Carleton University, Ottawa, Canada.

2009) and previous visits to the region in 1999 and 2004. As UN activities in both countries are ongoing, however, it is important to note that the analysis of this chapter is limited to the state of these programs to the end of 2009.[3]

The cases of Burundi and Tanzania were selected for conceptual and practical reasons. Practically, the fact that these are neighboring countries meant that fieldwork in both cases could be undertaken within the limited time and resources available for fieldwork. As already noted, however, there is a more important conceptual link between the two cases: development actors in Tanzania and peace-building actors in Burundi were both required to work with UNHCR to adopt new approaches to find solutions to the prolonged presence of Burundian refugees in the region. The benefit of this two-case study is that it provides the opportunity to consider contrasts between the plausibility probes as a means of identifying variation and suggesting factors that may help explain this variation. The limitation of this approach, especially considering cases from two different areas of UN activity, is primarily the limited ability to generalize from these findings to other cases. As such, the claims of this chapter are limited to arguing that that many of the causal mechanisms identified by Betts and Orchard as being significant in the norm implementation process were present in the cases of integrated development action Tanzania and integrated peace-building action in Burundi, and that preliminary results suggest that several of these factors may help explain why integrated action was constrained in Tanzania and enabled in Burundi.

THE "INTEGRATION" NORM IN THE UN SYSTEM

The last decade has witnessed the emergence of a new understanding that the appropriate behavior for UN agencies and programs is to adopt more integrated approaches. While it should be noted that this understanding has not been limited to the UN system,[4] this move towards integration has arguably been most pronounced within the UN system. Driven by calls for a more "efficient and effective" UN system, member states and senior members of the UN Secretariat, especially the Secretary-General, have adopted a "new" policy norm that UN agencies and programs should increasingly find ways to integrate their work at a global and local level.[5]

---

[3] For a more recent consideration of the state of refugee programming in Tanzania, see Milner (2013).

[4] Indeed, Patrick and Brown (2007) have detailed how a growing number of states have sought to develop approaches to their engagement in fragile states that integrate security, development, and humanitarian approaches.

[5] It should, however, be noted that efforts to better coordinate the work of various programs and agencies within the UN system have been a topic of discussion for several decades. See Hill (1978).

This norm has most clearly been codified through several recent initiatives, including the increased prevalence of "integrated missions" (UN 2006), humanitarian reform (Holmes 2007), the establishment of the UN PBC (UNGA 2005), and the conclusions of the High-Level Panel on United Nations System-Wide Coherence in the areas of development (UNSG 2006). While the development of integrated missions and the process of humanitarian reform are interesting case studies, this chapter considers the institutional changes relating to peace-building and development. After outlining the institutionalization of the policy norm of integrated approaches in these two issue areas, this section will introduce the challenge of cooperation between these actors and humanitarian actors, specifically UNHCR, before considering how these new institutional efforts at integrated approaches operated in the context of Tanzania and Burundi.

Peace-Building

While the importance of post-conflict reconstruction has been recognized for more than fifty years, the broader notion of peace-building became the focus of particular interest in the early 1990s when it was highlighted in the UN Secretary-General's report *An Agenda for Peace* (UNSG 1992). In his report, UN Secretary-General Boutros Boutros-Ghali added "peace-building" to the more established activities of preventive diplomacy, peacemaking and peacekeeping. He argued that such an innovation was required as the United Nations system needed to develop the capacity to "stand ready to assist in peace-building in its differing contexts: rebuilding the institutions and infrastructures of nations torn by civil war and strife; and building bonds of peaceful mutual benefit among nations formerly at war" (UNSG 1992: para. 15). While few of these activities were new, it became increasingly recognized that these longer-term undertakings were important elements in preventing a return to conflict. While the UN system contained a number of specialized agencies with mandates to undertake some of these activities, however, it became increasingly clear that stronger leadership and institutional coherence were required to ensure that peace-building was more effectively and systematically undertaken.

The establishment of a UN Peace-Building Commission was subsequently proposed as a means of ensuring better leadership and coordination of peace-building activities within the UN system. The initial proposal was included in the 2004 report of the UN Secretary-General's High-Level Panel on Threats, Challenges and Change. In his 2005 report, *In Larger Freedom*, UN Secretary-General Kofi Annan endorsed the creation of a Peace-Building Commission as an inter-governmental advisory body, which could ensure long-term political support and funding for post-conflict recovery programmes, in addition to advising on thematic issues and specific cases (Annan 2005). The UN General Assembly subsequently established the UN PBC, Peace-Building Support Office (PBSO), and the Peace-Building Fund (PBF) in December 2005.[6] In establishing the PBC, the UNGA recognized the "interlinked and mutually reinforcing" nature of peace and security, development, and human rights, and the benefits of "a coordinated, coherent and integrated approach to post-conflict peacebuilding" (UNGA 2005).

The PBC began work in 2006, initially concentrating on the cases of Burundi and Sierra Leone. By mid-2008, the PBC's Organizational Committee was comprised of thirty-one member states, including members of the Security Council, members from ECOSOC, representatives of the major donor countries, troop contributing countries, other members of the UNGA with experience in post-conflict reconstruction (UNGA 2008). Additional states directly implicated in particular peace-building operations were also granted membership in the country-specific configurations. Finally, meetings of the PBC have invited contributions from senior UN representatives in the field, representatives of other UN agencies, and representatives of major development institutions, including the World Bank, and representatives of civil society. In this way, the PBC brings together a wide range of institutional stakeholders implicated in peace-building initiatives and was hoped to serve as a clear example of the benefits of integrated approaches within the UN system.

Development

The need for reform and greater coordination has been a recurring criticism of the UN's various development initiatives for more than forty years (Hill 1978). As noted by Fomerand and Dijkzeul (2007: 561), "the UN 'system' is highly fragmented, rife with competition, and certainly not a harmonious cooperative whole in which the parts work towards a common purpose." Fomerand and Dijkzeul note that there are some fourteen specialized agencies under the supervision of ECOSOC, each with their own constitutions, governing bodies, budgets, and secretariats. Tensions and overlaps between these agencies have prompted frequent reform proposals for the UN's approach to development. In 1969, for example, Pearson's *Partners in Development* and Jackson's *Study of the Capacity of the United Nations System* highlighted the multitude of overlapping agencies, the difficulties posed by competition between agencies, and the general reluctance of specialized agencies to integrate their activities. Likewise, the Independent Commission on International Development Issues,

---

[6] See <http://www.un.org/peace/peacebuilding>, accessed Mar. 2011.

chaired by Willy Brandt in 1979, repeated concerns over the fragmentation of UN development bodies and called for large-scale reform.

As with approaches to peace and security issues, it was hoped that the end of the Cold War would usher in a new era of cooperation on development issues. Mirroring the *Agenda for Peace*, the 1992 *Agenda for Development* tried to articulate a convergence between the interrelated areas of security and development and called for a revitalization and reconsideration of the UN's development activities (UNSG 1994). Reforms were subsequently undertaken by Secretary-General Kofi Annan in 1997 and again in 2000 with the launching of the Millennium Development Goals. These reforms were promoted as a way of presenting a unified set of development priorities to guide all development activities undertaken under the flag of the UN. According to Fomerand and Dijkzeul (2007), some of these reforms have been effective. Specifically, they point to the innovation of the Chief Executive Board for Coordination (CEB) and its role in increasing coordination between twenty-eight UN funds, agencies, and specialized agencies, in addition to the Bretton Woods institutions. Coordination is also facilitated by the work of the Deputy Secretary-General, a position created in 1997, and the work of the UN Development Group.

These developments notwithstanding, the Secretary-General launched a new initiative to enhance the effectiveness and cohesion of the UN system in the mid-2000s. Building from the momentum of the 2005 World Summit, the Secretary-General invited the Prime Ministers of Pakistan, Mozambique, and Norway to co-chair a High Level Panel on United Nations System-Wide Coherence in the areas of development, humanitarian assistance, and the environment. Their final report, contained in the UN Secretary-General's follow-up report to the outcomes of the Millennium Summit (UNSG 2006), contained some telling reflections on the effectiveness of past reform efforts. According to the report (UNSG 2006: 18), there are "many reasons why the United Nations has become fragmented and weak: from a lack of buy-in and mixed messages from Member States between capitals and representatives in various bodies, to a proliferation of agencies, mandates and offices, creating duplication and dulling the focus on outcomes, with moribund entities never discontinued." The report continues (UNSG 2006: 19) that "even when mandates intersect, United Nations entities tend to operate alone with little synergy and coordination between them." This lack of synergy results in competition, overlap, incoherence and wastage at an international, regional, and country level.

Crucially, the report (UNSG 2006: 19) notes that this overlap is most evident at the country level where:

> operational incoherence between United Nations funds, programmes and agencies is most evident. More than one third of United Nations country teams include 10 or more United Nations agencies on the ground at any one time. Several teams

include 20 or more. This has led to incoherent programme interventions and excessive administrative costs. It also burdens the capacity of developing countries to deal with multiple agencies.

In response, the report called for a move towards a "One UN" system at the country and headquarters level. At a country level, the report called for a new approach premised on "the 4 Ones" (UNSG 2006: 22–3):

- *One Leader*, with a greater emphasis on the authority of the Resident Coordinator to coordinate the activities of UN programs in the country and to negotiate the One Country Program with the government on behalf of the whole UN;
- *One Program*, with the development of a single country strategy in consultation with the host government, responsive to the national development framework, strategy and vision, including the internationally agreed development goals, such as the MDGs;
- *One Budgetary Framework* that harmonizes the accounting procedures, budgetary cycles, and reporting mechanisms of UN agencies, with a view to insuring increased transparency and better resource management; and, where possible,
- *One Office*, with all UN programs and specialized agencies housed in a single premises, with a view to minimizing costs, increasing interaction between agencies, and increasing the security of UN personnel.

Shortly after the presentation of the report, eight countries expressed their willingness to be pilot countries for the One UN initiative: Albania, Cape Verde, Mozambique, Pakistan, Rwanda, Tanzania, Uruguay, and Vietnam.

Cross-Sectoral Cooperation within the UN system

As illustrated by these summaries, the establishment of the Peace-Building Commission and the launch of the One UN initiative were the result of the new policy norm of integrated approaches within the UN system. At the core of both initiatives is the desire to see closer cooperation not only between actors within a given sector or issue area, but also across sectors. Specifically, the policy norm has a stated objective of seeing all activities of the UN "deliver as one," especially in the field context. This policy norm was intended to help overcome significant tensions between UN agencies and programs working in a particular issue area, especially in the development sector. Perhaps more fundamental, however, is the challenge of overcoming tensions between sectors within the UN system more generally. One example of these tensions is the relationship between UNHCR and peace and security and development actors within the UN system.

UNHCR was created by a resolution of the UN General Assembly in December 1950 that detailed the place of the new organization within the UN system. The first paragraph of the Statute of the Office of the United Nations High Commissioner for Refugees states that the High Commissioner was to act "under the authority of the General Assembly" and was to pursue its mandate "under the auspices of the United Nations" (UNGA 1950). Although UNHCR is the only UN agency with a specific mandate to ensure the protection of refugees and to find solutions to their plight, it is unable to pursue its mandate independently. Instead, UNHCR has been structurally and operationally linked to a wide range of other actors in the international system, including donor and refugee-hosting states, other UN agencies, international, national, and local NGOs, and a number of other actors. That said, UNHCR's relationships with these actors have changed significantly over time and the organization's relations, especially with other UN agencies, has frequently been characterized by periods of tension and competition (Betts et al. 2012: 104–32).

For example, since the late 1990s, UNHCR has encouraged the Department of Peacekeeping Operations (DPKO) to consider the deployment of personnel to refugee-populated areas to address a range of security concerns relating to refugee movements. However, cooperation between the two agencies in the field remains limited as a result of the specific mandates given to particular peacekeeping missions and the significant challenges of funding, mandate, and access faced by UN peacekeepers. Likewise, there have been several key developments in the relationship between UNHCR and UNDP. In April 1997, for example, UNDP and UNHCR agreed to cooperate in five key areas, including early warning, mitigating the impact of refugee populations on local communities, and in a range of activities relating to post-conflict reconstruction and repatriation. While these areas of cooperation have been important, there have been numerous difficulties in the relationship between UNDP and UNHCR over the past decade, resulting from different priorities and programs in the field, stemming from the significant gap that remains between humanitarian and development activities within the UN system.

UNHCR's relations with other UN actors suggest that, while efforts at reform and cooperation have been pursued, important gaps between approaches, priorities, and mandates remain. One significant implication of these gaps is the challenge in finding solutions to large refugee situations, which have traditionally necessitated the strategic integration of approaches of these diverse actors and effective coordination and leadership at the field level (Loescher and Milner 2008; Betts 2008). In this way, the policy norm of integrated approaches within the UN system has been identified by UNHCR and states as an important basis upon which the UN system as a whole may cooperate to find solutions for longstanding refugee situations. In fact, a 2009

Conclusion on solutions for protracted refugee situations passed by UNHCR's Executive Committee (ExCom), which comprises eighty-seven UN member states, specifically called upon states, UNHCR, humanitarian, and development actors to

> pursue active and effective partnerships and coordination in implementation of durable solutions, and to develop new opportunities for partnership including through engaging in and implementing in full the objectives of the Delivering as One initiative; increased information exchange and advice given to the United Nations PBC; and partnerships with other actors such as international financial institutions, the Inter-Agency Standing Committee, the United Nations Development Group, regional bodies, parliaments, local governments, mayors, business leaders, the media and diaspora communities. (UNHCR ExCom 2010: operational para. n)

In this way, UNHCR's Executive Committee has not only recognized the norm of integrated approaches within the UN, but has called for its implementation to help find solutions for refugee situations. It is against this background that this chapter now turns to the case of solutions for Burundian refugees in Tanzania to consider what factors either enable or constrain the implementation of this norm in a field context.

Case Study: Burundian Refugees in Tanzania

The case of Burundian refugees in Tanzania is an important case study for the implementation of the norm of integrated UN approaches in a field context for three reasons. First, Tanzania's policy towards the hosting of Burundian refugees changed dramatically in 2007, with a shift from a very restrictive asylum policy to a willingness to offer citizenship to some 220,000 Burundians who had been in Tanzania since 1972. This shift introduced a number of opportunities for the implementation of integrated approaches at a field level in support of the resolution of this protracted refugee situations. Second, as one of the pilots for the One UN development initiative, Tanzania was thought to provide a useful start for developing integrated responses between development and humanitarian actors. Third, as one of the pilots for the UN Peace-Building Commission, Burundi was thought to provide a useful start for considering the implementation of integrated responses between humanitarian, development, and peace and security actors in a peace-building context. This section provides a brief background to Tanzania's asylum policies before introducing the shift that occurred in 2007–8. The section will then consider the implications of the One UN initiative for local integration in Tanzania and the implications of new peace-building initiatives in Burundi for repatriation and reintegration of refugees.

Tanzania: A Brief History of Asylum[7]

Through the 1960s and 1970s, Tanzania hosted tens of thousands of refugees fleeing both wars of national liberation in Southern Africa and post-colonial conflict and repression in neighboring states. Tanzania provided refugees with land, and refugees were encouraged to achieve self-sufficiency, with many entering the country's workforce. The openness of Tanzania's asylum policy during this period is perhaps best characterized by the mass naturalization of 36,000 Rwandan refugees in December 1980. This reputation changed dramatically in the context of renewed conflict and genocide in Burundi and Rwanda in the mid-1990s. Tanzania's refugee population reportedly climbed from 292,100 at the end of 1992 to 883,300 at the end of 1994. In response, and in advance of the country's first multi-party presidential elections, Tanzania ended its longstanding "open-door" asylum policy by closing its border with Burundi in March 1995 and by expelling the overwhelming majority of Rwandan refugees in December 1996. The expulsion of Rwandan refugees did not, however, lead to a return to Tanzania's previously open asylum traditions. Instead, the decade that followed witnessed the formulation and implementation of a series of increasingly restrictive asylum policies, characterized by the restrictive character of the 1998 Refugees Act and the 2003 National Refugee Policy.

Given this history, many observers of the refugee situation in Tanzania were stunned when, in February 2008, UNHCR announced that Tanzania had agreed to consider the naturalization of some 220,000 Burundian refugees who had been settled in Tanzania since 1972, and requested some US$34 million from donors to support the initiative. This appeal marked a key point in a dramatic shift in Tanzania's asylum policy. In June 2007, the Governments of Tanzania and Burundi announced that they sought a solution to the Burundian refugees who had lived in the Old Settlements of Katumba, Mishamo, and Ulyankulu since the early 1970s. Although UNHCR had not been present in the settlements for over twenty years, the organization then cooperated with the government in mid-2007 to conduct a census, registration, and survey of residents of the settlements asking if they would rather repatriate to Burundi or apply for Tanzanian citizenship. The findings of this process were endorsed by a Tripartite Commission meeting between UNHCR and the governments of Tanzania and Burundi in December 2007, with the initiative officially launched by the UN High Commissioner for Refugees, António Guterres, in March 2008.[8]

---

[7] For a more detailed analysis of the case of Tanzania between 1962 and 2008, see Milner (2009: 108–34).

[8] For a more detailed analysis of the naturalization programme in Tanzania, see Milner (2013).

Development and Local Integration

During the 2007 survey, approximately 75 percent of Burundians (some 165,000 individuals) living in the Old Settlements indicated their preference to pursue naturalization in Tanzania rather than return to Burundi. Many of these individuals had been born in Tanzania and grew-up speaking Kiswahili and English, not Kirundi and French, and felt more "Tanzanian" than "Burundian." The process of acquiring citizenship for these individuals was very different from the Rwandans in 1980: in 1980, refugees were granted citizenship through a mass naturalization declaration, whereas in 2008, refugees were required to make individual applications for citizenship. The result has been the challenge of processing some 76,000 individual citizenship applications, representing some 163,000 individuals. In June 2010, it was announced that 162,156 applications for naturalization—some 98 percent of applications—had been approved.

But the acquisition of citizenship is understood to be only the first of two steps for the integration of Burundian refugees. The second step is the much more difficult process of relocating the new citizens from the settlements where many have been resident for more than thirty-six years and establishing them in new communities across Tanzania. This relocation of Burundians from settlements where they have been self-reliant for more than twenty years raised a number of concerns for donor governments and NGOs in Dar es Salaam. It was frequently noted during interviews that the relocation and integration of such a large population would require the sustained engagement of a range of development actors in Tanzania and the possible integration of refugee issues into the UN's Tanzania Development Assistance Framework (UN-DAF).

Interviews with representatives of the One UN pilot in Dar es Salaam in 2009 suggested that such a step would be problematic. First, the planning cycle of the One UN program was negotiated five years in advance and would require a renegotiation with the Government of Tanzania. Second, such a renegotiation would require the Government of Tanzania to prioritize the needs of Burundians over the needs of its own citizens in key areas of health, education, and sanitation. Third, such an initiative would need to overcome many of the limitations encountered with one of the early phases of the One UN initiative in Tanzania: the transition from relief to development in Northwestern Tanzania, known as JP6.1 (Joint Program 6.1).

JP6.1 was focused on the rehabilitation of regions of Northwestern Tanzania formerly hosting refugees under the broad term "transition from humanitarian assistance to sustainable development." At the core of this initiative was an understanding that Northwestern Tanzania, especially Kigoma, Kasulu, and Ngara, had previously hosted some 800,000 refugees, resulting in strains on the local environment, infrastructure, and administration. Given that the local population of the area lacked access to many basic services, especially in the area of health and education, the objective of JP6.1 was to rehabilitate former refugee facilities and transfer their use to the benefit of the local population. One of the few projects under this initiative to be implemented was the rehabilitation and transfer of assets in Muyovosi Camp, near Kasulu. Working with WFP and UNICEF, UNHCR was the lead agency responsible for overseeing the conversion and upgrading of infrastructure formerly used by refugees for the local communities, such as health centres and schools. Working with the Kasulu District authorities and with an investment of invested TSh. 472,650,000 (US$330,000), projects were implemented to convert structures of the camp for use as a high school and a health post for the benefit of the local population.

While seemingly a worthwhile undertaking, a range of concerns were raised about this initiative by representatives of both the Government of Tanzania and UN agencies. First, there were a number of frustrations with the slow implementation of the project. Given the challenges of harmonizing programs and budget structures, funds for JP6.1 took many months to be released. It was also noted that requests for proposals for the initiative raised unrealistic expectations on the part of local government officials, who viewed the initiative as a means of pursuing broader and much more ambitious infrastructure development in the region. Finally, there was a slow deployment of additional staff to implement the initiative, meaning that many UN staff were required to develop and implement the initiative over and above their normal duties.

Several informants interviewed during fieldwork in 2009 raised concerns when asked if JP6.1 could serve as a basis for development engagement with the local integration of Burundians from the 1972 settlements. First, it was noted that JP6.1 was focused on the transfer of assets from refugee settings to a local population. Given that local integration initiatives would involve the allocation of resources to a "refugee population," there were concerns as to how such an undertaking would be received by Regional and District Commissioners. Second, there was a strong feeling that the planning cycles for development and humanitarian programs remained incompatible. As already noted, the inclusion of local integration initiatives into the broader One UN program would necessitate a renegotiation of the UN-DAF with the Government of Tanzania. Given that the quick response of UNCHR and the donor community to the funding requests was considered to be central to the earlier shift in Tanzania's asylum policy towards naturalization, it would seem probable that delays in funding for local integration initiatives could undermine the process.[9]

---

[9] Although activities to support the local integration of the "newly-naturalized Tanzanians" were ultimately included in the 2011–15 UN Development Assistance Plan, approved by the Government of Tanzania on 13 Dec. 2010, follow-up interviews in Dar es Salaam in June 2011 suggested that, in fact, the two-year delay in specifying the necessary funds as part of the One UN program in Tanzania has significantly undermined the momentum in concluding the naturalization of the 1972 Burundians (interviews, Dar es Salaam, June 2011; Milner 2013).

In this way, it is important to note that many of the constraints on the implementation of an integrated response to local integration through development for Burundian refugees in Tanzania reflect a number of the ideational, material, and institutional factors highlighted by Betts and Orchard in their introduction to this volume. Just as Betts and Orchard draw on the work of VanDeveer and Dabelko to suggest that "state capacity plays an important role in explaining variation in implementation," with limited capacity frequently associated with low levels of implementation or resource-dependent norms, the integration of refugees into development planning in Tanzania was constrained by concerns about the ability to spread limited development resources over a larger population. There were also significant bureaucratic constraints, especially relating to the differing planning cycles and program methods employed by development and humanitarian actors, reflecting many of the institutional constraints suggested by Betts and Orchard. In contrast, it is equally interesting to note how similar dynamics were present in Burundi, yet served to enable an integrated approach to humanitarian and peace-building issues.

Regional Relations, Peace-Building, and Repatriation

The most striking findings from fieldwork in 2009 was the extent to which institutional actors engaged in peace-building and refugee issues in Burundi and Tanzania were linked in dynamic and responsive ways that may have not been initially intended. In this way, the findings on peace-building and repatriation suggest that the dynamics of actor interests and bureaucratic identity highlighted by Betts and Orchard as having a positive effect on norm implementation may help explain the implementation of the norm of integrated approaches in the UN system's activities in Burundi.

From the signing of the Arusha agreements in 2000 to elections in 2010, Burundi has undergone a significant period of transition in the last decade. While a number of regional and international actors played an important role in guiding this transition, the United Nations played an especially important role in the coordination of peace-building activities following the establishment of the United Nations Integration Office in Burundi (BINUB) by the UN Security Council in October 2006 (UNSC Resolution 1719/2006). The purpose of BINUB was "to assist Burundian Government efforts towards peace and stability, through coherent and coordinated response of the UN system in Burundi." BINUB's work primarily focused on four priority areas: peace consolidation and democratic governance; disarmament, demobilization, reintegration, and reform of the security sector; promotion and protection of human rights; and UN agency coordination.

In addition to these activities, BINUB played a central role in helping Burundi respond to the scale of refugee repatriation. As illustrated by Table 12.1, nearly 500,000 refugees repatriated to Burundi between 2002 and 2009, primarily from Tanzania.

Table 12.1 Return of Burundian refugees by country of asylum, from 2002 to July 2009

Period	DRC	Rwanda	Tanzania	Others	Total
2002–3	4,284	219	130,824	322	135,649
2004	879	151	89,039	258	90,327
2005	1,002	4,489	62,338	279	68,108
2006	1,284	615	42,765	251	44,915
2007	45	111	39,506	136	39,798
2008	6	36	94,891	135	95,068
2009	55	2,268	19,741	118	22,182
Total	**7,555**	**7,889**	**479,104**	**1,499**	**496,047**

Source: UNHCR Burundi.

From 2008, an increasing number of these refugees were returning from the Old Settlements in Tanzania, where they had been self-reliant for some twenty years. There was consequently an expectation that they would return to Burundi with the resources necessary to support the process of reintegration with limited external support. These assumptions proved to be ill-founded, however, as repatriating refugees returned without the necessary means to re-establish themselves in Burundi. Repatriation consequently was suspended for the first four months of 2009 as temporary accommodation centres became overcrowded with refugees who could not be relocated to a final destination.

An assessment of the returning refugee population found that, while many had access to land in Burundi (14 percent) or had access to land with some need of support to re-establish themselves on that land (52 percent), 32 percent of refugees either had land that was already occupied or had no land at all. It soon became clear that responding to the needs of these landless returnees was not only a humanitarian concern but a potential challenge to stability in Burundi. It was frequently noted that this population had returned from settlements that had been under the influence of exiled political opposition groups, that their current vulnerability made them susceptible to mobilization by political and armed groups, and that the potential impact of such a population was heightened not only in the context of the tenuous peace in Burundi but also in the run-up to elections in 2010.

The Government of Burundi worked with the UN system, under the leadership of BINUB, and representatives of donor governments and NGOs, to establish two institutional responses to these concerns. First, the Government established the Commission National de Terres et Autres Biens (CNTB: the National Land Commission). The mandate of the CNTB was to mediate cases of occupied land and to arbitrate solutions to ensure that returnees could find a destination for return and reintegration as soon as possible. As of August 2009, the CNTB had ruled on approximately 5,600 of 12,000 cases received. While the enduring legitimacy of these rulings may be questioned by future generations, the work of the CNTB was identified as a useful short-term mechanism to address the challenge of land within the context of peace-building and return and reintegration in Burundi. Second, the experience of 2008 and the potential destabilizing role of landless returnees prompted the Government of Burundi and BINUB to establish the Commission Intégrée pour le Rapatriement, la Réintégration et la Réinsertion, which brings together five key government ministries, BINUB, key UN agencies, national and international NGOs, and donor governments.

The work of the Commission Intégrée was one of the most interesting findings of fieldwork in 2009. Interview respondents frequently mentioned that the Commission Intégrée had developed the ability to address both the political and policy issues relating to the return and reintegration of refugees, including the sensitive issues relating to the coordination of the relevant ministries and UN agencies, decisions on the allocation of scarce resources, a reconsideration of land policies, and the prioritization of reintegration and land issues within the broader peace-building agenda in Burundi. In fact, the collaborative efforts in the Commission Intégrée, resulting from strong leadership from within BINUB and the Government of Burundi, have succeeded in broadening the conceptual scope of the peace-building debate to view the issues of reintegration of war-affected populations, including refugees, not only as a humanitarian issue, but also as a development and peace-building issue. As noted by the fifth report of the Secretary-General on BINUB (May 2009), addressing the needs of returning refugees is central to the overall objective of peace-building in Burundi:

> Despite the progress achieved... the situation in Burundi remained fragile and the processes of consolidating peace and security continued to face some challenges, especially given the issues associated with the following processes... (a) the disarmament, demobilization and reintegration of FNL combatants and the integration of some of them into the Burundian security forces, coupled with the need to address the longer-term reintegration of this caseload and previously demobilized combatants, as well as returning refugees and others; (b) preparations for the 2010 elections; and (c) national consultations on the establishment of transitional justice mechanisms. (para. 65, p. 13)

More generally, findings from Burundi suggest how many of the ideational, material, and institutional factors identified by Betts and Orchard in the Introduction appeared to have a positive effect on the formulation and implementation of an integrated approach to returnees and peace-building in Burundi. Arguably the most significant factor was the convergence of the interests of a range of government and UN actors, especially at a senior level.

The fact that senior representatives of the Government of Burundi and the Special Representative of the Secretary-General to Burundi both identified a comprehensive response to refugee repatriation as essential to successful peace-building was clearly an important factor in motivating an integrated response. While this prioritization helped overcome a number of institutional challenges that constrained integration in Tanzania, it also played a central role in fostering a bureaucratic identity that valued creative problem-solving and the fostering of collaboration. Whereas development and humanitarian actors in Tanzania were encouraged by their managers to preserve the space within which their programs operated, senior managers of UN programs in Burundi valued staff who demonstrated the ability to reach out to and collaborate with counterparts in other UN agencies. This suggests that additional research on the role of individuals as "norm advocates" (Park and Vetterlein 2010: 21), "norm entrepreneurs," and "norm implementers" could usefully shed important light on variation between the implementation of common policy norms in different contexts.

CONCLUSION

The purpose of this chapter has been to consider the policy norm of integrated approaches within the UN system as an example of the potential gap between institutionalization and implementation, as proposed by Betts and Orchard in the Introduction. Drawing on the cases of peace-building in Burundi and development in Tanzania, the chapter has considered the plausibility of the causal mechanisms outlined by Betts and Orchard to explain variation between the implementation of the policy norm of integrated UN action. This chapter has argued that many of the ideational, material, and institutional dynamics that Betts and Orchard identify as enabling or constraining norm implementation were found to be active in the case studies.

Specifically, findings from Burundi suggest that strong leadership at a field level and the sustained engagement of the local state helped overcome a number of institutional divisions and gaps that initially frustrated an integrated response. Conversely, findings from Tanzania illustrate how efforts to integrate solutions for refugees into UN development activities in Western Tanzania were constrained by differences in institutional approaches, a lack of resources, and differences in expectations. In this way, the chapter has argued that integrated approaches to development in Tanzania were largely *constrained* by issues of capacity and bureaucratic contestation, while integrated approaches to peace-building in Burundi were *enabled* due to the interests of key actors and the bureaucratic identity created by senior institutional leaders.

Ultimately, the results of these plausibility probes illustrate the importance of the causal mechanisms outlined by Betts and Orchard and the potential benefits of additional research, especially field research, to more fully understand the factors that enable or constrain the implementation of policy norms.

These preliminary findings also suggest at least two aspects of norm implementation that may be usefully explored through future research. First, it is interesting to note the role that "pilot programs" played in the implementation of the policy norm of integrated approaches. Neither the UN PBC nor the One UN initiative were immediately responsible for all peace-building and development activities within the UN system. Instead, the implementation of the norm of integrated action was implemented through an incremental process, involving a limited number of pilot countries. Just as Betts and Orchard argue that "the implementation process itself can open up a new arena for interpretation and contestation of the norm by relevant actors," it would be useful to more systematically consider the specific role that pilot programs play in the implementation of policy norms and in the future shaping of that norm.

In the case of Burundi, for example, the experience of the pilot project highlighted the importance of solutions for displaced populations as part of the peace-building process. This lesson was communicated back to the global level through mission reports, which arguably contributed to additional precision in the application of the norm, including the issuance of the "Preliminary Framework for Supporting a More Coherent, Predictable and Effective Response to the Durable Solutions Needs of Refugees and Internally Displaced Persons," as endorsed by the UN Secretary-General on 4 October 2011. To this end, it may prove useful to more systematically understand on what basis these pilot countries are selected, the role that they play in providing a constructive space for "interpretation and contestation," and to what extent the lessons and experiences of these pilot programs feed back to the global level and potentially help specify or clarify the policy norm.

Second, more detailed understandings of the experience of norm implementation in specific contexts may offer additional insight on the role individuals play through the stages of the policy norm cycle. In the introduction to their edited volume on policy norms and the work of the IMF and World Bank, Park and Vetterlein (2010: 21) highlight the important role played by "norm advocates" in the emergence of particular policy norms and outline how these actors "used argument, persuasion and negotiation to influence the Fund and the Bank to adopt a much broader approach to development." In a similar way, the case of Burundi highlights the important role played by "norm implementers" in the realization of an integrated approach to peace-building, specifically in overcoming many of the institutional factors that could otherwise have constrained the implementation of the norm. Just as norm entrepreneurs are understood by constructivists as playing critical roles in the early stages of the norm life-cycle, the findings from Burundi illustrate how similar actors can play an important role in the implementation process.

These activities, however, may be understood to have not only contributed to norm emergence. Instead, through the actions of norm advocates, the integration of the needs of displaced populations in Burundi became normalized—or, in the words of Park and Vetterlein (2012: 22) habitualized—thereby contributing to norm stabilization both at the field level in Burundi and arguably at the global level. This suggests that future research on the role of individuals and the implementation of policy norms at the field level could not only make an important contribution to our understanding of the stages and mechanisms in the norm cycle proposed by Park and Vetterlein, but more generally make important contributions to our understanding of the significance of implementation in the meaning and endurance of policy norms.

13

Institutionalizing and Implementing the Disaster Relief Norm
The League of Red Cross Societies and the International Relief Union

Scott D. Watson

Every year, numerous natural disasters around the world overwhelm the capacity of states and local communities; affecting, on average, 200 million people and causing billions of dollars in damage to property and infrastructure (Saechao 2007: 663–4). Unlike the response to complex humanitarian emergencies, the response of the international community to these disasters is relatively predictable and stable, if insufficient. As an international norm, there is a "collective expectation that the proper behavior" (Katzenstein 1996: 5) in such circumstances is to offer assistance, either through multilateral or bilateral means, at the request of the receiving state.

While not strongly institutionalized in international law, international and domestic implementation of disaster relief is fairly robust. Kent (2004: 860) estimates that there are over 1,000 organizations (including state agencies, NGOs, and IGOs) that participate in the provision of international disaster relief. And disaster assistance is no longer primarily associated with OECD countries: over ninety governments responded to the 2004 Indian Ocean tsunami (Barnett and Weiss 2011: 29), while the recent disaster in Japan elicited offers of assistance from over 115 governments. Annual international humanitarian assistance (including but not limited to disaster relief) now exceeds $18 billion (Barnett and Weiss 2011: 29).

Yet a quick glance at the UN consolidated appeals process demonstrates that this vast disaster relief network is inadequate to the task. Few disasters are fully funded, and many garner less than 50 percent of the funding required to adequately meet the needs of those affected (United Nations 2011b). Furthermore, the increasing amount of resources devoted to disaster relief has not produced more effectively organized disaster relief (McEntire 1997: 228). There are gaps both in the development of "international law and IGO/NGO capabilities" (Fidler 2005: 462), and between the implicit goal of fully responding to all humanitarian emergencies and the inadequate support for and poor coordination of disaster relief. In this chapter I contend that understanding these gaps requires an understanding of how the norm of disaster relief was implemented and later institutionalized as a voluntary, charitable activity provided through a loose network of state and non-state entities.

According to Finnemore and Sikkink, institutionalization refers to the establishment of "international law, rules of multilateral organizations and bilateral foreign policies," "clarify[ing] what, exactly, the norm is and what constitutes violation.... and spell[ing] out specific procedures by which norm leaders coordinate disapproval and sanctions for norm breaking" (1998: 900). As it currently stands, international disaster relief is primarily institutionalized through soft law (Katoch 2003; Fisher 2007); and few binding international instruments pertain directly to disaster relief. While scholars of international norms do not dismiss soft law in the process of normative development, it is still generally understood as either a weaker form of international law that is less likely to produce normative compliance (Kirton and Trebilcock 2004) or as a "mechanism" for promoting new norms (Orchard 2010). Despite the collective establishment of principles and "policy norms" (Park and Vetterlein 2010) to guide disaster relief and humanitarian assistance by IGOs and INGOs, these do not address the fundamental questions of how much or what form of relief each actor should provide. This is not a failure of institutionalization or implementation, but rather an intentional form of institutionalization that followed from the American model of disaster relief implementation in the early twentieth century. This supports Betts and Orchard's assertion (this volume) that institutionalization and implementation should not be understood as sequential process, but as roughly parallel processes, in which implementation may precede, and profoundly influence, institutionalization.

In the first section of this chapter, I focus on the emergence and implementation of the disaster relief norm in the late nineteenth and early twentieth centuries. I show that three interrelated socio-political shifts profoundly shaped the emergence and implementation, and subsequently the institutionalization, of the disaster relief norm. In the second section I focus in detail on efforts to institutionalize the disaster relief norm in the post-First World War period—the establishment of the League of Red Cross Societies (LRCS) and the International Relief Union (IRU). These cases demonstrate both the impact of implementation on institutionalization, and the role of ideational and material power in the institutionalization process. In the concluding section I demonstrate how the current UN-based disaster relief system demonstrates normative and institutional continuity with the pre-UN disaster relief system. The narratives and normative commitments that influenced the creation of the LRCS and IRU, specifically the voluntaristic nature of disaster relief and the importance of maintaining state sovereignty, continue to animate the actions of the UN and limit the possibilities for the provision of disaster relief.

EMERGENCE OF THE DISASTER RELIEF NORM

The norm emergence and institutionalization process involves the exercise of power, is marked by competition and opposition (Jepperson et al. 1996: 56; Van Kersbergen and Verbeek 2007: 219), and proceeds in a non-linear fashion (Sundstrom 2005; Park and Vetterlein 2010; Krook and True 2012). In the institutionalization phase, the contested norms are imprecise and the institutionalization process is, if done effectively, meant to increase precision (Introduction to this volume; Percy 2007). Institutionalization is meant to resolve this contestation and produce relatively stable norms, though all norms remain "subject to future contestation" (Park and Vetterlein 2010: 19). How these emerging norms stabilize and the form of institutionalization they take is a product of human agency and patterns of implementation. In the case of the disaster relief norm, as is shown in the following section, its implementation was a product both of human agency and of ideational and material power configurations in international politics; these helped to both constitute relevant actors and constrain the actions of these actors.

In the case of disaster relief, norm advocates drew on three broad and inter-related discourses that were (and are) foundational to disaster relief: science, humanitarianism, and order. The disaster relief norm emerged with a scientific understanding of disaster, combined with and complemented by an emerging humanitarian ethos and an emphasis on order. The impetus for normative change was rooted in broader social changes in the late eighteenth and early nineteenth centuries that challenged existing explanations for the occurrence of natural disasters and how to appropriately respond to them. Writing of the 1755 Lisbon earthquake—the earliest recorded instance of international disaster relief in modern times—de Vattel argued that providing assistance was a "duty of humanity" among "civilized" nations (De Vattel and Chitty 1849: book II, ch. 1, principle 5). De Vattel was not articulating an entirely new norm: he was drawing on prominent frames such as "civilization" and "duties of humanity" that were prominent in European thought at that time (see Gong 1984; Bowden 2004).

The "standard of civilization" was a common frame that had varying and multiple meanings (Bowden 2004: 54). Yet one particularly strong "standard of civilization" was, and is, the standard of modernity, understood as the "application of science and technology to common problems" (Gong 1984: 93). Such a standard is clearly articulated in de Vattel's argument for disaster relief, which combined a humanitarian ethics and a rational, scientific understanding of natural disaster, in contrast to the dominant theological interpretation

(Hutchinson 2000: 4). This had important implications, in that it opened up the possibility of understanding the geological causes of disaster (and later the social causes of human vulnerability), and in turn the possibility of preventing and/or responding to natural disasters.

While the interpretation of natural disasters as punishment from God during the Middle Ages was not as hegemonic as is often suggested (Udias 2009: 41; Cutler 2009: 535), it remained a very popular and persuasive understanding into the eighteenth century. Udias (2009: 45) notes that an earthquake in Spain in 1680 was understood, without recorded contest, as punishment from God. In contrast, by 1755 the cause of the Lisbon earthquake was heavily contested by those promoting religious or scientific explanations. Prominent actors in Portugal explained the Lisbon earthquake as punishment from God (Udias, 2009) and the Dutch Government used this interpretation as the basis for their decision not to send disaster assistance to Portugal (Hutchinson 2000: 5).

By the end of the nineteenth century in Europe and the United States, however, the interpretation of natural disaster as punishment from God was clearly the marginal position. Few actors, political elites, or religious leaders resorted to this argument in reference to either the San Francisco earthquake of 1906 or the Messina earthquake in 1908 (Hutchinson 2000). This shift, which altered the meaning given to earthquakes and other natural disasters, contributed to a second shift in what was conceivable to do in preparation for and in response to natural disaster. Henry Davison, an influential norm entrepreneur of disaster relief whom I examine in further detail in the next section, understood the expansion of Red Cross societies in all nations as "throw[ing] the light of science upon every corner of the world" (quoted in Buckingham 1964: 70). Giovanni Ciarolo, another norm entrepreneur encountered in the next section, referred to his program as "enlightening through scientific research, the path of humanity amid the miseries of its great collective disasters" (Ciarolo 1924: 1462).

The promotion of a rational, scientific understanding of natural disasters remains a central component of disaster relief. For instance, the UN's disaster risk reduction program aims to "analyze and reduce the causal factors of disasters" (UNISDR 2011). In discussing the importance of disaster preparedness and relief, UN Secretary-General Ban Ki-moon (2011) stated "the more governments, UN agencies [etc.] understand risk and vulnerability, the better equipped they will be to mitigate disasters...and save more lives." The growing use of scientific techniques, such as disaster risk assessment, disaster mapping, architectural design, disaster simulation, and warning systems (Foster 1980; Blaikie 1994), indicates how thoroughly science has penetrated our understanding and response to natural disasters. Such an emphasis is neither universal nor neutral, but privileges particular cultures and types of knowledge (Hewitt 1983). Kent (1987: 16–17) observes that the scientific basis of the current disaster relief program is virtually uncontested and that it has resulted in an overemphasis on the necessity of aid, the categorization of disasters and imposition of common relief models regardless of local context, and the neglect of "psychological, social and economic" needs and capacities of those affected. The shift to a scientific understanding of disaster is one of the most important developments that made it possible to question what was the appropriate response to natural disaster events, and who may appropriately respond. This ultimately contributed to the emergence, implementation, and institutionalization of a disaster relief norm.

The resolution of these questions emerged from two other foundational discourses: humanitarianism and order. The importance of the state in the provision of order and public goods more generally was central to the emergence of the disaster relief norm. Assistance for victims of natural disasters was, and is, seen first and foremost as the responsibility of the affected state; the international community intervenes only when disaster overwhelms the capacity of the state. International disaster relief is used to physically establish and/or rhetorically re-establish order and the authority of the state in affected regions.

These concerns are evident in early efforts to respond to natural disasters and in current UN resolutions on disaster relief. Indeed, the IRU (1927) specifically applied to disasters that "exceed the limits and the powers of the stricken people." The UN's Guiding Principles for disaster assistance stress that the primary responsibility falls to the affected states, while the international community may respond when "the magnitude and duration are...beyond the response capacity of affected country."[1] The primary contribution that the LRCS, IRU, and UN make to disaster relief is that of coordination—the provision of order and authority in the re-establishment of order and authority. American disaster relief programs in the early 1900s stressed the importance of "coordination, centralized authority and order" in the immediate aftermath of natural disaster, and that reconstruction after relief was viewed as an opportunity to rebuild communities in a more orderly fashion (Hutchinson 2000: 12). Nearly one hundred years later, the same concerns were evident in the aftermath of the 2004 Indian Ocean tsunami, where states providing relief were concerned at the outset with establishing order and authority (preventing looting and crime) in affected areas and where post-disaster reconstruction presented an opportunity to rebuild communities in a more orderly and economically desirable fashion that would reduce vulnerability to natural disaster (Watson 2011).

The third discourse that remains a staple of disaster relief is that of humanitarianism. Beginning in the late eighteenth century, Haskett (1985: 335) notes that humanitarianism transformed Western societies and fundamentally altered attitudes to a wide range of vulnerable people, including the poor, the

---

[1] United Nations General Assembly 1991, Resolution 46/182, *Strengthening of the Coordination of Humanitarian Emergency Assistance at the UN.*

insane, and children. Yet the content and meaning of humanitarianism proceeded through various periods of contestation (Barnett and Weiss 2011) and it has never been settled or stable.[2] During the institutionalization phase of disaster relief, two aspects of humanitarianism were heavily contested: universality and voluntarism.

Whether humanitarian obligations were universal and compulsory was contested early on, as Finnemore (2004) clearly demonstrates in her work on humanitarian intervention. Similarly, understanding that the provision of disaster relief represents a universal and compulsory commitment to humanity has gradually and incrementally increased, though it is (and may necessarily always be) incomplete. In offering assistance after the Lisbon disaster, Spain and England's response was the exception, rather than the norm: most states did not provide assistance to Portugal, and numerous other devastating earthquakes during the eighteenth century received no international assistance (Hutchinson 2000: 4–5). Even de Vattel, the early disaster norm entrepreneur, "qualified the moral duty to provide disaster relief sufficiently to leave states with discretion on whether and how to provide relief" (Fidler 2005: 461). The original LRCS included only Allied states, and the IRU applied only to co-signatories. Even today, not all states respond to natural disasters in other states, and some disasters garner very little attention or international assistance.

The insistence on the part of some early disaster relief norm adopters that humanitarian assistance is voluntary (rather than compulsory) reflected and reinforced a strong resistance to both universality and international taxation. This encouraged instead an emphasis on the role of civil society and the freedom of choice in the provision of disaster relief, limiting compulsory obligations on states. It should be noted that various actors continue to argue in favour of disaster relief understood as a right (Hardcastle and Chua 1997) or as falling under the "responsibility to protect" (Saechao 2007), both of which involve moving away from a voluntaristic humanitarian understanding of disaster relief. I contend, however, that the lack of contestation at the UN reflects a relatively stable interpretation of humanitarianism, and in turn disaster relief, as a voluntary act.

These three broader narratives drawn on by early disaster relief entrepreneurs profoundly shaped how the norm was, and continues to be, institutionalized and implemented. In the case studies presented in the next section, I show how these broader narratives intersect with human agency, material and ideational power structures, and historical contingencies to shape how the

---

[2] Though various entities, particularly the Red Cross and the UN, have tried to fix its meaning, humanitarianism is generally understood in terms of humanity, neutrality, and impartiality (UNGA Res 46/182, 1991). The ICRC emphasizes the principles of humanity, neutrality, impartiality, and independence (ICRC 2008).

disaster relief was implemented and later institutionalized in two forms: the League of Red Cross Societies and the International Relief Union.

THE LRCS AND THE IRU

There is little evidence of routine international disaster relief until the late 1800s, and it emerges as a sort of by-product of the creation of humanitarian organizations designed for other purposes. In the mid to late 1800s, national Red Cross societies were created as means to alleviate suffering in wartime, but they also led efforts to provide disaster relief. Though Red Cross "founder" Henry Dunant was primarily concerned with wartime suffering, he had envisioned that these national societies could provide relief in cases of natural disaster as well (IFRC 2009: 3). The French Red Cross society provided relief during the 1876 floods in Paris (IFRC 2009: 3), while the American Red Cross was responding to disasters in the United States as early as 1881 (Gilbo 1987: 1) and played a pivotal role in the response to the devastating 1906 San Francisco earthquake (Deacon 1918; Hutchinson 2000: 4). These national Red Cross societies, along with other relief organizations such as the St John's Ambulance Association, founded in the UK in 1877, were part of a broader humanitarian movement that emphasized medical assistance in cases of crisis or disasters. Initially, however, they focused on domestic incidents.

It was the American Red Cross (ARC) under Clara Barton that expanded disaster relief to the international level, demonstrating that domestic implementation can precede and influence international institutionalization. The ARC first became involved in international disaster relief in 1890 in response to the famine in Russia, and was involved in several other international disasters during that decade (Moorehead 1998: 99).[3] In 1908, the ARC and numerous European Red Cross societies responded to the devastating Messina earthquake. These ad hoc efforts, as well as the work of the Red Cross societies during the First World War, led to two parallel approaches to institutionalizing an international disaster relief norm in the inter-war period. The director of the American Red Cross, William Davison, led one approach while the other was led by the director of the Italian Red Cross, Giovani Ciarolo. These two distinct efforts reveal much about norm implementation and institutionalization, such as the importance of material and ideational power in influencing the outcome of the institutionalization process and the centrality of contestation, adaptation, and mediation among

---

[3] Based on Moorehead's (1998) account, these early ventures were mostly funded by co-nationals and co-religionists of the affected groups in the United States, funnelled through the ARC.

norm entrepreneurs in producing an institutionalized norm (Krook and True 2012: 108).

The LRCS

With its greater experience of providing international disaster relief (Buckingham 1964: 2; Hutchinson 2000: 9), the ARC projected itself as the lead organization in the field by the early 1900s (Hutchinson 1996). In 1918, the ARC produced the first handbook on how to respond to natural disasters (Deacon 1918). By the outbreak of the First World War, the US Government had established firm control over the ARC,[4] and the organization was in a good position to lead efforts to institutionalize international disaster relief by virtue of its demonstrated expertise and influence in the field. This was buttressed by the enterprising efforts of Henry Davison, who was appointed the ARC's director in 1917 at the outset of American participation in the war, and had the moral and financial support of President Woodrow Wilson. Davison envisioned the creation of a "peacetime Red Cross," with a new or expanded Geneva Convention, the establishment of national Red Cross societies that would cooperate internationally, and a mandate to alleviate suffering associated with war, disease, and natural disasters (Hutchinson 1996: 289).

Davison first sought to alter the mandate of the International Committee of the Red Cross (ICRC) and to promote the creation of a new Geneva Convention that would institutionalize disaster relief in the same way that the previous Geneva Conventions had institutionalized norms of wartime protection for combatants (Hutchinson 1996: 293). However, the ICRC resisted expanding their mandate, which they saw as maintaining and expanding international law on inter-state war (Buckingham 1964). The Swiss-based ICRC saw Davison's proposal as a threat to the authority of the ICRC and an attempt to "assert American leadership" over the Red Cross movement (Forsythe 2005: 36). When it became apparent that Davison could not convince the ICRC to expand its mandate, he formed, with the Allied national Red Cross societies, a "real international Red Cross," the League of Red Cross Societies (LRCS), which would be representative of its membership (unlike the exclusively Swiss ICRC) and backed by American finances and expertise (Forsythe 2005: 36).

Davison's vision was promoted through a two-pronged strategy: diplomatic efforts aimed at leaders of the Allied States, led by President Woodrow Wilson and Colonel Edward House, Wilson's key advisor, combined with Davison's own efforts to bring the leaders of the national Red Cross societies on board

---

[4] Problems toward the end of Barton's time as head of the ARC, combined with the onset of the First World War, had resulted in the US Government asserting greater control over the ARC, with the director of the ARC officially appointed by the US President.

(Hutchinson 1996: 289). Wilson discussed the Red Cross at the Paris Peace Conference and managed to have the importance of national Red Cross societies written into the Covenant of the League of Nations (Forsythe 2005: 33). For his part, Davison gained the support of the leaders of the Allied Red Cross societies for his vision, by emphasizing the "truly international nature" of the LRCS and American financial support (Hutchinson 1996: 289).

The articles of association for the LRCS nicely demonstrate the institutional form preferred by the ARC: "national Red Cross societies in all states"; a mandate to "improve health, prevent disease, and mitigate suffering"; a call to "bring the benefits of the fields of science and medicine to humanity"; and to "coordinate relief work in the event of national and international disasters" (Hutchinson 1996: 304). Thus, the LRCS represented a continuation of the civilizing mission through the promotion of scientific knowledge and an emphasis on voluntary humanitarianism with only limited international obligations, epitomized by the American implementation of disaster relief. Davison's proposal maintained and reinforced the existing practice of promoting the interests of donating states by emphasizing the importance of bilateral relationships between states through their respective national Red Cross societies. The LRCS was to act only as an overarching organization charged with promotion of the Red Cross and relief coordination functions. In this system, national societies could choose whether to participate in an overseas disaster relief program and how much to provide, but were not required to respond to any particular disaster nor were individual societies under the auspices or control of the larger body (Buckingham 1964: 65). The LRCS system, which became the International Federation of the Red Cross (IFRC) in 1983, continues to operate on similar principles, though as with other humanitarian NGOs it has developed extensive policy norms regarding how humanitarian assistance is to be implemented.

Davison's proposal institutionalized American practice in disaster relief at the international level, though there remained a gap between Davison's vision, the principles of the LRCS, and its actual implementation of disaster relief. A number of internal and external developments contributed to this shift. Shortly after the First World War, there were internal divisions within the United States over its post-war position in the world which, combined with Wilson's incapacitation and the success of the Republicans in the 1920 American elections, resulted in the move to isolationism (Knock 1992). These divisions were evident in the ARC as well, which was divided over whether the LRCS should endorse a broad mandate including public health and disaster relief, or a narrower mandate specializing in health and medicine. Those holding a narrow and isolationist view ultimately succeeded, which meant that the ARC was less willing to engage in international disaster relief (Buckingham 1964: 107).

In addition, there were pressures to return to "normalcy" after the First World War that resulted in a significant reduction in spending on both military forces as well as national Red Cross societies (Buckingham 1964: 141).

Ideationally, the US was less interested in international disaster relief, and materially the ARC and LRCS faced a significant reduction in financial support. Furthermore, Davison's death in 1922 allowed those with a narrower vision for the ARC to gain control of the organization (Hutchinson 2000). Lastly, the world economic crisis and the onset of another world war severely limited the LRCS, by reducing funds available for international disaster relief and redirecting attention to traditional Red Cross wartime activities.

Despite these significant obstacles, the LRCS did coordinate disaster relief in response to several international disasters in the 1920s and through the 1930s, though the primary responder in these cases was the ARC (Buckingham 1964: 103–4). More importantly, the model of disaster relief based on cooperating national Red Cross societies became the foundation of international disaster relief in the League of Nations and, to a great extent, in the United Nations. The importance of setting up national societies was incorporated into the Covenant of the League of Nations in Article 25, and the IRU contracted the LRCS to implement disaster relief. After the Second World War, the United Nations' initial efforts to institutionalize and implement disaster relief also relied heavily on the Red Cross, as seen in the seminal 1965 UN General Assembly Resolution 2034, which called on all member states "to consider setting up national Red Cross or Red Crescent societies."[5] Katoch (2003: 49) contends that working with the Red Cross/Crescent is one of the "four foundations of UN General Assembly resolutions on disaster relief."

The "national societies" model encapsulated in the LRCS, and carried through to the League and UN, became a means to increase individual state capacity to act as first responders in their own states, a concern that has become even more explicit and prominent in the UN system. The LRCS model also reinforced a disaster relief system in which states could employ their national Red Cross societies to assist other Red Cross societies. This emphasis on bilateral disaster relief continues to be a prominent element of disaster relief under the UN, though it is no longer primarily Red Cross to Red Cross, but occurs through a wide range of organizations and mechanisms (Fischer 2003; Katoch 2003; Fisher 2007).

The ability of the LRCS to survive the economic depression and the Second World War reflected the flexibility of the Red Cross model in that it remained national in orientation, voluntaristic in its demands, and could be mobilized for peace and wartime activities. National Red Cross societies operated in their traditional capacity during the Second World War and the Red Cross brand survived relatively intact and ready to take up a more expansive mandate in the aftermath of the war. The LRCS served a number of important functions after the war, most notably by providing assistance for European refugees. Shortly thereafter, the LRCS returned to disaster relief, and it remains a central

---

[5] UNGA 1965, Resolution 2034 (XX), *Assistance in Cases of Natural Disaster.*

component of the current network of disaster relief (Kent 1987). The IFRC is the largest humanitarian aid organization in the world, consisting of 187 national societies; and in 2010 it spent over US$515 million in humanitarian aid (IFRC 2009).

However, the voluntary nature of obligations, the reliance on American financing, and the bilateral element of disaster relief emphasized through the LRCS proved to be a significant shortcoming, and an impetus for norm entrepreneurs to pursue other forms of institutionalization. Efforts at both the League of Nations and the United Nations emphasized the importance of national Red Cross societies, but also sought to create an alternative under-standing of the disaster relief norm, one in which commitments were compul-sory rather than voluntary and assistance was multilateral rather than bilateral. The IRU represents the closest the international community has come to real-izing this goal and it continues to shape the response of the UN to disaster relief.

The IRU

From a conventional norm institutionalization framework, the IRU enjoyed an enviable position compared with the LRCS in terms of consolidating and implementing disaster relief. According to David Fidler, the 1927 Convention and Statute Establishing an International Relief Union (IRU) was one of only two multilateral treaties on disaster relief that have ever been adopted; the other is the 1998 Tampere Convention on the Provision of Telecommunication Resources for Disaster Mitigation and Relief Operations, which applies to a highly specified type of activity (Fidler 2005: 462). Thus, the formation of the IRU in 1927 remains to this day the most successful attempt to institu-tionalize an international disaster relief norm through an international treaty (Fidler 2005: 462). In contrast, the LRCS emerged as a principle norm rather than treaty norm (Betts and Orchard, this volume). The IRU and the LRCS demonstrate that norms occupying similar ideational space and pertain-ing to a particular regulative ideal can be institutionalized through treaty or principle, and that institutionalization through treaty does not necessarily imply a more robust form of institutionalization, longevity, or more effective implementation.

The IRU came about due in large part to the entrepreneurship of Giovanni Ciarolo, the President of the Italian Red Cross. Having lost family in the Messina earthquake in 1908 and witnessed the Red Cross response to that disaster, Ciarolo became a leading proponent for international disaster relief (Moorehead 1998: 158, 264). As early as 1915, Ciarolo advocated for improvements in disaster response at both the national and international level. His efforts centred on disaster insurance and an international assistance organization (Hutchinson 2000: 14). In 1921, Ciarolo submitted a formal proposal to the ICRC that departed from the existing normative framework captured in the LRCS (Macalister-Smith 1986: 364). Rebuffed by the ICRC, Ciarolo was invited to submit a proposal to the League of Nations (Hutchinson 2000: 18–19). In it, he called for "an international organization for the relief and assistance of people overtaken by disaster," with "technical work...and administration entrusted to the Red Cross," paid for through a central fund based on annual assessed contributions "at the full and entire disposal of the ICRC" (Ciarolo 1922a).

Ciarolo's proposal shared the scientific approach to disaster relief[6] and the emphasis on centralized authority and order, but differed in his interpretation of humanitarianism, which he presented as universal and compulsory. This is evident in his call for annual assessed contributions from member states, and his initial proposal of "compulsory insurance of all citizens against such calamities" (Ciarolo 1922b). Ciarolo's goal was much more visionary and revolutionary than Davison's; though, like Davison, the actual institution that Ciarolo and his supporters/competitors succeeded in creating shifted over time in response to material and ideational forms of power. As noted earlier, the ICRC was hesitant to shift its focus to peacetime activities and unwilling to act as the primary driving force behind the proposal. At the same time, the LRCS was in no position to champion Ciarolo's vision; in 1921 it was suffering from lack of leadership due to the illness of both Davison and his successor, David Henderson. The interim leadership was focused on "public health and disease prevention" (Hutchinson 2000: 15–17).

Even more problematic was the opposition of the United States to the idea of the IRU. Increasing American isolationism after 1920 meant that they were not supportive of the League of Nations or the stronger international obligations contained in the IRU proposal. The United States Government and the ARC were opposed on several grounds, which were nicely summarized in the ARC's response to Ciarolo's proposal, presented to the League of Nations by the ARC as the official American governmental position. They strongly opposed the compulsory nature of the financial obligations, which the response referred to as a "tax." They questioned how the League would enforce tax collection, who would control its redistribution, and whether countries with higher risk of natural disaster would be taxed equally to those with lower risks. In summary, the ARC (1924) asserted "the Red Cross is a voluntary organization...its altruistic spirit would be lost and it would become merely a dispenser of money collected by compulsory taxation."

---

[6] On several occasions, Ciarolo emphasized the scientific nature of the project. In response to some concerns with his original proposal, Ciarolo emphasized the "carefully thought-out scientific basis" for his scheme and garnered support from the "learned societies" of the world (Clouzot 1924).

Hutchinson (2000) cites a number of reasons why the US was opposed to Ciarolo's proposal: the dominant powers in the United States were increasingly isolationist and skeptical of liberal internationalism; the US envisioned an "international order based on private capitalism and philanthropy" rather than public taxation; and the US saw "tactical advantages in keeping disaster relief a bilateral affair" to ensure its influence over regions prone to natural disaster (Hutchinson 2000: 30–1).

Other states also opposed Ciarolo's proposal. The British governmental representative, Lord Balfour, argued that the Red Cross should not be distracted by non-wartime activities and that the League Council "would never consent to collect money if it were not entrusted with its control" (League of Nations 1922). Most member states expressed their appreciation for Ciarolo's ideals, even as they identified a number of practical, economic objections to his proposal as it was presented.

Nonetheless, the proposal had enough support among the member states of the League to warrant further discussion and after a series of replies and revisions from Ciarolo, the League agreed to form a Preparatory Committee. This committee included representatives from the scheme's two largest and strongest opponents—the American Red Cross and the British Red Cross—and included international experts on insurance and international law. The Preparatory Committee quickly dismissed elements of the proposal that they saw as unrealistic, supporting Krook and True's (2012: 108) observation that the norm institutionalization process requires the "demarcation of that which is outside the limits of discourse."

In defining disasters, it excluded man-made disasters and disasters that "might have been avoided by prudent administration," wary of encouraging moral hazard (Preparatory Committee 1925: 1259). The Committee also dismissed Ciarolo's "universal right to relief" by stating that they "had no intention of introducing into international relations a positive obligation enforceable by penalties" (Preparatory Committee 1925: 1260). On the idea of insurance, the committee concluded that "international disaster relief can hardly take the form of insurance" because it "presupposes an estimate of risk" and in cases of natural disaster, these are "unforeseen by definition" (Preparatory Committee 1925: 1261). Lastly, on the matter of compulsory financial contributions, they concluded that "the IRU would run the risk of drying up the springs of generosity in the people at large" and that "more will be gained from freedom than obligation" (Preparatory Committee 1925: 1264).

The Preparatory Committee created a final proposal for the formation of the IRU that bore little resemblance to Ciarolo's original vision. Gone were the expansive conceptualization of disaster, the commitment to a universal right of disaster relief, the idea of disaster insurance, and fixed financial commitments from individual member states. In their place was an International Relief Union that prioritized state sovereignty and consent (IRU Convention,

Articles 3 and 4; Macalister-Smith 1986: 365; Fidler 2005: 463), and that consisted of an initial compulsory fund (Article 9), maintained by subsequent voluntary funding (Article 11 and 12; Macalister-Smith 1986: 366–8; Hutchinson 2001: 259). While the LRCS and national Red Cross societies were to implement disaster relief, the IRU would coordinate and distribute those funds to the Red Cross societies (Macalister-Smith 1986: 365). Working through the League of Nations had forced Ciarolo to engage with entrenched material and ideational forms of power, and resulted in a drastically revised version of disaster relief.

The IRU came into force in 1932, and concluded an agreement with the ICRC and the LRCS in 1933 to actually implement disaster relief operations. In its lifespan, the IRU made very modest contributions to two relief operations, an earthquake in India in 1934 and in Baluchistan in 1935; and it also began to compile preliminary data on disaster frequency (Macalister-Smith 1986: 370). By 1938, its agreement with the LRCS was altered, which effectively withdrew the LRCS from the IRU. By 1943 the IRU was in essence defunct and it was formally dissolved in 1966 (Macalister-Smith 1986: 370).

There are a number of insights to be gained from Ciarolo's effort to institutionalize an international disaster relief norm. It represented a radical departure from how disaster relief had been already implemented, suggesting that institutionalization may be profoundly influenced by implementation. In addition, American opposition (to the League and IRU), combined with concerns voiced by a number of other states and private actors, reaffirm that material and ideational power are both key factors in the norm institutionalization process. Some ideas, such as a universal right to relief and universal insurance schemes, were ultimately non-starters, excluded early on from serious consideration. Other ideas, namely compulsory multilateral aid, were more contested, but eventually dropped in favour of voluntarism. Ciarolo's vision for the IRU represented a significant challenge to the existing practice of disaster relief, namely its voluntary and bilateral elements. The multilateral nature of the IRU undermined the positive connotations associated with bilateral aid and relief reinforced through the LRCS model. From its early roots, disaster relief was an important aspect of state's foreign policy. Hutchinson (2001: 268) observes that, in response to the Tokyo earthquake in 1923, the US, France, and Sweden were insistent on keeping disaster relief "a bilateral affair." When Kissinger noted in 1976 that disaster relief "is becoming a major instrument of our foreign policy" (quoted in Kent 1987: 81), he was actually quite mistaken; it had been an important element of American foreign policy virtually since its inception.

While legal institutionalization did not weaken a previously strong norm (Percy 2007: 388–9), it did limit its growth. Ciarolo's push to legally institutionalize the norm required concessions that drastically weakened states' normative obligations and stunted the expansion of the disaster relief norm. The

UN made little effort to revive the IRU, though it readily adopted the model of the IRU for international disaster relief. This included relying on voluntary funds and an appeals process as its primary funding mechanism. The debates in the League negotiation over the IRU were not repeated in the UN—those debates for the most part had already been resolved. Thus, the resolution to debates during the creation of the IRU set the parameters for disaster relief for the UN, contributing, as Percy notes, to the stalled development of an international norm.

THE UN AND DISASTER RELIEF

Given the numerous changes in disaster relief since the Second World War,[7] it seems somewhat paradoxical to refer to disaster relief as a stalled norm. Yet, in this concluding section my purpose is to demonstrate the continuity between norm implementation and institutionalization in the nineteenth and twentieth centuries and in the UN system. After the Second World War, disaster relief was not high on the UN's agenda, though as it gained further attention, the international community adopted the basic institutional form negotiated in the IRU, largely without contestation. Since then, far more actors have become involved in disaster relief and continuing efforts to implement disaster relief have focused on increasing coordination capacity. This has led to "analytical institutionalization," in which IOs govern through the production of "technical knowledge" (Broome and Seabrooke 2011: 3), and the development of "policy norms" (Park and Vetterlein 2010). These developments aim to improve implementation, but have not altered the basic institutionalization of the disaster relief norm.

As outlined in the previous section, efforts during the inter-war period to institutionalize the disaster relief norm resulted in a two-tiered system comprised of a national system of disaster relief implementation operating bilaterally through government agencies and Red Cross/Crescent societies. This was supplemented by voluntary contributions to an international entity—the IRU. This basic system continues, though several important changes have occurred in the post-Second World War period. The first is the sheer number of actors involved in disaster relief. As Kent observes, the current system involves a complex network of actors, including states, the UN, and many NGOs. Indeed, since the late 1960s, and particularly post-Cold War, the international system has witnessed a drastic expansion of humanitarian activity, in terms of the amount of resources devoted to assistance and the number of actors involved

---

[7] For a good overview of disaster relief in the UN system, see Kent (1987, 2004), ICRC (2003), Fidler (2005), Fisher (2007), Saechao (2007).

(Barnett and Weiss 2011). In the UN system alone, the UNHCR, UNDP, WFP, UNFPA, UNICEF, FAO, WHO, IOM, and UNOCHA all play a fairly significant role in disaster relief. In addition to this, over 100 states contribute to disaster relief, and non-state entities which play a role number in excess of 2,500, with 260 described as "really serious players" (Barnett and Weiss 2011: 27).

The expansion of agencies and organizations of the UN involved in disaster relief occurred incrementally. Starting as early as 1949, the UN, through ECOSOC, began to consider how to respond to natural disasters, though revitalizing the IRU does not appear to have warranted serious consideration. After a series of ad hoc responses to various natural disasters in the 1950s and early 1960s (Green 1977: 30–1), the General Assembly, in its seminal 1965 Resolution 2034, explicitly identified the basic principles on which disaster relief should be institutionalized and implemented, once again reinforcing these processes as parallel rather than sequential. In this resolution, the General Assembly called on all states to develop disaster response capability, to establish a national Red Cross/Crescent society, to inform the UN of disaster relief they offer to other states, to set up a provisional fund to assist with disasters, and for the UN agencies to "continue and intensify their efforts to ensure the full coordination of assistance." Though the UN did not resurrect the IRU, the basic principles adopted clearly demonstrate continuity with the basic principles of the IRU.

Although other minor reforms followed throughout the 1970s and 1980s, General Assembly Resolution 46/182 in 1991 was the most substantial move toward institutionalizing the disaster relief norm.[8] Resolution 46/182 stands out because it is the most extensive articulation of the principles guiding disaster relief (and other forms of humanitarian assistance) and it created or consolidated the UN agencies involved in the coordination of disaster relief. This resolution established an extensive list of principles guiding disaster relief, and set up and consolidated a number of "analytic institutions" (Broome and Seabrooke 2011: 3) to study, facilitate, and coordinate disaster relief. The foundational guiding principles of disaster relief in section 1 of Resolution 46/182 were: humanitarianism, respect for state sovereignty and consent, the link between assistance and development, and the central importance of the UN as coordinating agency. To these ends, several institutions were created: the consolidated appeals process, the central emergency fund, the Inter-Agency standing committee, country-level coordinators, an emergency relief coordinator, and, eventually, the UN Office for the Coordination of Humanitarian

---

[8] UNGA Res. 46/182, 1991. Some other important measures include the creation of the Disaster Relief Office (UNDRO) in 1971, the Office of the Disaster Relief Coordinator (DRC) in 1978, the designation of 1990–9 as the International Decade for Natural Disaster Reduction, the Yokohama Strategy for Disaster Reduction in 1994, the 2005 Hyogo Framework for Action on Disaster Reduction, and the adoption of the cluster system of relief provision by UNOCHA in 2005.

Affairs (UNOCHA) in 1997. The basic form of disaster relief encapsulated in Resolution 46/182 was drawn more or less directly from the IRU—voluntary financial commitments with the international organization serving a coordinating role.

This is not to suggest that the particular form of institutionalization embodied in the IRU was fixed and uncontested after 1927. However, it is telling that many of the UN General Assembly resolutions and soft laws on disaster relief have been achieved through consensus (Smith 1999: 185; Katoch 2003: 49). Smith (1999: 189) notes that the primary point of contention concerning Resolution 46/182 was a minor difference between developed and developing states over the "precedence [given] to humanitarian assistance over state sovereignty." Ultimately a working group consisting of representatives from donor states and the G-77 agreed on compromise language in the guiding principles that allowed the Resolution to pass with consensus (Smith 1999: 191).[9]

Katoch (2003: 49) sums up the soft body of law that followed Resolution 2034, and that now spans nearly fifty years, based on four foundations: the primary responsibility for assisting victims of natural disaster falls on the affected country, the UN system is meant to "coordinate and facilitate" international offers of assistance, the UN disaster response system requires continued efforts for improvement, and lastly, the UN "works closely" with the Red Cross movement.[10] In these four foundations, the UN system retained the basic principles enshrined in the IRU and the LRCS model, the voluntaristic nature of disaster relief and a highly flexible system enabling states to favour bilateral disaster relief as part of their foreign policy. Indeed, the vast majority of disaster relief funds, operations, and relationships are bilateral (Fischer 2003; Fisher 2007: 12).

To be sure, these changes in disaster relief are important, and amount to increased institutional complexity, in terms of the number of actors involved and the profusion of policy norms emanating from these actors. Yet these many changes have done little to alter the basic institutional form of disaster relief, or to eliminate the gap between assessed need after a natural disaster and international assistance. This gap is the legacy of American implementation

---

[9] One of the most contentious debates over the balance between state sovereignty and the "right" to disaster relief occurred in response to Burma/Myanmar's refusal of aid in 2008. Thus the issue is clearly not uncontested, and there are some who evoke a right to relief (Hardcastle and Chua 1998) or a responsibility to protect (Saechao 2007) to override state sovereignty. Some scholars and practitioners have argued in favour of moving from voluntary funding for UN agencies to defined assessments (Walker et al. 2005). Thus far, neither amendment has been taken up at the UN.

[10] Though the relationship between the Red Cross and UN disaster relief agencies have not always been overly close or effective, the Red Cross continues to enjoy special status in the UN disaster relief system (Green 1977: 33–7).

of disaster relief in the late 1890s and the parallel implementation and institutionalization processes in the early decades of the twentieth century. This suggests that the basic foundations of the disaster relief norm were mostly settled during this period, while the disaster relief regime focuses on improving coordination, the production of technical knowledge, and the dissemination of best practices.

14

Status Determination and Recognition

Anna Schmidt

They are in transit. Anything can happen. The government could wake up
with a policy.[1]

Who is a refugee and who is not or no longer? This question lies at the heart of
the refugee regime: the international norms and related decision-making procedures and organizations, dealing with the definition and treatment of refugees. From its answer (can) flow the rights enshrined in the 1951 International
Refugee Convention, including that of non-refoulement, the ban on involuntary return or expulsion from the host country.

The refugee definition of the 1951 Convention (and that of the 1969 OAU
Convention Relating to the Specific Aspects of Refugee Problems in Africa)
is declaratory, i.e. not dependent on the formal recognition of status. As the
United Nations High Commissioner for Refugees (UNHCR) Handbook opti-
mistically puts it, a refugee "is recognised because he is a refugee" (UNHCR
1997).

In practice this means very little. Like any type of identity, refugee status—
like the corresponding rights—has only meaning when recognized and attributed, whether formally or informally. And while conferring upon refugees the
rights that should define asylum, the Refugee Convention only enshrines the
right to seek, not to obtain asylum. Hence, the importance of refugee status
determination (RSD). "The principles of asylum and non-*refoulement* cannot
be properly implemented without having refugee determination procedures"
(Goodwin-Gill in Rutinwa 2003: 12). Treaty norms here create the need for
policy norms to assure regime consistency.

This chapter describes how the gates of entry and exit are constructed for
the rural refugee populations in Tanzania and Uganda. It shows that under
similar levels of "international institutionalization" and broadly similar

---

[1] Interview, member of the Ugandan Refugee Eligibility Committee, Kampala, Mar. 2004.

structural challenges, different program set-ups and political contexts meant that, in each country, international, national, and non-state actors linked refugee policies and RSD differently—with direct consequences for refugee welfare and the understanding of core regime norms. The implementation of the international refugee regime in Africa is shaped by three broad features (1) high normative content and low textual precision of the international legal framework, (2) low implementation capacity of states involved and, partially as a result, (3) high degrees of delegation of implementation to international and non-state actors. Implementation is therefore not structured directly by international legal guidelines or government hierarchies: the dynamics of inter-organization networks filter both and the on-the-ground negotiation of refugee status hinges crucially on the constellation of interest, identities, and frames of the different organizational actors involved and the quality of their relationships. In analysing these dynamics, the chapter evaluates the strength of various resources—material, ideational, and institutional (legal/formal)—deployed by national, international, and local actors when implementing RSD.

GLOBAL AMBIGUITY: FROM TREATY TO POLICY AND IMPLEMENTATION

RSD is a "core technology" for the refugee regime. Yet its treaty framework is silent on the matter: "it says nothing about procedures for determining refugee status, and leaves to States the choice of means as to implementation at the national level" (Goodwin-Gill 1996: 34).[2] This absence affects both refugees and the global regime: debate has turned on procedural fairness or efficiency but also on the implications for international burden sharing.

The 1951 Refugee Convention defines a refugee as any person who "owing to a well-founded fear of being persecuted for reasons of race, religion, nationality, membership of a particular social group or political opinion is outside the country of his nationality and is unable or owing to such fear, is unwilling to avail himself of the protection of that country." Textually the main areas for interpretation relate to the meaning of "persecution" as well as "well-founded" fear, i.e. the credibility evaluation of the fear of the refugee in question. The grounds on which one may appeal for refugee status have also broadened, most notably in regards to gender and the notion of "social group." Regionally, the 1969 OAU Convention Governing Specific Aspects of Refugee Problems in Africa extends refugee status to people fleeing the effects of conflict,

---

[2] Jaeger (2003) argues that the drafting states had positive experiences with the mainly non-legal procedures managed by the League of Nations and voluntary agencies and thus felt no need for further codification.

violence, serious political upheaval, and unrest. National law and regulations add another layer of definition—many but by no means all countries signatory to the Convention directly copied its refugee definition into national law (D'Orsi 2006). Subsequent "regulatory" additions have further altered these for all practical purposes. Examples of these include the "safe third country" rule and various forms of "temporary protection" (Fitzpatrick 2000).

Globally, there is a paradoxical development: legal analysis and case law have furthered a broadening of the treaty-based refugee definition, notably with regards to gender or LGBT-related cases. Yet recognition *procedures* have become more restrictive, both in the north and in the south (Rutinwa 1999; UNHCR 2006). This includes eligibility procedures and other barriers that make it difficult for refugees to reach a potential country of asylum (UNHCR 2006). This is partially due to the increasing linkage of refugee issues to debates about migratory flows and, lately, global terrorism (Gibney and Hansen 2003), suggesting that RSD is easily affected by increased regime complexity or enmeshment.

Within this context, UNHCR and its Executive Committee (ExCom) promote international policy norms on RSD through more specific conclusions and international guidelines that list minimum benchmarks or essential guarantees for status determination procedures (e.g. UNHCR 2004). Yet no such norms exist with regards to mass influx or group determination procedures such as prima facie recognition, i.e. recognition "in the absence of evidence to the contrary" (UNHCR 1997: 13), based on an assessment of conditions in the country of origin rather than individual circumstance (Rutinwa 2002: 1). Yet prima facie recognition constitutes the main status recognition procedure across Africa.

This normative lacuna is filled through practice: "in the absence of international instruments providing for standards for recognition of refugees on a *prima facie* basis, states have devised their own procedures" (Rutinwa 2002: 7). These are not always obvious: "states do not always declare their intention to treat arriving groups as refugees, nor do they necessarily record such a determination in an official document" (Durieux and McAdam 2006: 11).

Procedures for *ending* refugee status show a tighter coupling of treaty and policy norms, certainly at global level: refugee status ceases when a "durable solution"—naturalization, resettlement, or voluntary repatriation—is found. It may also be terminated on the basis of the exclusion or cessation clauses. As Betts also describes in this volume, refoulement is explicitly forbidden (Art. 33). This conditions repatriation: "the involuntary return of refugees would in practise amount to refoulement" (UNHCR 1996: 10). The Refugee Convention only refers indirectly to repatriation when banning refoulement, whereas the UNHCR statute explicitly includes the facilitation of repatriation among the organizations' aims. ExCom Conclusion No. 40 (1985) exhorts return to be voluntary but also to take place in "conditions of safety and dignity" to an environment where "the causes of flight have been definitely and permanently removed" (UNHCR 1993: 104), while UNHCR (1996) provides guidance on how to meet these conditions.

Yet practice has not reflected such norms. Information collected by the United States Committee for Refugees suggests that at least twelve major repatriation movements took place under duress in 1998 alone, involving seven different countries of asylum, all in Africa (Crisp 2000). Indeed few issues in refugee protection have been debated more than the conditions of return and who should establish and judge "voluntariness" (Chimni 1993; Goodwin-Gill 1995; Harrell-Bond 1989).

Delegation: International Actors and RSD

The actual implementation of the attribution and the removal or ending of refugee status has long ceased to be a purely "domestic" matter. Particularly in the global South, UNHCR and other non-state actors play key roles in refugee policy implementation. In 2001, UNHCR conducted individual RSD on behalf of states in more than sixty countries (Kagan 2006: 4). It can also act in parallel with the state, assessing individual refugee claims on the basis of its mandate, or be an official "observer" to government-run refugee eligibility committees. With prima facie status, the role is often more diffuse but can be equally strong, especially when recognition processes are integrated in the administrative structures of registration within a given refugee assistance operation, including registration of bio-data or the issuance of ration cards. While in principle, "States have the primary responsibility to register and document refugees,"[3] UNHCR and its implementing partners often play important roles. International involvement in the implementation of registration is increasingly recognized in UNHCR ExCom conclusions (e.g. nos. 35 (1984); 91, (2001); 99 (2004)). The next section shows how the above macro conditions—ambiguity at international level and high involvement of international actors in "domestic" implementation—play out in Tanzania and Uganda.

TANZANIA AND UGANDA: CONTEXT AND NATIONAL FRAMEWORKS

In terms of formal "international institutionalization" Tanzania and Uganda appear fairly similar. Both are signatories to the 1951 and the OAU Convention, and both host refugee assistance programs largely managed and financed by UNHCR, the "guardian" of international refugee norms. At the time of

---

[3] "Practical Aspects of Physical and Legal Protection with Regard to Registration." Global Consultations on International Protection, 1st Meeting. EC/GC/01/6, 19 Feb. 2001, 72.

research both countries faced similar issues with respect to status determination. Some 99 percent of their refugees were recognized on a prima facie basis (UNHCR 2003), based on group determination procedures that formally designated refugees to spatially defined assistance programs: refugee camps in Tanzania, agricultural "rural settlements" in Uganda. Both countries also hosted large numbers of non-registered or "self-settled" refugees and both refugee operations were explicitly geared toward repatriation.[4] Finally, both operations faced the particular challenges of hosting Rwandese refugees.

The formal legal and administrative provisions of Uganda and Tanzania did little to fill the gaps left by the global regime. Historically, RSD was highly politicized and decisions were often implicit, rather than explicit (e.g. during Uganda's policy of "good neighbourliness" in the 1990s no Kenyan asylum seekers were officially accepted, but nor were they returned). Tanzania's first refugee Act lacked any definition of the term "refugee." The 1999 Act includes both the 1951 and the OAU definitions but also lets the minister declare *any* individual or group refugees.[5] There is no requirement for specific reasoning or deliberation. Equally, the 2003 Tanzanian refugee policy contains no commitment to specific procedures while transferring refugee screening to the security and defence committees at village and district level (United Republic of Tanzania 2003: 3). Existing ministerial declarations dating to the 1960s declared Rwandans, Congolese, Mozambicans, Malawians, South Africans, Namibians, Rhodesians, Ugandans, and Burundians prima facie refugees. It is unclear whether such recognition persists if it has not been officially revoked.[6]

In provisions difficult to reconcile with international treaty norms, Tanzania's 2003 National Refugee Policy enshrines repatriation as the primary solution[7] and restricts refugee status to one year.[8] Compared to the 1951 Convention or the Tanzanian Refugee Act it also widened the scope for deportation.[9] References to legal procedures remain vague: "In cases where refugee status has ceased, any final settlement will be concluded in an essentially humanitarian way."[10] On the other side, non-refoulement is affirmed in the policy's preamble.

In Uganda, similar tensions exist. As in Tanzania, newly arriving refugees had to register upon arrival. Formally, Uganda's long-time refugee law, the 1960 Control of Alien Refugees Act (CARA), did not contain a refugee

---

[4] Tanzania has offered naturalization to number of Somalis in 2003 and to some "old caseload" Burundi refugees.

[5] The Refugees Control Act, 1966 (Tanzania), sections 3 and 1.

[6] Rutinwa (2002) and Durieux and McAdam (2006) follow Jackson (1999) in arguing that its prima facie status is presumptive, i.e. conclusive unless or until state authorities decide a new procedure.

[7] United Republic of Tanzania, National Refugee Policy, p. 7, s. 14.

[8] United Republic of Tanzania, National Refugee Policy, p. 8.

[9] United Republic of Tanzania, National Refugee Policy, part 5, s. 28(4).

[10] United Republic of Tanzania, National Refugee Policy, p. 6.

definition and lacked provisions for RSD. But here (partial) implementation preceded formal incorporation: both UNHCR and the government affirmed that under CARA, deliberations generally "rely on international convention 1951 and the OAU convention" (D'Orsi 2006: 15). The new Refugee Act was adopted in 2006 and became operational in 2009. It introduces 1951 language but also contains new sections, notably on the recognition of gender-based persecution. Yet it maintains important discretion for refugee-related officials, including the right to restrict freedom of movement.

The Ugandan Refugee Eligibility Commission (REC) was created in 1988, but its composition, competence, and procedures were not legally codified (O'Neill et al. 2000: 164). The REC's importance increased after the Rwandan genocide and its membership expanded from four (Ministry of Culture and Community Development, Internal Affairs, Ministry of Justice, Police Special Branch) to include internal and external security organizations and the Ministry of Foreign Affairs. As in Tanzania, the relevant minister may grant status by declarations and declarations exist for the major groups of refugees: Sudanese, Rwandan, and Congolese. As in Tanzania, their continuous applicability was unclear.

THE PRACTICE OF STATUS DETERMINATION

The practical consequences of formal frameworks, national or international, have varied. In Tanzania, Burundian and Congolese refugees within the country continued to enjoy prima facie status in the early 2000s (Rutinwa 2002: 9). Yet a series of expulsions, border closures, and crackdowns against these and other refugees altered Tanzania's reputation as one of the world's most generous asylum countries from the mid-1990s onwards. In 1995 Tanzania officially closed its borders to Burundi but received around 60,000 new arrivals during the period of border closure (WFP and UNHCR 1996). In 2001, there was still confusion within UNHCR on whether or not the border closure persisted in some districts.[11] In both countries, as the senior legal officer of the Ugandan Office of the Prime Minister (OPM) put it: "Status determination is what we do in practice."[12]

This practice was influenced by different actors with very different, and often multiple, interests and varying interpretations of relevant norms. The next sections outline the constellation of actors and the factors structuring their interests in each country with regards to (a) the implementation of prima

---

[11] Minutes of Protection Meeting UNHCR Branch Office Tanzania, 27 June 2001.
[12] Interview OPM Legal Officer, Kampala, Mar. 2004. The UNHCR Protection Report of 1987 states that UNHCR has "no precise criteria" for granting mandate status except that it rejects "liars" and secondary movers.

facie recognition, including with regards to self-settled refugees and (b) the implementation of repatriation processes, i.e. the "end" of refugee status.

Implementation in Tanzania: Prima Facie Status and Registration

In Tanzania, arriving refugees were officially required to register with authorities within seven days and there were to be joint UNHCR/government "screenings" of new arrivals at the border "way stations." Yet the responsible Ministry of Home Affairs (MHA) did not participate in these visits and UNHCR's tours were sporadic.[13] In turn, registration at entry was mainly through NGO staff (Caritas) or later in the camps. This occasioned government complaints about aid workers who "were essentially deciding who was going to be admitted to Tanzania."[14] Particular procedures existed for Rwandans who, since 1998, were screened individually by the National Eligibility Committee (NEC), which included the various security organs of the state. The procedure was initially equivalent to prima facie status determination, with decisions based on objective circumstances in Rwanda, but it could also become more individualized (see Rutinwa 2005: 13).

In Dar Es Salaam, government officials followed politics when discussing recognition and had to explain refugee numbers to critical politicians. "In the old days the numbers were also high but the refugees were calm and the politicians were happy...don't fool yourself, the definition of a refugee it is not just the law. It changes and it is always political, no matter what the law says."[15] Outside the set-up of the refugee programme, and often bypassing MHA agents, government intervention at the border became more common. In June 2003 the Kibondo District Commissioner visited the border waystations. He drew a red line under the last name in the Caritas registration book, declaring access closed. The district's MHA representative denied any policy change.[16] The same month, an army contingent rejected a boat of Congolese asylum seekers in Kigoma district. After protests by international actors, both actions were officially revoked. Later that month, the Kigoma regional commissioner ordered any new arrivals to henceforth register with village authorities before screening. While MHA authorities insisted that this did not "substantially" change procedures, the districts created screening committees, which became de facto RSD organs. UNHCR could participate in some districts, not others (Rutinwa 2005: 22ff.). This varying participation matched directly the locally pre-existing

---

[13] "Minutes of Protection Meeting UNHCR Branch Office," Dar es Salaam, 27 June 2001.
[14] Interview, MHA, Dar es Salaam, Dec. 2003.
[15] Interview, MHA, Dar es Salaam, May 2003.
[16] Interview, MHA, Kibondo, Feb. 2003.

degree of conflict among actors (Schmidt 2006). In terms of results, such efforts to increase government control over RSD ironically increased its informalization and later politicization. Village authorities were largely ill-prepared or ignorant of their new duties, and the screening committees were untrained.[17]

Ultimately, because refugees officially had to reside in camps, registration for the purposes of recognition was closely tied to registration for the purposes of managing assistance. As a consequence, even though formal, prima facie represents a *procedure* for status determination, not a distinct form of refugee status (Durieux and McAdam 2006; Rutinwa 2002), the actual meaning of refugee status was described by the terms of the (international) assistance program that received them. This created feedback effects, such as when the smooth operation of assistance became a criterion in determining status, and actors implementing the assistance program could become gatekeepers for who "entered." For example, in Tanzania there was strong interest in preventing "recycling," i.e. refugees registering multiple times in order to obtain multiple rations or no-food items. Newly arrived refugees were screened by at least four different NGOs for registration purposes, each of which could declare them "recyclers." If this happened, they would sometimes wait for days to be interviewed by the MHA Settlement Commander (who tested credibility by their commitment to wait). At the time of research, a routine had been established whereby single boys and men were no longer registered, and thus not recognized but summarily categorized as "recyclers." This concern only increased when food rations were reduced by 50 percent in early 2004. Often unable to understand what they were told, they frequently just joined the queue again. On some days the (UNHCR) registration clerk registered ad hoc "families" of groups of young men, allocating them a plot and telling them to return for ration cards and food once they had built a hut on it. During their sporadic visits at the waystation UNHCR protection clerks also sometimes rejected asylum seekers suspected of "recycling."[18]

Historically, formal registration was not required for people coming as refugees to either Tanzania or Uganda (Daley 1991; Schmidt 2006; Malkki 1995). In 2006 the Burundi Government estimated there were some 190,000 Burundi refugees settled in Tanzanian villages.[19] There were also Congolese, many of whom had fled from war. These groups do not appear in UNHCR refugee statistics, but sometimes are recorded in government numbers. These unregistered, "self-settled" refugees point to fractures within the international regime: assistance, protection, and recognition were conditional on an initial suspension of the international right to freedom of movement, with the consequence that large numbers of refugees choose to remain outside the formal refugee

---

[17] Interview, UNHCR, Ngara, Nov. 2003.
[18] Interviews, UNHCR, at registration centre, Mar. 2003.
[19] IRIN News, 14 Aug. 2006: <http://www.reliefweb.org>.

regime. But they also highlight the different layers the state: in both countries, self-settled living required the complicity or toleration of local authorities.[20] "They don't exist [officially]. But the local officials know they do. If the local government gains from the presence of the refugees they won't report that they are there...since the locals and the local government keep silent it is very difficult to identify the refugees and to differentiate them from the locals."[21] In this sense, the "self-settled" were recognized and enjoyed a status that reflected in many ways the spirit of the old laws, giving wide-ranging, if arbitrary, powers to local officials to determine status. Difficult to classify in terms of migration status, in both countries self-settled refugees made use of various forms of documentation—graduated tax receipts in Uganda, ruling party membership cards in Tanzania. Two issues filtered policy implementation. First, the more refugees were framed as a security problem, the greater government pressure to get them into the camps. Secondly, increased political competition, such as the introduction of multi-party politics in Tanzania, increased the importance of national citizenship. There were recurrent claims in the refugee-affected areas that refugees were used as vote-fodder and questions of citizenship were raised over a number of aspirants for parliamentary seats, (Maliyamkono 1995). In 2001 a number of high-profile Tanzanians were "outed" as Rwandans.[22]

With regards to the self-settled, UNHCR's interpretation of its mandate changed over time and it saw them increasingly as outside its responsibilities. During round-ups in 1997, UNHCR had still documented their cases to help regularization of status outside the camps. In 2003, new round-ups were largely ignored. In Kibondo district the office did not record if "new arrivals" came from within Tanzania, merely indicating Burundi as place of origin.[23] Refugees who were returned to Burundi but were not previously registered in the camps were considered of no concern. On their side, NGOs interacted very little with the self-settled. However, after procedures at the waystations changed, the NGO forum in Kibondo wrote to the District Commissioner expressing concern over increasing restrictions on movement, including the self-settled.

Repatriation and the End of Status

The government push for repatriation differed by nationality. The Congolese were under no pressure to return, in contrast to the Burundese. Here pressures changed in line with different stages of the Burundi peace process.[24] The

---

[20] The 1999 round-ups in Tanzania showed how easily "foreigners" could be identified. On Uganda see Kaiser (2005).

[21] Interview, MHA, Dar es Salaam, Jan. 2003.

[22] See e.g. *The East African*, 12 Feb. 2001.

[23] Interview, UNHCR, Kibondo, Feb. 2003.

[24] UNHCR Annual Protection Report, Tanzania 1999.

central government and UNHCR differed on which border points would be officially opened for UNHCR repatriation convoys. The government urged the opening of more routes, whereas UNHCR resisted opening crossings to the more insecure south. Yet reports about ongoing insecurity were not shared with the refugees to avoid delaying returns. To show further support for repatriation, the UNHCR and government started registering people's *intention* to return.[25] Meanwhile government actors pursued implementation through signaling. In early 2002 the Minister of Home Affairs told refugees at Mtabila camp they "should now go back voluntarily and . . . not wait to be forced back."[26] Forced returns of Burundese refugees picked up at the border or potentially any outside the camps were intermittent but never en masse and again, were generally conducted without the direct participation of the MHA, thus cutting the formal link with "refugee policy." From May 2003 onwards, refugees increasingly returned "spontaneously." This was welcomed by the government, but UNHCR's response was ambivalent: in the most-affected district it refused any involvement and warned of using UNHCR assets to assist the returnees. In parallel the High Commissioner for Refugees visited Tanzania in December 2003 and urged the speedy repatriation of the Burundese, brushing aside the concerns of the country office.

NGOs felt the tension and spoke in hushed voices about the possibility of mass refoulement. In Kibondo especially, they grew increasingly critical of UNHCR's information management, seeking out independent assessments. Some tried to increase the refugees' access to independent information, including through organized visits by Burundi NGOs. In Ngara, the Jesuit Refugee Service's Radio Kwizera jealously guarded its role as an independent source of information, refusing funding by UNHCR.[27]

When the returnees passed through Kibondo, UNHCR ordered its guards to chase the refugees away from the sub-office. The Tanganyika Christian Refugee Service (TCRS) cleared out its truckyard and provided some 300 people safety and access to sanitation and water. In the absence of government or UNHCR support it acted on "humanitarian grounds." It also established three similar spaces en route to the border and provided increased information about the situation in Burundi to the refugees.[28]

If the return of the Burundese was a story of push and pull, the strongest pressures were on the Rwandans. In the government's public view the remaining Rwandese refugees had "no valid reason, unless they are criminals."[29] Their repatriation was to have concluded in 2002. This was confirmed by a

[25] Interview, UNHCR, Kibondo, Mar. 2003.
[26] Minister of Home Affairs during joint visit with Burundi Minister in Charge of Repatriation, 25 Feb. 2002.
[27] Interview, Jesuit Refugee Service, Ngara, June 2003
[28] IRIN Africa News Clippings, 4 May 2003.
[29] Interview UNHCR, Kibondo, Jan. 2003.

January 2003 announcement that only 150 remained, and a feature story in UNHCR Tanzania's magazine titled "Rwanda Refugee Saga Over."[30] However, a February 2003 tripartite meeting set another deadline for "voluntary repatriation" of some 2,000 remaining Rwandans, while a Rwandan delegation reportedly visited some 2,600 Rwandans in Ngara's Lukole camp.[31] In 2003 the Kibondo District Commissioner announced the closure of a camp hosting many Rwandans (even though the MHA had transferred refugees there just the previous day). The measure caused considerable upheaval prior to being revoked. Security forces continuously rounded up Rwandese self-settled refugees, pushing them back into Rwanda, often across the Rusumo river crossing. Those in camps were eventually "deported" after their cases had been reopened by the REC and more or less summarily rejected. On 2 September 2004 the Rwandese refugees in Lukole camp were forced into trucks and transported across the border while their huts in the camps were burned down.

Officially, UNHCR agreed that the Rwandans should go home and repeatedly indicated its willingness to invoke the cessation clause for these purposes.[32] Yet many local staff believed they were witnessing—and tacitly supporting—another case of forced repatriation. In December 2002 a report from Ngara noted: "the voluntary nature of the repatriation was totally disregarded. Instruction was given to Rwandese refugee families to demolish their homes and proceed home. Police visited house to house to put pressure upon the refugees. This led to a massive deportation-like movement [and] congested camps at Nyakarambi in Rwanda."[33] However, the country office criticized the report and one month later congratulated the same sub-office on organizing repatriation in "safety and dignity." Subsequently, an email by the head of the UNHCR Africa Bureau also thanked Ngara in particular, noting that he had "rarely seen a repatriation operation like this done so rapidly and effectively." UNHCR leadership saw no alternative to returns while lower-level staff acquiesced and often informally advised refugees to leave Tanzania and try to make a living elsewhere, possibly Zambia or Malawi. Logistics NGOs that filled critical resource gaps for the government and UNHCR were sometimes directly involved in these issues. Concerning the Rwandese, the main logistics NGO in Ngara strongly raised the matter of norms governing the *process* of return. A letter to UNHCR stated: "we were imposed by UNHCR Ngara very bad conditions of transports, particularly in terms of safety and dignity. It was clearly obvious that the Rwandan repatriation was not made according to the tripartite agreement, namely a voluntary repatriation."[34] Yet they saw their

---

[30] UNHCR Tanzania Newsletter, 14 (Jan. 2003).

[31] IRIN chronology at <http://www.irinnews.org/print.asp?ReportID=38809>.

[32] However, during the NEC assessment of Rwandese cases in 2003, the UNHCR declared some "mandate refugees" and helped resettle them.

[33] Interview, UNHCR, Ngara, Dec. 2002.

[34] Letter from Atlas Logistique to UNHCR, 15 Oct. 2002.

influence as limited: "the only thing we can do is control the number of people that are being put in the vans. And refuse to do the work should that become necessary."[35]

STATUS RECOGNITION IN UGANDA

In Uganda, prima facie refugees generally registered within the districts of arrival.[36] Before 2001–2 NGOs registered and screened arrivals in the northern refugee settlements, after which this responsibility was officially transferred to the OPM. However, in practice this still varied among districts.[37]

Again, prima facie recognition was integrated into the mode of assistance, with the move to the refugee settlements a condition for registration. Again, ration cards provided the only proof of refugee status for the vast majority: "Your ration card is the ID. You need your ration card to get your permit to go out."[38] According to the UNHCR deputy country representative: "we have a specific area for refugees because it gives official recognition to refugees, and an interest as a point of departure."[39] In turn, the different assistance set-up changed the resulting concerns and political pressures.

Instead of ration cards and recycling, in Uganda debates about refugee status were linked to debates over land allocation. In the southwest, this included the complex negotiation of citizenship and land rights of the different waves of Rwandese arrivals who were part of the political fabric of the area.[40] Refugees were supposed to be clearly identified and settled on designated land essentially governed by the OPM and UNHCR. Yet this land was coveted, including, ironically, by some Rwandan "old refugees," who had not returned with the Rwandese Patriotic Front in the 1990s. In the north, local politicians pursued contradictory agendas: Adjumani district saw the simultaneous attempt to restrict refugees to the settlements, limit the amount of land provided to them, *and* avoid its demarcation. "This land, OPM wanted to trick us... we said no surveyors and no stones. UNHCR with their technical people. We told them, no stones."[41] In Arua, the RDC had a different attitude: "To avoid a crisis is to allow refugees to work with nationals. Let them look around for jobs and be integrated in the local population."[42] Different pressures pulled both for and

---

[35] Interview, Atlas Logistique, Ngara, Dec. 2003.
[36] Interview, OPM, Kampala, Apr. 2004.
[37] Interviews, Arua and Adumani, Feb. 2004.
[38] Interviews with refugees, Rhino camp, Arua, Feb. 2004.
[39] Interview UNHCR, Kampala, Jan. 2004.
[40] Interview RDC, Mbarara, Apr. 2004; Bagenda et al. (2003).
[41] Interview, LC 5 official, Adjumani, Apr. 2004.
[42] Interview RDC, Arua, Feb. 2004.

against refugee registration and the settlement system. As long as the two were linked, pressures on one created pressures for the other.

Due to close cross-border ties, the "liberal" leanings of President Museveni and an existing relative lack of registration, government agents frequently tolerated non-registered and self-settled refugees. However, this "benign neglect" was unpredictable. As in Tanzania, electoral periods increased tensions. Locally, previously disregarded laws could suddenly be enforced. In March 2005 the Hoima District Security Committee ordered refugees to register within a month: "if not they will be arrested as criminals and deported."[43]

Although within UNHCR some regretted that Uganda's relatively benign neglect of the self-settled was not formalized, it did not challenge the situation. Again the operational focus on specific locations supported that those outside were considered an issue for immigration, not the refugee regime. On the Congolese border, UNHCR helped push arrivals into the designated settlements. It was keenly aware that more routine recognition independent of the settlement system risked exposing its struggling urban refugee program to increasing demands. Some NGOs worried: "There is a gap in the mandate. UNHCR does protection but it is used in terms of basic needs. But there are always unregistered. Here protection officers are completely ineffective... [and] we have no legitimacy for that."[44] Among them the Refugee Law Project explicitly advocated the formalization of self-settlement.

Ending Status

As in Tanzania, refugee status was seen as a stage preceding repatriation. In the settlements, refugees were banned from planting permanent crops or building permanent housing, could not own land, and their movement was controlled. Yet pressures for actual return were limited. In the north the government's sympathy with the SPLA reduced pressures. In the southwest, the Rwandan Government and UNHCR both pushed for a repatriation. Yet for domestic and foreign policy reasons the government remained lukewarm: "Repatriation is no priority for us. Uganda as a country is not anxious to return refugees to an unsafe situation."[45] Powerful central actors, including President Museveni, publicly promoted more liberal, pan-regional attitudes where refugees were seen as deeply enmeshed in the (ongoing) story of African state-building. This echoed at district level: "we may have refugees for many years, [we are] not closing the chapter today, but tomorrow. The process of democracy takes time and [the creation of] one area of integration. In one Africa, an African union,

---

[43] Press release by district security committee and OPM, dated 17 Mar. 2004.
[44] Interview international NGO, Kampala, Apr. 2004.
[45] Interview OPM, Kampala, Mar. 2004.

the issue of refugees might not be there."[46] At the same time, on a variety of issues, the self-settled and the "Kibati" group, government actors were experiencing conflicting pressures and avoided a public definition of policy.

Rwandese who feared refoulement from Tanzania had been arriving in Uganda since 1996 and had generally been recognized as refugees by UNHCR and the government. A new wave arrived in early 2002, providing an instructive window onto the negotiated nature of RSD implementation. In contrast to previous practice, in late 2002 Uganda declared it would not accept Rwandans from Tanzania.[47] Thus "Kibati" emerged, a makeshift camp just outside the official settlement Nakivale. Uganda signed a tripartite repatriation agreement with Rwanda in July 2003 and announced the repatriation of its 23,000 officially remaining Rwandans by the end of the year—in practice only a few hundred returned. In early 2004, some 5,000 Rwandese lived in Kibati. They were refused RSD and recognized as neither refugees nor asylum seekers. Discussion about their status went up to cabinet level, but with no result.[48] Ugandan officials felt caught. Many noted that, while they allowed the group to stay against UNHCR wishes, this meant they could not accord them formal status. "We cannot. For these refugees were refugees in Tanzania, recognized by UNHCR and their repatriation was fully blessed by UNHCR, the government of Rwanda and Tanzania. We cannot give them status. [They stay] on humanitarian grounds, humanitarian law comes in. They've been harassed. We are assisting them on humanitarian grounds."[49]

For UNHCR repatriation was a general priority, but most strongly for the Rwandans. The country representative had worked in Rwanda and supported its strong interest in repatriation. "Most of them are economic refugees and some of them, but not many, might be reluctant because they fear legal consequences. The repatriation will be voluntary of course... [but] UNHCR is interested in finally closing this chapter."[50] UNHCR seemingly informed the government in 2003 that it would declare the "cessation" of status for all Rwandans by July 2004.[51] It also announced in February 2003 that it would "not provide assistance or international protection to Rwandans moving from Tanzania to Uganda," declaring them "irregular movers from a first country of asylum."[52] UNHCR thus strictly opposed recognition for the Kibati group.

---

[46] Interview RDC, Mbarara, Apr. 2004.
[47] IRIN News, 19 Dec. 2002 "Great Lakes: Uganda says No to Rwandan Refugees from Tanzania": <http://www.reliefweb.org>.
[48] Interview, UNHCR, Kampala, Apr. 2004.
[49] Interview, OPM, Mbarara, Apr. 2004.
[50] Interview, UNHCR head of Branch Office, Kampala, Jan. 2004.
[51] Appeal no. 01.12/2003 Programme Update No.1: IFRC appeal. <http://www.ifrc.org/docs/appeals/annual03/01120301.pdf>.
[52] The UNHCR Uganda public information officer, 3 Feb. 2003. Quoted in "Tanzania 2003 Chronology," IRIN News. In 1999 UNHCR still advocated that Rwandans arriving from Tanzania be admitted on a prima facie basis—advice followed by the Ugandan Government.

According to its senior protection officer: "The [Ugandan] government was ready to accept [them], UNHCR prevented that."[53]

Given the non-decisions of UNHCR and the government, the two operating agencies, URC and WFP took on de facto responsibility for the Kibati group. Both were concerned about the refugees' health and safety.[54] "They have spent two years here now and have not gotten asylum. We are currently catering for an unregistered 5000 people."[55] Both pushed to give them some bureaucratic identity. "Politically HCR did not want them... but WFP then registered them. We did an EFNA [Emergency Food Needs Assessment]... things become more complicated once you have data. EFNA [served to] formalize and increased the likelihood for the minister to call."[56] "The government should decide. They should either be forced to repatriate or become legal refugees."[57] Yet they also recognized the politics involved: "There were accusations that Uganda was harbouring Interahamwe and giving Rwandese status would have brought it crashing down."[58] Without UNHCR support, the situation was at an impasse. As WFP explained: "HCR wants a cessation date. Politically, UNHCR did not want them to be given asylum again."[59]

EXPLAINING OUTCOMES

What was the effect of ambiguity within the macro regime? The formal or procedural vagueness of RSD was "resolved" when status recognition and socio-economic provision were "aggregated" into one operational logic. But each assistance operation developed its own needs in terms of who would be integrated and who would not. This could lead to a neglect of proper registration and RSD, even of the prima facie sort. At a basic level, prima facie status attribution became a form of temporary protection, where some rights of the Refugee Convention were no longer considered constitutive of refugee status. Although opinions differed on whether this was "right," a shared understanding existed that it was so. Status was considered neither comprehensive nor conclusive. The self-settled refugees were almost completely outside formal normative scope of the regime. This "implementation" effect reflects a recasting of regime norms: it effectively elevated blanket restrictions on freedom of movement at odds with international refugee law into

---

[53] Interview, UNHCR senior protection officer, Kampala, Apr. 2004.

[54] In June 2003 a fire erupted in the Kibati camp. A third of the huts were destroyed and nine children died.

[55] Interview, URC, Mbarara, Mar. 2004.   [56] Interview, WFP, Kampala, Jan. 2004.

[57] Interview, URC, Nakivale settlement, Apr. 2004.

[58] Interview, URC, Mbarara, Mar. 2004.   [59] Interview, WFP, Kampala, Jan. 2004.

an ordering principle. But the consensus regarding such implementation procedures and results was unstable. Over time, relationships among regime actors at all levels were increasingly strained, including because local politics and regional political pressures impacted differently on UNHCR, NGOs, and host state agencies.

As noted, Rwandan refugees presented a special challenge to status attribution and termination. Again, implementation processes reprioritized closely linked treaty norms and introduced normative fault lines across levels. In Tanzania, a double adjustment took place for UNHCR, the international norms-promoting institution: in Geneva and the country headquarters, involuntary repatriation was redescribed as voluntary and thus the significance of the norm of non-refoulement symbolically maintained. On the ground, staff failed to make this leap and described actions as refoulement, as a breach of the norm. Here adjustment eventually meant shifting the perceived significance of the norm—its breach was no longer perceived as abnormal or even consequential. In the eyes of many, refoulement had been routinized. As noted, some personnel advised refugees to escape the regime itself and try their luck "underground." Within local relationships, the standing and credibility of UNHCR suffered, including with government officials who themselves promoted speedy returns. Yet in Uganda, similar external pressures and regime norms played out quite differently. Problems with status determination crystallized around the Kibati group, starkly revealing the different prioritizations of core actors despite their public agreement on the goal of repatriation. Where the government's stance was "softer," UNHCR's organizational preferences produced mutual strategies of non-decisions and the institutional limbo for the Kibati group. Again other actors negotiated informal "solutions" that altered outcomes at the margin and led to increasing exit from the international refugee regime. Unregistered, informal living in the camp came within the purview of NGOs covered by wider humanitarian norms. In both countries, non-refoulement remained a recognized standard in the sense that nobody wanted to be seen to engage in it. However, in both countries, UNHCR's (central) interpretation of compliance reflected a regional strategy of return, justified in the name of Rwandan reconstruction.

Beyond aggregate outcomes, these case studies show inherently dynamic practices which represented the momentary outcome of bargaining among interdependent actors. None could impose their preferred policy on the other but their actions together made "implementation." Which kind of relations or resources mattered in this "negotiation"? The next section reviews the different relational resources which actors deployed; from formal institutional ones based on law to material or normative/professional standing, and, finally, access to information.

Law and Legality

At first glance, the question of status is fundamentally tied to the formal-legal aspects of the regime. Its attribution is predicated on rule-bound, authoritative determination that an individual or group satisfies the relevant criteria. Yet in both countries, the legal realm lacked autonomy and no single administrative structure had the capacity—or will—to establish it. Legal arguments formed part of the discussions between UNHCR, the government, and IPs. Yet legal guidelines remained highly malleable. Caritas's gatekeeper role at the Tanzanian border was largely unsupervised and not measured against any criteria; similarly, registration in the camps was defined by non-legal logics. If treaty norms seemingly created the necessity for legal procedure and argument regarding the Rwandans, this frequently seemed more an adaptation of means than a shift in justification requirements.

Tanzania's new refugee policy announced greater formalization or even "legalization" of RSD and deportation procedures. Yet it was largely perceived as a political gesture. Its relevance vis-à-vis other bodies of law and regulation remained unclear, as did its implementation. Even senior officials were sometimes at pains to downplay its significance. The creation of the ad hoc registration committees effectively increased the role of local politicians and security agents. In the words of the senior MHA lawyer: "that was supposed to be a matter for the [legal] professionals, but they [the politicians] don't trust us."[60] Ultimately, legal expertise was frequently useless when negotiating refugee status on the ground.

In Uganda, government practice reflected "legalism à la carte," with a menu containing three different legal sources: international refugee law, the draft new refugee bill, and finally the actual national law, the CARA.[61] Whenever possible, policies were framed in terms of international refugee law or the new bill.

However, which law was *used* often depended on their fit with a specific predetermined action, not vice versa: "we incorporate that part of international law which we like."[62] Also, as UNHCR's senior legal officer in Uganda observed: "how generous or strictly obligations are implemented is due to personalities."[63] Personal fiat was tempered less by law then by history: "where refugees are concerned different regimes in Uganda have showed continuity. Perhaps institutions as such are not developed fully in terms of [there being] almost a legal vacuum. But [de facto] Uganda is maybe a bit more advanced." Others deplored the lack of legalization. "We don't have legislation but policies

---

[60] Interview, MHA, Dar es Salaam, May 2003.
[61] Carlos Twesigomwe, *Uganda's Refugee Policy and Practice*. N.d. On file with the author.
[62] Twesigomwe, *Uganda's Refugee Policy*.
[63] Interview, UNHCR, Kampala, Apr. 2004.

have been exemplary—so we say. But we must stop depending on good will of officials, [and] introduce accountability."[64]

While not implementing legal procedures, both governments used the threat of enforcing national law. UNHCR had a similar resource arising from its international legal mandate. Its recurrent announcements of a future formal "cessation" for the Rwandese shaped behaviour and procedures without providing the procedural guarantees of formal cessation.

The formal tripartite repatriation agreements codified actors' commitments to certain actions. Yet other relationships mattered more. The head of the sub-office in Ngara described repatriation as "a political issue that is decided by the international community. If both countries agree but UNHCR does not agree, then UNHCR cannot put pressure. As far as I'm concerned we just carry out instructions by the government."[65] This is an interpretation, incidentally, that the Ugandan Government refugee department would not have shared.

Material Power

What does money buy? The material dimension of refugee assistance directly created and sustained the registration process, itself the site at which, for all practical purpose, status was accorded. Computer systems and registration procedures were all externally financed. It is unclear whether, without the externally financed aid set-up, registration would have happened or have been as systematic.

Yet as a power resource, the benefits were decidedly mixed. The head of UNHCR Uganda was adamant that the only limits to negotiation were financial. For repatriation, UNHCR needed to increase incentives: "UNHCR is pushing, their condition [is] it should benefit Uganda in some sort."[66] In Tanzania, when the Kibondo district commissioner decided the closure of a refugee camp, UNHCR's ability to influence a reversal was partially due to divisions within government, but also its material clout.[67] Yet material flows also created sunk costs and could produce resentment and subterfuge instead of gratitude and compliance. In 2005, heavily dependent on UNHCR financing, the Ugandan refugee department suspended registration and land allocation in the north to protest against UNHCR budget cuts.[68]

For NGOs, material independence provided power, albeit not by itself. The TCRS's own funds and wide local linkages permitted them at times to act independently and against the wishes of UNHCR, whilst also engaging

---

[64] Norbert Mao, then member of Ugandan Parliament.
[65] Interview, UNHCR, Ngara, Nov. 2003.
[66] Interview, UNHCR, Kampala, Apr. 2004.
[67] Interview, UNHCR, Kibondo, Mar. 2003.   [68] Interview, UNHCR, Apr. 2004.

in critiques of the government, via the NGO forum. Enabled by independent resources, together with a longstanding embeddedness in Uganda's aid sector, WFP and the URC provided the Kibati group with some degree of assistance, despite UNHCR's opposition and the government's hands-off strategy. The regime-adjacent norms of "humanitarian relief" based on need constituted an additional normative resource when justifying policies opposed by the official (refugee) norm-interpreters.

Moral Clout and Professional Ties

Legal and material ties were heavily embedded in the "non-contractual terms of the contract," such as degrees of trust and social consensus—or mistrust and conflict—among actors. Here history or precedent shaped both relationships and practices. In Tanzania, the 1996 Rwandan repatriation left a lasting and controversial legacy, especially with regards to status determination and its cessation. It was possibly the single most important issue affecting the credibility and influence of UNHCR, and by extension the norms it was mandated to promote. Its aftermath affected perceived performance benchmarks and the mutual understanding of roles. The role of professional ties was relatively insignificant in this policy realm. The entry of rural refugees seemingly required little expert knowledge and reception staff in both countries were relatively untrained. Instead, more intangibly, "diplomatic" elements structured relationships.

Information Networks

Structurally, a great difficulty for the negotiation and coordination of RSD practices in Tanzania and Uganda related to unevenly shared information, including about small-scale expulsions, round-ups, or the self-settled. Information flows were shaped by bureaucratic boundaries and politics as well as qualitative relationships. Their relevance was due to implementation and problem structure. In all cases, timing of information was crucial: decisions once made or actions once taken were often irreversible. Many arising status issues were negotiated locally and integrated into day-to-day activities rather than distinctively flagged. The organizational ability to shape information was underlined with the Kibati case. WFP and URC could raise the issue through a formal needs assessment even though the two most central actors wanted to ignore it (ultimately though, this strategy reached its limits). In Tanzania, the broader lack of trust and understanding between UNHCR and the government meant that no information was seen as neutral. In the example of security assessment for Burundi, the government relied on information received directly from Burundese politicians, and disregarded UNHCR and its sources. [69] This increased disagreement over the implementation of the norm of non-refoulement.

CONCLUSION

The most obvious observations from the above are the large diversity of "implementation" across and within the country cases, and the fact that actor interests during norm implementation cannot be derived simply from pre-established roles. UNHCR did not always support broader recognition or access for refugees, and government interests were not always toward more restrictions or less refugees.

Implementation results—including the meaning and ranking of RSD norms and the de facto decision-making structures on the ground—were influenced by a number of logics. For once, broad pressures such as democratization, state consolidation, regional politics, or material shortages all influenced trends in status recognition to varying degrees. This chapter documents an inability to insulate the refugee regime by recourse to its specific norms. With regards to the Rwandan case, even senior UNHCR staff acknowledged: "These are regional geopolitics all the way on top there is a priority with international conveniences. All [official] reasons are given to address discrepancies in reason."[70]

Yet broader structural factors were channeled through localized configurations of the "international refugee regime," i.e. the assistance set-up organized by the UNHCR offices, state actors, and international and national NGOs all operating under the umbrella of broad norms. Here different network dimensions played out at different times and across policy levels. Ultimately, not one of the central actors could impose their interest over time, but also, no one type of resource—be it financial transfers, legal frameworks, information, or trust—was primary. In terms of formalized norms, both UNHCR and central government actors referred to higher legal frameworks, while avoiding the procedural guarantees of legalism. This is visible in UNHCR's use of the threat of cessation, Tanzanian RSD procedures, and the legalism à la carte in Uganda.

Implementation structures are informed by the enmeshment of international and "domestic" or local logics and practices. Due to the heterogeneity of interests and actors involved, here norm interpretation can remain unstable over a long time. These implementation settings can arguably be described as "conflictive negotiation systems" where (a) high interdependence does not necessarily lead to increased agreement and (b) non-decisions and uncertainty

---

[69] Interview, Regional Police Commander, Kigoma, May 2003.
[70] Interview, UNHCR, Kampala, Apr. 2004.

about preferences figure prominently. In the two cases here, key actors often avoided formulating clear policies but acted through non-decisions or plausible deniability. The mode of decision-making was "diplomacy-based."

For an overall analysis, the conceptual distinctions introduced by Betts and Orchard provide much clarity for analytical engagement. However, the findings here question whether international and domestic levels of (international) norm use belong in fundamentally different conceptual categories. Many actors involved engaged on various levels and were driven by both international and local or domestic pressures. At the level of international policy-making, other modes of interaction may be prominent "on the ground" (Weber would have highlighted the different importance of paperwork). Yet the qualitative processes at both sites include those of norm-making, norm interpretation, and norm negotiation. From a sociological perspective Philip Selznick (1957) provided an early and influential definition of "institutionalization" as a process in which formal norms or organizational structures are "infused with value," i.e. gain meaning or importance in and of themselves. This key process seems worth investigating, whether in international treaty-making or its remaking (or "pre-making") in other arenas "on the ground." This investigation is possibly most fruitful across levels. Institutionalization and implementation would thus not be located at different levels of analysis (international or domestic), but describe *qualitatively* different processes, with the former presumably preceding the latter. Such an approach would also strengthen the mutual legibility of concepts across the political science subdisciplines of international relations, comparative politics and sociology.

15

Conclusions
Norms and the Politics of Implementation

Alexander Betts and Phil Orchard

When constructivists discuss norms, the scholarship frequently focuses on international measures: the ratification of an international treaty; acceptance of an issue by an international organization; adoption of a policy within a crucial actor or network. This is the theme of Finnemore and Sikkink's norm emergence life-cycle: that these processes of institutionalization help to cement the emergence of a new norm.

In this volume, we have sought to challenge this premise. Institutionalization at the international level is an important marker for norm emergence. But it is not an end state. It does not equal compliance. Norms once institutionalized remain ill-defined and imprecise. Even with clear norms, states may signal adoption at the international level, but find further efforts stymied by a lack of capacity or by domestic opposition. Or they may signal adoption purely as a rhetorical move with no further plans.

A gap exists between institutionalization and subsequent implementation efforts. Implementation, we have suggested, is a parallel process to institutionalization, which draws attention to the steps necessary to introduce the new international norm's precepts into formal legal and policy mechanisms within a state or organization in order to routinize compliance. As we have argued, almost all new norms go through an implementation process at the domestic level before they can be considered as internalized or settled within the state. This process helps to clarify the norms and to create clear and observable standards. This process can also open up renewed contestation, leading to the norm being redefined at the domestic level or even stalling out.

The goal of this book has been twofold: first, to identify whether this institutionalization–implementation gap exists and, second, to see how it affects state practice. To test this, we have examined a range of norms within the sphere of people-centered issues, issues designed primarily to assist and protect individuals within the spheres of human rights, aid, humanitarianism, peacekeeping, intervention, and displacement. These norms are based in international treaties, in informal principles and practices, and in policy within organizations. The individual chapters began with puzzles—variations in state practice that cannot be explained by institutionalization alone. The chapters have generally used qualitative approaches as a way to unpack complex causal mechanisms (George and Bennett 2005). Some chapters focus on in-depth and multi-sited fieldwork using interviews and ethnographic methods. Others use historical research as ways to examine the evolution of the relationship between institutionalization and implementation.

In this final chapter, we re-evaluate our theoretical framework in light of the findings of the empirical chapters, and consider what the chapters mean collectively for research and policy. We structure the conclusion in four parts: defining, explaining, theorizing, and practising implementation.

DEFINING IMPLEMENTATION

In the introductory chapter, we argued that it was useful to analytically distinguish between institutionalization, which primarily reflected an international process, and the implementation process, which is triggered at the domestic level or within organizations once the state or organization commits to the emerging norm. Approaching these as distinct *processes* allows us to problematize normative change in a nuanced way. While Finnemore and Sikkink note that completion of the life-cycle is not inevitable (1998: 895), the nature of the life-cycle itself does suggest a pattern of forward, linear movement: that we should expect the inevitable progression of a fixed and understood norm. Considering these as separate but linked processes alters this linear story in several ways. Processes not only slow down or halt, but can also reserve. Similarly, between these two processes we can expect to see unexpected, unanticipated, and perhaps even unnoticed feedback effects (see Chapter 8 by Job and Shesterinina and Chapter 14 by Schmidt). Contestation within one process can directly affect the other. This view therefore has three advantages.

First, as we noted, institutionalization as a term is frequently used to denote separate—and even competing—processes. Whereas for Finnemore and Sikkink (1998: 900) it was focused on the international level, for others (see Acharya 2004; Checkel 1999, 2007; Cortell and Davis 2000; Weiner 2007, 2010) it was primarily a domestic-level process. With our view, implementation becomes a separate process from norm institutionalization, a process which enables us to avoid the international "end-point" that institutionalization suggests (McKeown 2009) and thereby allows us to take seriously the role of domestic institutions and actors as well as the continued contestation of core elements of a given norm.

Second, the framework set out an explanation for implementation at the domestic level. It offered a parsimony framework highlighting the role of structure (material, institutional, and ideational) and agency in explaining variation in the institutionalization–implementation gap. The chapters in the volume have followed and built upon that framework but also nuanced it and highlighted a range of additional causal mechanisms that explain variation in implementation.

Third, we proposed that the inherent nature of the norm itself affects how implementation proceeded. In the introductory chapter, we argued in favor of a typology of norms. We hypothesized that different normative forms—institutionalized through different processes—would affect the implementation process in different ways and, potentially, by mobilizing different sets of proponents and opponents at the domestic level. In other words, the form of the norm, as opposed to its content, could affect whether it would be implemented.

Dynamic Contestation

Throughout the chapters, treating institutionalization and implementation as separate processes opened up the possibility of ongoing norm contestation. Schroeder and Tiemessen, for example, found that, with respect to the Rome Statute, the implementation campaign required a distinct, domestically oriented process which empowered and worked "with supportive state actors to reassure domestic audiences, develop domestically appropriate interpretations of the Rome Statute, and pass complex implementing reforms" (Schroeder and Tiemessen, Chapter 3). Aneja (Chapter 5) similarly saw implementation as providing for contestation *within* an actor (such as an organization), seeking to interpret new norms in line with their existing policies and identity, and then at the domestic level as the actor puts forward their interpretation of the new norm.

Other authors, however, found that this formulation was too simple, arguing instead for a range of different contestations between these two policies. Anderson (Chapter 11), examining the norm on property restitution, argued that there can be several implementation cycles. In her case, she suggests that implementation efforts predated any attempts at international institutionalization (within the Pinheiro Principles). This meant that the institutionalization process reflected too closely individual implementation events, most notably in Bosnia-Herzegovina. Weaver and Peratsakis (Chapter 10) suggested that feedback can occur within the implementation process as well. Successful implementation of a new norm may cause outside actors to "move the goal line": the World Bank becoming a champion of transparency has led transparency norm advocates to move away from a view of transparency as an end in itself to transparency as a means to greater accountability. Betts (Chapter 2) finds that outside factors—massive numbers of Zimbabwean survival migrants—can cause states to re-evaluate even settled norms, leading to a renewed implementation process.

Further, the implementation process can create feedback effects in international institutionalization efforts. Job and Shesterinina (Chapter 8) pointed to the need to pair a typical "top-down" model with a complementary "bottom-up dynamic" which allows for a feedback loop to develop from the national to the international level. Thus, they suggest that, for many norms, implementation is not realized through domestic action, but through "international actions, e.g. enforcing UNSC resolutions, imposing sanctions, or providing humanitarian relief," a view echoed by Welsh (Chapter 7).

This suggests that implementation processes may have no clear end point, and instead be iterative in nature, with new periods of contestation continually reinterpreting the norm. This follows Krook and True's view that norms are a process exposed to ongoing contestation and this means that "co-optation, drift, accretion and reversal of a norm—including disputes over whether it a norm at all—are constant possibilities" (Krook and True 2012: 104); norms are never fixed.

If this is the case, however, how can norms ever reach a settled state? The implementation process is linked to legal and policy processes within the state. Implementation can, therefore, be retriggered by new events or crises not considered when the norm was originally implemented can trigger renewed contestation. At the extreme, crisis events can trigger the wholesale replacement or transformation of new norms as they disrupt policy stasis within government (Milner and Keohane 1996: 16; Orchard 2014). This then leads to "short bouts of intense ideational contestation in which agents struggle to provide compelling and convincing diagnoses of the pathologies afflicting the old regime/policy paradigm and the reforms appropriate to the resolution of the crisis" (Hay 2008: 67). Lesser events will not require replacement, but can be used by local agents to reinitiate the implementation process as the state seeks to understand how norms apply to a given situation.

Material and Ideational Structures

Structures at the national level matter both for constraining and enabling implementation and shaping what norms do in practice. At the ideational level, we suggested that domestic cultural understandings, the political environment, and political institutions (such as the legal system) would all have effects on efforts to implement new norms. Equally, however, ideas (and how they were framed) would also play a part in critical efforts by domestic norm entrepreneurs to promote (or block) implementation efforts. At a material level, we suggested that interests and capacity would matter. Here we expected to find efforts by the state and other domestic actors to reinterpret new norms through their own parochial sets of interests which might shape how the norm was implemented. State capacity, including its economic strength and simple ability to actually implement change, but also its institutional structure and ability to respond to corruption and rent-seeking, was also likely to be an explanatory factor. Finally, we hypothesized that the institutional structure of the state, including not only its constitutional framework and bureaucratic structure, but also other variations due to the contingences of history, would also be an important set of factors.

The emphasis on material versus ideational structure varies across the cases. Betts (Chapter 2) provided an interest-based account of the conditions under which "regime stretching" takes place at the national level in the refugee regime, highlighting the role of elite interests in responding to international and domestic incentives. The argument is effectively a "two-level Steve Krasner" argument showing how ambiguous or imprecise norms are reconciled by interests at the national level just as they are at the international level (Krasner 1999). Orchard also offered a predominantly material account of the structures that shape variation in the implementation of IDP protection norms. For him, institutionalization opens up a "Trojan Horse" which "provides an opening to domestic and international actors to pressure governments to conform to the legislation" but institutionalization "is only a step" (Chapter 6). After this, two further material conditions have been necessary for implementation: international pressure (willingness) and domestic capacity (ability).

Paddon (Chapter 9) argued that a mix of material and institutional factors explain the UN's implementation of the protection of civilians norm in the Democratic Republic of the Congo. In particular she points to concerns over risk (including risk of expulsion, of escalating hostilities, and of property damage or personal injury) as explaining implementation failures, while these are countered by clear capacity, including resources, clear mandates, local knowledge, but also "top cover"—clear backing from the institution itself defined as the UN Secretariat and the Security Council.

Ideas also matter. Schroeder and Tiemessen demonstrated how the idea of sovereignty matters at the national level, and can be used to contest or shape the accountability norm. In their words, "criticism that the Court is biased against Africa and is a form of Western judicial colonialism in weak states" has been used to support norm contestation and non-implementation in states like Sudan and Kenya (Chapter 3). However, part of the implementation story elsewhere has been the way in which transnational advocacy groups, such as the Coalition to the International Criminal Court, have worked to dispel or coopt prevailing ideas in positive ways in states such as Uganda.

Aneja emphasized the important role of actor identity in defining how norms are interpreted and hence implemented by those actors: "even a treaty norm with constant institutionalization has to first be interpreted by the actors responsible for implementing the norm" (Chapter 5). INGO identities and self-understandings have defined whether the norm of emergency assistance has been implemented on a needs-based or rights-based basis during different phases of the Sri Lanka conflict. As well as recognizing the role of non-material structures in shaping implementation, the chapter also usefully highlights how and why implementation cannot be seen in purely state-centric terms but is also determined, often significantly, by contestation among non-state actors.

In Schmidt's (Chapter 14) account of the refugee regime, both material and ideational structures at every level of governance mattered. They also interacted in complex ways, demonstrating the highly contingent and localized nature of the structures that define norm contestation and reinterpretation. Watson pointed to a mix of ideational and material power affecting the implementation of the disaster relief norm and that an expansive view of disaster relief was blocked by states concerned about the material costs and obligations of such an international organization. The recognition that both ideas and material structures matter, and interact in highly political and contested ways, takes understandings of how norms move from the global to the national and local levels beyond the predominantly cultural and ideational accounts of norm localization (Acharya 2004).

Agency and the Role of Individuals

Beyond structure, agency matters for implementation, and examples of the role of individuals abound across the chapters. Terms such as "enablers of implementation" or "norm implementers" are used to highlight a similar phenomenon: the role of individuals in enabling (or in some cases constraining) implementation. Although Paddon (Chapter 9) recognized the centrality of structural variables—based on risk and capacity—individuals ultimately define how these variables translate into practice. In her account, Major General Patrick Cammeart and Dominique McAdam, the head of the UN office in Ituri, were central to the more robust and successful implementation of the protection of civilians norm.

Within the World Bank, the "successful engineering of the implementation process" is partly the product of an auspicious structural context, including a general trend and external pressure for aid transparency (Chapter 10). However, Weaver and Peratsakis demonstrated how individuals such as former Executive Director Robert Zoellick and Managing Director Carolyn Anstey matter for turning this structural context into AI policy reform in-house. Milner's account likewise did not gainsay the importance of structure but shows how leadership, absent from the Tanzania case, was central for overcoming institutional divisions to inter-agency coordination in Burundi.

As well as coming from individuals, agency may also be generated by state strategies at the inter-governmental level. Job and Shesterinina, for example, demonstrated how China's strategic engagement with norms has had a bearing on the contestation of R2P at implementation. As they explain, having accepted the norm "as it was institutionalized at the World Summit in 2005...China has consistently advanced a particular interpretation of R2P, impacting the evolution in the understanding of the norm and conditioning its implementation" (Chapter 8).

Far from being purely within the black box of the state or within a single institution, though, the actors exercising agency in shaping implementation can be transnational in nature. For Schroeder and Tiemessen (Chapter 3), non-state actors such as the Coalition to the International Criminal Court (CICC) played a crucial role in determining the prospects for implementation by assisting, shaming, and persuading state parties. Thus, non-state actors may facilitate or obstruct norm implementation but, either way, they may be significant in shaping contestation and hence implementation.

As well as agency, contingency also matters; history, circumstances, and luck can all play critical roles. This is not a novel finding—constructivists have long argued that "social systems can get 'locked in' to certain patterns by the logic of shared knowledge, adding a source of social inertia or glue that would not exist in a system without culture" (Wendt 1999: 188). As Crawford notes, this may mean that there are no good ethical or practical reasons for a norm, and yet:

> for some accidental reason, the practice is accepted and expected. In this situation, no one seems to have what might be recognized as an ethical or logical argument to justify the practice, though *post-hoc* rationalizations for the practice might spring to mind if practitioners are pressed. (2002: 88)

Such contingencies may assist the norm institutionalization and implementation processes, but they can also derail them. For Percy (Chapter 4), the anti-mercenary norm was significantly affected by outside events, including the decline in mercenary use overall and the Convention's inability to police the few new mercenary-like actors that emerged. For Watson (Chapter 13), disaster relief is a voluntaristic activity because of debates held in the 1920s, debates themselves framed by earlier rational scientific understandings of natural disasters. This debate was "won" by the American Red Cross, based on the vision of its by then-dead director, Henry Davison.

The Inherent Nature of the Norm

The empirical chapters reveal that the distinction between treaty, principle, and policy norms is more fundamental than we had anticipated—not only does the form of the norm affect its implementation; it also introduces a range of unanticipated interaction effects. With respect to treaty norms, the most concretely institutionalized norms at the international level, we expected that the clear *legalization* of the norm would have three important benefits for implementation: it would increase the legitimacy of the norm and thereby its compliance pull (Franck 1990: 24; Finnemore 2000: 702–3; Deitelhoff 2009: 34); it would lead to increased *precision* of the norm as states clarified their understandings through negotiation (Lutz and Sikkink 2000; Percy 2007: 389); and a legal treaty was more likely to have *clear implementation mechanisms* (Diehl et al. 2003: 45).

These benefits, however, are countered by a growing literature which points to continued vagueness in what a norm means and how it should be applied, even when institutionalized through a legal treaty (Van Kersbergen and Verbeek 2007: 218–19, 22; Sandholtz 2008: 101; Krook and True 2012: 104).

The individual chapter contributors demonstrate that this holds: without clear implementation, treaty norms can be quite weak. Thus, Schroeder and Tiemessen (Chapter 3) demonstrated with respect to the Rome Statute that the legitimacy of a treaty norm, its precision, and international pressure have not been enough. Rather, they find the ongoing efforts of the CICC to work with domestic NGOs and governmental actors—and, at times, to allow the redefinition of critical concepts such as complementarily—was critical to the implementation process. Aneja similarly found that the clear legal obligations for humanitarian assistance established in the Geneva Conventions (which have been ratified in whole or with reservations by 194 countries) are in practice subject to "tremendous variation."

Precision can also impede or prevent implementation. Percy (Chapter 4) argued that, with respect to mercenaries, precision led to so many loopholes that it made the treaty functionally useless. Watson found that concessions as part of negotiations drastically weakened states' normative obligations with respect to disaster relief. And while focused on a policy norm, Weaver and Peratsakis (Chapter 10) noted that norm precision actually began to disintegrate *following* successful implementation steps as contention increased over what marks a success.

This suggests that rather than the gold standard for institutionalization, the precision introduced by legal treaties may actually make the implementation process more difficult for some norms. This finding is counterintuitive; much of the work on norm emergence has focused on the importance of law to ban landmines (Price 1998), chemical weapons, (Price 1997), and to help establish human rights (Keck and Sikkink 1998; Thomas 2001), to mention only a few examples. Given the relatively small number of cases, clearly, further research is necessary. But a few implications can be drawn out. First, there is the issue of time: Percy (Chapter 4) flags the length of time it first took to negotiate the Convention against the use of mercenaries and then the decade-long ratification process in which outside factors changed considerably. Equally, though, examining the implementation process associated with some of these "strong" legal norms, such as landmines, may demonstrate that they remain less settled than anticipated, a finding already echoed in the human rights field (see Hafner-Burton and Ron 2009).

We argued in favor of distinguishing principle norms from treaty norms for two reasons. The first was that, even without a process of legal codification, these more informal norms were clearly both important and institutionalized. The second was that this might actually be more advantageous for the norm emergence process, as Orchard (2010: 285–6) had earlier argued. That such soft institutionalization might reflect a deliberate decision was confirmed in the chapters by Orchard (Chapter 6) and Watson (Chapter 13). In both cases, this allowed for individual states to have more flexibility and less normative constraint on their actions.

Principle norms are more likely to be complex or cluster norms, containing, as Welsh noted, "more than one prescription." This introduces three issues unique to this type of norm. First, it "raises questions for how scholars should measure the strength of principle norms" (Chapter 7). In looking at R2P, Welsh called into question how successful implementation of R2P could actually be measured, suggesting that even the presence or absence of military intervention could not be taken as a good proxy. Hence for principle norms, as Aneja suggested, a range of methodological challenges remain on how to specify the norm, identify the benchmark of institutionalization, and measure implementation (Chapter 5). Weaver and Peratsakis suggested that to a lesser extent, policy norms also pose methodological challenges, especially once policies are identifiable within multiple documents of varying degrees of normative authority (Chapter 10).

Second, as Job and Shesterinina noted, proponents of principle norms are inherently seeking to combine competing norms, to replace existing and established norms, and to create new standards of responsibility. Thus the R2P brought into contestation fundamental principles of sovereignty and state responsibilities. They suggested that some principle norms are designed to operate at a deeper level, to establish new fundamental or metanorms. In effect, principle norms are more complex and less precise specifically because they seek to do more than most treaty or policy norms and hence are subject to significantly higher levels of contestation at both stages. Therefore, because of their construction and role, principle norms "are seldom articulated definitively through institutionalization" (Chapter 8).

Whereas principle norms were found to be more complex than treaty norms in many cases, the chapter authors found policy norms frequently to be nested, based on reinterpretations of existing treaty or principle norms. Policy norms play the critical role of representing the shared expectations of relevant actors which are encapsulated in policy, usually within international organizations (Park and Vetterlein 2010: 13). Here, the implementation process can be critical, however, as it brings about significant reinterpretation of these norms by implementing actors. We saw this with respect to aid organizations and the rights-based approach in Aneja's chapter (Chapter 5), UN peacekeeping and the protection of civilians in the Congo in Paddon's (Chapter 9), with respect to aid transparency and the World Bank in Weaver and Peratsakis's (Chapter 10), and with respect to integrated approaches and the United Nations in Milner's (Chapter 12).

These findings suggest that this division of norms is useful, but that rather than simply reflecting different institutionalization processes, the norm content may actually trigger a particular form of implementation. This echoes Wiener's (2007: 9) earlier argument as noted by Job and Shesterinina (Chapter 8): "Norms 'remain flexible by definition', and not surprisingly the most contested norms, such as R2P, are those that concern fundamental understandings of international relations." Equally, while policy norms may be the least contested, in that they are nested and reflect broader normative understandings, even here the implementation process brings about (potentially significant) reinterpretation. This suggests that the implementation process may introduce significant feedback at the international level and into the institutionalization process, a point we shall discuss further.

THEORIZING IMPLEMENTATION

Our original conceptual framework is intended to serve as a parsimonious starting point for thinking about implementation. To our delight, rather than simply apply the framework, many of the chapters push the framework in new directions and in some cases even openly challenge it. Some of the main areas of theoretical development that emerge from the chapters relate to exploring ways in which a theory of norm implementation can be made both non-linear and dynamic, capturing feedbacks from implementation to institutionalization or from the national level to the global level, and capturing temporality and normative change. Furthermore, some of the chapters also sought to explore ways in which the concept of implementation can be analogously applied beyond the national level to other levels of governance, including the global level or within particular organizations or institutions.

Towards a Dynamic Approach

One of the key findings of the chapters was that, by taking a dynamic approach and considering feedback effects seriously, we can observe the implementation process affecting international institutionalization over time. As anticipated within the Introduction, the implementation process can involve a range of actors at the domestic level. Schmidt (Chapter 14), Milner (Chapter 12), and Betts (Chapter 2) highlighted the roles played by government, UNHCR, and implementation partners. As Schmidt argues, none of the actors' interests can be understood as derived simply from pre-established roles: "UNHCR did not always support broader recognition or access for refugees, and government interests were not always towards more restrictions or less refugees" (Chapter 14). Instead, what emerges in terms of implementation is the result of ongoing and highly contingent localized processes of negotiation, in which the very identity of the local actors is endogenous to those negotiations.

Dynamism, however, can also lead to actors driving both the implementation and institutionalization processes. Job and Shesterinina, for example, highlighted the idea of a "bottom-up-and-back" dynamic of norm-shaping to reflect "the tensions in contemporary contestation over international norms, especially the complex principle ones" (Chapter 8). Emerging powers like China and India, they highlighted, are becoming norm-makers rather than norm-takers, actively reshaping prevailing Western liberal norms. These states are internalizing and implementing norms but are also deliberately impacting the nature of those norms through the ways in which they pursue implementation.

Implementation is not solely a state-based activity. Rather, in many of the chapters, *non-state actors* are central to the process. Far from a unitary state's action or inaction defining what norms do in practice, a range of non-state actors—whether INGOs, transnational civil society, UN peacekeepers, rebel groups, or elites within a disaggregated state—matter for the negotiation and (re)contestation of norms at the domestic level (see the chapters by Aneja, Milner, Paddon, Betts). The role of such non-state actors and the need to recognize the disaggregated nature of the state becomes all the more important in the context of the weak states in which this volume's people-centered norms are generally implemented. For example, Schroeder and Tiemessen's (Chapter 3) analysis suggested that transnational actors may also simultaneously play roles in both the institutionalization and implementation of new norms. The embeddedness of CICC within the inter-governmental debates on institutionalization was a central element in what enabled it to contribute to implementation, playing a similar top-down and a bottom-up role. CICC was effectively an illustration of "the transnational within the domestic": being an actor able to "bridge the gap" between early institutionalization and implementation. This empirical observation has theoretical implications insofar as it highlights the ways in which institutionalization and implementation are not necessarily stages, phased one after the other, but may take place in parallel, in ways that can be complementary or contradictory, and in which different or, in the case of CICC, occasionally the same actors may play an active role.

Feedback effects are not only actor-driven, however, but can be created through the implementation process itself. Thus Percy found that institutionalization did little to "fix" the content of normative prohibitions against mercenary use. The "combat" provision of anti-mercenary law had been historically silent. Yet private military and security companies (PMSCs) have deliberately used this as a core distinction from mercenaries: "the idea that the use of private force is acceptable only as long as those employed do not use force is increasingly internationally accepted" (Chapter 4). In this case, feedback through the implementation process has actually changed the basic state understandings of the norm. Anderson also demonstrated that implementation can shape institutionalization with the Pinheiro Principles for property restitution. These Principles serve as the outcome of recognition of gaps in practice and they "required prior attempts at implementation before they could be framed in their current form" (Chapter 11). While implementation and institutionalization may be parallel processes, this suggests that the earlier stages of the implementation process can have important legacy effects on the form and basic understandings embedded in the norm itself.

Implementation beyond the Domestic Level

Some of the chapters argue that implementation occurs not just at the domestic level but may occur within international organizations or at the global level, for example. Weaver and Peratsakis (Chapter 10) looked at international organizations' internal policies and practices. In doing so, they analogously apply our concept of implementation to the parallel and distinct processes of policy development and policy implementation. This is an approach that certainly pushes the scope of how and where the concept of implementation can be used and applied beyond the scalar levels of global/national/local.

In their analysis of R2P in particular, both Welsh (Chapter 7) and Job and Shesterinina (Chapter 8) demonstrated that implementation can also be understood to take place at regional and international levels. Welsh, for instance, showed how the establishment of "early warning" capacity within the international community would be an example of implementation at R2P that takes place at the global level, arguing for "the development of stronger capacity for effective mediation among conflicting parties so as to end violence against innocent civilians."

Our response to Welsh's argument is to recognize that different types of norms are implemented in different ways and on different geographical bases. In some cases, this might involve recognizing that implementation can take place at the global level. However, for most norms implementation has to happen somewhere, and this "somewhere" is usually a particular national context. Of course, this is not to say that actions cannot be taken collectively or even transnationally (see Schroeder and Tiemessen, Chapter 3) that support implementation but that, in our conceptual framework, "early warning" mechanisms, for example, might instead be understood as developing the capacity to support implementation rather than implementation itself.

Beyond Institutionalization, Compliance, and Localization

One of the central theoretical claims of this book is that it is possible and worthwhile to develop a concept of "norm implementation" as distinct from other established concepts such as "compliance," "localization," and "institutionalization." The intention is not to critique or reject these concepts but to complement and in some ways connect them.

We argued that compliance reflects an act of rule-following or norm obeyance; it is separate from the mechanisms which cause the state to do so. This view of compliance is adopted in many of the authors' chapters (see Schroeder and Tiemessen, Chapter 3; Welsh, Chapter 7). Thus, while acts of non-compliance (or defection) are easier without constraints set in place to stop it, even a fully institutionalized and implemented norm may not be complied with. As Schroeder and Tiemessen noted in their chapter, "parties may face political obstacles to compliance irrespective of the degree of implementation," but in the case of Kenya, implementation helped to empower domestic judicial institutions and civil society which were able to keep pressure on the government. By contrast, Paddon (Chapter 6) found that, even with improved implementation efforts around the protection of civilians norm in the Congo, rates of compliance were variable.

However, this notion of compliance-as-act is also problematized by examining implementation processes. Different actors will hold different interpretations of the same norm: violation for one may represent compliance for another. This suggests, as Aneja (Chapter 5) noted (see also Job and Shesterinina (Chapter 8)), that the notion of compliance-as-act, as a "binary categories of compliance or violation", itself is based on a fixed notion of a given norm, and hence cannot be analytically useful until both implementation and institutionalization processes are concluded. "Contestation over implementation and monitoring of compliance," Job and Shesterinina noted, therefore "take on whole new dimensions of complexity."

Further, the chapters see Acharya (2004)'s work on norm localization as reflecting a special case of implementation. His work recognizes how norms are changed in their encounters with particular national and local contexts and the complexity of such processes. Acharya's focus, however, is mainly on the role of culture and ideas as mechanisms for norm translation at the regional level. Therefore, it represents a top-down approach (Job and Shesterinina, Chapter 8). By contrast, implementation moves beyond cultural focus or a notion of "grafting" to recognize implementation as a political process of contestation in which a range of structures and actors shape and channel what norms do in practice. Further, it can better account for the dynamic process by which implementation processes lead to changed international norms, a piece missing from Acharya's framework.

Across all the chapters, there is recognition that implementation serves to usefully highlight processes that are rendered invisible with a reliance on "institutionalization." The mark of a useful concept is that it can explain puzzles or render empirical processes visible that would otherwise be obscured. The chapters show how the distinction of implementation from institutionalization serves this analytical purpose.

First, on a spatial level, distinguishing implementation from institutionalization helps explain *variation in practice* that is otherwise unexplained. In Welsh's words, it highlights how "institutionalization does not necessarily represent a moment of triumph for norms" (Chapter 7). Seeing implementation as a distinct process allowed puzzles of variation in practice despite common levels of institutionalization to be unpacked and understood in ways that are impossible with a standard norm life-cycle approach, which ends the account at the point at which states sign and ratify norms, or with accounts of institutionalization that burrow into the domestic realm to varying degrees (see e.g. the chapters by Betts, Orchard, Paddon, Schmidt, Milner, and, Schroeder and Tiemessen).

Second, on a temporal level, the chapters further suggested that seeing institutionalization and implementation as distinct but parallel processes helps to explain *normative change* that is otherwise rendered invisible. Where institutionalization can assume the content of a norm is fixed, a number of the chapters find implementation useful as a way of highlighting a parallel process in which the content of institutionalized norms can evolve as a result of changes in practice and feedback from implementation (see e.g. the chapters by Percy, Job and Shesternina, Anderson, Aneja, and Watson).

PRACTICING IMPLEMENTATION

One of the big "so what?" motivations behind this volume was that implementation matters for practice. If we work only with the lens of Finnemore and Sikkink's norm life-cycle model, we risk failing to explain how norms actually affect people's lives. In the case of the people-centered norms in this volume, what ultimately matters is not whether states sign and ratify norms but what those norms do in practice. As such, the volume makes both academic and practical contributions to these debates. With that in mind, it would be remiss to close without five reflections on general lessons the chapters might offer for policy and practice. Of course, there is no generic roadmap for successful norm implementation, and policy implications will vary with the type of norm and a range of other contingencies; nevertheless, some basic lessons stand out.

Treaty Design

The chapters highlight that the way in which norms are conceived has implications for the ways in which they are implemented. Imprecision and ambiguity may reduce the costs of an agreement at the global level, but they can have serious implications for what norms ultimately do (or do not do) in practice. Percy's (Chapter 4) analysis of the "unimplementable" anti-mercenary norm was a stark illustration of what can happen if a treaty norm is conceived with too many loopholes or with too little regard for implementation. On the other hand, as Watson (Chapter 13) highlighted, some norms may be deliberately institutionalized by states in ways that are intended to maximize state discretion and preserve sovereignty. Yet some of the chapters were able to offer insights of good practice. Weaver and Peratsakis (Chapter 10) discussed how implementation of the aid transparency norm was consciously "engineered" by the World Bank, while Anderson (Chapter 11) highlighted the role that iterative learning can play in ensuring that, when norms are institutionalized, they are informed by a body of practice and an awareness on the part of actors of the dynamics of implementation.

Alliances with Non-State Actors

The distinction between institutionalization as an international process and implementation is often implicit in the approach of international public policy-makers. Many norm creators within the "international community"—like international relations scholars—tend to regard their task as complete once states sign and ratify norms, and stand back from engagement with domestic politics. In analytically transcending the international/domestic divide, the chapters offered guidance on ways in which international public policy-makers can influence norm implementation without overtly transgressing state sovereignty. Schroeder and Tiemessen (Chapter 3) highlighted the role that can be played by forming alliances with transnational advocacy groups, for example. Meanwhile, many of the other chapters hinted at ways in which "the international at the domestic level"—a form of Trojan Horse presence—might enable the international community to more effectively influence norm implementation (Orchard, Chapter 6). In some regimes such as the refugee regime, international organizations like UNHCR may already have a national presence (see Schmidt, Chapter 14). In other contexts, ad hoc alliances may need to be considered.

Multi-Level Political Analysis

International organizations, often created as the guardians of particular international norms, rarely have significant capacity for political analysis. Many international organizations, including a number of those covered by this volume, are conceived with mandates that are explicitly non-political. Frequently, this is overinterpreted to imply that such organizations should limit their degree of political awareness or the resources they allocate to political analysis. Yet, this is a mistake, because the very process of insuring the norms that they uphold have impact is inherently political. In order to understand and influence the impact of the norms they uphold, international organizations cannot limit their analysis to legal or normative analysis because to do so is to misunderstand how norms relate to practice. The chapters in this volume collectively highlighted the importance for international organizations of undertaking high-quality political and stakeholder analysis at every level at which they operate, not least the national and local levels (see in particular the chapters by Betts, Paddon, Milner, and Schmidt).

Ongoing Incentives

The chapters revealed that, in thinking about normative impact on practice, international law cannot do the work by itself. Norms are transformed in their movement from the global to the national to the local level. At each stage, ideas, interests, and power all matter. In order to make norms work as intended, international public policy-makers cannot just release international law into the domestic sphere, like a feral animal, and hope that it will find its own way. Instead, there is a need to consider the sets of incentives that may be required to shape domestic elite interests, and thereby render the domestic political environment more auspicious for norm implementation (see the chapters by Betts, Orchard, and Schroeder and Tiemessen).

Empowering Individuals

One of the overriding themes of the chapters is that individual leadership matters for implementation. "Implementation enablers" or "norm implementers" are central to many of the stories in the book (see the chapters by Milner, Paddon, Weaver, and Peratsakis). Leadership and the role of individuals remain among the least theorized aspects of international relations and yet they are endemically recognized as crucial for normative change, within states, national bureaucracies, and international organizations. "Institutional intrapreneurship" seems to be crucial to allowing adaptation within organizations like the World Bank or across UN organizations at the field level, or within the governments of developing countries. Part of this is always likely to be related to the personality, values, and talents of those particular individuals. However, it is certain that structural conditions may constrain or enable individual initiative to take root and have an impact on norm implementation. If individual agency is so important, then it is something that international public policy-makers should thrive to promote, beginning within their own organizations.

CONCLUSIONS

The premise of this volume has been that implementation matters deeply in the ways in which new international norms are understood by states and by organizations. Treating institutionalization and implementation as distinct processes provides a way of understanding variability in state and organization practice in spite of common levels of normative institutionalization. By focusing on a range of treaty, principle, and policy-based human protection norms, the individual chapters have both identified this variability and sought to explain it. Our answers have not been easy ones. Examining implementation requires a different set of foci than most international relations scholarship: it privileges the domestic, the internal. And yet, this is not simply a shift in the level of analysis. Implementation is dynamic: as a process, it can feed back into international institutionalization efforts, as states and other actors push their understandings of new norms. It can open contestation at both the domestic and the international levels. And implementation sacrifices an easy end point for understanding when a new norm is settled: contestations can continue, or re-emerge, years or even decades after a norm is first introduced.

The agency and structures at play in such contestations can be identified. The ideational, material, and institutional factors at play in each case vary, but they are present. This volume has sought to introduce implementation as a distinct process in order to better understand the puzzles that appeared in our own work. In introducing this concept, we do not suggest we have all the answers, but rather we seek to begin a conversation. This conversation will be a challenging one: it redefines core ideas; it changes where we look for empirical data; and it increases dramatically the complexity of our work. By introducing implementation as a process, however, it helps to shift our perspectives, broaden our views, and improve our understanding of the world.

References

Abbott, K. W., and Snidal, D. 2003. "Hard and Soft Law in International Governance," *International Organization*, 54(3): 421–56.

Abbott, K. W., Keohane, R., Moravcsik, A., Slaughter, A.-M., and Snidal, D. 2000. "The Concept of Legalization." *International Organization*, 54(3): 401–19.

Abebe, A. M. 2010. "The African Union Convention on Internally Displaced Persons: Its Codification Background, Scope, and Enforcement Challenges," *Refugee Survey Quarterly*, 29: 28–57.

Acharya, A. 2004. "How Ideas Spread: Whose Norms Matter? Norm Localization and Institutional Change in Asian Regionalism," *International Organization*, 58: 239–75.

Acharya, A. 2011. "Norm Subsidiarity and Regional Orders: Sovereignty, Regionalism, and Rule Making in the Third World," *International Studies Quarterly*, 55(1): 95–123.

Adams, T. K. 1999. "The New Mercenaries and the Privatization of Conflict. Parameters," *US Army War College Quarterly*, 29: 1–12.

Adhikari, Y. P., and Joshi, U. 2008. *Rapid Assessment of Conflict Induced Internally Displaced Persons (IDPs) for the Return, Resettlement and Reintegration*. Kathmandu: National Human Rights Commission, Nepal.

Agence France-Presse. 2003. "War in Northern Uganda World's Worst Forgotten Crisis: UN." 11 Nov.

Akhavan, P. 2009. "Are International Criminal Tribunals a Disincentive to Peace? Reconciling Judicial Romanticism with Political Realism," *Human Rights Quarterly*, 31: 624–54.

Albert, S. 1997. "The Return of Refugees to Bosnia and Herzegovina: Peacebuilding with People," *International Peacekeeping*, 4(3): 1–23.

Allcock, J. B., Milivojevic, M., and Horton, J. J. 1998. *Conflict in the Former Yugoslavia: An Encyclopedia*. Denver, CO: ABC-CLIO.

American Red Cross. 1924. "Reply from the Government of the United States of America. Resolution XVI, Articles V and VI. Insurance of Peoples Against Calamities, etc.," *League of Nations—Official Journal*, Geneva.

Amit, R. 2010. *Protection and Pragmatism: Addressing Administrative Failure's in South Africa's Refugee Status Determination Decision*. FMSP Report, Apr. Johannesburg: Forced Migration Studies Programme, University of the Witwatersrand.

Amnesty International. 2004. *The Failure of States to Enact Effective Implementing Legislation*. London: Amnesty International. <http://www.amnesty.org/en/library/asset/IOR40/019/2004/en/e1410df4-d580-11dd-bb24-1fb85fe8fa05/ior400192004en.pdf>.

Amnesty International. 2010. *International Criminal Court: Rome Statute Implementation Report Card*. London: Amnesty International. <http://www.amnesty.org/en/library/asset/IOR53/011/2010/en/22fab440-cf1e-4ac2-a1ff-2a4ad9527b87/ior530112010en.pdf>.

Anderson, M. J. 2011. "The UN Principles on Housing and Property Restitution for Refugees and Displaced Persons (The Pinheiro Principles): Suggestions for Improved Applicability," *Journal of Refugee Studies,* 24(2): 304–22.

Annan, K. 1999. *Report of the Secretary-General Pursuant to General Assembly Resolution 53/35: The Fall Of Srebrenica,* A/54/549 (15 Nov.).

Annan, K. 2005. *In Larger Freedom: Toward Development, Security and Human Rights for All,* UN doc. A/59/2005 (21 Mar.).

Annan, K. 2006. "A Progress Report on UN Renewal," *New World* (Spring), 6–11.

Arnold, G. 1999. *Mercenaries: The Scourge of the Third World.* London: Macmillan.

Arraiza, J.-M., and Massimo, M. 2009. "Getting the Property Questions Right: Legal Policy Dilemmas in Post-Conflict Property Restitution in Kosovo," *International Journal of Refugee Law,* 21(3), 421–52.

Asian Tribune. 2009. "India Offers More Aid to Lanka for IDPS," *Asian Tribune,* 18 Oct.

Asia-Pacific Centre for the Responsibility to Protect (APCRP). 2008. *Burma Briefing: Cyclone Nargis and the Responsibility to Protect.* Brisbane: Global Centre for the Responsibility to Protect.

Assembly of States Parties, International Criminal Court. 2006. *Strategic Plan for Outreach of the International Criminal Court.* The Hague: Assembly of States Parties.

Autesserre, S. 2009. "Hobbes and the Congo: Frames, Local Violence, and International Intervention," *International Organization,* 63: 249–80.

Autesserre, S. 2010. *The Trouble with the Congo: Local Violence and the Failure of International Peacebuilding.* Cambridge. Cambridge University Press.

Avant, D. 2000. "From Mercenary to Citizen Armies," *International Organization,* 54: 41–72.

Badescu, C., and Bergholm, L. 2009. "Responsibility to Protect and the Conflict in Darfur: The Big Let Down," *Security Dialogue,* 40: 287–309.

Badescu, C. G., and Weiss, T. G. 2010. "Misrepresenting R2P and Advancing Norms: An Alternative Spiral?," *International Studies Perspectives,* 11(4): 354–74.

Bagenda, E., Naggaga, A., and Smith, E. 2003. *Land Problems in Nakivale Settlements and the Implications for Refugee Protection in Uganda.* Refugee Law Project Working Paper. Kampala: Refugee Law Project.

Ballard, M. J. 2010. "Post Conflict Property Restitution: Flawed Legal and Theoretical Foundations," *Berkeley Journal of International Law,* 28(2): 462–96.

Banda, M. 2007. *The Responsibility to Protect: Moving the Agenda Forward.* Ottawa: United Nations Association in Canada.

Bank Information Center. 2010. *Unlocking the World Bank's Access to Information Policy: Your Key to the Vault.* Bank Information Center, Sept. <http://www.bicusa.org/en/Document.102341.aspx>.

Barakat, S., Evans, M., and Strand, A. 2002. *Back to Basics: Reconstruction and Development in Sri Lanka.* York: University of York.

Barber, R. J. 2008. "Protecting the Right to Housing in the Aftermath of Natural Disaster: Standards in International Human Rights Law," *International Journal of Refugee Law,* 20(3): 432–68.

Barnett, M. 2011. *Empire of Humanity: A History of Humanitarianism.* New York: Cornell University Press.

Barnett, M., and Coleman, L. 2005. "Designing Police: Interpol and the Study of Change in International Organizations," *International Studies Quarterly,* 49(4): 593-620.

Barnett, M. N., and Finnemore, M. 2004. *Rules for the World: International Organizations in Global Politics*, Ithaca, NY: Cornell University Press.

Barnett, M., and Ramalingam, B. 2010. *The Humanitarian's Dilemma: Collective Action or Inaction in International Relief*. London: Humanitarian Policy Group.

Barnett, M., and Weiss, T., eds. 2008. *Humanitarianism in Question: Politics, Power, Ethics*. Ithaca, NY: Cornell University Press.

Barnett, M. N., and Weiss, T. G. 2011. *Humanitarianism Contested: Where Angels Fear to Tread*. London: Routledge.

Barnett, Michael. 2009. "Evolution without Progress? Humanitarianism in a World of Hurt," *International Organisation*, 63(4): 621–63.

Bassiouni, M. C. 1996. "Searching for Peace and Achieving Justice: The Need for Accountability," *Law and Contemporary Problems*, 59(4): 9–28.

Bastian, S., ed. 1994. *Devolution and Development in Sri Lanka*. Colombo: Konark Publishers.

Bastian, S. 1999. *The Failure of State Formation, Identity Conflict, and Civil Society Responses: The Case of Sri Lanka*. Bradford: University of Bradford.

Bayley, C. C. 1977. *Mercenaries for the Crimea: The German, Swiss and Italian Legions in British Service, 1854–1856*. London: McGill-Queen's University Press.

Beauchamp, S. 2008. *Defining the Humanitarian Space through Public International Law: On the Edges of Conflict*. Vancouver: Liu Institute for Global Studies and Canadian Red Cross. <http://www.redcross.ca/cmslib/general/obeoc_beauchamp.pdf>.

Beck, U. 1999. *World Risk Society*. Cambridge: Polity Press.

Béland, D. 2005. "Ideas and Social Policy: An Institutionalist Perspective," *Social Policy and Administration*, 39: 1–18.

Bell, C. 2000. *Peace Agreements and Human Rights*. Oxford: Oxford University Press.

Bell, P. 2001. *Presentation on Rights-Based Approaches*. Washington, DC: Interaction.

Bellamy, A. J. 2009. *Responsibility to Protect: The Global Effort to End Mass Atrocities*. Cambridge: Polity Press.

Bellamy, A. J. 2010. "The Responsibility to Protect—Five Years on," *Ethics and International Affairs*, 24: 143–69.

Bellamy, A. J. 2011. *Global Politics and the Responsibility to Protect: From Words to Deeds*. London and New York: Routledge.

Bellamy, A. J. 2012. "Mainstreaming the Responsibility to Protect in the United Nations System: Dilemmas, Challenges, and Opportunities." *Conference on Norms and Practice of Humanitarian Interventions: Operationalizing the Responsibility to Protect*. Konstanz: University of Konstanz.

Bellamy, A. J., and Davies, S. E. 2009. "The Responsibility to Protect in the Asia-Pacific Region," *Security Dialogue*, 40(6): 547–74.

Bellamy, A. J., and McLoughlin, S. 2009. *Preventing Genocide and Mass Atrocities: Causes and Paths of Escalation*, Asia-Pacific Centre for the Responsibility to Protect. Brisbane: University of Queensland.

Bellamy, A., and Williams, P. 2011. "The New Politics of Protection? Côte d'Ivoire, Libya and the Responsibility to Protect," *International Affairs*, 87(4): 825–50.

Bellamy, A., Williams, P., and Griffin, S., eds 2010. *Understanding Peacekeeping*. 2nd edn, Cambridge: Polity Press.

Benner, T. 2013. *Brazil as a Norm Entrepreneur: The "Responsibility While Protecting" Initiative*. Berlin: Global Public Policy Institute.

Bennett, A., and Checkel, J. (Forthcoming) "Process Tracing: From Philosophical Roots to Best Practices," in A. Bennett and J. Checkel (eds), *Process Tracing in the Social Sciences: From Metaphor to Analytic Tool*. Cambridge: Cambridge University Press. Ch. 1 available online at <http://www.sfu.ca/internationalstudies/checkel.html>

Bethlehem, D., and Weller, M., eds. 1997. *The "Yugoslav" Crisis in International Law: General Issues, Part I*. Cambridge: Cambridge University Press.

Betts, A. 2008. "Historical Lessons for Overcoming Protracted Refugee Situations," in G. Loescher, J. Milner, E. Newman, and G. Troeller (eds), *Protracted Refugee Situations: Political, Human Rights and Security Implications*, 162–85. Tokyo: United Nations University Press.

Betts, A. 2010. "Survival Migration: A New Protection Framework," *Global Governance*, 16(3): 361–82.

Betts, A. 2013. *Survival Migration: Failed Governance and the Crisis of Displacement*. Ithaca, NY: Cornell University Press.

Betts, A., and Kaytaz, E. 2009. *National and International Responses to the Zimbabwean Exodus: Implications for the Refugee Protection Regime*. New Issues in Refugee Research, 175. July. Geneva: UNHCR.

Betts, A., Loescher, G., and Milner, J. 2012. *UNHCR: The Politics and Practice of Refugee Protection*. 2nd edn, New York: Routledge.

Beyani, C. 2006. "Recent Developments: The Elaboration of a Legal Framework for the Protection of Internally Displaced Persons in Africa," *Journal of African Law*, 50(2): 187–97.

Bigombe, B., and Predergast, J. 2006. "Stop the Crisis in Northern Uganda," *Philadelphia Inquirer*, 21 Feb.

Birdsall, N., Kharas, H., and Perakis, R. 2011. "Measuring the Quality of Aid: QuODA Second Edition." Executive Summary for the Fourth High-Level Forum on Aid Effectiveness, Busan, Korea, 29 Nov.–1 Dec.

Bissell, R. E. 2009. "Regarding the World Bank's Policy on Disclosure of Information." Committee on Financial Services, US House of Representatives, Washington, DC, 10 Sept.

Blaikie, M. 1994. *At Risk: Natural Hazards, People's Vulnerability, and Disasters*. London: Routledge.

Bob, C. 2009. *The International Struggle for New Human Rights*. Philadelphia: University of Pennsylvania Press.

Bob, C. 2010. "Packing Heat: Pro-Gun Groups and the Governance of Small Arms," in D. D. Avant, M. Finnemore, and S. K. Sell (eds), *Who Governs the Globe?*, 183–201. Cambridge: Cambridge University Press.

Bolton, J. 2005. *Letter to UN Member States Conveying U.S. Amendments to the Draft Outcome Document Being Prepared for the High Level Event on Responsibility to Protect*, 30 Aug. Available at: <http://www.responsibilitytoprotect.org> (accessed June 2013).

Bowden, B. 2004. "In the Name of Progress and Peace: The "Standard of Civilization" and the Universalizing Project," *Alternatives: Global, Local, Political*, 29(1): 43–68.

Brauer, J. 1999. "An Economic Perspective on Mercenaries, Military Companies and the Privatization of Force," *Cambridge Review of International Affairs*, 13: 130–45.

Brauman, R. 2006. *Dangerous Liaisons Bearing Witness and Political Propaganda: Biafra and Cambodia—the Founding Myths of Medecins Sans Frontiers*. Paris: MSF.

Brookings-Bern Project on Internal Displacement and Republic of Uganda. 2006. *Workshop on the Implementation of Uganda's National Policy for Internally Displaced Persons, Kampala, Uganda, 3-4 July 2006*. Washington, DC: Brookings Institution.

Broome, A., and Seabrooke, L. 2011. "Seeing like an International Organisation," *New Political Economy*, 17(1): 1–16.

Brown, M. 2006. "The Failing Humanitarian Response in Northern Uganda," *Humanitarian Exchange*, 36(2). <http://www.odihpn.org/humanitarian-exchange-magazine/issue-36/the-failing-humanitarian-response-in-northern-uganda>

Brunmee, J., and Toope, S. 2010a. *Legitimacy and Legality in International Law*. Cambridge: Cambridge University Press.

Brunnee, J., and Toope, S. 2010b. "The Responsibility to Protect and the Use of Force: Building Legality?" *Global Responsibility to Protect*, 2: 191–212.

Buckingham, C. E. 1964. *For Humanity's Sake: The Story of the Early Development of the League of Red Cross Societies*. Washington, DC: Public Affairs Press.

Busby, J. W. 2007. "Bono Made Jesse Helms Cry: Jubilee 2000, Debt Relief, and Moral Action in International Politics," *International Studies Quarterly*, 51: 247–75.

Busby, J. W. 2010. *Moral Movements and Foreign Policy*. Cambridge: Cambridge University Press.

Calland, R., and Neuman, L. 2007. "Making the Law Work: The Challenges of Implementation," in A. Florini (ed.), *The Right to Know: Transparency for an Open World*. 179–213. New York: Columbia University Press.

Cammaert, P. 2008. "A Peacekeeping Commander's Perspective," *RUSI Journal*, 153(3): 68–71.

CARE International. 2007. "CARE International: Strategic Plan 2007–2012." Geneva: CARE International, http://www.care-international.org/index2.php?option=com_content&do_pdf=1&id=51 accessed Feb. 2012.

CARE International. 2010. *Aid Reform: Addressing Conflict and Situations of Fragility*. Geneva: CARE International.

CARE—World Food Program. 2000. *Household Livelihood and Security Assessment in the Wanni District*. Colombo: CARE-WFP.

Carpenter, R. C. 2010. "Governing the Global Agenda: 'Gatekeepers' and 'Issue Adoption' in Transnational Advocacy Networks," in D. D. Avant, M. Finnemore, and S. K. Sell (eds) *Who Governs the Globe?*, 202–37. Cambridge: Cambridge University Press.

Carr, S. 2009. "From Theory to Practice: National and Regional Application of the Guiding Principles." *International Journal of Refugee Law*, 21(1): 34–47.

Caverzasio, G., ed. 2001. *Strengthening Protection in War: A Search for Professional Standards. Summary of Discussions among Human Rights and Humanitarian Organizations*. Workshops at the ICRC, 1996–2000. Geneva: ICRC.

Centre for Policy Alternatives (CPA). 2003. *Humanitarian Concerns on the Road to Peace Workshop Report*. Colombo: Centre for Policy Alternatives (CPA).

Centre on Housing Rights and Evictions. <www.cohre.org> (accessed Aug. 2013).

Center for Policy Research (CPA). 2007. *Policy Brief on Humanitarian Issues.* Colombo: CPA.

Center for Policy Research (CPA). 2009. *A Profile of Human Rights and Humanitarian Issues in the Vanni and Vavuniya.* Colombo: CPA.

Centre for the Study of Forced Migration. 2003. *The Impact of the Presence of Refugees in Northwest Tanzania.* Dar es Salaam: University of Dar es Salaam.

Cesner, R. E., and Brant, J. W. 1977. "Law of the Mercenary: An International Dilemma," *Capital University Law Review*, 6: 339–70.

Chandler, D. 2001. "The Road to Military Humanitarianism: How the Human Rights NGOs Shaped a New Humanitarian Agenda," *Human Rights Quarterly*, 23(3): 678–700.

Chayes, A., and Chayes, A. H. 1993. "On Compliance," *International Organization*, 47(2): 175–205.

Checkel, J. 1997. "International Norms and Domestic Politics: Bridging the Rationalist—Constructivist Divide," *European Journal of International Relations*, 3: 473–95.

Checkel, J. T. 1999. "Norms, Institutions, and National Identity in Contemporary Europe," *International Studies Quarterly*, 43(1): 83–114.

Checkel, J. 2005. "International Institutions and Socialization in Europe," *International Organization*, 59(4): 801–26.

Chimni, B. S. 1993 "The Meaning of Words and the Role of UNHCR in Voluntary Repatriation," *International Journal of Refugee Law*, 5(3): 442–60.

Chin, G., and Thakur, R. 2010. "Will China Change the Rules of Global Order?" *Washington Quarterly*, 33(4) (Oct.): 119–38.

Chinkin, C. 1989. "The Challenge of Soft Law: Development and Change in International Law," *International and Comparative Law Quarterly*, 38: 850–66.

Ciarolo, G. 1922a. "Scheme for an international organization to assist in the Relief of Peoples Overcome by Disaster," *League of Nations—Official Journal*, Nov., Geneva.

Ciarolo, G. 1922b. "Proposal by the President of the Italian Red Cross Society," *League of Nations—Official Journal*, July, Geneva.

Ciarolo, G. 1924. "Letter from Senator Ciarolo to the Secretary-General, submitted to the Council on August 30, 1924," *League of Nations—Official Journal*, Geneva.

CICC (Coalition for the International Criminal Court). 2006. *The International Criminal Court Monitor*, 2. New York: CICC.

CICC. 2011. *Proposal for 2012–2014 (Draft)*. New York: CICC.

Cilliers, J. 2001. "Still…France versus the Rest in Africa?," *African Security Review*, 10(3): 123–6.

Clapham, C. 1996. *Africa and the International System: The Politics of State Survival.* Cambridge: Cambridge University Press.

Clapham, C. 1999. "African Security Systems: Privatization and the Scope for Mercenary Activity," in G. Mills and J. Stremlau (eds), *The Privatization of Security in Africa*, 23–46. Johannesburg: South African Institute of International Affairs.

Clark, A.-M. 2001. *Diplomacy of Conscience: Amnesty International and Changing Human Rights Norms.* Princeton: Princeton University Press.

Clouzot, E. 1924. "Letter of September 1923 and Resume of Replies to the Appeal Addressed to the Learned Societies," *League of Nations—Official Journal*, Geneva.

Cohen, R. 2007. *Northern Uganda: National and International Responsibility.* Washington, DC: Brookings Institution.

Cohen, R., and Deng, F. M. 1998. *Masses in Fight: The Global Crisis of Internal Displacement.* Washington, DC: Brookings Institution.

Collin, M., Zubairi, A., Nielson, D., and Barder, O. 2009. *Costs and Benefits of Aid Transparency.* Wells, UK: AidInfo. Available at <http://www.aidinfo.org/files/aidinfo-Costs-and-Benefits-October-2009.pdf>

Collinson, S., Elhawary, S., and Muggabe, R. 2010. *States of Fragility: Stabilization and its Implications for Humanitarian Action.* London: Humanitarian Policy Group.

Commission of the European Communities. 2009. *Report on the Findings of the Investigation with Respect to the Effective Implementation of Certain Human Rights Conventions in Sri Lanka.* Brussels: Commission of the European Communities.

Commission on Human Rights, Sub-Commission on the Promotion and Protection of Human Rights. 2002. *The Return of Refugees' or Displaced Persons' Property.* Working Paper Submitted by Mr Paulo Sérgio Pinheiro Pursuant to Sub-Commission Decision 2001/122*.

Commission on Human Rights, Sub-Commission on the Promotion and Protection of Human Rights. 2003. *Housing and Property Restitution in the Context of the Return of Refugees and Internally Displaced Persons: Preliminary Report of the Special Rapporteur, Paulo Sérgio Pinheiro,* submitted in accordance with Sub-Commission Resolution 2002/7*. Geneva: United Nations.

Consortium of Humanitarian Agencies (CHA). 2003. *Practitioners Kit for Return, Resettlement, Rehabilitation, and Development.* Colombo: CHA.

Consortium of Refugees and Migrants in South Africa (CoRMSA). 2008. *Protecting Refugees, Asylum Seekers and Migrants in South Africa,* 18 June. Johannesburg: CoRMSA.

Cooley, A., and Ron, J. 2002. "The NGO Scramble: Organizational Insecurity and the Political Economy of Transnational Action," *International Security,* 27(1): 5–39.

Cornish, S. 2008. "No Room for Humanitarianism in 3D Policies: Have Forcible Humanitarian Interventions and Integrated Approaches Lost their Way?" *Journal of Military and Strategic Studies,* 10(1): 1–48.

Cortell, A. P., and Davis, J. W. J. 2000. "Understanding the Domestic Impact of International Norms: A Research Agenda," *International Studies Review,* 2(1): 65–87.

Cortell, A. P., and Davis, J. W. J. 2005. "When Norms Clash: International Norms, Domestic Practices, and Japan's Internalisation of the GATT/WTO," *Review of International Studies,* 31(1): 3–25.

Crawford, N. C. 2002. *Argument and Change in World Politics: Ethics, Decolonization, and Humanitarian Intervention.* Cambridge: Cambridge University Press.

Crisp, J. 2000. *Africa's Refugees: Patterns, Problems and Policy Challenges.* New Issues in Refugee Research, 28. Geneva: UNHCR.

Crisp, J., and Dessalegne, D. 2002. *Refugee Protection and Migration Management: The Challenge for UNHCR.* New Issues in Refugee Research, 64. Geneva: UNHCR.

Crisp, J., and Kiragu, E. 2010. *Refugee Protection and International Migration: A Review of UNHCR's Role in Malawi, Mozambique and South Africa.* Geneva: UNHCR Policy Development and Evaluation Service (PDES).

Crush, J., and Tevera, D. S. 2010. *Zimbabwe's Exodus: Crisis, Migration, Survival.* Cape Town: Southern African Migration Project; Ottawa: International Development Research Centre.

Cumming, G. 2011. "Burying the Hatchet? Britain and France in the Democratic Republic of Congo," *Journal of Modern African Studies*, 49: 547–73.

Cutler, A. 2009. "Acts of God? Review of Geology and Religion: A History of Harmony and Hostility," *Nature Geoscience*, 2: 535.

Daley, P. 1991. "Gender, Displacement and Social Reproduction: Settling Burundi Refugees in Western Tanzania," *Journal of Refugee Studies*, 4(3): 248–66.

Davies, J. E. 2011. "From Ideology to Pragmatism: China's Position on Humanitarian Intervention in the Post-Cold War Era," *Vanderbilt Journal of Transnational Law*, 44(2): 217–83.

Deacon, J. B. 1918. *Disasters and the American Red Cross in Disaster Relief.* New York: Russell Sage Foundation.

De Chaine, Robert. 2002. "Humanitarian Space and the Social Imagery: Medecins Sans Frontiers/Doctors without Borders and the Rhetoric of International Community," *Journal of Communication Enquiry*, 26(4): 354–69.

Deere, C. 2009. *The Implementation Game: The TRIPS Agreement and the Global Politics of Intellectual Property Reform in Developing Countries.* Oxford: Oxford University Press.

Deitelhoff, N. 2009. "The Discursive Process of Legalization: Charting Islands of Persuasion in the ICC Case," *International Organization*, 63: 33–65.

Demusz, K. 2000. *Listening to the Displaced: Action Research in the Conflict Zones of Sri Lanka.* Oxford: Oxfam.

Deng, F. M. 1993. *Protecting the Dispossessed.* Washington, DC: Brookings Institution.

De Vattel, E., and Chitty, J. 1849. *The law of nations: or, Principles of the law of nature, applied to the conduct and affairs of nations and sovereigns.* Philadelphia: T. & J. W. Johnson.

Diebert, R. J. 1997. *Parchment, Printing and Hypermedia: Communication in World Order Transformation.* New York: Columbia University Press.

Diehl, P. F., Ku, C., and Zamora, D. 2003. "The Dynamics of International Law: The Interaction of Normative and Operating Systems," *International Organization*, 57: 43–75.

Dolan, C. 2011. *Social Torture: The Case of Northern Uganda, 1986–2006.* Oxford: Berghahn Books.

Dolan, C., and Hovil, L. 2006. *Humanitarian Protection in Uganda: A Trojan Horse?* London, Overseas Development Institute: Humanitarian Policy Group.

Donini, A., ed. 2012. *Golden Fleece: Manipulation and Independence in Humanitarian Action.* Sterling, VA: Kumarian Press

Dorney, S. 1998. *The Sandline Affair: Politics and Mercenaries in the Bougainville Crisis.* Sydney: ABC Books.

D'Orsi, C. 2006. *La Definition de 'refugie' dans les legislations africaines: Une analyse comparative critique.* New Issues in Refugee Research. Geneva: UNHCR.

Doss, A. 2010. "MONUC and Civilian Protection in the Democratic Republic of Congo," in *The UN Security Council and the Responsibility to Protect: Policy, Process, and Practice.* 98–102. New York: International Peace Institute.

Duffield, M. 1994. "Complex Emergencies and the Crisis of Developmentalism," *IDS Bulletin*, 25(4): 37–45.

Duffield, M. 2007. *Development, Security and Unending War.* Cambridge: Polity Press.

Dunigan, M. 2011. *Victory for Hire*. Stanford, CA: Stanford University Press.

Durieux, J., and McAdam, J. 2006. "Non-Refoulement through Time: The Case for a Derogation Clause to the Refugee Convention in Mass Influx Emergencies," *International Journal of Refugee Law*, 16(1): 4–24.

Eade, D., and Williams, S. 1995. *The Oxfam Handbook of Development and Relief*. Oxford: Oxfam.

Easterly, W., and Williamson, C. 2011. "Rhetoric versus Reality: The Best and Worst of Aid Agency Practices," *World Development*, 39(11): 1930–49.

Elhawary, S. 2011. *The Failure of Humanitarianism in Sri Lanka*. London: Overseas Development Institute.

Erskine, T. 2003. "Making Sense of 'Responsibility' in International Relations: Key Questions and Concepts," In T. Erskine (ed.), *Can Institutions Have Responsibilities?* Houndsmill: Palgrave Macmillan.

Evans, G. 2003. "The Responsibility to Protect: When is it Right to Fight?" *Progressive Politics*, 3(31): 68–72.

Evans, G. 2008a. "Facing up to our Responsibilities," *Guardian*, 12 May.

Evans, G. 2008b. "The Responsibility to Protect: An Idea Whose Time has Come...and Gone?" *International Relations*, 22: 283–98.

Evans, G. 2008c. *The Responsibility to Protect: Ending Mass Atrocity Crimes Once and for All*. Washington, DC: Brookings Institution.

Evans, G. 2011. *The RtoP Balance Sheet After Libya*. Available at: <http://www.globalr2p. org/publications/205> (accessed June 2013).

Evans, G., and Steinberg, D. 2007. *China and Darfur: Signs of Transition*. London: Guardian Unlimited and International Crisis Group.

FAO, NRC, OCHA, UN-HABITAT, and UNHCR. 2007. *Handbook on Housing and Property Restitution for Refugees and Displaced Persons: Implementing the "Pinheiro Principles."* Available from <http://www.ohchr.org/Documents/ Publications/pin-heiro_principles.pdf>

Fehl, C. 2004. "Explaining the International Criminal Court: A 'Practice Test' for Rationalist and Constructivist Approaches," *European Journal of International Relations*, 10(3): 357–94.

Ferguson, J. 1990. *The Anti-Politics Machine: "Development," Depoliticization, and Bureaucratic Power in Lesotho*. Cambridge: Cambridge University Press.

Ferris, E. 2011. *The Politics of Protection: The Limits of Humanitarian Action*. Washington, DC: Brookings Institute Press.

Ferris, E., Mooney, E., and Stark, C. 2011. *From Responsibility to Response: Assessing National Approaches to Internal Displacement*. Washington, DC: Brookings Institution—LSE Project on Internal Displacement.

Fidler, D. P. 2005. "Disaster Relief and Governance After the Indian Ocean Tsunami: What Role for International Law," *Melbourne Journal of International Law*, 6: 458.

Finnemore, M. 2000. "Are Legal Norms Distinctive?" *New York University Journal of International Law and Policy*, 32: 699.

Finnemore, M. 2004. *The Purpose of Intervention: Changing Beliefs about the Use of Force*. Ithaca, NY: Cornell University Press.

Finnemore, M., and Sikkink, K. 1998. "International Norm Dynamics and Political Change," *International Organization*, 52(4): 887–917.

Fischer, H. 2003. "International Disaster Law Treaties: Trends Patterns and Lacunae," in Victoria Bannon (ed.), *International Disaster Response Laws, Principles and Practice. Reflections, Prospects and Challenges,* 25. Geneva: International Federation of Red Cross and Red Crescent Societies.

Fisher, D. 2007. *Law and Legal Issues in International Disaster Response: A Desk Study.* Geneva: IFRC.

Fitzpatrick, J. 2000. "Temporary Protection of Refugees: Elements of a Formalized Regime," *American Journal of International Law,* 94(2): 279–306.

Flanigan, S. Teresa. 2008. "Non-Profit Service Provision by Insurgent Organizations: The Cases of Hizbullah and the Tamil Tigers," *Studies in Conflict and Terrorism* 31(6): 499–519.

Florini, A. 1996. "The Evolution of International Norms," *International Studies Quarterly,* 40(3): 363–89.

Focarelli, C. 2008. "The Responsibility to Protect Doctrine and Humanitarian Intervention: Too Many Ambiguities for a Working Doctrine," *Journal of Conflict and Security Law,* 13(2): 191–213.

Fomerand, J., and Dijkzeul, D. 2007. "Coordinating Economic and Social Affairs," in T. Weiss and S. Daws (eds), *The Oxford Handbook of the United Nations,* 561–81. Oxford: Oxford University Press.

Foot, R. 2011. "The Responsibility to Protect and its Evolution: Beijing's Influence on Norm Creation in Humanitarian Areas," *St Anthony's International Review,* 6(2): 47–66.

Foot, R., and A. Walter. 2011. *China, the United States, and Global Order.* Cambridge: Cambridge University Press.

Forsythe, D. P. 2005. *The Humanitarians: The International Committee of the Red Cross.* Cambridge: Cambridge University Press.

Foster, H. D. 1980. *Disaster Planning: The Preservation of Life and Property with 48 Figures.* New York: Springer-Verlag.

Foster, M. 2009. *International Refugee Law and Socio-Economic Rights: Refuge from Deprivation.* Cambridge Studies in International and Comparative Law. Cambridge and New York: Cambridge University Press.

Fox, J. 2007. "The Uncertain Relationship between Transparency and Accountability," *Development in Practice,* 17(4): 663–71.

Francis, D. J. 1999. "Mercenary Intervention in Sierra Leone: Providing National Security or International Exploitation?" *Third World Quarterly,* 20: 319–38.

Franck, T. M. 1990. *The Power of Legitimacy among Nations.* New York: Oxford University Press.

Frost, M. 1996. *Ethics in International Relations: A Constitutive Theory.* New York: Cambridge University Press.

Gaer, F. D. 2003. "Implementing International Human Rights Norms: UN Human Rights Treaty Bodies and NGOs," *Journal of Human Rights,* 2(3): 339–57.

Gegout, C. 2009. "The West, Realism and Intervention in the Democratic Republic of Congo (1996–2006)," *International Peacekeeping,* 16(2): 231–44.

General Framework Agreement for Peace in Bosnia and Herzegovina. 1995.

George, A. L., and Bennett, A. 2005. *Case Studies and Theory Development in the Social Sciences.* Cambridge, MA: MIT Press.

George, Hannah. 2012. "Raising the Bar on Transparency, Accountability and Openness." Blog entry on World Bank's "Inside the Web", 16 Feb. Available <http://blogs.worldbank.org/insidetheweb/raising-the-bar-on-transparency-acco untability-and-openness>.

Ghosh, A., and Kharas, H. 2011. "The Money Trail: Ranking Donor Transparency in Foreign Aid," *World Development*, 39(11): 1918–29.

Gibney, M. J., and Hansen, R. 2003. *Asylum Policy in the West: Past Trends, Future Possibilities.* Wider Discussion Paper, WDP 2003/68. Helsinki: United Nations University.

Gilbo, F. 1981. *The American Red Cross.* New York: Harper & Row.

Gill, B., and Huang, Chin-hao. 2009. "China's Expanding Presence in UN Peacekeeping Operations and Implications for the United States," in R. Kamphausen, D. Lai, and A. Scobell (eds), *Beyond the Strait: PLA Missions Other than Taiwan.* Carlisle: Strategic Studies Institute of the US Army War College (SSI), 99–125.

Glanville, L. 2010. "The Antecedents of 'Sovereignty as Responsibility,'" *European Journal of International Relations,* 17: 233–55.

Glasius, M. 2006. *The International Criminal Court: A Global Civil Society Achievement.* New York: Routledge.

Glasius, M. 2008. "Global Justice Meets Local Civil Society: The International Criminal Court's Investigation in the Central African Republic," *Alternatives,* 33(4): 413–33.

Glasius, M. 2009. "We Ourselves, we are Part of the Functioning': The ICC, Victims, and Civil Society in the Central African Republic," *African Affairs,* 108(430): 49–67.

Global Center for the Responsibility to Protect. 2009. *Open Letter to the Security Council on the Situation in Sri Lanka.* New York: Global Center for the Responsibility to Protect. Available at: <http://www.globalr2p.org/publications> (accessed June 2013).

Global Centre for the Responsibility to Protect (GCR2P). 2009. "Implementing the Responsibility to Protect." GCR2P, 19 Aug. <http://www.globalr2p.org/publications/42>.

Global Centre for the Responsibility to Protect (GCR2P). 2012a. "UN General Assembly Informal Interactive Dialogue on the Responsibility to Protect: Timely and Decisive Action, 2012," Global Centre for the Responsibility to Protect, 5 Sept. Available at: < http://www.globalr2p.org/resources/278> (accessed June 2013).

Global Centre for the Responsibility to Protect. 2012b. *"Early Warning, Assessment, and the Responsibility to Protect": Informal Interactive Dialogue of the General Assembly Held on 9 August 2010,* Global Centre for the Responsibility to Protect. Available at: <http://www.globalr2p.org/publications/37> (accessed June 2013).

Global Centre for the Responsibility to Protect and Stanley Foundation. 2012. *PreparatoryWorkshop for the Second Meeting of the R2P Focal Points Network.* New York: Global Center for the Responsibility to Protect and Stanley Foundation, 12 Mar. Available at: <http://www.stanleyfoundation.org/resources> (accessed June 2013).

Global Transparency Initiative. 2009. *Model World Bank Policy on Disclosure of Information.* GTI, May 2009.

Goertz, G. 2003. *International Norms and Decisionmaking: A Punctuated Equilibrium Model.* Lanham, MD: Rowman & Littlefield.

Goldstein, J., Kahler, M., Keohane, R. O., and Slaughter, A.-M. 2000. "Introduction: Legalization and World Politics," *International Organization*, 54: 385–99.

Gong, G. W. 1984. *The Standard of "Civilization" in International Society*. Oxford: Clarendon Press.

Goodhand, J. 2001. *Aid, Conflict and Peacebuilding in Sri Lanka*. London: Centre for Defence Studies, Kings College.

Goodhand, J. 2006. *Aiding Peace: The Role of NGOs in Armed Conflict*. Warwick: Practical Action Publishing.

Goodhand, J. 2010. "Stabilizing a Victor's Peace? Humanitarian Action and Reconstruction in Eastern Sri Lanka," *Disasters*, 34(3): 342–67.

Goodhand, J., and Klem, B. 2005. *Aid, Conflict and Peacebuilding in Sri Lanka, 2000-2005*. Colombo: Asia Foundation.

Goodhand, J., and Lewer, B. 1999. "Sri Lanka: NGOs and Peacebuilding in Complex Political Emergencies," *Third World Quarterly*, 20(1): 69–87.

Goodhand, J., Hulme, D., and Lewer, N. 1999. *NGOs and Peacebuilding: Sri Lanka Study*. Bradford and Manchester: Institute for Development Policy and Management, University of Bradford and University of Manchester.

Goodwin-Gill, G. 1995. "Asylum: The Law of Politics and Change," *International Journal of Refugee Law*, 7(1): 6–7.

Goodwin-Gill, G. 1996. *The Refugee in International Law*. Oxford: Clarendon Press.

Goodwin-Gill, G., and McAdam, J. 2007. *The Refugee in International Law*. Oxford: Oxford University Press.

Gordenker, L., and Weiss, T. G. 1996. "Pluralising Global Governance: Analytical Approaches and Dimensions," in T. G. Weiss and L. Gordenker (eds), *NGOs, the UN, and Global Governance*. 17–50. Boulder, CO: Lynne Rienner Publishers.

Gorlick, B. 2005. *Improving Decision-Making in Asylum Determination*. New Issues in Refugee Research, 119. Geneva: UNHCR.

Gourevitch, P. 1978. "The Second Image Reversed: The International Sources of Domestic Politics." *International Organization*, 32: 881–912.

Government of Sri Lanka. 2000. *The Framework for Relief, Rehabilitation, and Reconciliation: A Progress Report*. Colombo: Government of Sri Lanka.

Gow, J. 1997. *Triumph of Lack of Will: International Diplomacy and the Yugoslav War*. London: Hurst & Co.

Green, S., and Council on Foreign Relations. 1977. *International Disaster Relief: Toward a Responsive System*. New York: McGraw-Hill.

Grono, N. 2006. "Briefing—Darfur: The International Community's Failure to Protect," *African Affairs*, 105(421): 621–31.

Guéhenno, J. M. 2002. "On the Challenges and Achievements of Reforming UN Peace Operations," *International Peacekeeping*, 9(2): 69–80.

Haas, P. M. 1992. "Introduction: Epistemic Communities and International Policy Coordination," *International Organization*, 46: 1–35.

Haddad, E. 2008. *The Refugee in International Society: Between Sovereigns*. Cambridge: Cambridge University Press.

Hafner-Burton, E. M., and Montgomery, A. H. 2009. "Globalization and the Social Power Politics of International Economic Networks," in M. Kahler (ed.), *Networked Politics: Agency, Power, and Governance*, 23–42. Ithaca, NY: Cornell University Press.

Hall, P., and Thelen, K. 2009. "Institutional Change in Varieties of Capitalism," *Socio-Economic Review Special Issue: Changing Institutions in Developed Democracies: Economics, Politics and Welfare*, 7(1): 7–34.

Halliday, T. C. 2009. "Recursivity of Global Normmaking: A Sociolegal Agenda," *Annual Review of Law and Social Science*, 5: 263–89.

Hameiri, S., and Kühn, F. P. 2011. "Special Issue: Risk, Risk Management and International Relations," *International Relations*, 25(3): 275–9.

Hammar, A., McGregor, J., and Landau, L. B. 2010. "Introduction. Displacing Zimbabwe: Crisis and Construction in Southern Africa," *Journal of Southern African Studies*, 36(2): 263–83.

Hardcastle, R., and Chua, A. 1997. "Victims of Natural Disasters: The Right to Receive Humanitarian Assistance," *International Journal of Human Rights*, 1(4): 35–49.

Hardcastle, R. J., and Chua, A. T. L. 1998. "Humanitarian Assistance: Towards a Right of Access to Victims of Natural Disasters," *International Review of the Red Cross*, 38: 589–610.

Harff, B. 2003. "No Lessons Learned from the Holocaust? Assessing Risks of Genocide and Political Mass Murder since 1955," *American Political Science Review*, 97: 57–73.

Harrell-Bond, B. E. 1989. "Repatriation: Under What Conditions is it the Most Desirable Solution for Refugees? An Agenda for Research," *African Studies Review*, 32(1): 41–69.

Harris, R. 2011. "Knowledge is Power: Transparency and Participation will Be the Drivers of Effective Development." *Huffington Post*, 19 Apr. <http://www.huffingtonpost.com/rebecca-harris/knowledge-is-power-transp_b_851020.html>.

Harris, S. 2000. "Listening to the Displaced: Analysis, Accountability and advocacy in action," *Forced Migration Review*, 8: 20–1.

Harris, S., and Lewer, N. 2002. *Operationalizing Peacebuilding and Conflict Reduction: Case Study. Oxfam in Sri Lanka*. Bradford: University of Bradford.

Harris, S. 2010. *Humanitarianism in Sri Lanka: Lessons Learned?* Boston: Feinstein International Centre, Tufts University.

Hasenclever, A., Mayer, P., and Rittberger, V. 1997. *Theories of International Regimes*. Cambridge: Cambridge University Press.

Haufler, V. 2010. "Disclosure as Governance: The Extractive Industries Transparency Initiative and Resource Management in the Developing World," *Global Environmental Politics*, 10(3): 53–73.

Hawkins, V. 2003. "History Repeating Itself: The DRC and the Security Council," *African Security Review*, 12(4): 47–55.

Hayden, R. M. 1996. "Schindler's Fate: Genocide, Ethnic Cleansing, and Population Transfers," *Slavic Review*, 55(4): 727–48.

Heertens, L. 2009. "The Biafran War in Britain: An Odd Alliance of Late 1960s Humanitarian Activists," *Journal of the Oxford University History Society*, 7: 1–18.

Hehir, A. 2012. *The Responsibility to Protect: Rhetoric, Reality and the Future of Humanitarian Intervention*. Houndmills: Palgrave.

Henry, K. 1999. "CARE International: Evolving to Meet the Challenges of the 21st Century," *Nonprofit and Voluntary Sector Quarterly*, 28(1): 109–20.

Hewitt, K. 1983. *Interpretation of Calamities: From the Viewpoint of Human Ecology*. Boston: Allen & Unwin.

Hill, M. 1978. *The United Nations System: Coordinating its Economic and Social Work.* Cambridge: Cambridge University Press.

Hoffman, P., and Weiss, T. 2006. *Sword and Salve: Confronting New Wars and Humanitarian Crises.* Lanham, MD: Rowman & Littlefield.

Holmes, J. 2007. "Humanitarian Action: A Western-Dominated Enterprise in Need of Change," *Forced Migration Review,* 29 (Dec.): 4–5.

Holt, V., and Taylor, G. 2009. *Protecting Civilians in the Context of UN Peacekeeping Operations: Successes, Setbacks and Remaining Challenges.* New York: UN OCHA and DPKO.

Hovil, L., and Okello, M. C. 2006. *Only Peace Can Restore the Confidence of the Displaced.* 2nd edn, Geneva: Internal Displacement Monitoring Centre.

Hultman, L. 2013. "UN Peace Operations and Protection of Civilians: Cheap Talk or Norm Implementation?," *Journal of Peace Research,* 50(1): 59–73.

Human Rights Watch. 2002a. "Congo: Kisangani Residents Again Under Fire," press release, New York.

Human Rights Watch. 2002b. *War Crimes in Kisangani: The Response of Rwandan-Backed Rebels to the May 2002 Mutiny.* New York: HRW.

Human Rights Watch. 2004a. *The International Criminal Court: How Non-Governmental Organizations Can Contribute to the Prosecution of War Criminals.* New York: HRW.

Human Rights Watch. 2004b. *War Crimes in Bukavu..* Human Rights Watch Briefing Paper. New York: HRW.

Human Rights Watch. 2005. *Uprooted and Forgotten: Impunity and Human Rights Abuses in Northern Uganda.* New York: Human Rights Watch.

Human Rights Watch. 2008. *Neighbors in Need: Zimbabweans Seeking Refuge in South Africa.* Washington, DC: HRW.

Human Rights Watch. 2009a. *You will be Punished: Attacks on Civilians in Eastern Congo.* New York: HRW.

Human Rights Watch. 2009b. "UN Human Rights Council Victims," <http://www.hrw.org/en/news/ 2009/05/27/sri-lanka-un-rights-council-fails-victims> (accessed Jan. 2012).

Human Rights Without Frontiers International. 2005. *Internally Displaced Persons in Nepal: The Forgotten Victims of the Conflict.* Brussels: Human Rights Without Frontiers International.

Hurd, I. 1999. "Legitimacy and Authority in International Politics," *International Organization,* 53: 379–408.

Hutchinson, J. F. 1996, *Champions of Charity: War and the Rise of the Red Cross.* Boulder, CO: Westview Press.

Hutchinson, J. F. 2000. "Disasters and the International Order: Earthquakes, Humanitarians, and the Ciraolo Project," *International History Review,* 22(1): 1–36.

Hutchinson, J. F. 2001. "Disasters and the International Order-II: The International Relief Union," *International History Review,* 23(2): 253–98.

Hyde, S. D. 2011. "Catch us if you Can: Election Monitoring and International Norm Diffusion." *American Journal of Political Science,* 55: 356–69.

IFRC. 2009. *Ninety Years of Improving the Lives of the Most Vulnerable.* Geneva: International Federation of Red Cross and Red Crescent Societies.

Independent International Comission on Kosovo. 2000. *The Kosovo Report: Conflict, International Response, Lessons Learned.* Oxford: Oxford University Press.

Informal Sector Service Center. 2011. *Trend Analysis: July–September 2011.* Kathmandu: Informal Sector Service Center.

Informal Sector Service Center. 2012. *Nepal Human Rights Yearbook 2011.* Kathmandu: Informal Sector Service Center.

Interaction. 2007. *Interaction Member Activity Report: A Guide to Humanitarian and Development Efforts of Interaction Member Agencies in Sri Lanka.* Colombo: Interaction.

Internal Displacement Monitoring Centre. 2006. *Only Peace Can Restore the Confidence of the Displaced.* 2nd edn, Geneva: Refugee Law Project, Norwegian Refugee Council.

Internal Displacement Monitoring Centre. 2010a. *Nepal: Failed Implementation of IDP Policy Leaves Many Unassisted.* Geneva: Norwegian Refugee Council.

Internal Displacement Monitoring Centre. 2010b. *Uganda: Difficulties Continue for Returnees and Remaining IDPs as Development Phase Begins.* Geneva: Internal Displacement Monitoring Centre.

Internal Displacement Monitoring Centre. 2013. *Global Overview 2012: People Internally Displaced by Conflict and Violence.* Geneva: Internal Displacement Monitoring Centre.

International Commission on Intervention and State Sovereignty (ICISS). 2001a. *The Responsibility to Protect: Report of the International Commission on Intervention and State Sovereignty.* Ottawa: International Development Research Centre.

International Commission on Intervention and State Sovereignty (ICISS). 2001b. *The Responsibility to Protect: Research, Bibliography, Background. Supplementary Volume to the Report of the International Commission on Intervention and State Sovereignty.* Ottawa: International Development Research Centre.

International Crisis Group (ICG). 2005. *The Congo's Transition is Failing: Crisis in the Kivus.* Africa Report, 91, Brussels: ICG.

International Crisis Group. 2006. *Sri Lanka: The Failure of the Peace Process.* Colombo/Brussels: ICG.

International Crisis Group. 2009a. *Development Assistance and Conflict in Sri Lanka: Lessons from the Eastern Province.* 2009. Colombo/Brussels: ICG.

International Crisis Group. 2009b. *Sri Lanka: A Bitter Peace.* Colombo/Brussels: ICG.

International Crisis Group. 2010a. *Congo: No Stability in Kivu Despite a Rapprochement with Rwanda.* Africa Report, 165. Brussels: ICG.

International Crisis Group. 2010b. *War Crimes in Sri Lanka.* Asia Report, 91. Brussels: ICG, 17 May.

International Relief Union. 1927. *The Convention and Statute Establishing an International Relief Union.* Geneva: UN Treaty Series, 480.

IOM. 2009. *Towards Tolerance, Law and Dignity: Addressing Violence Against Foreign Nationals in South Africa.* Geneva: IOM.

IRIN. 2010. "NEPAL: Stalled Government Policy Leaves IDPs in Limbo," 4 Mar. <http://www.irinnews.org/Report.aspx?ReportId=88310>.

IRIN. 2011. "South Africa: Deportations of Zimbabwean Migrants Set to Resume," 7 Oct. <www.irinnews.org>.

IRIN News. 2011. "Nepal: Political Impasse Stalls Disaster Preparedness Bill," 25 Feb. <www.irinnews.org/Report/92030/NEPAL-Political-impasse-stalls-disaster-preparedness-bill>.

Jackson, R. 1993. *Quasi-States: Sovereignty, International Relations, and the Third World*, Cambridge: Cambridge University Press.

Jackson-Preece, J. 1998. "Ethnic Cleansing as an Instrument of Nation-State Creation: Changing State Practices and Evolving Legal Norms," *Human Rights Quarterly*, 20(4): 817–42.

Jaeger, G. 2003. "Opening Keynote Address: The Refugee Convention at Fifty," in J. van Selm, K. Kamanga, J. Morrison, A. Nadig, S. Spoljar-Vrzina, and L. van Willigen (eds).,*The Refugee Convention at Fifty: A View from Forced Migration Studies*, 9–22. New York: Lexington Books.

James, I. 1990. *Peacekeeping in International Politics*. London: Macmillan.

Jenkins, B. 2009. *World Bank and IMF Launch Disclosure Reviews*. Bretton Woods Project Update, 65: 12 (23 Apr), <http://old.brettonwoodsproject.org/update/65/bwupdt65.pdf>.

Jepperson, R., Wendt, A., and Katzenstein, P. 1996. "Norms, Identity, and Culture in National Security," in P. Katzenstein (ed.), *Culture of National Security: Norms and Identity in World Politics*, 33–77. New York: Columbia University Press.

Jinks, D. 2003. "The Temporal Scope of Application of International Humanitarian Law in Contemporary Conflicts," at informal high level expert meeting on the reaffirmation and development of international humanitarian law, Cambridge, MA, Harvard Program of Humanitarian Policy and Conflict Research.

Jones, B. 2005. "Implementing 'in Larger Freedom'," in P. Heinbecker and P. Goff (eds), *Irrelevant or Indispensible? The United Nations in the 21st Century*, 33–42. Waterloo: Wilfred Laurier University Press.

Jones, L. 2012. *ASEAN, Sovereignty and Intervention in Southeast Asia*. Basingstoke: Palgrave Macmillan.

Jörgens, H. 2004. "Governance by Diffusion: Implementing Global Norms through Cross-National Imitation and Learning," in W. M. Lafferty (ed.), *Governance for Sustainable Development: The Challenge of Adapting Form to Function*. Northampton, MA: Edward Elgar Publishing.

Joshi, A. 2011. "Review of Impact and Effectiveness of Transparency and Accountability Initiatives: Annex 1 Service Delivery," paper prepared for the Transparency and Accountability Initiative Workshop, Oct. Available at <www.transparency-initiative.org/workstream/impact-learning> (accessed Mar. 2012).

Kagan, M. 2006. "The Beleaguered Gatekeeper: Protection Challenges Posed by UNHCR Refugee Status Determination," *International Journal of Refugee Law*, 18(1): 1–29.

Kaiser, T. 2005. "Participating in Development? Refugee Protection, Politics and Developmental Approaches to Refugee Management in Uganda," *Third World Quarterly*, 26(2): 351–67.

Kaldor, M. 1999. *New and Old Wars: Organized Violence in a Global Era*. Stanford, CA: Stanford University Press.

Kälin, W. 2005. "The Guiding Principles on Internal Displacement as International Minimum Standard and Protection Tool," *Refugee Survey Quarterly*, 24(3): 27–36.

Kälin, W. 2008. *Guiding Principles on Internal Displacement: Annotations*. Washington, DC: American Society of International Law.

Kälin, W. 2010. *Internal Displacement in Peace Processes: Addressing Internal Displacement in Peace Processes and Agreements*. Washington, DC: Brookings.

Katoch, A. 2003, "International Natural Disaster Response and the United Nations," in *International Disaster Response Laws, Principles and Practice*. Geneva: International Federation of the Red Cross and Red Crescent Societies, IFRC.

Katzenstein, P. 1996. *The Culture of National Security: Norms and Identity in World Politics*. New York: Columbia University Press.

Keck, M. E., and Sikkink, K. 1998. *Activists Beyond Borders: Advocacy Networks in International Politics*. Ithaca, NY: Cornell University Press.

Kelley, J. 2008. "Assessing the Complex Evolution of Norms: The Rise of International Election Monitoring," *International Organization*, 62: 221.

Kelly, L., Kilby, P., and Kasynathan, N. 2004. "Impact Measurement for NGOs: Experiences from India and Sri Lanka," *Development in Practice*, 14(5): 696–701.

Kenkel, K. M. 2012. "Brazil and R2P: Does Taking Responsibility Mean Using Force?" *Global Responsibility to Protect*, 4(1): 5–32.

Kent, R. C. 1987. *Anatomy of Disaster Relief: The International Network in Action*. London: Pinter Publishers.

Kent, R. C. 2004. "International Humanitarian Crises: Two Decades Before and Two Decades Beyond," *International Affairs*, 80(5): 851–69.

Keohane, R. O. 1984. *After Hegemony: Cooperation and Discord in the World Political Economy*. Princeton: Princeton University Press.

Khagram, S., Riker, J. V., and Sikkink, K. 2002. *Restructuring World Politics: Transnational Social Movements, Networks, and Norms*. Minneapolis: University of Minnesota Press.

Kikoler, N. 2008. *Responsibility to Protect*. London: Humanitarian Policy Group.

Ki-moon, B. 2009. *Implementing the Responsibility to Protect: Report of the Secretary General*, UN doc. A/63/677 (12 Jan.).

Ki-moon, B. 2010. *Early Warning, Assessment, and the Responsibility to Protect: Report of the Secretary General*, UN doc. A/64/864 (14 July).

Ki-moon, B. 2011a. "Remarks at Breakfast Roundtable with Foreign Ministers on 'The Responsibility To Protect: Responding to Imminent Threats Of Mass Atrocities'", UN News Centre (23 Sept.). Available at: <http://www.un.org//apps/news/infocus/sgspeeches> (accessed June 2013).

Ki-moon, B. 2011b. *The Role of Regional and Sub-Regional Organizations in Implementing the Responsibility to Protect: Report of the Secretary-General*, UN doc. A/65/877-S/2011/393 (27 June).

Ki-moon, B. 2011c. "Human Protection and the 21st Century United Nations," Cyril Foster Lecture, University of Oxford (2 Feb.).

Ki-moon, B. 2011d. "Remarks at General Assembly informal thematic debate on Disaster Risk Reduction" 9 Feb. <http://www.un.org/apps/news/infocus/sgspeeches/statments_full.asp?statID=1068#.Ux77goWuCQs>.

Ki-moon, B. 2012. *Responsibility to Protect: Timely and Decisive Response. Report of the Secretary General.*, UN doc. A/66/874-S/2012/578 (25 July).

Ki-Moon, B. 2013. Responsibility to Protect: State Responsibility and Prevention. Report of the Secretary General., UN doc. A/67/269 (9 July).

Kirsch, P., and Holmes, J. T. 1999. "The Rome Conference on an International Criminal Court: The Negotiating Process," *American Journal of International Law*, 93(2): 2–988.

Kirton, J. J., and Trebilcock, M. J. 2004. *Hard Choices, Soft Law: Voluntary Standards in Global Trade, Environment, and Social Governance*. London: Ashgate.

Kiwanuka, Monica, and Tamlyn Monson. 2009. *Zimbabwean Migration into Southern Africa: New Trends and Responses*. FMSP Research Report, Nov. Johannesburg: Forced Migration Studies Programme, University of the Witwatersrand.

Klein, A. 2012. "Northern Uganda's Displaced People are Left to Fend for Themselves," *Guardian*, 24 Jan.

Knock, T. J. 1992. *To End All Wars: Woodrow Wilson and the Quest for a New World Order*. New York: Oxford University Press.

Koh, H. 1997. "Why do States Obey International Law?" *Yale Law Journal*, 106: 2599–659.

Koser, K. 2007. *Addressing Internal Displacement in Peace Processes, Peace Agreements, and Peace-Building*. Washington, DC: Brookings-Bern Project on Internal Displacement.

Kovach, H., Neligan, C., and Burall, S. 2003. *Global Accountability Report: Power without Accountability?* London: One World Trust.

Krahmann, E. 2013. "The United States, PMSCs and the State Monopoly on Violence: Leading the Way towards Norm Change," *Security Dialogue*, 44: 53–71.

Krain, M. 1997. "State-Sponsored Mass Murder: The Onset and Severity of Genocides and Politicides," *Journal of Conflict Resolution*, 31: 331–60.

Krasner, S. D. 1982. "Structural Causes and Regime Consequences: Regimes as Intervening Variables," *International Organization*, 36: 185–205.

Krasner, S. D. 1999. *Sovereignty: Organized Hypocrisy*. Princeton: Princeton University Press.

Kratochwil, F. V. 2001. "How do Norms Matter?" in M. Byers (ed.), *The Role of Law in International Politics*. Oxford: Oxford University Press.

Krebs, R. R., and Jackson, P. T. 2007. "Twisting Tongues and Twisting Arms: The Power of Political Rhetoric," *European Journal of International Relations*, 13: 31.

Kritsiotis, D. 1998. "Mercenaries and the Privatization of Warfare," *Fletcher Forum of World Affairs*, 22; 1–11.

Krook, M. L., and True, J. 2012. "Rethinking the Life Cycles of International Norms: The United Nations and the Global Promotion of Gender Equality," *European Journal of International Relations*, 18(1): 103–27.

Kshetry, R. 2009. "Displaced Choose Urban Homelessness over Rural Insecurity," Inter Press Service, 9 Apr.

Landau, L. B., and Misago, J. P. 2009. *Towards Tolerance, Law and Dignity: Addressing Violence Against Foreign Nationals in South Africa*, Feb. Johannesburg: IOM Regional Office for South Africa.

Lawyers Committee for Human Rights. 2002. *Refugees, Rebels and the Quest for Justice*. New York: Lawyers Committee for Human Rights.

Leckie, S. 2001. *Returning Home: Housing and Property Restitution for Refugees and Internally Displaced Persons*. International, Regional and National Legal Resources, 7. Amsterdam: Primavera.

Legro, J. W. 1997. "Which Norms Matter? Revisiting the 'Failure' of Internationalism," *International Organization*, 51(1): 31–63.

Loescher, G. 2001. *The UNHCR and World Politics: A Perilous Path*. Oxford: Oxford University Press.

Loescher, G., and Milner, J. 2008. "A Framework for Responding to Protracted Refugee Situations," in G. Loescher, J. Milner, E. Newman, and G. Troeller (eds), *Protracted Refugee Situations: Political, Human Rights and Security Implications,* 353–77. Tokyo: United Nations University Press.

Luck, E. C. 2012. "From Promise to Practice: Implementing the Responsibility to Protect," in J. Genser and I. Cotler (eds), *The Responsibility to Protect: The Promise of Stopping Mass Atrocities in our Time,* 85–108. Oxford: Oxford University Press.

Luopajarvi, K. 2003. "Is there an Obligation on States to Accept International Humanitarian Assistance to Internally Displaced Persons under International Law?" *International Journal of Refugee Law,* 15(4): 678–714.

Lutz, E. L., and Sikkink, K. 2000. "International Human Rights Law and Practice in Latin America," *International Organization,* 54: 633–59.

McAdam, D., McCarthy, J. D., and Zald, M. N. 1996. *Comparative Perspectives on Social Movements: Political Opportunities, Mobilizing Structures, and Cultural Framings.* Cambridge: Cambridge University Press.

Macalister-Smith, P. 1986. "Reflections on the Convention Establishing an International Relief Union of July 12, 1927," *Legal History Review,* 54: 363, 374.

McCrummen, S. 2010. "Abusive Congolese Colonel Got Aid," *Washington Post,* 9 Mar.

McEntire, D. A. 1997. "Reflecting on the Weaknesses of the International Community during the IDNDR: Some Implications for Research and its Application," *Disaster Prevention and Management,* 6(4): 221–33.

McGee, R. 2013. "Aid Transparency and Accountability: 'Build it and They'll Come?'" *Development Policy Review,* 31: s107–s124. doi: 10.1111/dpr.120222.

Macfarlane, N. 1999. "Humanitarian Action and Conflict," *International Journal,* 54(4): 537–61.

McGee, R., and Gaventa, J. 2011. *Shifting Power? Assessing the Impact of Transparency and Accountability Initiatives.* IDS Working Paper, 383. Brighton: IDS. Available at <http://www.ids.ac.uk/files/dmfile/Wp383.pdf>.

McGee, R., and Gaventa, J. 2010. "Review of Impact and Effectiveness of Transparency and Accountability Initiatives," synthesis report prepared for the Transparency and Accountability Initiative Workshop, 14–15 Oct., Institute of Development Studies.

McKeown, R. 2009. "Norm Regress: US Revisionism and the Slow Death of the Torture Norm," *International Relations,* 23: 5–25.

Mackintosh, K. 2000. *The Principles of Humanitarian Action in International Humanitarian Law.* London: Humanitarian Policy Group.

Macrae, J. 1998. "The Death of Humanitarianism: An Anatomy of the Attack," *Refugee Studies Quarterly,* 17(1): 24–32.

Mahoney, J., and Thelen, K. 2010. *Explaining Institutional Change: Ambiguity, Agency and Power.* Cambridge: Cambridge University Press.

Major, M.-F. 1992. "Mercenaries and International Law," *Georgia Journal of International and Comparative Law,* 22: 103–50.

Maliyamkono, T. L. 1995. *The Race for the Presidency: The First Multiparty Democracy in Tanzania.* Dar es Salaam: Tanzania Publishing House.

Mallaby, S. 2012. "The Quiet Revolutionary Who Saved the World Bank." Council on Foreign Relations op-ed. 17 Feb. Available at <http://www.cfr.org/international-finance/quiet-revolutionary-saved-world-bank/p27398> (accessed Oct. 2013).

Malkki, L. K. 1995. *Purity and Exile: Violence, Memory, and National Cosmology among Hutu Refugees in Tanzania.* Chicago: Chicago University Press.

Manning. R. 2010. *AidInfo Evaluation, Final Report,* 14 Sept. <http://www.aidinfo.org/wp-content/uploads/2011/06/Aidinfo-Evaluation_Final-Report.pdf>.

Marino, J. 2008. *Is the PRDP Politics as Usual? Update on the Implementation of Uganda's Peace, Recovery and Development Plan.* Kampala: Beyond Juba Project.

Martens, K. 2005. *NGOs and the United Nations: Institutionalization, Professionalization and Adaptation.* New York: Palgrave Macmillan.

Mawowa, S., and Matongo A. 2010. "Inside Zimbabwe's Roadside Currency Trade: The 'World Bank' of Bulawayo," *Journal of Southern African Studies,* 36(2): 319–37.

Mayer, M., Rajasingharn-Senanayake, D., and Thangarajah, Y. eds. 2003. *Building Local Capacities for Peace: Rethinking Conflict and Development in Sri Lanka.* Delhi: Macmillan India.

Mearsheimer, J. 1993. "The Answer," *New Republic,* 203: 22–7.

Merry, S. 2006. "Anthropology and International Law," *Annual Review of Anthropology,* 35: 99–116.

MSF. 2008. *No Refuge, Access Denied: Medical and Humanitarian Needs of Zimbabweans in South Africa.* Brussels: MSF-Belgium.

Meredith, M. 2002. *Robert Mugabe: Power, Plunder and Tyranny in Zimbabwe.* Johannesburg: Jonathan Ball.

Milner, H. V., and Keohane, R. O. 1996. "Internationalization and Domestic Politics: An Introduction," in H. V. Milner and R. O. Keohane (eds), *Internationalization and Domestic Politics,* 3–24. Cambridge: Cambridge University Press.

Milner, J. 2009. "Refugees and the Regional Dynamics of Peacebuilding," *Refugee Survey Quarterly,* 28(1): 13–30.

Milner, J. 2013. *Two Steps Forward, One Step Back: Understanding the Shifting Politics of Refugee Policy in Tanzania.* New Issues in Refugee Research, Working Paper, 255. Geneva: UNHCR.

Ministry of Foreign Affairs of the People's Republic of China. 2003. "China's Independent Foreign Policy of Peace." Available at: <http://www.fmprc.gov.cn/eng/wjdt/wjzc/t24881.htm> (accessed June 2013).

Ministry of Foreign Affairs of the People's Republic of China. 2004. "Carrying Forward the Five Principles of Peaceful Coexistence in the Promotion of Peace and Development: Speech by Wen Jiabao Premier of the State Council of the People's Republic of China at Rally Commemorating the 50th Anniversary of The Five Principles of Peaceful Coexistence." Available at: <http://www.fmprc.gov.cn/eng/topics/seminaronfiveprinciples/t140777.htm> (accessed June 2013).

Ministry of Foreign Affairs of the People's Republic of China. 2007. "The Chinese Government's Special Representative on the Darfur Issue Holds a Briefing to Chinese and Foreign Journalists." Available at: <http://www.fmprc.gov.cn/eng/wjb/zzjg/xybfs/gjlb/2883/2885/t414377.shtml> (accessed June 2013).

Mitchell, R. B. 2005. "Flexibility, Compliance and Norm Development in the Climate Regime," in O. S. Stokke, J. Hovi, and G. Ulfstein (eds), *Implementing the Climate Regime: International Compliance.* Sterling, VA: Earthscan.

Mooney, E. 2003. "Bringing the End into Sight for Internally Displaced Persons." *Forced Migration Review,* 17: 4–7.

Mooney, E. 2005. "The Concept of Internal Displacement and the Case for Internally Displaced Persons as a Category of Concern," *Refugee Survey Quarterly*, 24(3): 9–26.

Moorehead, C. 1998. *Dunant's Dream: War, Switzerland and the History of the Red Cross*. Cambridge: Cambridge University Press.

Morais, N., and Ahmad, M. M. 2010. "Sustaining Livelihoods in Complex Emergencies: Experiences of Sri Lanka." *Development in Practice* 20(1): 5–17.

Muggah, R. 2008. *Relocation Failures: A Short History of Displacement and Resettlement in Sri Lanka*. London: Zed Books.

Mulley, S. 2010. "Donor Aid: New Frontiers in Transparency and Accountability," Transparency and Accountability Initiative. Available at <http://www.transparency-initiative.org/wp-content/uploads/2011/05/donor_aid_final.pdf>.

Musah, A. F., and Fayemi, J. K., eds. 2000. *Mercenaries: An African Security Dilemma*. London and Sterling, VA: Pluto Press.

Musoni, F. 2010. "Operation Murambatsvina and the Politics of Street Vendors in Zimbabwe," *Journal of Southern African Studies*, 36(2): 301–17.

Nadelmann, E. A. 1990. "Global Prohibition Regimes: The Evolution of Norms in International Society," *International Organization*, 44: 479–525.

Nepal IDP Working Group. 2009. *Distant from Durable Solutions: Conflict Induced Internal Displacement in Nepal*. Kathmandu: Nepal IDP Working Group.

Norris, J., and Malknecht, A. 2013. *Atrocities Prevention Board: Background, Performance, and Options*. Washington D.C.: Center for American Progress, 13 June. Available at <http://www.americanprogress.org> (accessed June 2013).

Norwegian Refugee Council. 2009. "NRC Nepal—Official Closure", Kathmandu: Norwegian Refugee Council. Available at <http://reliefweb.int/node/315025> (accessed Feb. 2012).

Nossal, K. R. 1998. "Roland Goes Corporate: Mercenaries and Transnational Security Corporations in the Post-Cold War Era," *Civil Wars*, 1: 16–35.

Nye, J. S. 2008. *The Powers to Lead*. Oxford: Oxford University Press.

O'Callaghan, S., and Pantuliano, S. 2007. *Protective Action: Incorporating Civilian Protection into Humanitarian Response*. London: Humanitarian Policy Group.

Odinkalu, C. 2003. "Back to the Future: The Imperative of Prioritizing the Protection of Human Rights in Africa," *Journal of African Law*, 47(1): 1–37.

Office for the Coordination of Humanitarian Affairs. 1999. *Guiding Principles on Internal Displacement*. New York: UNOCHA.

Office for the Coordination of Humanitarian Affairs. 2010. *Nepal 2010: Humanitarian Transition Appeal*. New York: UNOCHA.

Office of the Press Secretary. 2011. "Presidential Study Directive on Mass Atrocity Prevention," press release (4 Aug.), Washington, DC.

OHR, UNHCR, and OSCE. 2004. *Statistics: Implementation of the Property Laws in Bosnia and Herzegovina*. Sarajevo: OHR, UNHCR, and OSCE.

OHR, OSCE, UNHCR, and CRPC. 2003. "Implementation of the Property Laws in Bosnia and Herzegovina Reached 90 per cent," 1 Nov.. <http://www.ohr.int/ohr-dept/presso/pressr/default.asp?content_id=31164. (accessed Nov. 2003).

O'Neill, K., Balsiger, J., and VanDeveer, S. 2004. "Actors, Norms, and Impact: Recent International Cooperation Theory and the Influence of the Agent-Structure Debate," *Annual Review of Political Science*, 7: 149–75.

O'Neill, W., Rutinwa B., and Verdirame, G. 2000. "The Great Lakes: A Survey of the Application of the Exclusion Clauses in the Central African Republic, Kenya and Tanzania," *International Journal of Refugee Law*, 12 (suppl. 1): 135–70.

Orchard, P. 2010. "Protection of Internally Displaced Persons: Soft Law as a Norm-Generating Mechanism," *Review of International Studies*, 36(2): 281–303.

Orchard, P. 2014. *A Right to Flee: Refugees, States, and the Construction of International Society*. Cambridge: Cambridge University Press.

OSCE. 2001. *Report of the OSCE Mission to the Republic of Croatia on Croatia's Progress in Meeting International Commitments since 18 April 1996*. Zagreb: Organization for Security and Co-operation in Europe.

OSCE Croatia. 2005. *Status Report No. 17 on Croatia's Progress in Meeting International Commitments since July 2005*. Zagreb: Organization for Security and Co-operation in Europe, Mission to Croatia Headquarters.

Ostrom, E. 1990. *Governing the Commons: The Evolution of Institutions for Collective Action*. Cambridge: Cambridge University Press.

Owen, D. 1995. *Balkan Odyssey*. London: Victor Gollancz.

Oxfam. N.d. "Oxfam International Policy Compendium Note on Humanitarianism." <http://www.oxfam.org/en/policy/humanitarian-policy-notes> (accessed Jan. 2011).

Pace, W. R., and Schense, J. 2004. "International Lawmaking of Historic Proportions: Civil Society and the International Criminal Court," in P. Gready (ed.), *Fighting for Human Rights*, 104–16. New York: Routledge.

Paddon, E., and Lacaille, G. 2011. *Stabilising the Congo*. Refugee Studies Centre Policy Brief, 8. Oxford: University of Oxford.

Paglione, G. 2008. "Individual Property Restitution: from Deng to Pinheiro—and the Challenges Ahead," *International Journal of Refugee Law*, 20(3): 391–412.

Pandit, S. 2008. *National Policy on Internally Displaced Person[s], 2063. Implementation for Rehabilitation, Resettlement and Reintegration [of] Internally Displaced Persons in Nepal: I/NGOs Perspective: Initiation, Present Situation and Way Forward*. Geneva: Norwegian Refugee Council.

Panke, D., and Petersohn, U. 2012. "Why International Norms Disappear Sometimes," *European Journal of International Relations*, 18(4): 719–42.

Park, R. 2011. "The Responsibility to Protect and North Korea," *Harvard International Review*, 7 Dec. Available at: <http://hir.harvard.edu/responsibility-to-protect-in-north-korea> (accessed June 2013).

Park, S., and Vetterlein, A. 2010. "Owning Development: Creating Policy Norms in the IMF and the World Bank," in S. Park and A. Vetterlein (eds), *Owning Development: Creating Policy Norms in the IMF and the World Bank*, 3–26. Cambridge: Cambridge University Press.

Patrick, S., and Brown, K. 2007. *Greater than the Sum of its Parts? Assessing "Whole of Government" Approaches to Fragile States*. New York: International Peace Academy.

Pattison, J. 2010. *Humanitarian Intervention and the Responsibility to Protect: Who should Intervene?* Oxford: Oxford University Press.

Percy, S. 2007a. *Mercenaries: The History of a Norm in International Relations*. Oxford: Oxford University Press.

Percy, S. V. 2007b. "Mercenaries: Strong Norm, Weak Law," *International Organization*, 61: 367–97.

Permanent Mission of the People's Republic of China to the UN. 2000a. Letter dated 4 Aug. 2000 from Mr Wang Yingfan to the Secretary-General of the United Nations on the Question of Taiwan.

Permanent Mission of the People's Republic of China to the UN. 2000b. Statement by Ambassador Shen Guofang at the 55th GA Session on Causes of Conflict and the Promotion of Durable Peace and Sustainable Development in Africa.

Permanent Mission of the People's Republic of China to the UN. 2001. Statement by Ambassador Wang Yingfan, Permanent Representative of China to the UN, at the Plenary Meeting of the UN GA on the Review of the Report of the Secretary-General on Armed Conflict Prevention.

Permanent Mission of the People's Republic of China to the UN. 2004a. Statement by Ambassador Zhang Yishan, Head of the Chinese Delegation, at ECOSOC Substantive Session on Human Rights (item 14g).

Permanent Mission of the People's Republic of China to the UN. 2004b. Statement by Mr LA Yifan, Alternate Representative of the Chinese Delegation on Agenda Item 105(a): Implementation of Human Rights Instruments at 3rd Committee during GA 59th Session.

Permanent Mission of the People's Republic of China to the UN. 2005a. Statement by Ambassador Wang Guangya at the Security Council's Open Debate on "Cooperation between the United Nations and Regional Organizations in Maintaining International Peace and Security."

Permanent Mission of the People's Republic of China to the UN. 2005b. Statement by Ambassador Zhang Yishan at the General Committee of the 60th GA Session.

Permanent Mission of the People's Republic of China to the UN. 2005c. Statement by Ambassador Zhang Yishan at the Security Council's Open Debate on "Protection of Civilians in Armed Conflict."

Permanent Mission of the People's Republic of China to the UN. 2005d. Statement by Ambassador Zhang Yishan of the Chinese Mission to the UN at the first informal consultation on follow-up to the World Summit Outcome on Development and ECOSOC Reform.

Permanent Mission of the People's Republic of China to the UN. 2006. Statement by Ambassador Liu Zhenmin at the Security Council Open Debate on "Protection of Civilians in Armed Conflict."

Pierson, P. 2004. *Politics in Time: History, Institutions, and Social Analysis.* Princeton: Princeton University Press.

Pollentine, M. 2012. "Constructing the Responsibility to Protect," Ph.D. thesis, Cardiff University.

Polzer, T. 2008. "Responding to Zimbabwean Migration in South Africa: Evaluating Options," *South African Journal of International Affairs,* 15(1): 1–15.

Polzer, T., Kiwanuka, M., and Takavirwa, K. 2010. "Regional Responses to Zimbabwean Migration, 2000–2010," *Open Space: On the Move: Dynamics of Migration in Southern Africa,* 3: 30–4.

Prantl, J., and Nakano, R. 2011. "Global Norm Diffusion in East Asia: How China and Japan Implement the Responsibility to Protect," *International Relations,* 25(2): 204–33.

Preparatory Committee for the Ciarolo Scheme. 1925. "Report of the Preparatory Committee for the Ciarolo Scheme," *League of Nations—Official Journal*, Geneva.

Price, M. E. 2009. *Rethinking Asylum: History, Purpose, and Limits.* Cambridge: Cambridge University Press.

Price, R. 1998. "Reversing the Gun Sights: Transnational Civil Society Targets Landmines," *International Organization*, 52(3): 613–44.

Price, R. 2003. "Transnational Civil Society and Advocacy in World Politics," *World Politics*, 55(4): 579–606.

Price, R., ed. 2008. *Moral Limit and Possibility in World Politics.* Cambridge: Cambridge University Press.

Price, R., and Tannenwald, N. 1996. "Norms and Deterrence: The Nuclear and Chemical Weapons Taboo," in P. J. Katzenstein (ed.), *The Culture of National Security*, 114–52. Ithaca, NY: Cornell University Press.

Prunier, G. 2009. *Africa's World War: Congo, the Rwandan Genocide, and the Making of a Continental Catastrophe.* New York: Oxford University Press.

Publish What You Fund. 2009. *Briefing Paper 1: Why Aid Transparency Matters, and the Global Movement for Aid Transparency.* Available at <http://www.publishwhatyoufund.org/files/BP1_final.pdf>.

Publish What You Fund. 2011. *Pilot Aid Transparency Index 2011.* Available at <http://www.publishwhatyoufund.org/resources/index/2011-index> (accessed Mar. 2012).

Rae, H. 2002. *State Identities and the Homogenisation of Peoples.* Cambridge: Cambridge University Press.

Ramji-Nogales, J., Schoenholtz, A., and Schrag, P. 2009. *Refugee Roulette: Disparities in Asylum Adjudication and Proposals for Reform.* New York: NYU Press.

Rathmell, A. 2005. "Planning Post-Conflict Reconstruction in Iraq: What Can we Learn?" *International Affairs*, 81: 1013–38.

Raustiala, K., and Slaughter, A.-M. 2002. "International Law, International Relations and Compliance," in W. Carlsnaes, T. Risse-Kappen, and B. A. Simmons (eds), *Handbook of International Relations*, 538–58. London: Sage.

Ravallion, M. 2010. "Wholesaling Research for Development," blog entry, 29 Sept. Available at <http://blogs.worldbank.org/developmenttalk/wholesaling-research-for-development> (accessed Mar. 2012).

Refugee Law Project. 2005. *"There are No Refugees in This Area": Self-Settled Refugees in Koboko."* Refugee Law Project Working Paper, 18. Kampala: Refugee Law Project.

Rehman, B. 1999. "Constructing Humanitarianism: An Investigation into Oxfam's Changing Humanitarian Culture, 1942–1994," Ph.D., University of Wales.

Reinold, T. 2010. "The Responsibility to Protect: Much Ado about Nothing?" *Review of International Studies*, 36: 55–78.

Republic of Uganda. 2004. "National Policy for Internally Displaced Persons." Available at: <http://www.brookings.edu/~/media/Projects/idp/Uganda_IDPpolicy_2004.PDF> (accessed Oct. 2012).

Responsibility to Protect Engaging Civil Society (R2PCS). 2008. "9 May 2008 R2PCS Message on R2P and Burma/Myanmar." Available at: <http://responsibilitytoprotect.org/index.php/component/content/article/1652> (accessed June 2013).

Reus-Smit, C., ed. 2004. *The Politics of International Law.* Cambridge: Cambridge University Press.

Reynaert, J. 2010. "MONUC/MONUSCO and Civilian Protection in the Kivus," Antwerp: International Peace Information Services. Available at <http://www.ipis-research.be/publications_internpapers.php>.

Reyntjens, F. 2009. *The Great African War: Congo and Regional Geopolitics, 1996–2006*. New York: Cambridge University Press.

Ribeiro Viotti, M. L. 2011. *Responsibility While Protecting: Elements for the Development and Promotion of a Concept*, New York: United Nations General Assembly A/66/551-S/2011/701 (11 Nov.).

Rieff, D. 2011. "R2P, R.I.P.," *New York Times*, 7 Nov.

Risse, T., and Sikkink, K. 1999. "The Socialization of International Human Rights Norms into Domestic Practice," in T. Risse, S. C. Ropp, and K. Sikkink (eds), *The Power of Human Rights: International Norms and Domestic Change*, 1–38. Cambridge: Cambridge University Press.

Risse-Kappen, T. 1995. *Bringing Transnational Relations Back in: Non-State Actors, Domestic Structures, and International Institutions*. Cambridge: Cambridge University Press.

Roberts, A. 2006. *The Wonga Coup*. London: Profile Books.

Roberts, A. 2011. "The Civilian in Modern War," in H. Strachan and S. Scheipers (eds), *The Changing Character of War*, 357–80. Oxford: Oxford University Press.

Roberts-Moore, J. 1986. "Studies in Documents: The Office of the Custodian of Enemy Property: An Overview of the Office and its Records, 1920–1952," *Archivaria*, 22: 95–106.

Rosand, E. 1998. "The Right to Return under International Law Following Mass Dislocation: The Bosnia Precedent," *Michigan Journal of International Law*, 19 (Summer): 1091–139.

Rosenberg, S. P. 2009. "Responsibility to Protect: A Framework for Prevention," *Global Responsibility to Protect*, 1: 422–77.

RSIS. 2010. *Regional Consultation on the Responsibility to Protect*. Singapore: RSIS Centre for Non-Traditional Security Studies.

Rutinwa, B. 1999. *The End of Asylum? The Changing Nature of Refugee Policies in Africa*. New Issues in Refugee Research, 5. Geneva: UNHCR.

Rutinwa, B. 2002. *Prima Facie Status and Refugee Protection*. New Issues in Refugee Research, 69. Geneva: UNHCR.

Rutinwa, B. 2003. *Response to SGBV and SE in Kibondo: Some Policy and Legal Implications* (Annex to TCRS Programme Evaluation 2003). Dar Es Salaam: Tanzanian Christian Refugee Service.

Rutinwa, B. 2005. *Identifying Gaps in Protection Capacity—Tanzania*. Geneva: UNHCR.

Saechao, T. R. 2007. "Natural Disasters and the Responsibility to Protect: From Chaos to Clarity," *Brookings Journal of International Law*, 32(2): 663–707.

Sandholtz, W. 2007. *Prohibiting Plunder: How Norms Change*. Oxford: Oxford University Press.

Sandholtz, W. 2008. "Dynamics of International Norm Change: Rules Against Wartime Plunder," *European Journal of International Relations*, 14: 101–31.

Sandholtz, W., and Sweet, A. S. 2004. "Law, Politics, and International Governance." In C. Reus-Smit (ed.), *The Politics of International Law*, 238–72. Cambridge: Cambridge University Press.

Schechtman, J. B. 1962. *Postwar Population Transfers in Europe: 1945–1955*. Philadelphia: University of Pennsylvania Press.

Schiff, B. N. 2008. *Building the International Criminal Court*. Cambridge: Cambridge University Press.

Schimmelfennig, F. 2001. "The Community Trap: Liberal Norms, Rhetorical Action, and the Eastern Enlargement of the European Union," *International Organization*, 55: 47–80.

Schmidt, A. 2006. *From Global Prescription to Local Treatment: The International Refugee Regime in Tanzania and Uganda*. Berkeley, CA: Department of Political Science, University of California.

Schreier, T. H. 2008. "An Evaluation of South Africa's Application of the OAU Refugee Definition," *Refuge*, 25(2): 53–63.

Scott, A. S. 2009. *Laurent Nkunda et la rébellion du Kivu*. Paris: Karthala.

Selznick, P. 1957. *Leadership in Administration: A Sociological Interpretation*. Evanston, IL: Row Peterson.

Shacknove, A. E. 1985. "Who is a Refugee?" *Ethics*, 95(2): 274–84.

Sharman, J. C. 2008. "Power and Discourse in Policy Diffusion: Anti-Money Laundering in Developing States," *International Studies Quarterly*, 52: 635–56.

Shearer, D. 1997. "Exploring the Limits of Consent: Conflict Resolution in Sierra Leone," *Millennium*, 26: 845–60.

Shelton, D. 2000. "Introduction: Law, Non-Law and the Problem of 'Soft Law'," In D. Shelton (ed.), *Commitment and Compliance: The Role of Non-Binding Norms in the International Legal System*, 1–18. Oxford: Oxford University Press.

Shesterinina, A. 2012. "Evolving Norms of Protection: China, Libya, and the Problem of Civilians in Armed Conflict," International Studies Association Annual Convention, San Diego, CA.

Shneiderman, S., and Turin, M. 2012. "Nepal and Bhutan in 2011," *Asian Survey*, 52: 138–46.

Shue, H. 1980. *Basic Rights: Subsistence, Affluence, and U.S. Foreign Policy*. Princeton: Princeton University Press.

Shukla, K. 2008. "The International Community's Responsibility to Protect," *Forced Migration Review*, 30: 7–9.

Sikkink, K. 2011. *The Justice Cascade: How Human Rights Prosecutions are Changing World Politics*. New York: W. W. Norton & Co.

Simmons, B. A. 2009. *Mobilizing for Human Rights: International Law in Domestic Politics*. Cambridge: Cambridge University Press.

Simmons, B. A., Dobbin, F., and Garrett, G. 2007. "The Global Diffusion of Public Policies: Social Construction, Coercion, Competition or Learning?" *Annual Review of Sociology*, 33: 449–72.

Singer, P. W. 2004. "War, Profits and the Vacuum of Law: Privatized Military Firms and International Law," *Colombia Journal of Transnational Law*, 42: 521–49.

Singh, S., Sharma, S. P., Mills, E., Poudel, K. C., and Jimba, M. 2007. "Conflict Induced Internal Displacement in Nepal," *Medicine, Conflict and Survival*, 23: 103–10.

Smit, A. 2012. *The Property Rights of Refugees and Internally Displaced Persons: Beyond Restitution*. Abingdon: Routledge.

Smith, C. B. 1999. "The Politics of Global Consensus Building: A Comparative Analysis," *Global Governance*, 5: 173–201.

Smith, D. 2010. "Congo Conflict: 'The Terminator' Lives in Luxury while Peacekeepers Look on," *Guardian*, 5 Feb.

Solidarity Peace Trust. 2012. *Perils and Pitfalls: Migrants and Deportation in South Africa.* Johannesburg: Solidarity Peace Trust, <www.solidaritypeacetrust.org/perils-and-pitfalls>.

Spicer, T. 1999. "Interview with Lt. Col. Tim Spicer," *Cambridge Review of International Affairs,* 13: 165–71.

Sriskandarajah, D. 2003. "The Returns of Peace in Sri Lanka: The Development Cart Before the Conflict Resolution Horse," *Journal of Peacebuilding and Development,* 1(2): 21–35.

Stahn, C. 2007. "Responsibility to Protect: Politic Rhetoric or Emerging Legal Norm?" *American Journal of International Law,* 101: 99–120.

Stanger, A. 2009. *One Nation under Contract.* New Haven and London: Yale University Press.

Stanley Foundation. 2010. *Implementing the Responsibility to Protect.* Available at <http://www.stanleyfoundation.org> (accessed June 2013).

Stanley Foundation. 2011. *Structuring the U.S. Government to Prevent Atrocities: Considerations for an Atrocities Prevention Board.* Available at <http://www.stanleyfoundation.org> (accessed June 2013).

Stearns, J. 2008. "Laurent Nkunda and the National Congress for the Defence of the People (CNDP)," in S. Marysse, F. Reyntjens, and S. Vandeginste (eds), *L'Afrique des Grands Lacs: Annuaire 2007–2008.* Paris: L'Harmattan, 127–45.

Stearns, J. 2011. *Dancing in the Glory of Monsters: The Collapse of the Congo and the Great War of Africa.* New York: Public Affairs.

Steinberg, D. 2009. "Responsibility to Protect: Coming of Age?" *Global Responsibility to Protect,* 1: 432–41.

Stoddard, Abby. 2003. "Humanitarian NGOs: Challenges and Trends," In J. Macrae and A. Harmer (eds), *Humanitarian Action and the Global War on Terror,* 25–36. London: Humanitarian Policy Group.

Stoffels, R. A. 2004. "Legal Regulation of Humanitarian Assistance in Armed Conflict: Achievement and Gaps," *International Review of the Red Cross,* 86(855): 515–45.

Stokke, K. 2006. "Building the Tamil Eelam State: Emerging State Institutions and Forms of Governance in LTTE Controlled Areas in Sri Lanka," *Third World Quarterly,* 27(6): 1021–40.

Stone, L., and du Plessis, M. 2008. *The Implementation of the Rome Statute of the International Criminal Court in African Countries.* Pretoria: Institute for Security Studies (ISS).

Strauss, E. 2009. "A Bird in the Hand is worth Two in the Bush: On the Assumed Legal Nature of the Responsibility to Protect," *Global Responsibility to Protect,* 1: 291–323.

Sunday Times. 2009. "Dragon's Share of Lankan Development Projects Given to China," 6 Dec.

Sundstrom, L. M. 2005. "Foreign Assistance, International Norms, and NGO Development: Lessons from the Russian Campaign," *International Organization,* 59(2): 419–49.

Sweeney, J. A. 2012. "Restorative Justice and Transitional Justice at the ECHR," *International Criminal Law Review,* 12(3): 313–37.

Tannenwald, N. 2005. "Ideas and Explanations: Advancing the Theoretical Agenda," *Journal of Cold War Studies*, 7(2): 13–42.

Taulbee, J. 1985. "Myths, Mercenaries and Contemporary International Law," *California Western International Law Journal*, 15: 339–63.

Taulbee, J. L. 2000. "Mercenaries, Private Armies and Security Companies in Contemporary Policy," *International Politics*, 37: 433–56.

Teitt, S. 2008. *China and the Responsibility to Protect*. Brisbane: Asia-Pacific Centre for the Responsibility to Protect.

Teitt, S. 2009. "Assessing Polemics, Principles and Practices: China and the Responsibility to Protect," *Global Responsibility to Protect*, 1(2): 208–36.

Teitt, S. 2011. "The Responsibility to Protect and China's Peacekeeping Policy," *International Peacekeeping*, 18(3): 298–312.

Thakur, R. 2008. "Should the UN Invoke the 'Responsibility to Protect'?" *Globe and Mail*, 8 May.

Thakur, R. 2009. "West shouldn't Fault Sri Lankan Government Tactics." *Daily Yomiuri*, 12 June.

Thakur, R. 2011. *The Responsibility to Protect: Norms, Laws and the Use of Force in International Politics*. New York: Routledge.

Thakur, R., and Weiss, T. G. 2009. "R2P: From Idea to Norm—and Action?" *Global Responsibility to Protect*, 1: 22–53.

The East African. 2001. "Shock as Tanzania Acts Against 'Aliens'," 12 Feb.

Thomas, D. C. 2001. *The Helsinki Effect: International Norms, Human Rights, and the Demise of Communism*. Princeton: Princeton University Press.

Thomson, J. E. 1994. *Mercenaries, Pirates, and Sovereigns: State-Building and Extraterritorial Violence in Early Modern Europe*. Princeton: Princeton University Press.

Tiefer, C. 2009. "The Iraq Debacle: The Rise and Fall of Procurement-Aided Unilateralism as a Paradigm of Foreign War," *University of Pennsylvania Law Review*, 29: 1–58.

Torpey, J. C. 2003. *Politics and the Past: On Repairing Historical Injustices*. Lanham, MD: Rowman & Littlefield.

Tsebelis, G. 2002. *Veto Players: How Political Institutions Work*. Princeton: Princeton University Press.

Udias, A. 2009. "Earthquakes as God's Punishment in 17th and 18th-Century Spain," in M. Kolbl-Ebert (ed.), *Geology and Religion: A History of Harmony and Hostility*, 41–8. London: Geological Society of London.

Uganda Coalition for the International Criminal Court (UCICC). (2007). *Approaching National Reconciliation in Uganda: Perspectives on Applicable Justice Systems*. London: UCICC/Redress. <http://www.iccnow.org/documents/ApproachingNatio nalReconciliationInUganda_07aug13.pdf>.

United Nations. 1958. *United Nations Treaty Series*. New York: United Nations.

United Nations. 1985. *Charter of the United Nations and Statute of the International Court of Justice*. New York: United Nations, Department of Public Information.

United Nations. 1995. *Yearbook of the United Nations: 1994*, vol. 48. New York: Martinus Nijhoff Publishers.

United Nations. 1999. *Report of the Independent Inquiry into the Actions of the United Nations during the 1994 Genocide in Rwanda*, UN doc. S/1999/1257 (16 Dec.).

United Nations. 2002. *Final Report of the Panel of Experts on the Illegal Exploitation of Natural Resources and Other Forms of Wealth of the Democratic Republic of the Congo*, S/2002/1146.

United Nations. 2004. *A More Secure World: Our Shared Responsibility. Report of the High-Level Panel on Threats, Challenges and Change*. New York: United Nations General Assembly.

United Nations 2005a. *2005 World Summit Outcome*, UN doc. A/Res/60/1 (16 Sept.).

United Nations 2005b. *Debate on the Protection of Civilians in Armed Conflict*, UN doc. S/PV.5319 (9 Dec.).

United Nations 2005c. *World Summit Achieved Concrete, Significant Gains in Human Rights, Rule of Law, Secretary-General Says in Address to Universidade Nova de Lisboa*, UN doc. SG/SM/10161 (10 Oct.).

United Nations. 2006. "Note of Guidance on Integrated Missions Clarifying the Role, Responsibility and Authority of the Special Representative of the Secretary-General and the Deputy Special Representative of the Secretary-General/Resident Coordinator/Humanitarian Coordinator," issued by the Secretary-General, 9 Feb.

United Nations. 2008. *United Nations Human Resources Structures must be Adapted to Meet Growing Demands of Peacekeeping, Other Field Operations, Budget Committee Told*, UN doc. GA/AB/3837 (4 Mar.).

United Nations. 2009a. *Implementing the Responsibility to Protect, Report of the Secretary General* (A/63/677).

United Nations. 2009b. *Interactive Thematic Dialogue of the United Nations General Assembly on the Responsibility to Protect*, UN doc. A/63/PV.9823 (24 July).

United Nations. 2009c. *Report of the Secretary-General on the Protection of Civilians in Armed Conflict*. New York: United Nations.

United Nations. 2010. *Special Rapporteur on Extrajudicial, Summary or Arbitrary Executions—Mission to the Democratic Republic of the Congo*, A/HRC/14/24/Add.3.

United Nations. 2011a. *Report of the Secretary General's Panel of Experts on Accountability in Sri Lanka*. New York: United Nations.

United Nations. 2011b. *Humanitarian Appeal 2011*. New York: United Nations Office for the Coordination of Humanitarian Affairs.

United Nations. 2011c. *Peace-Building Strategy for Nepal, 2011–12*. Kathmandu: United Nations.

United Nations. 2012. *International Strategy for Disaster Reduction 2011*, ISDR Mandate. Available <http://www.unisdr.org/who-we-are/mandate>

United Nations Commission on Human Rights. 2002. *Report of the Representative of the Secretary-General on Internally Displaced Persons, F.M. Deng*. Geneva: United Nations Commission on Human Rights.

United Nations, DPKO (Best Practices Unit). 2005. *MONUC and the Bukavu Crisis 2004* (Internal). New York: UN.

United Nations, DPKO. 2008. *United Nations Peacekeeping Operations: Principles and Guidelines*. New York: UN.

United Nations General Assembly. 2005. *Resolution 60/1: World Summit Outcome*. New York: United Nations.

United Nations General Assembly. 2008. *Report of the Peacebuilding Commission on its Second Session*. UN Doc. A/63/92-S/2008/417, 24 June.

United Nations General Assembly. 2009. *Follow-up to the Outcome of the Millennium Summit*. UN Doc. A/63/PV.98, 24 July.

United Nations General Assembly. 2011. *Resolution 65/133: Strengthening of the Coordination of Emergency Humanitarian Assistance of the United Nations*.

United Nations High Commissioner for Refugees (UNHCR). 1992, 1997. *Handbook on Procedures and Criteria for Determining Refugee Status under the 1951 Convention and the 1967 Protocol Relating to the Status of Refugees*. Geneva: UNHCR.

UNHCR. 1993. *The State of the World's Refugees, 1993: The Challenge of Protection*. New York: Penguin Books.

UNHCR. 1994. *Registration: A Practical Guide for Field Staff*. Geneva: UNHCR.

UNHCR. 1996. *Handbook on Voluntary Repatriation*. Geneva: UNHCR.

UNHCR. 2003. *Statistical Yearbook*. Geneva: UNHCR.

UNHCR. 2004. *Protection Gaps Framework for Analysis—Enhancing Protection for Refugees—Strengthening Protection Capacity Project*. Geneva: UNHCR.

UNHCR. 2006. *The State of the World's Refugees 2006: Human Displacement in the New Millennium*. Oxford: Oxford University Press.

UNHCR. 2007. *Handbook for the Protection of Internally Displaced Persons*. Geneva: UNHCR.

UNHCR Executive Committee of the High Commissioner's Programme (ExCom). 2010. "Summary Record of the 637th meeting held at the Palais des Nations, Geneva, on Tuesday, 8 December 2009, at 10am," A/AC.96/SR.637, 25 Jan.

United Nations Human Rights Council. 2006. *Report of the High-Level Mission on the Situation of Human Rights in Darfur Pursuant to Human Rights Council Decision S-4/101*, UN doc. A/HRC/4/80 (7 Mar.).

United Nations Human Rights Council. 2007. *Report on the Situation of Human Rights in Darfur*, UN doc. A/HRC/5/6 (8 June).

United Nations International Strategy for Disaster Reduction. 2011. *Our Mandate*. <http://www.unisdr.org/who-we-are/mandate>.

United Nations Office for the Coordination of Humanitarian Affairs. 2006. *Guidelines on the Use of Foreign Military and Civil Defence Assets in Disaster Relief: "Oslo Guidelines"* New York: UNOCHA.

United Nations Secretary-General. 1992. *An Agenda for Peace: Preventive Diplomacy, Peacemaking and Peace-Keeping*. Report of the Secretary-General pursuant to the statement adopted by the Summit Meeting of the Security Council on 31 January 1992, A/47/227, 17 June.

United Nations Secretary-General. 1994. *An Agenda for Development*. Report of the Secretary-General, A/48/935, 6 May.

United Nations Secretary-General. 1998. *Report of the Secretary-General on the Situation in Africa*, S/1998/318.

United Nations Secretary-General. 1999a. *Report of the Secretary-General pursuant to General Assembly Resolution 53/35: The Fall of Srebrenica*, A/54/549.

United Nations Secretary-General. 1999b. *Report of the Secretary-General on Rwanda*, S/1994/728.

United Nations Secretary-General. 1999c. *Observance by the UN of IHL*, ST/SGB/1999/13.

United Nations Secretary-General. 2001. *Sixth Report of the Secretary-General on MONUC*, S/2001/128.

United Nations Secretary-General. 2005. *In Larger Freedom: Towards Security, Development and Human Rights for All.* Report of the Secretary-General of the United Nations for decision by Heads of State and Government in September 2005, A/59/2005, 21 Mar.

United Nations Secretary-General. 2006. *Follow-up to the Outcome of the Millennium Summit*, including "Delivering as One: Report of the High Level Panel on United Nations System-wide Coherence in the areas of development, humanitarian assistance and the environment," Report of the Secretary-General of the United Nations to the Sixty-first session of the United Nations General Assembly, A/61/583, 20 Nov.

United Nations Secretary-General. 2009. *Fifth report of the Secretary-General on the United Nations Integrated Office in Burundi*, S/2009/270, 22 May.

United Nations Security Council. 2006a. *Debate on the Protection of Civilians in Armed Conflict*, UN doc. S/PV.5577 (4 Dec.).

United Nations Security Council. 2006b. *Resolution 1674* UN doc. S/RES/1674 (28 Apr.).

United Nations Security Council. 2006c. *Resolution 1706*, UN doc. S/Res/1706 (31 Aug.).

United Nations Security Council. 2006d. *Update Report No. 1: Protection of Civilians in Armed Conflict*, Security Council Report, 8 Mar. Available at <http://www.security-councilreport.org> (accessed June 2013).

United Nations Security Council. 2009. *Resolution 1894*, UN doc. S/Res/1894 (11 Nov.).

United Nations Security Council. 2011. *Thematic Debate on the Protection of Civilians in Armed Conflict*, UN doc. S/PV.6531 (10 May).

United Republic of Tanzania, Ministry of Home Affairs. 2003. *The National Refugee Policy*. Dar Es Salaam: Government of Tanzania.

Unruh, J. 2008. "Land Policy Reform, Customary Rule of Law and the Peace Process in Sierra Leone," *African Journal of Legal Studies*, 2(2): 94–117.

Urpelainen, J. 2010. "Regulation under Economic Globalization," *International Studies Quarterly*, 54: 1099–121.

US Congress 2010. *Concurrent Resolution*, 111th Congress, 2nd Session, S.CON. RES.71 (22 Dec.).

US Department of State 2010. *The First Quadrennial Diplomacy and Development Review (QDDR): Leading through Civilian Power*. Available at <http://www.state.gov/s/dmr/qddr/index.htm> (accessed June 2013).

Van Kersbergen, K., and Verbeek, B. 2007. "The Politics of International Norms: Subsidiarity and the Imperfect Competence Regime of the European Union," *European Journal of International Relations*, 13(2): 217–38.

VanDeveer, S. D., and Dabelko, G. D. 2001. "It's Capacity, Stupid: International Assistance and National Implementation," *Global Environmental Politics*, 1: 18–29.

Victor, D. G., Raustiala, K., and Skolnikoff, E. B. 1998. *The Implementation and Effectiveness of International Environmental Commitments: Theory and Practice.* Cambridge, MA: MIT Press.

Vigneswaran, D., Araia, T., Hoag, C., and Tshabalala, X. 2010. "Criminality or Monopoly? Informal Immigration Enforcement in South Africa," *Journal of Southern African Studies,* 36(2): 465–85.

Volcker, Paul A., et al. 2007. *Independent Panel Review of the World Bank Group Department of Institutional Integrity.* Washington, DC: World Bank.

Vrasti, W. 2008. "The Strange Case of Ethnography and International Relations," *Millennium-Journal of International Studies,* 37: 279.

Waal, A. D. 2007. "Darfur and the Failure of the Responsibility to Protect," *International Affairs,* 83: 1039–54.

Walker, P., Wisner, B., Leaning, J., and Minear, L. 2005. "Smoke and Mirrors: Deficiencies in Disaster Funding," *BMJ* 330: 247–50.

Wapner, P. 1996. *Environmental Activism and World Civic Politics.* Albany, NY: State University of New York Press.

Watson, S. 2011. "The 'Human' as Referent Object? Humanitarianism as Securitization," *Security Dialogue,* 42(1): 3–20.

Weaver, C. 2008. *Hypocrisy Trap: The World Bank and the Poverty of Reform.* Princeton: Princeton University Press.

Weeks, W. 2002. *Pushing the Envelope: Moving Beyond "Protected Villages" in Northern Uganda.* New York: UN Office for the Coordination of Humanitarian Affairs.

Weiss, T. G., and Pasic, A. 1998. "Dealing with the Displacement and Suffering Caused by Yugoslavia's Wars," in R. Cohen and F. M. Deng (eds), *The Forsaken People: Case Studies of the Internally Displaced.* Washington, DC: Brookings Institution Press, 175–225.

Welch, C. E., and Watkins, A. 2011. "Extending Enforcement: The Coalition for the International Criminal Court," *Human Rights Quarterly,* 33(4): 927-1031.

Welsh, J. M. 2007. "The Responsibility to Protect: Securing the Individual in International Society?" in B. Gould and L. Lazarus (eds), *Security and Human Rights.* 363–83. Oxford: Hart.

Welsh, J. M. 2010. "Turning Words into Deeds? The Implementation of the 'Responsibility to Protect,'" *Global Responsibility to Protect,* 2: 149–54.

Welsh, J. M. 2012. "Who Should Act? Collective Responsibility and the Responsibility to Protect," In W. A. Knight and F. Egerton (eds), *The Routledge Handbook of the Responsibility to Protect,* 103–14. New York: Routledge.

Welsh J. (2013) "Norm Contestation and the Responsibility to Protect," Global Responsibility to Protect, 5 (4): 365–96.

Welsh, J. M. Forthcoming. *Sovereignty as Responsibility.*

Welsh, J. M., and Banda, M. 2010. "International Law and the Responsibility to Protect: Clarifying or Expanding States' Responsibilities," *Global Responsibility to Protect,* 2: 213–31.

Welsh, J. M., Sharma, S., and Reike, R. 2012. *The Prevention of Mass Atrocity Crimes: A Strategic Framework.* July. Available at <http://www.elac.ox.ac.uk>.

Welsh, J. M., Thielking, C., and Macfarlane, S. N. 2002. "The Responsibility to Protect: Assessing the Report of the International Commission on Intervention and State Sovereignty," *International Journal,* 57: 498–512.

Wendt, A. 1992. "Anarchy is What States Make of it: The Social Construction of Power Politics," *International Organisation,* 46(2): 391–425.

Wendt, A. 1999. *Social Theory of International Politics*. Cambridge: Cambridge University Press.

Weyland, K. 2008. "Toward a New Theory of Institutional Change," *World Politics*, 60(2): 281–314.

WFP/UNHCR. 1996. *Joint WFP/UNHCR Food Assessment Mission in the Great Lakes Region*. Tanzania: WFP/UNHCR.

Whitaker, Ben. 1983. *A Bridge of People: A Personal View of Oxfam's First Forty Years*. London: Heinemann.

Whitfield, L., and Fraser, A. 2009. "Introduction: Aid and Sovereignty," in L. Whitfield (ed.), *The Politics of Aid: African Strategies for Dealing with Donors*, 1–26. Oxford: Oxford University Press.

Wiener, A. 2007. "Contested Meanings of Norms: A Research Framework," *Comparative European Politics*, 5(1): 1–17.

Wiener, A. 2008. *The Invisible Constitution of World Politics*. Cambridge: Cambridge University Press.

Wiener, A. 2009. "Enacting Meaning-in-Use: Qualitative Research on Norms and International Relations," *Review of International Studies*, 35: 175–93.

Williams, D. 2000. "Aid and Sovereignty: Quasi-States and the International Financial Institutions," *Review of International Studies*, 26: 557–73.

Williams, P. D., and Bellamy, A. J. 2005. "The Responsibility to Protect and the Crisis in Darfur," *Security Dialogue*, 6: 27–47.

Williams, R. C. 2010. "The Pinheiro Principles Take a Licking (and Keep on Ticking?)" <terra0nullius.wordpress.com/2010/11/18/the-pinheiro-principles-take-a-licking-and-keep-on-ticking> (accessed May 2003).

Wills, S. 2009 *Protecting Civilians: The Obligations of Peacekeepers*. Oxford: Oxford University Press.

Winter, P. 2012. *A Sacred Cause: The Inter-Congolese Dialogue 2000–2003*. Edinburgh: Librario.

World Bank. 2011b. "World Bank's Financial Data, Open and Transparent." World Bank Press Release No. 2012/148/CTR, 9 Nov.

World Bank. 2005. *World Bank Disclosure Policy: Additional Issues: Follow-Up Consolidated Report (Revised)*. World Bank Operations Policy and Country Services, 14 Feb.

World Bank. 2007. *Implementation Plan for Strengthening World Bank Engagement on Governance and Anticorruption*. Washington, DC: World Bank.

World Bank. 2009. *Towards Greater Transparency: Rethinking the World Bank's Disclosure Policy: Approach Paper*. World Bank Operations Policy and Country Services, 29 Jan.

World Bank. 2010a. "New World Bank Access to Information Policy Takes Effect July 1," press release no. 2010/448/EXC, 3 June.

World Bank. 2010b. "World Bank Policy on Access to Information Progress Report, November 2009 through September 2010." Legal Vice Presidency, 16 Dec.

World Bank. 2010c. "World Bank Policy on Access to Information Progress Report, October through December 2010." Legal Vice Presidency, 28 Mar.

World Bank. 2012. *FY2011 Access to Information Annual Report*. Washington, DC: World Bank.

World Vision. 2012a. "Grass Root Efforts to Prevent and Resolve Violence." <http://www.worldvision.org.uk/what-we-do/advocacy/publications/research-reports> (accessed Dec. 2012).

World Vision. 2012b. "World Vision's Response." <http://www.worldvision.org/content.nsf/about/press-development-peace> (accessed June 2012).

World Vision International (WVI) (2012) *Minimum Inter-Agency Standards for Protection Mainstreaming*. Available at <http:// reliefweb.int/sites/reliefweb.int/files/resources/Full_Report_3752.pdf>

Wyckoff, M., and Sharma, H. 2009. *Trekking in Search of IDPs and Other Lessons from ICLA Nepal: Evaluation Report*. Geneva: Norwegian Refugee Council.

Wyndham, J. 2006. "A Developing Trend: Laws and Policies on Internal Displacement," *Human Rights Brief*, 14: 7–11.

Xinhua. 2005. "Full text of China's Position Paper UN Reforms," part III.1, 8 June. <http://news.xinhuanet.com/english/2005-06/08/content_3056817_3.htm>.

Zarate, J. C. 1998. "The Emergence of a New Dog of War: Private International Security Companies, International Law, and the New World Disorder," *Stanford Journal of International Law*, 34: 75–162.

Zoellick, R. 2010. "Democratizing Development Economics," Speech delivered at Georgetown University, 29 Sept.

Zoellick, R. 2011. "The Middle East and North Africa: A New Social Contract for Development," Speech delivered to the Peterson Institute for International Economics, Washington, DC, 6 Apr. Available at <http://www.piie.com/events/event_detail.cfm?EventID=176> (accessed Mar. 2012).

Zolberg, A. R. 1983. "The Formation of New States as a Refugee-Generating Process," *Annals of the American Academy of Political and Social Science*, 467: 24–38.

Index

The page numbers in italics denotes the tables and figures